D0948888

WITHDRAWN

SUNKEN TREATIES

Emily O. Goldman

SUNKEN TREATIES

Naval Arms Control Between the Wars

The Pennsylvania State University Press
University Park, Pennsylvania

Library of Congress Cataloging-in-Publication Data

Goldman, Emily O., 1961–
    Sunken treaties : naval arms control between the wars / Emily O.
Goldman.

        p.   cm.
    Includes bibliographical references and index.
    ISBN 0-271-01033-9 (cloth) — ISBN 0-271-01034-7 (pbk.)
    1. Nuclear arms control.   2. United States—Foreign relations
—Treaties—History.   I. Title.
JX1974.7.G6525   1994
327.1'74—dc20   93-31953
                                                               CIP

Published by The Pennsylvania State University Press,
University Park, PA 16802-1003

It is the policy of The Pennsylvania State University Press to use acid-free paper for the
first printing of all clothbound books. Publications on uncoated stock satisfy the minimum requirements of American National Standard for Information Sciences—Permanence of Paper for Printed Library Materials, ANSI Z39.48–1984.

CONTENTS

PREFACE

When I first began to think about naval arms control and the interwar period, it was not a particularly fashionable topic. Anyone who wrote about arms control during the Cold War wrote about Cold War arms control, particularly nuclear arms control. Only occasionally did scholars drift back between the wars to snatch up tidbits of information to reconfirm hypotheses they were making about the then-current period. Few dared do something so unfashionable as writing an entire book about pre–Cold War arms control. But fashion is just that, fashion; and it changes. Now scholars, journalists, and policymakers are reaching back into history, searching fervently for maps to guide them through the murky, uncertain post–Cold War future. So, for reasons beyond my control, my topic has become very fashionable. However, I probably have not approached the topic in a very fashionable way. Perhaps my treatment will endure for that very reason.

My initial motivation for studying naval arms control between the world wars was to reconcile diametrically opposing judgments about the period. There are those who hold up the interwar experiment as one of the few successful episodes in arms control, as a shining light during a turbulent period in the international system. There are also those who brand the whole experiment an unmitigated failure. This latter group also uses the history of the 1920s and 1930s as evidence that arms control itself is a fundamentally flawed undertaking. I look back into history with neither of these beliefs about the interwar period or arms control in general, with no political cause to champion, and with no ideological ax to grind.

From my reading of events, I conclude that naval arms control between the wars was a limited success. The failures of the 1930s should not detract from the accomplishments of the 1920s. The frustrations of negotiating naval limits among the European powers should not discredit the more farsighted and innovative approaches to arms control pursued in the Far East. What became even more apparent to me as I studied the period was that it was possible to distinguish two strategies of arms control, one in which efforts to diffuse political conflicts were integrated with force reductions; another in which force reductions were pursued alone. The second approach shares much with the philosophy that the founders of modern arms control theory expounded in the 1960s. The interwar naval experiment offered a unique opportunity to test the validity of these two approaches, assess the repercussions of each, and examine the biases in the Cold War approach to arms control that we have come to accept as truths. So, an inquiry that began out of historical curiosity evolved into a theoretical critique of arms control theory and the neoclassical economic approach to politics that spawned it.

The post–Cold War world confronts scholars and practitioners with much of the uncertainty and fluidity we have become accustomed to associating with the interwar period. The global structure of conflict is less clear as we stand somewhere between the precarious unipolarity of U.S. predominance and the evolving multipolarity of regional centers of power. Former enemies are becoming friends, and former allies are becoming adversaries. Military power remains an important currency of international influence but economic prosperity and the nonmilitary dimensions of security have increased in salience among leaders and their publics. Between the wars, arms control was used to reorient perceptions of power, status, and influence among states in order to transcend sources of conflict and enlarge the scope for cooperation. This approach did not always succeed, but to the degree that it did, it deserves far more careful consideration and study by those interested in building robust regional and global security orders for the future.

In writing and rewriting this book more times than I would have ever imagined, I had the good fortune to have had the support and advice of a number of individuals through the years. The final product of this book is more a testament to the insights I gained from my adviser, Alexander George, than I ever anticipated when I first began my dissertation. For the core of my book rests on the power of "process" and the insights that a process perspective can give us that static approaches to understanding politics and policymaking ignore, obscure, or deem irrelevant. Anyone who knows Alex George will be familiar with the intensity with which he strives to unpack the "black box" of the policy- and decision-making processes. It has taken me years to recognize the tremendous power of his ideas, and I hope I have done them justice.

While writing my dissertation at Stanford University, I benefited from the advice of Robert North, Condoleezza Rice, and David Holloway. Christopher Gacek has been a thoughtful critic and supporter throughout the years. While completing my dissertation at the Center for International Affairs, Harvard University, as a John M. Olin fellow, I came into contact with a group of very bright individuals: Michael Desch, Ted Hopf, Chaim Kaufman, Kimberly Nolan, and Kevin Sheehan. I thank them for their suggestions and insights. While I was a Secretary of the Navy fellow at the U.S. Naval War College, Bob Kaufman provided me with support, motivation, and a very healthy dose of sarcasm that saw me through the conclusion of the project. I thank John Maurer for always reminding me of the importance of the topic. Andrea Gates provided critical assistance at the conclusion of the project.

Generous fellowships from the MacArthur and Olin foundations and from the Institute for Global Conflict and Cooperation at the University of California allowed me to complete my research and writing. The Herbert Hoover Presidential Library awarded me a research travel grant.

Several individuals deserve special mention. My parents, Carolyn and Elmer Goldman, have always supported me and believed in me. I could not have sustained this endeavor without them. My husband, Barry Forrest, was unfortunate in that he was broken into the life of living with an academic, probably at one of the most stressful times in an academic's career. He worked very hard to help me keep it all in perspective.

Finally, I owe a very special debt of gratitude to Leslie Eliason. Leslie was my most severe critic, yet my greatest champion. She constantly kept the faith when I lost sight of it. She helped me to uncover the ideas buried in my work and remained convinced of its importance all along the way. While I alone am responsible for the contents of this book, it would not have reached the point it did without her support. I dedicate this book to a true friend and colleague, Leslie Eliason.

Davis, California
April 1993

LIST OF MAPS AND TABLES

1 Shattering the Arms Control Orthodoxy

ON JUNE 8, 1928, Chinese Nationalist forces entered Peking after their long march northward. The Nationalists officially took over the capital on July 3, parading the streets past a throng of expressionless onlookers. Chiang Kai-shek and the four principal generals of the second northern expedition then paid a ceremonial visit to a temple in the Western Hills where the remains of Sun Yat-sen lay. In an atmosphere charged with emotion, they presented the father of the Chinese nation with the consummation of his dreams. The Nationalist unification of China, a revolution that Sun had ordained, had been achieved, at least nominally. Several months later that same year and thousands of miles to the west, the groundwork for a second revolution was being laid. In November 1928, in Germany, the Weimar government authorized funds to construct *Panzerkreuzer* A, the first of Germany's revolutionary pocket battleships, a vessel able to outshoot any vessel that could outrun it and outrun any vessel that could outshoot it. Both of these revolutions, the culmination of one and the initiation of another, heralded the demise of the Washington treaty system. The first rendered its political premises obsolete. The second rendered its technical premises irrelevant.

Throughout the 1920s and into the 1930s, sea power in the Far East was regulated by a system of treaty agreements that had been negotiated at the Washington Conference of 1921–22 by the five leading naval powers of the period, Great Britain, the United States, Japan, France, and Italy. With the defeat of Germany in World War I, British eyes turned toward the Far East and China, the region of the most extensive global rivalry. It was also in the Pacific rather than the Atlantic that two new naval powers had emerged with the ability to challenge Britain's global naval hegemony. With the acquisition of the Philippine Islands from the Spanish in 1898, the strategic frontier of a continental United States had become global, and the wartime construction program of the United States had positioned it to subvert Britannia's rule of the waves. Japan had made significant territorial gains in the Pacific during the First World War and had emerged predominant in the western region. The Japanese longed to be admitted to the great-power club, with all that it entailed. These three, the so-called Big Three, embarked on a great experiment in 1921 in the Far East, with implications for the global balance of naval power. They were unaware of the rocks of Chinese nationalism, worldwide depression, and German ambition that lay beneath the surface of the waters they were sailing. For them, arms control and political accommodation in the Far East offered a way to achieve economic prosperity and imperial security peacefully and cheaply.

The three most significant treaties signed at the Washington Conference limited the primary naval combatants of all five naval powers based on ratios of total capital ship tonnage, demilitarized the western Pacific, and committed the Far Eastern powers to work to help China develop into a strong independent nation that could promote stability in the region. In 1930, the Washington powers reconvened at the first London Naval Conference and extended the coverage of technical limitation to ancillary combatants—cruisers, destroyers, submarines—which had not been done at Washington. But in the intervening eight years, the Chinese Nationalists had unified their country and were committed to revoking all the unequal treaties that the imperial powers had imposed on China in the past. And Germany was preparing for complete and overt rearmament. A second London Conference was scheduled for December 1935, and by the time it convened, the Washington treaty system had ceased to exist. In 1934, Japan had given notification of its intent to withdraw from the system by 1936, following the prescribed procedures for withdrawal. The Japanese had already expelled the Chinese Nationalists from China's northern provinces and replaced local rulers with puppet governments. France had begun to rearm against Germany, and in January 1935, the French formally abrogated the Washington treaty after Mussolini refused to surrender parity to France.

In retrospect we might wonder why the system failed to prevent the outbreak of war in the Pacific and dismiss the experience as a failure because of its "brief" duration. We should not be too hasty. The naval arms control experiment is one of few historical precedents of its kind, and its value today has risen precisely because it preceded the Cold War. With the burgeoning of nuclear arsenals after World War II, the logic and nature of arms control changed fundamentally. Arms control became tightly linked to the Cold War political landscape, which was characterized by bipolarity, irreconcilable political differences, an overriding concern with nuclear technology, and an obsession with the military dimensions of security. Arms control was relegated to a technical exercise of fine-tuning force structures to manage a relationship characterized above all by immutable conflict. The Cold War arms control orthodoxy has bequeathed a set of intellectual and strategic blinders to the role that arms control may play above and beyond the technical dimensions to which it has been relegated for the past forty-five years. Beyond the academic interest that such a critique of arms control theory may engender, the policy implications for today are perhaps of greater relevance because mainstream arms control theory offers little guidance for navigating the complex political landscape of the post–Cold War world.

To appreciate the interwar naval arms control experiment as it unfolded, we must understand the political, economic, and domestic as well as military and strategic considerations that shaped the treaty powers' decision-making processes. I lay these out in Chapters 2 and 3. In Chapter 4 I discuss the negotiations at the Washington Conference. In Chapters 5 and 6 I examine the military and political developments that followed in the 1920s, and which laid the groundwork for the collapse of the system in the 1930s. Although the Washington treaty system is generally treated as one arms control event, it is really several. True, in 1922, negotiations for arms control in the Far East and in Europe took place at the same conference, and their provisions were interrelated, but the processes were different. In the Far East the arms control processes of the 1920s and the 1930s were fundamentally different. It is in these differences that the nature of the Cold War arms control orthodoxy is revealed and challenged. It is from these cases that

I identify two fundamentally different strategies of arms control, one that may have worked during the Cold War, another that holds far more promise for the post–Cold War world.

GAINING PERSPECTIVE ON THE COLD WAR

For three decades, the ideas introduced in Thomas Schelling and Morton Halperin's book *Strategy and Arms Control* (1961) dominated the discourse of the arms control debate. These ideas comprise one of the most entrenched bodies of Cold War thought and illustrate how deeply the Cold War has become "hard-wired into our strategic mentality."[1] With the end of the Cold War, scholars have been driven back into history to find guides for charting future policy. Some scholars have optimistically called for the return to collective security systems like the Concert of Europe. Others, pessimistically, see in the post–Cold War disorder the balance of power politics and communal rivalries characteristic of the pre–World War I era and the 1930s. The 1920s have valuable insights and lessons that have gone underexamined to date. That period in history may prove surprisingly illuminating for the complex, multilateral, and politically charged landscape in which future arms control initiatives will be forged.

Interwar naval arms control, the single most prominent pre–Cold War example of force limitation, has relevance for the multilateral and regional dimensions of arms control today. The political landscape within which that arms control process developed resembles in significant ways the forces shaping the contemporary arms control environment. In both periods, the international system was moving through a period of political transition with traditional great powers disappearing or experiencing limited retrenchment and new powers emerging and assuming more prominent postures. In both periods, the devolution of power, and movement toward multipolarity and regional centers of influence, coexisted with strong incentives for cooperative economic relationships and a less competitive international order. Both periods can be characterized by a high degree of uncertainty. Finally, in both periods there developed an enhanced appreciation for the nonmilitary di-

1. Eliot Cohen, "The Future of Force," *National Interest* 21 (Fall 1990): 9.

mensions of security. It was under a set of circumstances of this nature that post–World War I leaders negotiated a military-economic-political package regulating arms control, commerce, and diplomacy in the Far East, an area of the world, it was recognized, that could potentially become the primary locus of postwar instability. The hope was that robust cooperative regional orders would pave the way toward a new world order once regional force ratios were extended to the global level.

What do the differences between the Cold War and post–Cold War political landscapes mean for the future relevance and direction of arms control initiatives? The differences are a sign that the new political-diplomatic-strategic landscape requires a radically different approach to arms control. In contrast to the Cold War "military-based" approach to the arms control process, the new era calls for a "political-based" orientation. The military-based approach to arms control was defined and shaped by the Cold War structure of conflict. Because political consensus proved so difficult to forge, much of the cooperative effort focused on regulating the military relationship and mitigating the destabilizing characteristics of nuclear weapons and their delivery systems. As Lawrence Freedman characterizes it, "The main concern was with the safe management of the military aspects of the Cold War, and therefore no provision was made in the theory for overcoming the basic antagonism."[2] At best, arms control could only manage a status quo. Arms control matured as a military mechanism that addressed questions of strategy, weaponry, deployments, and doctrine. Arms control, from this Cold War perspective, encompasses all forms of military cooperation in the interest of furthering the political goal of avoiding war.[3] In general, these remain the terms of the arms control discourse today. The focus is disproportionately on the relationship between instabilities in military balances and the outbreak of war.

By contrast, the political-based approach to arms control is designed to enhance general political stability and to reduce the nonmilitary incentives to resort to force or to intimidation by the threat of force, rather than just the military incentives to resort to force. To do this

2. Lawrence Freedman, "Weapons, Doctrines, and Arms Control," *Washington Quarterly* (Spring 1984): 9; see also Lawrence Freedman, *The Evolution of Nuclear Strategy* (New York: St. Martin's Press, 1981), especially Section 5.

3. Thomas C. Schelling and Morton H. Halperin, *Strategy and Arms Control* (New York: The Twentieth Century Fund, 1961; reprint, Washington, D.C.: Pergamon Press, 1985), p. 2; page references are to reprint edition.

successfully, the arms control process must link military and nonmilitary arrangements. As examples, the arms control process may marry settlements over (1) spheres of influence, (2) security guarantees, (3) new security structures, (4) norms and procedures for intervention in areas of conflict, (5) containment and resolution of conflict, and (6) economic relations with the more familiar mechanisms of (1) limitations and reductions, (2) bans on use and deployments, and (3) confidence- and security-building measures. The political-based approach expands the scope of the arms control process beyond the restrictions imposed by the Cold War structure of conflict. The arms control process, from this perspective, can function as an important tool for shaping a new status quo.

Most critical, the political-based approach to arms control differs from the military-based approach by stressing the importance of building a consensus among the parties' strategic visions or conceptions of stability and security. Restraint is a property of the political, diplomatic, and strategic landscape and is shaped by the strategic visions of the participants. The bipolar nuclear confrontation, because it simplified the strategic situation between the superpowers in important ways, also oversimplified our notions of arms control. Restraint was understood as a property inhering in and traveling with technology. The world is more complex now. No objective definition of "stability" exists today, as the logic of mutual assured destruction (MAD) would have us believe at the strategic nuclear level. Rather, state-specific definitions of stability and security compete with as well as complement one another. Stability and security are defined subjectively by each state in terms of its unique political, economic, and strategic circumstances; hence, the importance of understanding how arms control is affected by different and potentially competing strategic visions and of forging a political consensus for arms control that creates and builds on mutually conceived understandings of the role of military force.

Our contemporary theories of arms control are driven largely by the technical properties (and consequences) of nuclear weapons. If we restrict ourselves to a military-based approach to arms control, we will be interested predominantly in the technical characteristics of weapons and how they influence military strategy. Restraint, however, is a product of understandings, interpretations, and perceptions of people involved in bargaining about weapons use and limitation. Contemporary theorists have missed many important aspects of the dynamics of the arms control process because they have focused almost exclusively on the consequences of nuclear technology and on the behavior of the states possessing the largest nuclear arsenals, the superpowers. By looking at the security system of the 1920s and 1930s, we can critique prevailing notions of arms control that are part of the Cold War orthodoxy without the fog of the nuclear dimension obscuring our analytic view.

The interwar experience in the Far East offers one pattern of political-based arms control, combining force reductions with security guarantees, nonaggression pacts, spheres of influence, norms and procedures for intervention in third areas, and economic arrangements. Since the major arena of potential conflict between the great naval powers was China, deep force reduction was part and parcel of a general security package in the region. The interwar experience demonstrates that the security-enhancing capacity of treaties depends less on how technical provisions affect the military balance than on how the entire arms control exercise supports broader foreign policy and national security goals, and that technical agreements which simplify highly nuanced political dialogues may exacerbate insecurity. The successes and failures of the interwar experience yield both encouraging and cautionary lessons for today. On the encouraging side, the arms control process facilitated and codified a shift in political relations among Great Britain, the United States, and Japan. The process was a means of transition from an alliance relationship that legitimated Japanese imperialism and created friction between Great Britain and the United States to one that formalized Anglo-American alignment as a basis for regional and world order. On the cautionary side, we see how agreements between former long-standing allies (Great Britain and Japan) rapidly deteriorated, at a time when we are struggling to forge agreements between former, even longer-standing enemies. As a case study of the rise and decline of a multilateral security system during a period of political transition, the arms control process of the 1920s and 1930s forces us to reconsider assumptions about arms control that we have accepted for three decades, assumptions that may be constraining our ability to think creatively about building robust and durable security systems after the Cold War.

How did the statesmen of the interwar years negotiate and structure the Far Eastern security system? What cautionary lessons may we draw from their failure to maintain that security system over time? Both political-based and military-based arms control strategies were pursued at

the Washington Conference of 1921–22. In the European arena, negotiations were confined to technical force balances because the British
refused to grant the French security guarantees on the Continent. In
the Far East, the negotiators were very conscious of the fact that force-
balance agreements would not be viable unless integrated with discussions of conflict resolution in China. A comparative analysis of the Far
Eastern and European components of the Washington treaty system
permits us to evaluate the extent to which each approach mitigated or
exacerbated interstate tensions. The Washington treaty system collapsed in the 1930s under a series of pressures, primarily economic, that
were out of the hands of negotiators to predict and influence. However,
the actual arms control process itself was not without levers of influence
for policymakers. We can learn from their successes and failures in
managing the arms control process, particularly by pinpointing poor
strategies that may have exacerbated the impact of situational factors,
such as revolution in China and worldwide depression, on the threat
perceptions of states.

INTERWAR ARMS CONTROL—AN OVERVIEW

The interwar naval arms control experiment was a complex process that
spanned fifteen years, embraced six major treaties, and included five
great powers. The treaty powers sought to regulate great-power political, military, and economic relations in the Far East and western Pacific
and extend the security system to the global level by linking Pacific and
European force balances. The technical arms control provisions of the
security system were codified in the Five Power treaty of 1922. Built on
the premise that the battleship remained the strategic system of the day
and the index of great power, the Five Power treaty was also supported
by a consensus among the three leading maritime powers on the validity
of Alfred Thayer Mahan's doctrine of battleship supremacy. Endorsement of Mahan's strategic doctrine provided a shared understanding of
the role of naval power in national security and a common basis to
establish the limitation of naval forces.

The Five Power treaty laid out a series of procedures for orchestrating
a new naval balance. Capital ship tonnage was to be used as the index
of naval power with proportionate allowances for auxiliary, or ancillary,
combatants. Calculation of total tonnage levels was to be based on an

assessment of relative and existing strength in terms of ratios. Actual and projected capital ship building programs were halted for the duration of a ten-year naval holiday. Armaments were reduced by scrapping older vessels. Anglo-American naval parity was established. Britain, the United States, and Japan agreed not to fortify their bases in the western Pacific.

The Four Power treaty demilitarized the western Pacific and superseded the long-standing Anglo-Japanese alliance with a nonaggression pact. Premised on the principle of security without resorting to alliance, force, or the combination of any two nations against another, this treaty proved indispensable for naval limitation. The United States would not limit its navy if the Anglo-Japanese alliance remained intact because the alliance enabled Japanese imperialism in the Far East and endangered U.S. interests. Yet the Japanese refused to accept an inferior capital ship ratio if the alliance was not renewed or if some other corresponding compensation was not offered. The Four Power treaty supplied this compensation by forbidding British and U.S. collusion in the Orient. When coupled with treaty limits on force projection by virtue of both the 5:5:3 battleship ratio among the British, U.S., and Japanese navies and the prohibition of base fortifications in the western Pacific, the Four Power treaty left the Japanese with indisputable local superiority. Acquiescing to the inferior capital ship ratio became possible.

Finally, the Far Eastern powers recognized that the Four and Five Power treaties would not promote confidence unless linked to specific understandings regarding China. Naval agreements were made contingent on political detente. In particular, the western powers needed formal assurances that Japan was ready to curtail its ambitions on the mainland. The Nine Power treaty advanced three principles: the open door in China, renunciation of particularistic diplomacy and pursuit of cooperative action among the great powers in China, and noninvolvement in China's internal affairs. To promote stability, the treaty powers outlined the "Washington formula," a series of steps for raising duties on Chinese imports to create a financial base for a strong central government.[4]

4. The "Washington formula," embodied in the Washington Customs Treaty, pledged the signatories to "raise the duty on China's imports by a surtax not exceeding 5 percent ad valorem on luxuries and 2½ percent on other articles. The treaty also contemplated a further increase in the tariff to a 12½ percent rate on condition that the Chinese abolished the system of likin," an internal transit tax on goods moving between different provinces. Dorothy Borg, *American Policy and the Chinese Revolution, 1925–1928* (New York: Macmillan, 1947), pp. 95–96.

This network of agreements formed the basis for a new security framework for the Far East and represented a first step toward world order and reconstruction based on great-power cooperation. Military agreements stabilized a balance of naval power by granting each Pacific power defensive superiority in its respective sphere and by reducing the ability to bring war to one's adversary. Accordingly, one might conclude that arms control successfully enhanced security. Nevertheless, because fundamental political interests that mirrored this new military equilibrium, particularly those of the Americans and Japanese, failed to converge over the life of the treaty system, perceptions of enhanced security diminished over time.

At the Washington Conference of 1922, the treaty powers—Great Britain, the United States, Japan, France, and Italy—recognized that by enhancing the ability to defend and curtailing the ability to attack maritime communications and respective spheres of influence in the Pacific, arms control would reinforce mutual security and bolster deterrence. The Washington treaties were designed to reduce navies to defensive forces by restricting fighting capability and by limiting the major offensive weapon system of the day: the battleship. For Great Britain, the United States, and Japan, rigid limits on their navies largely removed threats to their home territories and vital overseas interests. For the most part, each was seriously threatened by a very limited number of adversaries: one another. Security was further enhanced by their relative geographical isolation.[5]

The 5:5:3 ratio of total battleship tonnage offset the advantages the Japanese had in the western Pacific by virtue of geographic proximity. The nonfortification clause froze naval base fortifications in the western Pacific at the status quo. Both provisions were orchestrated to safeguard respective national interests in the Far East by creating defensive superiority in respective Pacific spheres. The Four Power treaty demilitarized the western Pacific and committed the signatories to refrain from allying with, or colluding against, one another. This measure further reduced the risk of war in the western Pacific because the United States relinquished the option of colluding with the British, which significantly curtailed U.S. power projection capability.

Nevertheless, interwar naval arms control was only a limited success,

5. Christopher Hall, *Britain, America, and Arms Control* (New York: St. Martin's Press, 1987), p. 115.

and it has become part of the folklore to call it an unmitigated failure. Interestingly, an assessment based exclusively on military or technical criteria cannot tell us why the treaty process failed, since the indicator of success a military-based approach uses is force-posture stability, not general stability. The causes of failure in the 1920s and 1930s that a military-based arms control approach would logically omit include the pursuit of overly ambitious and clashing foreign policy objectives by the treaty powers and how this influenced their orientation toward arms control, and failure to accommodate changes over time in the domestic political, diplomatic, economic, and strategic constraints facing the treaty powers. Rather than address the dilemma of Japanese insecurity created by the unification of China, the Anglo-Saxon powers separated political questions from arms control issues at the London Naval Conference of 1930 in what we now think of as the modern arms control mode. These examples of the causes of failure highlight political sources of instability that are not addressed by military-based strategies of arms control.

By contrast, a political-based approach to the arms control process would evaluate the success of the interwar experience by also asking whether or not the treaties had aligned, or at least temporarily bridged, the conflicts of political interest that fueled military rivalries, and how political interests were codified in the treaties. In 1922, Great Britain and the United States had compatible political expectations about how to enhance security, which were codified in the Washington treaties. Political expectations between the United States and Japan converged only temporarily, however.

The Washington treaties succeeded in mitigating tensions in Anglo-American relations, which facilitated the peaceful evolution away from British naval superiority to Anglo-American parity. The treaties eliminated the possibility of conflict between the two superpowers of the interwar period, which at the time was a major contingency contemplated by naval planners on both sides of the Atlantic. One might assume that neither the United States nor Britain was in fact committed to an arms race because they did not build to the full extent permitted by treaty limits in the ensuing years.[6] Yet the degree of competition

6. Bruce D. Berkowitz makes such an argument in *Calculated Risks: A Century of Arms Control, Why It Has Failed, and How It Can Be Made to Work* (New York: Simon & Schuster, 1987), pp. 147–49.

in Anglo-American relations during the interwar period remains a hotly contested issue among historians.[7] Had there been no Washington treaty, the United States might have proceeded with its 1916 building program and the British might have built four battle cruisers and four battleships, neither of which happened. The naval agreements succeeded in defusing Anglo-American conflict because political compromises were forged and codified during the treaty process that mirrored the technical codification of parity in the 5:5:3 capital ship ratio. The Washington treaties superseded the Anglo-Japanese alliance that had shielded Japan's and served Britain's Far Eastern policies since 1902.[8] Great Britain abandoned its major Far Eastern ally and became a nominal adversary with Japan in order to restructure its military relationship with the United States. Arms control managed the transformation of this political-military relationship and was grounded in an emerging political consensus among British and U.S. leaders.

At the same time, the Five Power treaty established only a very delicate political consensus to support the new U.S.-Japanese military relationship. Although the technical provisions agreed to between the United States and Japan enhanced deterrence, failure to more effectively bridge political conflicts of interest over time renewed perceptions of insecurity and contributed to system breakdown. Tokyo was determined to prevent western intervention in the Far East and to dominate East Asia's raw material markets.[9] Washington wanted to preserve

7. Thomas A. Buckley, *The United States and the Washington Conference, 1921–1922* (Knoxville: University of Tennessee Press, 1970), p. 20, discusses the tensions of Anglo-American relations. The subtitle of Stephen Roskill's first volume on naval policy in the 1920s, a classic in the field, tells the story. Roskill writes, "In spite of this community of interest between Britain and the United States naval rivalry between them played a very large part in the disarmament negotiations, and at times came near to wrecking the close association which had been achieved during the war. The events leading to the British-American alliance of World War II, in which an unprecedented degree of military, economic and political co-ordination was for a time achieved, have resulted in a tendency by historians to underplay, if not actually ignore, the serious differences of opinion and the rivalry in many fields which arose between the two nations during the inter-war period." The fundamental causes of naval rivalry between the two lay in the "challenge of the United States to the long-standing maritime and mercantile predominance enjoyed by Britain." Stephen Roskill, *Naval Policy Between the Wars*, vol. 1, *The Period of Anglo-American Antagonism, 1919–1929* (New York: Walker, 1968), p. 20.

8. Ian Nish, *The Anglo-Japanese Alliance: The Diplomacy of Two Island Empires, 1894–1907* (London: Athlone Press, 1966); Ian Nish, *Alliance in Decline: A Study in Anglo-Japanese Relations, 1908–23* (London: Athlone Press, 1972).

9. Sadao Asada, "Japan's Special Interests and the Washington Conference, 1921–1922," *American Historical Review* 67 (October 1961): 62–70.

its influence in the Far East to restrain Japanese activities and defend U.S. interests.[10] The United States promoted the Nine Power treaty and Washington formula for tariff revision as the new mechanisms to regulate and coordinate great power interaction in China. U.S. desires to preserve Chinese territorial and administrative integrity and to se-cure the open door clearly clashed with the Japanese vision of hege-mony in the Far East. For the Japanese, neither agreement on arms limitation nor on the Nine Power treaty reflected a firm rejection of long-term imperial aspirations.[11] Rather, cooperation was perceived as a safer, more expedient way to achieve those objectives with minimum force and as a means to enhance long-term strategic and economic se-curity.[12]

More than a technical question of limiting and monitoring force levels, security in the Far East required understandings to regulate great-power interaction on the mainland because of the potential for insta-bility that existed in China. At the Washington Conference, the treaty process included policy deliberations on China and the Pacific, but in the ensuing years the treaty powers failed to cultivate an enduring polit-ical consensus to reorient great-power strategic interaction in China.[13] An important first step, the Nine Power treaty outlined general princi-ples of behavior but it left enough latitude for different interpretations. The treaty did not represent a consensus on policy objectives parallel to the technical provisions of the Five Power treaty because no shared conception of a future vision for China ever evolved. Britain and the United States remained committed to the independence and stability of China[14] to neutralize Japanese claims to special interests that the Japa-nese were determined to preserve.[15] Though calling for restraint and

10. Buckley, *United States and the Washington Conference*, p. 27.

11. James B. Crowley, *Japan's Quest for Autonomy: National Security and Foreign Policy, 1930–1938* (Princeton: Princeton University Press, 1966), pp. xiv–xvii.

12. Michael Barnhart, "Japan's Economic Security and the Origins of the Pacific War," *Journal of Strategic Studies* 4 (June 1981): 105–24; Nish, *Alliance in Decline*, p. 280.

13. With the failure of the Peking Tariff Conference in 1926, the Washington signatories abandoned cooperation in China based on the Washington formula and began pursuing unilateral strategies in the Far East. Akira Iriye, *After Imperialism: The Search for a New Order in the Far East, 1921–1931* (Cambridge: Harvard University Press, 1965), pp. 57–88.

14. W. G. Beasley, *Japanese Imperialism, 1894–1945* (Oxford: Clarendon Press, 1987), p. 19; W. Roger Louis, *British Strategy in the Far East, 1919–1939* (Oxford: Clarendon Press, 1971), pp. 19–25; A. Whitney Griswold, *Far Eastern Policy of the United States* (New York: Harcourt, Brace, 1938).

15. Raymond Leslie Buell, *The Washington Conference* (New York: D. Appleton, 1922), pp.

noninterference in the internal affairs of China, the Nine Power treaty lacked meaningful substantive provisions, and its ambiguities permitted conflicting interpretations by states with incompatible agendas.

Eight years later, at the London Naval Conference of 1930, the signatories addressed strictly military questions, and though the treaty process reduced the potential for conflict in narrow military terms,[16] it failed to ground its provisions in a political consensus. Militarily, the London treaty actually codified Japanese superiority until 1936. Though the Japanese accepted a 10:6 ratio in heavy cruisers with the United States, they actually secured at least a de facto 10:7 ratio until 1936 because the United States, under the provisions of the Reed-Matsudaira compromise,[17] agreed to defer construction of its sixteenth cruiser until 1934, the seventeenth until 1935, and the eighteenth until 1936. The Japanese derived little comfort from the fact that their military supremacy in the western Pacific had been guaranteed until 1936. The London Conference did not cause Japanese insecurity but it certainly exacerbated Tokyo's security concerns, despite the force ratio in cruisers that Japan could have enjoyed through the mid-1930s.

The success of arms control depends on the degree to which agreements enhance the security of the signatories *as each of them defines it.* For the Japanese, the Washington naval treaties enhanced security as long as they codified Japanese hegemony in the Far East. Even though one could argue that Japan would retain naval superiority in the Far East until 1936, failure to reach a political consensus with the Anglo-Saxon powers on policy in China undermined the durability of arms control by creating a crisis of confidence in Japan. Since 1925, Japanese leaders had feared the effects of the Nationalist unification of China and wanted cruisers in excess of the 10:6 ratio to supplement their fleet. "Generally the appeals were based on the China operations or on Japan's emergence as a major Power."[18] It is doubtful that the difference

240–41; William Reynolds Braisted, *The United States Navy in the Pacific* (Austin: University of Texas Press, 1971), p. 569.

16. At London, for the first time an agreement was reached that limited all categories of warships of Great Britain, the United States, and Japan, quantitatively in all classes and qualitatively in each class. A major loophole, the failure to place quantitative restrictions on ancillary vessels, which had been exploited for renewed competition during the 1920s, was blocked.

17. Raymond G. O'Connor, *Perilous Equilibrium: The United States and the London Naval Conference of 1930* (Lawrence: University of Kansas Press, 1962), pp. 76–83.

18. Gerald E. Wheeler, *Prelude to Pearl Harbor: The United States Navy and the Far East, 1921–1931* (Columbia: University of Missouri Press, 1963), p. 169. On the last point, O'Connor argues

between a 10:6 and 10:7 ratio in a secondary category of ship could have significantly enhanced Japan's security, but it reveals how the Japanese defined their security. The higher ratio and acknowledgment of special interests in China were tightly linked in a political definition of great-power status. Arms control policy could only be understood according to this definition of Japanese national security.

Focusing on military questions and excluding related political issues in 1930 at the first London Conference was one way to close loopholes in the arms-limitation component of the security system. It succeeded in broadening the scope of technical agreement but failed to address the political sources of conflict, and this eventually destroyed the carefully spun web of security understandings. In essence, subjective definitions of security among states must converge over time for arms control to succeed, and one should not assume that agreements that enhance only military stability necessarily enhance security. In 1930 the Japanese delegates accepted the inferior ratio in cruiser tonnage in a tenuous and politically unpopular compromise, yet received no political compensation.[19] Concessions were confined to ships alone, and this failed to address the political sources of instability in the Far East, particularly Japanese fears about a unified Nationalist China. In the end, this military-based approach and its failure to relate the political and military dimensions of security contributed to the fall from power of those leaders in Japan committed to arms limitation and cooperation with the West. In a parallel fashion, the legacy of naval arms control in Europe between the wars provides a study in the persistent failure to relate the political and military dimensions of security.

The interwar naval arms control experience demonstrates the destabilizing consequences of pursuing military-based arms control in the absence of developing, or moving toward, a consensus on the political architecture that arms control, at best, can only bolster. This period teaches us that whether or not arms control will enhance security de-

---

that with population increases and rising unemployment "Japan appeared to have reached the limits of industrial expansion. In the nineteenth century a nation faced with this situation could find relief through imperialism, but the Western powers had denied this solution to Japan at the Washington Conference. Only China appeared to offer the opportunity which Japan so desperately sought, but the economic exploitation of this huge and politically chaotic nation was bound to meet with resistance from the Western powers and Russia." O'Connor, *Perilous Equilibrium*, p. 53.

19. Sadao Asada, "Japanese Admirals and the Politics of Naval Limitation: Kato Tomosaburo vs Kato Kanji," in Gerald Jordan, ed., *Naval Warfare in the Twentieth Century, 1900–1945* (New York: Crane Russak, 1977), pp. 147–48.

pends not only on the impact of technical provisions related to the military balance but also on how arms control is assimilated into definitions and perceptions of national security. State-specific perceptions of what security entails and the role arms control is perceived to play in enhancing security are important factors that must enter into the arms control process to produce useful security-enhancing treaties. These perceptions will vary from state to state and over time, but clearly conflicting definitions of national security adversely affect treaty interpretation and compliance. In the 1920s and 1930s, the U.S. definition of national security differed in crucial respects from the Japanese.

For a self-sufficient post–World War I United States, a global order based on political independence, self-determination, equal opportunity, and free trade would enhance national security.[20] This definition was incompatible with Japan's belief that legitimate exclusive rights in Asia were indispensable for its economic survival. For the United States, the conclusion of an arms-limitation agreement itself was perceived as a significant step toward the approach of a global order based on international law and unfettered economic activity.

The Japanese, by contrast, were committed to achieving great-power status. Acceptance of an inferior naval ratio in the Pacific region could be only temporary. Clearly, economic and domestic political pressures made cooperation with the West an attractive strategy, but arms control was never valued as an end in itself. Germany had been competitive militarily yet still vulnerable to economic blockade, impressing on the Japanese the necessity of economic security. Despite debate over tactics and strategy, the Japanese remained committed to pursuing what they perceived as eminently reasonable objectives: imperial security and economic self-sufficiency. Arms control and cooperation with the West could enhance their perceived security, but only as long as the treaties contributed to these goals. In the end, arms control would produce the ends of U.S. national security, but for Japan it represented only a means for achieving great-power status.

As the military-based approach implies, agreements among states based solely on military-technical considerations may reduce tension in the international system. However, this occurs only if their definitions of national security are compatible. (They need not be identical.) An

---

20. Michael A. Barnhart, *Japan Prepares for Total War: The Search for Economic Security, 1919–1941* (Ithaca: Cornell University Press, 1987), pp. 50–51.

approach focusing only on the military-technical priorities for arms control cannot explain what agreements represent to different states, because a military-based arms control approach assumes a narrow and temporally independent notion of stability and security, rather than inductively examining the political, diplomatic, economic, and strategic assumptions that influence how states define security.

ARMS CONTROL THEORY—THE PREVAILING ORTHODOXY

The intellectual foundations of contemporary U.S. arms control theory may be traced to the late 1950s and early 1960s when scholars and practitioners became consumed with managing the strategic nuclear relationship between the United States and Soviet Union.[21] The assumptions of this approach, most clearly articulated by Thomas Schelling and Morton Halperin, have driven the discourse of the arms control debate for three decades. This ahistorical body of thought possesses serious analytical deficiencies; nevertheless, its assumptions have continued to guide theory and prescriptions for the arms control process into the post–Cold War era.

Schelling, Halperin, and the Cold War arms control school that their ideas spawned base their prescriptions on a deductive theory of the sources of instability in the nuclear age. They posit that under conditions of intense political tension between states, the likelihood of war increases as the level of force-posture stability decreases. Because the level of political tension is assumed to be constant and high enough to preclude the resolution of political conflict (a situation called deadlock), these theorists focus on mitigating the destabilizing characteristics of nuclear weapons and their delivery systems, that is, reducing force-posture instability, as a more modest, practical alternative. By

21. In 1961, seven books were published that reflected the new arms control approach: Bernard B. Bechhoeffer, *Postwar Negotiations for Arms Control* (Washington, D.C.: The Brookings Institution, 1961); Donald G. Brennan, ed., *Arms Control, Disarmament, and National Security* (New York: George Braziller, 1961); Hedley Bull, *The Control of the Arms Race* (New York: Praeger, 1961); David H. Frisch, ed., *Arms Reduction: Program and Issues* (New York: The Twentieth Century Fund, 1961); Arthur T. Hadley, *The Nation's Safety and Arms Control* (New York: Viking, 1961); Louis Henkin, ed., *Arms Control: Issues for the Public* (New York: Prentice-Hall, 1961); and Thomas C. Schelling and Morton H. Halperin, *Strategy and Arms Control* (New York: The Twentieth Century Fund, 1961).

eliminating first-strike weapons and encouraging the deployment of weapons less vulnerable to preemptive attack,[22] technical treaties can lessen the likelihood that in a crisis, one state will be tempted to initiate military action to reap the advantages of striking first.[23] By reducing the military incentives to strike first, arms control reduces the risk of war. Because of the bias in this argument for the "military" requirement of enhancing security defined narrowly as force-posture stability, I refer to the Schelling-Halperin prescriptions, and the orientation their approach fosters, as "military-based" arms control. Arms control is a "military" tool that enhances the "political" goal of international security by offsetting the destabilizing characteristics of weapons through the design of military strategy, weaponry, deployments, and doctrine. Freedman describes the approach as an essentially managerial one that "offered no image of a world getting better" and "did not therefore set out a long-term agenda for action, but more a guide to the paradoxes of the nuclear age which wise statesmen would be wise to acknowledge."[24] Freedman argues that by the 1970s, there was a move away from the earlier assumption of steady antagonism.[25] Much of subsequent writing on arms control, however, remained wedded to the earlier beliefs.

Three central assumptions of the military-based orientation make it a weak and misleading model for the arms control process in general. First, the approach focuses to near exclusion on a situation of bipolar, superpower conflict. Because the players are involved in a game of deadlock, in game-theoretic terms this means they both "prefer firmness to either appeasing the opponent or compromising with him."[26] This reduces the opportunities for cooperation based on compatible political premises, elevating to preeminence technical arms control strategies. Though developing out of a perception in the mid-1950s that political-based arms control with the Soviet Union was impossible, this historically bounded Cold War assumption about the arms control process has been sustained as an objective truth about the enterprise in general.

22. Schelling and Halperin here make the assumption of rational deterrence, that deterrence will work if these goals are met.
23. Joseph Kruzel, "Arms Control, Disarmament, and Stability of the Postwar Era," in Charles W. Kegley, Jr., ed., The Long Postwar Peace: Contending Explanations and Projections (New York: HarperCollins, 1991), p. 257.
24. Freedman, "Weapons, Doctrines, and Arms Control," p. 9.
25. Ibid., pp. 10–11.
26. Glenn H. Snyder and Paul Diesing, Conflict Among Nations (Princeton: Princeton University Press, 1977), p. 45.

Second, the approach is obsessed with nuclear arms control. The very existence of nuclear weapons, as distinct from the fear of another conventional war, creates an overriding interest in avoiding war because the main determinant of the likelihood of war is "the character of modern weapons and the expectations they create."[27] In other words, nuclear weapons impose a "certain lethal symmetry," as Joseph Kruzel describes it, that overwhelms differences in doctrine and ideology.[28] The presumption is that restraint is a property of technology rather than of the strategic, diplomatic, and political context.

Third, nuclear weapons make it imperative to separate arms control from the broader political context to an unprecedented degree to reduce the chances that irreconcilable political agendas will interfere with the arms control process, and more broadly with efforts that serve mutual interests in reducing the risk of war. The approach isolates the military aspects of arms competitions, and this allows its adherents to deal with the technical dimensions of interstate rivalry separate from the broader political context within which that particular form of competition takes place. This assumption does not deny that certain types of linkage may develop in practice in conjunction with military-based approaches to arms control. Linkage did occur in U.S.-Soviet arms control relations.[29] Linkage was employed as a bargaining strategy with arms control at times the object, at times the lever of policy modification, as with U.S. grain sales to the Soviet Union. Linkage developed inadvertently, the result of unplanned interactions between arms control and developments in other policy areas, as in President Carter's request that the Senate table the SALT II treaty as a signal of U.S. displeasure with the Soviet invasion of Afghanistan. However, military-based arms control precludes intrinsic linkage, or the packaging of issues that cannot be easily decoupled from one another, as a strategy for arms negotiations.

The combination of these premises allows Cold War arms controllers to retreat into an analytical stance that isolates the technical/technological dimensions of arms racing. From this rather limited perspective, they generalize about the arms control process, which is unjustified for two reasons. First, from a case selection perspective, one cannot gener-

27. Schelling and Halperin, *Strategy and Arms Control*, p. 3.
28. Joseph Kruzel, "What's Wrong with the Traditional Approach?" *Washington Quarterly* 8 (Spring 1985): 124.
29. Kiron K. Skinner, "Linkage," in Albert Carnesale and Richard N. Haass, eds., *Superpower Arms Control: Setting the Record Straight* (Cambridge: Ballinger, 1987), pp. 275–302.

alize from a very specific kind of arms racing to all kinds of arms racing. Second, this approach rips nuclear arms control out of its broader historical and political context, as if it were possible in practice to divorce arms racing, nuclear or otherwise, from all other dimensions of interstate rivalry.

This approach has many pitfalls. First, one winds up assuming that the characteristics of the military aspects of a bipolar, nuclear arms race between two superpowers apply more generally to all interstate rivalries. The conventional arms control process in Europe has focused on achieving "conventional stability," equating this objective with the first-strike stability of strategic nuclear analysis.[30] Theorists of arms control have stretched the idea of stability, which is problematic even in the strategic nuclear context, to the non-nuclear arena.

Second, because the argument fixates on the destabilizing characteristics of weapons technology, it ignores how political crises might evolve into conventional confrontations that could escalate to the nuclear level.

Third, because it isolates the subset of strategic nuclear stalemate, the Cold War argument creates an artificial distinction between the arms control process at the strategic nuclear level and the arms control processes at all other levels.

Finally, because the Cold War argument focuses disproportionately on the relationship between the military balance and the outbreak of war, it narrowly confines the methods of the enterprise of arms control, which may lead to unwarranted disillusionment and to a belief that arms control is no longer relevant to the post–Cold War world. Mutual vulnerability may be a powerful motive to avoid a situation that could lead to a devastating war, but stability is multidimensional. If one advocates arms control strategies based on a deductive model of the incentives that lead to conflict, and if reality fails to mirror the predictions of the model, one may declare arms control irrelevant or a failure.

An evaluation, however, is only as valid as the assumptions of the model on which the prescriptions are based. The Cold War thesis is based on a deductive model that equates security with strategic stability, deduced from the logic of mutual assured destruction (MAD). Cold

---

30. Paul K. Davis et al., *Variables Affecting Central-Region Stability: The "Operational Minimum" and Other Issues at Low Force Levels* (N-2976-USDP) (Santa Monica: The RAND Corporation, September 1989), pp. 2–3.

War arms control prescriptions assume that bolstering the state of MAD minimizes the chances of nuclear war and enhances international security. However, does reinforcing MAD, with little attention to the level of conflict in the broader political relationship, enhance security as states define it subjectively?[31] An inductive approach examining the political, diplomatic, economic, and strategic assumptions that influence how states define security and how they utilize arms control and interpret treaties to enhance their security, reveals that the military-based deductive argument lacks validity. Whether arms control agreements enhance security in the estimation of political leaders remains an empirical question to be answered rather than an analytical assumption to be deduced.

An approach that reintegrates the nonmilitary and military components of security into the arms control process—both of which are critical foundations of sound arms control—supports different arms control strategies. Technical provisions must be coupled with understandings, however limited, that manage or moderate the differences that created and sustain the military rivalry. Political arrangements do not require a completely harmonious resolution of conflict. States may reach limited accommodations in specific issue areas. In the 1920s, for example, the Pacific powers negotiated spheres of influence and policies regulating commerce in China to support technical agreements managing the balance of naval power. Today, regulating the future balance of forces in Eurasia for the great powers, not to mention the lesser powers, requires understandings about the scope of great-power commitment there, the types of military forces that will be required to support that political commitment (e.g., highly mobile forces for crisis response), the management and organization of those forces, and the codification of norms of intervention and restraint for the use of those forces. Political-based arms control strategies are designed to forge a consensus on the premises of a military and political state of affairs, neither of which exists in isolation from the other. Political-based arms control prescriptions

31. Helga Haftendorn, "The Security Puzzle: Theory-Building and Discipline-Building in International Security," *International Studies Quarterly* 35 (March 1991): 3–17. Haftendorn discusses the shift in paradigm from "national" security to "international" security, based on the realization of mutual vulnerability in a nuclear world. She notes, however, that "though a concept of international security offers a better prescription for current security affairs than a strategy of national security, in its present form it has serious conceptual deficits and cannot be applied globally. It carries with it the notion of its origin, the preoccupation with nuclear weapons and deterrence, and is highly ethnocentric, based on U.S. perceptions and values." Haftendorn, pp. 10–11.

emerge from different theoretical premises about the sources of instability in interstate relations and the relationship between arms control
and the outbreak of war.

Cold War arms control advocates might counter with the analogy of
two gangs disarmed before attending a high-school dance. Although the
agreement could be strained by sneaking in knives or by a confrontation
outside the dance, the query is raised, "What is wrong with a technical
agreement to disarm as one component of a detente?" The danger under
these circumstances, empirically demonstrated in the 1920s and 1930s
but dismissed by Cold War arms control theory, is that a strategy of
technical arms control may enhance *insecurity*, because under such a
strategy only the military relationship becomes an issue of mutual responsibility, but the political goals remain unilateral responsibilities and
are neither assured nor compensated for. In this manner, technical arms
control treaties may make a state feel more vulnerable in the military
realm *and* in the political realm. Failure to grant political assurances to
counter the drop in capability and prestige caused by the reduction in
military assets may, to return to the analogy, undermine the prestige of
one gang disproportionately or shift the constellation of forces within a
gang adversely.

Leaders need not reach consensus on long-term political, economic,
or strategic objectives in order to agree on the technicalities of arms
control. Clearly, arms control agreements have been reached without
the harmonious resolution of political agendas and while political
agendas remained incompatible.[32] The post–World War II record veri-
fies this. But when is arms control, under these circumstances, a success? Agreements may be reached and tensions may be reduced for a
short time, but differences in underlying national agendas may restructure competition under the new security arrangements with potentially
deleterious effects on the level of general stability and political tension
among states. The Washington treaty process demonstrates how this
may develop.

At the Washington Conference of 1922, three different interest constellations supported agreements on various force-structure provisions.
Cooperation between "similar" interests was built on a consensus of
long-term political, economic, and/or strategic objectives. The Five

---

32. One example is that of SALT I. See George Breslauer, "Why Detente Failed," in Alexander
L. George, ed., *Managing U.S.-Soviet Rivalry: Problems of Crisis Prevention* (Boulder: Westview
Press, 1983), pp. 319–40.

Power treaty, which among other things codified Anglo-American naval parity, reflected a similar strategic objective for the United States
and Great Britain. The United States was determined to have a navy
second to none, and the British were committed to a fleet at least equal
to that of the next largest naval power. Since both powers agreed that
the battleship was the index of naval power, establishing parity in battleship strength was relatively easy. The long-term strategic objective of
moving from British naval superiority to Anglo-American parity, as Britain relinquished naval superiority for the first time in its history, codified a shift in the worldwide balance of naval power. Most important,
the Five Power treaty reflected a political consensus between the Anglo-Saxon powers that Anglo-American cooperation was the only firm
foundation for supporting a new postwar order.

Cooperation between "convergent" interests was built on different
yet not contradictory objectives that were satisfied within a single
agreement. The Four Power treaty was built on such convergent interests. The agendas of the signatories in the Pacific differed in important
respects yet were satisfied within the framework of a single agreement
that established their respective spheres of influence. The Four Power
treaty required significant concessions from the major Pacific powers.[33]
The United States, by forgoing any possibility of collusion with the
British, significantly curtailed its ability to project power into the western Pacific, which strengthened Japanese defensive superiority there.[34]
The British and Japanese abrogated the Anglo-Japanese alliance, the
cornerstone of their respective Far Eastern policies since 1902,[35] which
represented a major political realignment as the British and Japanese,

33. Since the British and Japanese had been allies for twenty years, the French were included in
the Four Power Treaty, at U.S. insistence, to prevent the isolation of the United States should
disputes arise.

34. Buell, The Washington Conference, pp. 182–200. Buell states, "I do not know whether the
American delegation realized the exact import of the Four Power Treaty or not. Certainly the fact
that it constitutes a pledge of non-intervention in the Orient was not brought out in the debates
on the Treaty. Nevertheless, it is difficult to see how the conclusion can be avoided that in the
future the United States will be forced to follow this policy, so much desired by Japan." The U.S.
delegates denied the existence of any secret understanding with Great Britain regarding the Four
Power Treaty which created "such a basis of sympathy . . . between Great Britain and the United
States that both sides assume that in all future emergencies they can both count on having the
very closest cooperation."

35. Ira Klein, "Whitehall, Washington, and the Anglo-Japanese Alliance, 1919–1921," Pacific
Historical Review 41 (November 1972): 460–83; M. G. Fry, "The North Atlantic Triangle and the
Abrogation of the Anglo-Japanese Alliance," Journal of Modern History 39 (March 1967): 46–64;
Nish, Alliance in Decline.

long-standing allies, became nominal adversaries. The abrogation of this alliance ameliorated a potential source of conflict in the Far East because the Japanese could no longer use the alliance with Britain to shield their imperialist ambitions in the Far East.

Cooperation despite "conflicting" interests emerged when a temporary convergence of conflicting preferences was accommodated in a treaty. This last scenario differs from that described by Cold War arms control theorists where cooperation in arms control emerges despite conflict in *other* issue areas. The situation described here is one in which cooperation emerges despite conflicting agendas in that *same* issue area.

The Five Power treaty bridged temporarily the conflicting foreign policy objectives and strategic interests of the United States and Japan. Convergence on means occurred between them despite failure to reconcile political and strategic differences. Tokyo wanted to maintain the status quo in the Far East for the time being and prevent Western intervention. Washington wanted to assure its ability to project power into the Far East to restrain Japanese activities[36] and defend U.S. interests. Though both states favored or found useful certain types of arms limitation, this policy preference reflected divergent strategic objectives. The Five Power treaty demonstrates that though convergence on interests may be absent, states may still cooperate. They may believe that in the short run, a diplomacy of cooperation is useful as a step in a particular political maneuver. Ideally, agreement could be a first step toward further arms control, security arrangements, or political accommodations. For the Japanese, however, arms limitation did not extinguish the competitive thrust of their foreign policy.

The Nine Power treaty is another example of how limited forms of ostensible cooperation developed though national agendas conflicted. Yet unlike the Five Power treaty, the Nine Power treaty demanded no positive actions of the signatories. The Nine Power treaty reflected a compromise between the conflicting interests of Great Britain and the United States, who sought to enhance the independence, stability, territorial and political integrity of China, and the Japanese, who were determined to preserve special interests on the mainland inconsistent with the principle of the open door endorsed by the treaty. Though calling for restraint and abstention, the Nine Power treaty lacked meaningful substantive provisions and remained sufficiently ambiguous

36. Buckley, *United States and the Washington Conference*, p. 27.

to accommodate differing interpretations and to support conflicting national agendas.

Cooperation is a multifaceted construct that varies with the nature of the interests served. The Five Power treaty codified the similar interests of Britain and the United States while temporarily bridging the conflicting interests of the United States and Japan. The Four Power treaty illustrates the ways dissimilar interests may converge and be fully satisfied in an agreement. The Nine Power treaty created the broad outlines for cooperation in China, even though the agendas of the Anglo-Saxon powers differed in fundamental ways from Japanese desires for hegemony in the Far East, and despite the lack of consensus on positive methods to cultivate and further cooperation in specific contingencies. Arms control may develop despite political conflict; however, the consequences of negotiating agreements that address numbers of weapons and neglect underlying differences may feed and even exacerbate competition unintentionally.

In the 1920s, the degree to which treaties succeeded in managing rivalry, reducing tension, and enhancing security depended in part on whether similar, convergent, or conflicting interests underlay treaty compromises. Disentangling the incentives that motivate states to engage in arms control clarifies the different types of political, economic, strategic, and military objectives that may contribute to the initiation of the process. The goals with which states enter arms control negotiations, however, do not predetermine the outcome of the process. Rather, the process itself is politically relevant for international actors because of the perceptions and understandings that may develop as part and parcel of the process and because of how the process may reshape the preferences and the strategic visions of the participants. Arms control is not simply a logical puzzle with agreements merely manifestations of national interests or objectives that can be deduced from the starting positions of the actors in the negotiating process. Arms control, rather, is a social process in which human beings may adjust their perceptions, understandings, and preferences over time. The nature of the process, therefore, is relevant to the nature of the outcomes. Arms control agreements are not epiphenomena, emerging only in areas where the initial preferences of the parties involved do not conflict. The strategies of arms control employed influence the outcome of the process and whether or not the process will enhance the security of the participants and reduce tensions among them. Although arms control may appear ephemeral as presently conceived—binding only when it is really unnecessary—this need not be the case if the process is shaped to include broader political considerations.

Two primary types of arms control strategies can be identified: (1) military-based strategies, designed to stabilize the balance of forces among adversaries and reduce the military incentives to resort to force, and (2) political-based strategies, designed to stabilize the overall political-military relationship among adversaries through the coupling of nonmilitary and military means in the arms control process. Arms control may be bilateral or multilateral; strategic or nonstrategic; nuclear or non-nuclear. The military-based/political-based dichotomy assumes that the important analytic distinction is whether the means implemented focus on regulating the military balance exclusively to enhance force-posture stability or on orchestrating a relationship between nonmilitary and military understandings to enhance general stability. This distinction should not be misconstrued to suggest that military-based arms control agreements are apolitical in either their domestic context or their negotiating objectives. Military-based strategies may be politically motivated. The distinction revolves around the means employed to secure those negotiating objectives.

Table 1 demonstrates how different types of interest constellations and arms control strategies resulted in different treaties in the 1920s and 1930s. Along the left axis, "resolution" of agendas encompasses similar and convergent interest constellations, whereas "contention" of agendas signifies conflicting interest constellations. The major agreements of the Washington treaty system fall across the four cells.

Table 1 Strategies and interests

Interest Constellation	Arms Control Strategy	
	Military and Nonmilitary Means	Military Means Only
Resolution (Agendas aligned)	U.S. and Britain • Five Power treaty, 1922 U.S., Britain, and Japan • Four Power treaty, 1922	Britain and France • Submarine treaty, 1922 Britain and France • London, 1930
Contention (Agendas in dispute)	U.S. vs. Japan • Five Power treaty, 1922 U.S. and Britain vs. Japan • Nine Power treaty, 1922	U.S. vs. Japan • London treaty, 1930 Britain vs. Germany • Anglo-German naval agreement, 1935

Table 2 Approaches to arms control

Scope of Arms Control Process	Arms Control Agreements (Outputs)	Arms Control Success (Outcomes)
	Political-Based Arms Control	
Political Economic Diplomatic Strategic Military-technical	(1) agreement/no agreement (2a) military content (i.e., parity, defensive superiority) (2b) political content (i.e., intervention norms, security guarantees, eco- nomic arrangements)	Security/insecurity (agendas aligned and codified; aligned but not codified; in dispute but bridged; in dispute and not bridged)
	Military-Based Arms Control	
Military-technical	(1) Agreement/no agreement (2) Military content	force posture stability/instability

The interesting analytic question is how successful were each treaty specifically and the overall system in general in diffusing tension, managing conflict, and enhancing the security of states involved in a mixed competitive-collaborative relationship? Agreements may, indeed, reduce expenditures but be counterproductive along these other criteria. The answer requires addressing how success should be operationalized and how a military-based approach to arms control differs from a political-based one in terms of fostering success.

By definition, military-based arms control treaties enhance international security if they effect a stable military balance and reduce force-posture instability, in short, if they reduce the military incentives to resort to force. However, whether those agreements enhance security in the estimation of national leaders depends on more than just the nature of the military balance. Deducing stability from the condition of the military balance is an analytical assumption of the military-based model rather than an empirical conclusion derived by examining how states define the requisites of their security.

The military-based arms control approach is analytically deficient for three reasons, and these reasons are compensated for in the political-based arms control approach. First, because of its Cold War focus, the military-based approach restricts the scope of the arms control negotiating process in crucial ways. Although inadvertent linkage may exist, intrinsic linkage is absent (see Tables 2, 3, and 4).

Table 3   The Washington Pacific treaties

Scope of Arms Control Process	Arms Control Agreements	Arms Control Success
Great Britain • Parity with U.S. • Imperial security • Commercial interests in China	*Military Content* Five Power treaty • Anglo-American parity • Defensive superiority in Pacific spheres	*Five Power Treaty* • G.B. and U.S. Agendas aligned and codified • U.S. vs. Japan Agendas in dispute bridged temporarily
United States • Navy second to none • New world order • Philippines and China	*Political Content* Four Power treaty • Security without collusion, alliance, force	
Japan • Hegemony in western Pacific • Special interests in China	*Political Content* Nine Power treaty • Open door • Renunciation of particularistic diplomacy • Noninvolvement in internal affairs of China	*Four Power Treaty* Agendas converge and codified *Nine Power Treaty* • G.B. and U.S. vs. Japan Agendas in dispute bridged temporarily

Table 4   The Washington European treaties

Scope of Arms Control Process	Arms Control Agreements	Arms Control Success
Great Britain • 2-power standard or superiority over France and Japan • Abolish submarine • Secure approaches to home islands	*Military Content* Five Power treaty • Franco-Italian parity • Great Britain 2-power standard Submarine treaty • Rules for conduct of warfare on merchant shipping	*Five Power Treaty* • France vs. Italy Agendas in dispute bridged temporarily *Submarine Treaty* • France and Britain Agendas aligned but not codified
France • Superiority over combined strengths of German and Italian fleets • Security guarantees in Europe	*Political Content* None	
Italy • Parity with France		

The military-based approach is concerned to near exclusion with regulating the destabilizing characteristics of military technology while slighting the importance of the political, diplomatic, economic, and strategic factors that influence behavior in the conflict and arms control arenas. The approach assumes that arms control is relevant if the state of the military relationship is a decisive factor in whether or not a crisis might transform a cold into a hot war. Arms control, more broadly conceived, may speak to a range of incentives rather than one purported overriding incentive.

Second, again because of its Cold War focus, the military-based approach focuses on achieving sound technical provisions that are, indeed, an important dimension of treaty content, but in the process, it omits important dimensions of arms control content. This military focus obscures the question of whether the treaties constitute a movement toward, or achievement of, the resolution of interstate political differences. The fallacy lies in assuming that the most dangerous threat to state security is strategic instability rather than broader conflicts of interest.

The Cold War assumption that the major threat to state security is force-posture instability might be reasonable for nuclear-armed powers if it were not for a third problem. Because the Cold War approach focuses on enhancing force-posture stability, it assumes away the multidimensional and nonmilitary dimensions of security that are encompassed by the concept of "general" stability. As a result, the argument has omitted important criteria of arms control success.

Like the deterrence literature in general, Cold War arms control theory is preoccupied with military considerations and, as John Mueller describes it, concentrates on "crisis stability, the notion that it is desirable for both sides in a crisis to be so secure that each is able to wait out a surprise attack fully confident that it would be able to respond with a punishing counterattack. In an ideal world, because of its fear of punishing retaliation, neither side would have an incentive to start a war no matter how large or desperate the disagreement, no matter how intense the crisis."[37] Mueller continues by juxtaposing crisis stability with "a more general form of stability . . . that is derived from broader needs, desires, and concerns. It prevails when two powers, taking all potential benefits, costs, and risks into account, greatly prefer peace to war . . . whether crisis stability exists or not." Rather than assume that security is achieved in the arms control process above all by a condition of strategic stability, we must ask how states define security (in its political, diplomatic, economic, and strategic as well as military dimensions), what role, if any, they see arms control playing in enhancing

---

37. John Mueller, "The Essential Irrelevance of Nuclear Weapons," *International Security* 13 (Fall 1988): 69–71.

their security, and whether those definitions are consistent with one another. Agreements that ignore the sources of general instability and political tension among states may undermine international security, despite their positive impact on strategic stability.

The interwar patterns of arms control demonstrate how focusing exclusively on managing the military balance may itself be a contributing factor to instability and the collapse of cooperation. Although it seems true that arms control should enhance security, arms control agreements that meet the criteria for success of the military-based approach may not necessarily do so or be perceived as such. Paradoxically, by ignoring underlying sources of conflict, technical agreements may exacerbate insecurity. The London Naval Treaty of 1930 reaffirmed Japan's defensive superiority in the western Pacific. Yet in the long run, it exacerbated insecurities in Japan because the treaty process ignored the differences between the Anglo-Saxon powers and Japan over policy toward a unified China. A military-based model is too conceptually restricted to serve as a measure for the success or failure of the enterprise in general, or to provide standards for the challenges of arms control that lie ahead.

As Table 2 summarizes, the military-based approach focuses on the technical scope of the arms control process and defines the enterprise as successful if agreements are reached that enhance force-posture stability. Clearly, technical agreements may be reached that are destabilizing, but there will be success only if the military-technical requirements of stability are met. Political-based arguments encompass a more comprehensive set of priorities for the arms control process, of which the technical dimension is but one. The arms control enterprise succeeds if it enhances security more broadly defined, if it encodes in the military agreement or in related political arrangements understandings about what constitutes security for the parties, and if those security requirements are aligned or temporarily bridged. This means that although agreements may be technically sound according to the requirements of military-based arms control, they may not be successful according to the political-based approach if the process does not represent or support movement toward a convergence of political agendas among the signatories. Sound technical agreements, in sum, may be counterproductive for political reasons. One should never assume that arms control is "technical." Arms control is only technical when political consensus among the parties makes it so.

Because states have traditionally derived power and prestige from the mere possession of arms, the decision to limit or reduce those weapons is never a purely technical exercise. The great strength of a political-based approach to the arms control process is that it has the potential to reorient perceptions of status and power. Weapons themselves are not the only source of instability and danger. It is the political situation and perceptions of threat and potential conflict that make any armament a contributing factor to instability in the international system.

LEARNING FROM NAVAL ARMS CONTROL

Returning to the interwar naval arms control experience in a thorough, systematic, and comprehensive manner, informed by the concerns of contemporary arms control theorists and practitioners, can deepen and enrich our understanding of the arms control process. The legacy of the rise and decline of the Washington treaty system provides insights into the obstacles of creating and maintaining a multilateral security and arms control system in an international environment of political transition. The interwar case illustrates the comparative effectiveness of military-based and political-based strategies of arms control because both approaches were implemented within the same arms control system.

We can also see how the arms control process exerts a causal influence on political relations. Treaties, by affecting the military balance and perceptions of that balance, may have the perverse effect of re-channeling military programs and competition. Treaties may also influence the threat perceptions of states through the mechanisms they create, or fail to create, for responding to changing internal and external pressures. In both cases, treaty interpretation is critical and is influenced by how states define security, what role they see arms control playing in enhancing their security, and how they assess the risks and perceive the implications of diverging from the letter and spirit of arms control treaties.

The Washington treaty system illustrates that creating a new security system is a momentous challenge; but it is only the first. Maintaining that system may be an equally great, if not greater, challenge. Robert Keohane argues that "the conditions for maintaining existing international regimes are less demanding than those required for creating them."[38] The interwar experience suggests that the reverse may be true. These differing assessments turn, in part, on divergent conceptions of maintenance. Equating maintenance and compliance,[39] Keohane argues that even an imperfect regime may be worth preserving rather than struggling to form a new regime. Compliance may be a very important component of treaty and regime maintenance, but maintenance extends beyond compliance. Maintenance involves changing rules and procedures to adapt to new security problems, foreign policy objectives, and technological developments. Where system formation may be relatively easy because of the various types of interest constellations that may converge in the short term, and because formation does not require actors to reach a consensus on the spirit and intent of an agreement at the outset, maintenance requires the development of just such a consensus. One must, therefore, be attentive to the motivations that drive the process of treaty creation and how they evolve over time.

From the pre–Cold War past we learn that political-based arms control strategies prove to be more effective than military-based arms control strategies for enhancing security because they are sensitive to and seek to accommodate different conceptions of security. With the end of the Cold War, the collapse of bipolarity, the implosion of the Soviet Union, the rise of formidable economic competitors, and the distinct prospect of several nuclear-capable states, the United States must reassess its political, economic, and military relationships worldwide and should also reconsider its approach to the arms control process. Although a recognition of the need to break with Cold War approaches has been espoused by scholars and practitioners, much of current arms control discourse and practice remains locked in the Cold War mode of thought. The arms control process can be an instrument for forging consensus on the requisites of security systems at the subregional, regional, and global levels. But to remain relevant and to be exploited to its fullest potential, the arms control process must speak to the dynamics currently shaping political and military relations around the world.

38. Robert O. Keohane, *After Hegemony: Cooperation and Discord in the World Political Economy* (Princeton: Princeton University Press, 1984), p. 50.
    39. Ibid., pp. 98–100.

2 The Allure of Arms Control

IN THE LATE 1950s, the term *arms control* acquired a technical meaning. As Coit D. Blacker and Gloria Duffy define it, arms control involves "limitations on the number or types of armaments or armed forces, or on their deployment or disposition, or on the use of particular types of armaments; arms control also encompasses measures designed to reduce the danger of accidental war or to reduce concern about surprise attack."[1] Most contemporary theorists would concur that arms control is a diplomatic strategy for regulating the military balance. In 1922, by contrast, the Washington treaty powers used the arms control process to reduce the political incentives, as well as the military incentives, to resort to force or to intimidation by the threat of force. Rather than excluding or ignoring thorny and seemingly intractable political issues, the Washington treaty process embraced them and struggled to confront much of what was intentionally precluded from arms control negotiations during the Cold War. A careful analysis of the 1920s and 1930s reveals that military agreements proved most effective in mitigating interstate tensions when supported with political understandings and least successful when pursued alone.

Because the Washington treaty system represented an attempt to create a new system of diplomacy and a new framework of regional order and peaceful interaction, the process created a complex web of strate-

1. Coit D. Blacker and Gloria Duffy, eds., *International Arms Control: Issues and Agreements* (Stanford: Stanford University Press, 1984), p. 3n.

gic, economic, political, and military relationships. The treaty powers were struggling to fill the vacuum created by the demise of imperial diplomacy in the Far East, which had peacefully regulated interstate relations. The Washington treaty system represented their efforts to adapt, control, and limit shifts in the Far Eastern regional balance of power and to coordinate those shifts with changes in the global balance of power. In 1922, the Washington powers assumed the burdens of restructuring interstate relations in the Far East and of relating this regional order to a broader global order. Like their counterparts in the 1990s, they faced the daunting challenge of designing a new world order and viewed the arms control process as integral to their endeavor.

END OF THE OLD ORDER

The pre–World War I structure of international action in the Far East has been described alternatively as a diplomacy of imperialism, as cooperative imperialism, as an imperialism of free trade, and as informal empire. The imperialism of free trade is associated primarily with the British policy of establishing, in parts of the world such as China, security for trade without using paramount force or colonial rule,[2] but rather by developing an informal empire codified by protectorates, spheres of influence, and privileges embodied in treaties. These privileges were unequal, not reciprocal. The Chinese were not granted equivalent rights in Britain or elsewhere. But from the perspective of the imperial powers, arrangements were cooperative. Gains secured by one foreign power were shared with the rest by virtue of the most-favored-nation clause. Because the treaty rights were not exclusive to any particular power, it was easy for the powers to cooperate and extend them.[3]

Up until the First World War, a multipolar regional system of Western imperial powers, a weak China, and a modernizing Japan functioned relatively peacefully. Imperial powers maintained an equilibrium through alliances, ententes, and agreements that reaffirmed mutual spheres of influence and harmonized the interests of as many imperial

2. John Gallagher and Ronald E. Robinson, "The Imperialism of Free Trade," *Economic History Review*, 2d series, 6 (August 1953). The "diplomacy of imperialism" is Iriye's phrase. Iriye, *After Imperialism*, pp. 5–6.
3. Beasley, *Japanese Imperialism*, p. 17.

powers as possible. World war destroyed the balance of power that had supported the diplomacy of imperialism. Traditional imperial powers disappeared, too weak to sustain their Far Eastern commitments. New powers emerged, seeking greater influence and creating impediments to the reestablishment of the old order. Massive shock crippled the interlocking system of political and military relationships, leaving individual states to their own devices to reconstruct new regional and international relationships.

Germany, a major imperial power, disappeared from the Far East altogether. With the realization that it could no longer operate as an imperial power, Germany rejected all vestiges of the diplomacy of imperialism and became the first country to offer China more than mere verbal assurances of equality. In May 1921, the Germans signed an agreement granting China tariff autonomy and abolishing extraterritoriality in return for most-favored-nation treatment and the liquidation of German property in China.

The Soviet Union launched an equally strong assault on the old order. Immediately after the October Revolution, Russia repudiated all secret and open agreements made by the tsarist regime with other imperial powers at the expense of China. With the Karakhan manifestos of 1919 and 1920, Lenin nullified the old treaties. Revolutionary communism became the rallying cry for a new international order.

China for its part was struggling to overcome the internal weakness that had made the prewar diplomacy of imperialism possible. The Chinese rejected the major premise of the old pattern of international relations in the Far East, namely, that diminution of Chinese sovereignty was an acceptable price to pay to facilitate cooperative imperialism. Chinese nationalism offered an alternative conception of order in the Far East.

The United States emerged from the war as a formidable actor supported by a vast naval establishment. Because of the preponderance of its power in 1917, any framework of cooperation in the Far East had to be amenable to U.S. inclinations, and this precluded cooperation in the form of a military alliance. Stimulated by war, U.S. naval power grew in leaps and bounds, and with it, Wilsonian attempts to redefine the international order. The United States rejected the particularistic arrangements concluded by the great powers in the Far East at the expense of China, frustrating Japanese postwar efforts to return to prewar methods of diplomacy. Unwilling to grant China complete and uncon-

ditional sovereignty, the Wilson administration nevertheless rejected a
status quo based on a balance of power among imperialists. Instead, it
championed a new order founded on pledges to cooperate, to refrain
from expansion, and to assist China along the road to independence.

As the war swept away multilateral equilibrium in the Far East, significant checks to Japanese imperialism disappeared, checks that had
supported a semblance of commercial harmony in China. The war
strengthened the military power and strategic position of Japan and left
the Japanese a vast empire on mainland Asia and in the Pacific.[4] Up
until the war, Japan had acted as a responsible imperialist, working
within the framework of Far Eastern diplomacy and seeking understanding with the West. Japanese civilian leaders were willing to cut back
their wartime excesses and return to these methods of prewar diplomacy.[5] However, the structure of international relations Japanese civilian leaders wished to restore was thwarted by Wilsonianism, Soviet revolutionary communism, and Chinese nationalism. Frustrated in their
attempts to return to prewar practices, many Japanese advocated independent action in China and Manchuria to consolidate hegemony.

Finally, the war undermined the old order by demonstrating that
Great Britain no longer commanded worldwide maritime supremacy. In
the prewar Far East, British naval power supported the structure of informal empire. War gave tremendous impetus to navalism worldwide,
stimulating U.S. and Japanese building programs and challenging British naval superiority in the Atlantic and Pacific. These naval developments abroad threatened the Royal Navy's global command of the sea
and Britain's scattered empire and highly specialized internal economy,
which depended upon overseas commerce. If not dominant on the seas,
Britain needed to reevaluate its strategic posture and devise new
methods to support its overseas commerce. Because of its global maritime position, shifts in Britain's force posture would necessarily have
implications for the worldwide balance of naval power.

World War I also taught a fundamental lesson, "that twentieth century technical progress, especially the phenomenal development of submarines and aircraft, had progressively narrowed the geographical area
within which any navy could establish an indisputable command of the

4. See Cpt. A. W. Hinds, "Changes in the Naval Situation of the Pacific Due to the World
War," *Army and Navy Journal* 59 (October 15, 1921): 149.
5. Iriye, *After Imperialism*, p. 9.

sea."[6] The latest technologies threatened to place insurmountable "obstacles in the way of landing and maintaining large expeditionary forces on distant hostile shores."[7] As a result, command of the western Pacific had definitively passed to Japan. Coupled with the destruction of the multilateral balance of power in China and Japanese wartime expansion in the Far East, the emergence of Japan as a regional naval hegemony created the need for dramatically new policies, practices, and patterns of international relations.

THE BRITISH POSITION

Checking Japanese imperialism in China emerged as a cardinal feature of Britain's Far Eastern policy by the 1920s. The weakness of China, a major source of instability in the Far East and an invitation to Japanese incursions, required a constructive policy of rehabilitation. The British hoped to cure the economic and political ills of China, halt Japanese aggression into China's interior, and secure their piece of the China market.

British economic interests in China had developed along with the "treaty port system," a structure of informal empire established by the Western powers in East Asia in the nineteenth century. Although the treaty port system rested on force that Britain, in the interwar years, had neither the strength nor will to maintain, the nineteenth-century relics of the system persisted: treaty ports, concessions, and settlements.[8] Treaty ports, two to three dozen in China altogether, were areas open to foreign residence and trade by agreement between the Chinese and a foreign government. Concessions were areas at treaty ports leased in perpetuity to a foreign government for occupation by its nationals. Settlements were areas at treaty ports where foreigners could reside and acquire land. In settlements and concessions, administrative authority

6. Harold Sprout and Margaret Sprout, *The Rise of American Naval Power, 1776–1918* (Princeton: Princeton University Press, 1939), pp. 372–78.
7. Harold Sprout and Margaret Sprout, *Toward a New Order of Sea Power: American Naval Policy and the World Scene, 1918–1922* (Princeton: Princeton University Press, 1940), p. 22.
8. Sir Eric Teichman, *Affairs of China: A Survey of the Recent History and Present Circumstances of the Republic of China* (London: Methuen Publishers, 1938), pp. 137–39.

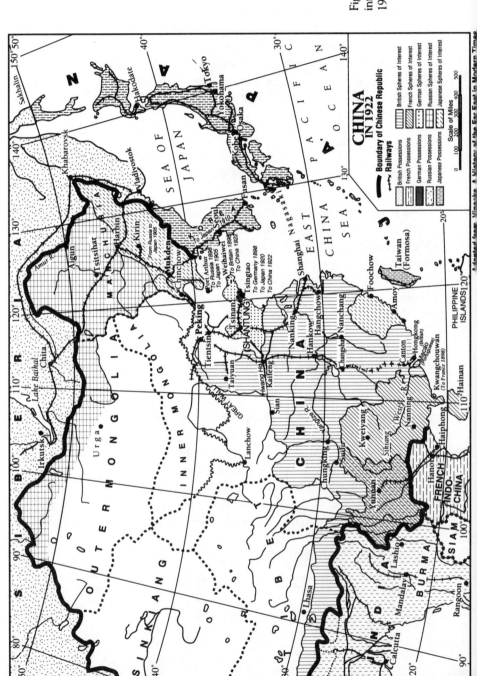

Fig. 1. Spheres of
influence in China,
1922

CHINA
IN 1922

Boundary of Chinese Republic
Railways

British Possessions
French Possessions
German Possessions
Russian Possessions
Japanese Possessions

British Spheres of Interest
French Spheres of Interest
German Spheres of Interest
Russian Spheres of Interest
Japanese Spheres of Interest

Scale of Miles
0   100   200   300   400   500

was exercised by the foreign power. The treaty port system presumed a variety of foreign impingements that undermined the territorial integrity and administrative independence of China.

Since Britain's ability to operate as a nineteenth-century imperial power was gradually eroding in the early decades of the twentieth century, it was to Britain's advantage to readjust the treaty port system, restore tariff autonomy to the Chinese, and abolish consular jurisdiction whereby foreigners were accorded extraterritorial rights.[9] From the British perspective, a stable regime in China had been a prerequisite for the structure of informal empire established in the 1840s. Only a strong and united China could sustain trade while the treaty port system was being dismantled. The British were reluctant to rely on military solutions that might destroy political stability in the region to the detriment of the imperial powers. The challenge was

> to identify a middle path, namely, a policy that would not draw Britain into territorial control, as in India, but would avoid the opposite extreme of having to fight occasional wars to reassert its interests. Positively, their conclusion was that China must be helped to undertake reforms: of the tax system, in order to provide a stable revenue; of administration, to eliminate endemic corruption and irresponsibility; and of the military establishment, to provide the means for suppressing unrest. Such measures would benefit foreign trade as well as China. Negatively the powers should refrain meanwhile from actions that would undermine the Manchu dynasty's position.[10]

Building a strong China, however, conflicted with Japanese wishes to keep China weak, disunited, and ideally under Japanese hegemonic control. As Sir Victor Wellesley explained, "If we want to understand the Japanese attitude, we cannot do better than ask ourselves how we would welcome a Japanese invitation to cooperate in a policy aiming at the unification of a strong and unfriendly Europe."[11]

The demands of British imperial defense, however, in particular the role of the Anglo-Japanese alliance, collided with the long-term thrust

9. Iriye, *After Imperialism*, p. 5.
10. Beasley, *Japanese Imperialism*, p. 19.
11. Quoted in Louis, *British Strategy*, p. 6.

of London's China policy. Though British policies in China were driven predominantly by economic considerations, its security policies in the Far East during the first two decades of the twentieth century were intimately linked to naval requirements in the European theater and to the demands of imperial defense in the Pacific.[12] In many instances, policies pursued in China stemmed from considerations divorced from the Far East and more directly associated with global naval commitments.

The Anglo-Japanese alliance was signed on January 30, 1902, out of a desire to cooperate against Russia in China, Manchuria, and Korea. The alliance was revised in 1905 and 1911, renewed in 1920, and officially terminated at the Washington Conference.[13] The alliance possessed significance beyond what the treaty text suggested because it symbolized that Tokyo had entered the ranks of the world powers. The alliance also marked Britain's first break with its traditional policy of splendid isolation as it prepared to share the burden of maintaining the Pax Britannica in the Far East with another power.

Though initially part of an anti-Russian front in Asia, for Britain, the chief value of the alliance increasingly became naval.[14] From the alliance, Britain derived both security and economy. The alliance ensured the security of the Pacific dominions at a minimum cost. With the Japanese victory over Russia in 1905 in the Battle of the Japan Sea, the British withdrew their battleships to European waters, leaving only a squadron of five cruisers in the Pacific, a very modest presence given the volume of British trade with China and the defense requirements of Britain's far-flung empire in the south Pacific. By 1913, the China

12. For general background, see Howard L. English, Jr., "Great Britain and the Problem of Imperial Defense" (Ph.D. diss., Fordham University, 1971); Ian Hamill, *The Strategic Illusion: The Singapore Strategy and the Defense of Australia and New Zealand, 1919–1942* (Kent Ridge: Singapore University Press, 1981); Malcolm D. Kennedy, *The Estrangement of Great Britain and Japan, 1917–1935* (Berkeley and Los Angeles: University of California Press, 1969); Paul M. Kennedy, *The Realities Behind Diplomacy: Background Influences on British External Policy, 1865–1980* (Glasgow: William Collins Sons, 1981); Peter Lowe, *Britain in the Far East: A Survey from 1819 to the Present* (London: Longman, 1981); Peter Lowe, *Great Britain and Japan, 1911–1915: A Study of British Far Eastern Policy* (London: St. Martin's Press, 1969); B.J.C. McKercher and D. J. Moss, eds., *Shadow and Substance in British Foreign Policy, 1895–1935* (Edmonton: University of Alberta Press, 1984).

13. Nish, *Anglo-Japanese Alliance*, p. 1.

14. For general background, see Arthur J. Marder, *From the Dardenelles to Oran: Studies of the Royal Navy in War and Peace, 1915–1940* (London: Oxford University Press, 1974); Arthur J. Marder, *From the Dreadnought to Scapa Flow: The Royal Navy in the Fisher Era, 1904–1919*, 5 vols. (London: Oxford University Press, 1961–70).

squadron had been reduced to two armored cruisers, a level inferior to the German Pacific Squadron. Although increasing naval weakness in the Pacific enhanced Britain's dependence on Japan and Japanese good faith, the economies provided by the alliance were a valuable asset when the Admiralty was forced to concentrate naval power in European waters against Germany. After all, exercising force over a distance of several thousand miles was neither easy nor cheap. And "the point of having an 'informal empire' was that it should be economical to run."[15]

As an ally of Japan, Britain tacitly acknowledged a degree of Japanese expansion on the Asian continent. Moreover, to prevent Japan from expanding into Britain's Pacific empire, Japanese continental policies received a wide margin of toleration. Foreign Secretary Sir Edward Grey struggled to balance British mercantile interests, which were threatened by the latitude Japan derived from the Anglo-Japanese alliance, with what he perceived as the justified natural expansion of a loyal ally. The two became increasingly difficult to reconcile when after 1913, Britain and Japan became territorial and financial rivals in China for the first time.[16] Having supported the victorious south party during the second Chinese Revolution of 1913, Japanese enterprise exploded in south and central China, along with demands to create a rail network in the heart of Britain's sphere from Nanchang to Hankow.

The alliance, in theory, could jeopardize not only British economic interests in China but also the safety of Britain's Pacific dominions. Britain's dominions differed with the imperial center on the requisites of security. From the perspective of the Pacific dominions, security in the western Pacific was imperiled by an alliance that rendered naval benefits outside the Far East. Although the alliance might deter Japanese advances into Britain's Pacific empire, it could as easily free up Japan to dominate the western Pacific. The British homeland was immune from direct Japanese aggression but Australia and New Zealand were not.

During World War I, Japan exploited western preoccupation in the European theater to secure commercial and political supremacy on mainland Asia under the pretext of the Anglo-Japanese alliance. World War I gave the Japanese free play in China, and the foothold acquired in the German sphere of Shantung (Shandong) permitted the Japanese

---

15. Beasley, *Japanese Imperialism*, p. 15.
16. Nish, *Alliance in Decline*, p. 100.

to realize their ambitions. In the postwar era, British views of the balance of power in Asia reflected concerns similar to those in Europe. If Japan harnessed the manpower and exploited the resources of China, British commerce and strategic position would suffer catastrophically.[17] Japan's position in Shantung—the heart of China—created a serious risk. Control of the railways in Shantung had political and strategic, as well as commercial, consequences because economic concessions fostered political control. The British most feared Japanese control of the harbor of Tsingtao (Qingdao) and territorial expansion along the Tsingtao-Tsinan (Qingdao-Jinan) railway. The British projected this railroad would control the approaches to Peking, connect with future railways of southern Manchuria and eastern Mongolia, and eventually join railways from Korea and possibly the Yangtze valley. Japan could systematically choke off all Western trade from China. As Sir John Jordan, one of the most distinguished China experts of the century, wrote to Secretary of State for Foreign Affairs George N. Curzon on September 5, 1919, "I have been a close observer of railway construction in Korea and Manchuria during the past twenty years, and I have no hesitation in affirming that a railway running from the principal port of China [Tsingtao] to the capital of a province [Shantung province] containing 35,000,000 people, owned, policed and controlled by Japanese, is not an economic concession, but a political one. . . ."[18] While condemning Japan's use of railways for territorial aggrandizement, British leaders considered railway construction a solution to China's problems of communication and political disunity. If railway construction was regulated by international oversight, the China trade could flourish and the British dream of a vast China market would become a reality.[19]

London's view of the international dynamics affecting East Asia had to include the emerging role of the United States—an actor brought onto the scene in a new and direct way in 1917 and the only Far Eastern power capable of checking Japanese ambitions. British policymakers viewed Anglo-American cooperation in regulating commercial competition as a solution to the "China problem." An international consortium could govern the financial affairs of China, eliminate spe-

---

17. Louis, *British Strategy*, p. 17.
18. Quoted in ibid., p. 24.
19. Ibid., p. 25.

cial claims in spheres of influence, and secure the open door. Naturally, the Japanese objected to the inclusion of Manchuria and Mongolia within the sphere of the consortium's activities.[20] Yet from Britain's perspective, it was precisely railway construction in Manchuria and Mongolia that required regulation.

Four major strands of British policy were woven into the future of the Anglo-Japanese alliance: (1) protecting commercial interests in China, (2) checking Japanese imperialism, (3) imperial defense, and (4) forging a new Anglo-American understanding. The alliance had freed the Royal Navy to focus on the European balance at the turn of the century. After World War I, however, the alliance posed greater risks for Anglo-American and Anglo-Dominion relations than it provided benefits.

The alliance also appeared incompatible with the new postwar Far Eastern balance of power. In the postwar years, the British were caught between both the conflicting interests of their ally and dominions and the escalating tensions between Japan and the United States. Given naval weakness in the Pacific, vulnerability of Pacific possessions, and defense requirements in China and India, Britain needed a friendly Japan. Yet London's financial weakness required U.S. goodwill. Indeed, the defeat of Germany made concentration in European waters no longer necessary. However, though Britain possessed more than forty dreadnoughts, a number greater than that of the United States and Japan, the pace of U.S. and Japanese building programs coupled with demands at home for fiscal retrenchment made it inconceivable to realistically expect to maintain a fleet commensurate with Japan's in the Far East and with that of the United States across the globe.

On the eve of the Imperial Conference of 1921, Foreign Secretary Curzon reviewed the arguments for and against renewal of the Anglo-Japanese alliance, an issue that telescoped many of the tensions in the Anglo-American-Japanese triangle.[21]

Against the alliance, it could be said that its original function—to act as a counter-balance to an aggressive Russia—had disappeared; its existence was a source of irritation to the United

---

20. By 1920, the Japanese had backed down in the face of U.S. threats to withdraw financial assistance from Japan.

21. See Klein, "Whitehall, Washington, and the Anglo-Japanese Alliance," pp. 460–83.

States; it was alienating the sympathy of China and encouraging Japanese forward policy which Britain ought to be resisting. . . . In favor . . . the alliance had over the years proved a great substantial success; in the future we might be faced with a combination of a resuscitated Russia and a revived Germany in the Far East; the alliance gave Britain the means of putting a check on Japan's ambitions; it absolved Britain from maintaining large naval and military forces in the Far East; and the Japanese were in favor of renewal.[22]

More than any other power in the postwar world, the British faced severe economic, strategic, and geographic constraints. The very survival of the British economy and the demands of imperial defense required the protection of thousands of miles of maritime communications.[23] Yet the war had left the British with insufficient resources to sustain naval competition or to defend imperial interests from the challenges posed by U.S. and Japanese building programs. The postwar slump was severe. Rising unemployment, stagnating trade and industry, falling prices, and mounting pressures for social reform all combined to urge fiscal retrenchment.[24] The scattered nature of the empire imposed demands incomparable to those faced by any other state. For two decades, British diplomacy had relied upon the Anglo-Japanese alliance to protect imperial interests in East Asia, and the alliance had become integral to Britain's perceptions of its security. The reaction of Arthur J. Balfour, former prime minister, former First Lord, and foreign secretary at the time of the Washington Conference, to the alliance's abrogation in 1922 demonstrates how much British foreign policy had come to depend upon an understanding with Japan.

Through the forest of black coats and white collars I could see in profile, motionless and sober, the distinguished head of Mr. Balfour. As the last sentence sounded and the Anglo-Japanese Alliance publicly perished, his head fell forward on his chest exactly

22. Nish, *Alliance in Decline*, pp. 328–29.

23. See Geoffrey Kemp and John Maurer, "The Logistics of the Pax Britannica: Lessons for America," in Uri Ra'anan, Robert L. Pfaltzgraff, Jr., and Geoffrey Kemp, eds., *Projection of Power: Perspectives, Perceptions, and Problems* (Hamden: Archon, 1982), pp. 28–48.

24. See John Robert Ferris, *Men, Money, and Diplomacy: The Evolution of British Strategic Policy, 1919–26* (Ithaca: Cornell University Press, 1989).

as if the spinal chord had been severed. It was an amazing reve-
lation of what the Japanese Treaty had meant to the men of a
vanished age. It was the spinal chord that had been severed. . . . The head of a stereotyped diplomacy had fallen forward—the vital chord severed—and new figures hereafter would
monopolize the scene.[25]

By 1922, the alliance had become a mirror, reflecting the tensions
inherent in Britain's strategic requirements. On the one hand, the security of Canada, hostage to Anglo-American relations, would be enhanced with the termination of the alliance. Prime Minister Arthur
Meighen of Canada opposed renewing the alliance, for Canada faced
no Japanese naval threat, whereas deteriorating relations between the
United States and Britain created a more proximate source of conflict.
The alliance was exacerbating U.S.-Japanese enmity, and this rivalry
threatened to upset the Asian balance. Ascendancy in Asia by either
power would be dangerous for the British empire. Critically, hopes for a
future world order based on Anglo-American cooperation required termination of the alliance.[26] On the other hand, security of the Pacific
dominions, hostage to Anglo-Japanese relations, in theory might be
enhanced by the alliance's existence. Prime Minister William Hughes
of Australia feared Japanese sea power in the Pacific if the alliance were
not renewed. Further, by threatening the possibility of a united naval
front against the United States, the alliance served to check what the
Admiralty feared might be U.S. aspirations to naval supremacy. A pri-

25. Putnam Weale, *An Indiscreet Chronicle from the Pacific* (New York: Dodd, Mead, 1922), pp.
186–87.
26. It is easy to assume that Anglo-American cooperation was a foregone conclusion. This view
is based more upon hindsight than the record of past relations between Britain and the United
States. Buckley traces the rivalry between the two that threatened to erupt after the war. "The two
great Anglo-Saxon countries had argued with each other at one time or another since before the
Revolution when the English-speaking peoples in North America began to consider themselves a
separate nation and to challenge the government of London. After the War of 1812 the Americans tended to believe that the British were tampering with their territorial claims in the Western
Hemisphere, trying to Balkanize . . . the North American subcontinent. During the Civil War the
Palmerston ministry [had not] behaved in a neutral fashion. . . . Only toward the end of the
century, . . . did the British and Americans drop their enmities and move toward friendship."
Though war between these two was unlikely, past cooperation had been short-lived and it was not
at all clear that it would last into the 1920s. Besides the postwar commercial struggle, America's
decision not to join the League exacerbated tensions. Buckley, *United States and the Washington
Conference*, p. 20.

mary objective of the British delegation at the Washington Conference was to resolve the tensions in their strategic requirements by replacing the alliance with an arrangement providing the same benefits without the accompanying liabilities, particularly since both renewing and not renewing the alliance were losing propositions. "The former would cause suspicion and difficulties with the United States while the latter might turn an ally into an enemy who could directly threaten British interests from Yangtze to Singapore."[27] The most desirable alternative—a tripartite agreement among London, Tokyo, and Washington—faced several obstacles: a strong anti-British contingent in the United States; probable failure in the U.S. Senate; and the instability and discontinuity of U.S. policy across administrations. The British came to Washington hoping that resulting agreements would deal with the messy issue of the alliance's future.

The British recognized the linkages between Far Eastern and disarmament issues and believed the fate of the Anglo-Japanese alliance had to be resolved first. Yet disarmament had to be orchestrated in two theaters. Britain was the sole link between the European and Pacific naval balances. Their strategic dilemma in the Pacific and East Asia could not be solved in isolation from strategic requirements in the Atlantic and Europe. "If Britain restricted her navy, there was no guarantee that France would curtail her military force, which might have the eventual capacity to devastate Britain by air attack. If Britain limited [its] capital ships, France might continue to develop the weapon capable of paralysing the British fleet and merchant marine—the submarine."[28] The British press during the Conference was consumed with the fears generated by the submarine issue.

The British were committed to parity with the United States and to a revised two-power naval standard: superiority over the next two naval powers, Japan and France. The British came to the Washington Conference demanding a fleet at least equal to any other. Their Far Eastern objectives, having evolved out of meetings with the empire's prime ministers during the summer of 1921, were to bring the United States into a tripartite arrangement and supplant the Anglo-Japanese alliance. Failing this, the British would stand by Japan. Supreme importance was

27. Ibid., p. 34.
28. Louis, *British Strategy*, p. 97.

attached to continuing, in some form, the Anglo-Japanese alliance, or the purposes it served.

Britain's delegates to the Washington Conference—Lord Arthur Balfour, Sir Auckland Geddes, Lord Arthur Lee (first lord of the Admiralty, 1921–22) Sir Robert Borden (prime minister of Canada, 1911–20), and George F. Pierce (Australian minister of defense)—appreciated as well the technological constraints the submarine and airplane had imposed on the Royal Navy. Both undermined Britain's security, which had, in the past, rested on naval superiority and insular position. The inability of Britain to sustain the naval superiority of the Pax Britannica was evident far earlier than the First World War. During the war, however, British supremacy was challenged even in European waters by the marine mine, the self-propelled torpedo, and submarine. Britain retained command of the sea but only at short range and with distance and geography in its favor. As Harold and Margaret Sprout put it, "The war reemphasized the importance of geography as a factor limiting hostile operations against a strong naval power. The British Navy's success in confining the German battle fleet within the North Sea was attributable not merely to the former's superior power, but also to the size and configuration of the North Sea. And it is extremely doubtful if even the British Navy could have duplicated this achievement against the smaller Navy of the United States."[29] Though Britain emerged after the war dominant in European waters, technological developments spurred by the war had profound political and strategic consequences for the world order of sea power. Airpower and the submarine challenged the conventional theory and practice of naval warfare, weakened Britain's strategic position, and made it tremendously more difficult to maintain command of the sea over several thousand miles. The British were determined to abolish the submarine in order to maintain secure approaches to the home islands.[30] At the very least, the Washington Conference offered a financially attractive way for the Royal Navy to retain a fleet at least equal to any other, a strategic and symbolic re-

29. Sprout and Sprout, Rise of American Naval Power, p. 370.

30. Lord Balfour, head of the British delegation, was cognizant of the Admiralty's view that as long as France retained submarines, the Grand Fleet would not be safe in European waters. The British Cabinet, concerned about the French submarine threat instructed Balfour "not to impair Britain's strength unless France took corresponding measures to disarm." Since "only a strong British fleet of destroyers and light cruisers could protect Britain from [the submarine] menace, . . . Britain could accept no proposal to limit auxiliary craft unless submarines were abolished." See Louis, British Strategy, pp. 99–102.

quirement threatened by the economic, strategic, and geographic constraints facing the British after the war.

THE U.S. POSITION

The Spanish-American War of 1898 revolutionized the strategic and
political situation of the United States and profoundly altered U.S.
interests. The insular accessions extended the strategic frontier of the
United States several hundred miles eastward into the Atlantic and
several thousand westward across the Pacific. This war transformed the
United States "from a geographically isolated continental Power into a
scattered empire with a strategic problem virtually insoluble without
recourse to alliances absolutely incompatible with the traditions of
American foreign policy."[31] This, in a nutshell, captures the dilemma
that faced the United States. The Washington treaty system appeared
to be a solution.

The United States lacked the political will to maintain fleets and
naval bases in Far Eastern waters. Yet the Department of State insisted
on unqualified most-favored-nation treatment for American commerce
in, and with, each Far Eastern nation. Simply put, American traders
should enjoy rights and privileges equal to those embodied in the most
favorable terms granted to any of their competitors. As A. Whitney
Griswold puts it, "Only the phrase by which it was to become identified
in the Far East—the open door policy—made it peculiar to that region.
The open door meant, from the very beginning, the open door to equal
commercial opportunity via the most-favored-nation clause."[32] The
methods toward this end included respect for the territorial integrity of
Far Eastern nations and detachment from their internal politics. The
United States sought to win by propitiation what Europe had extorted
by force.

The special rights and privileges claimed by each imperial power in
its sphere consisted primarily of preferential rights to construct railroads
and exploit mines. Special rights had not yet been extended to impose
a differential tariff on merchandise consumed or passing through these

31. Sprout and Sprout, *Rise of American Naval Power*, p. 230.
32. Griswold, *Far Eastern Policy*, p. 6.

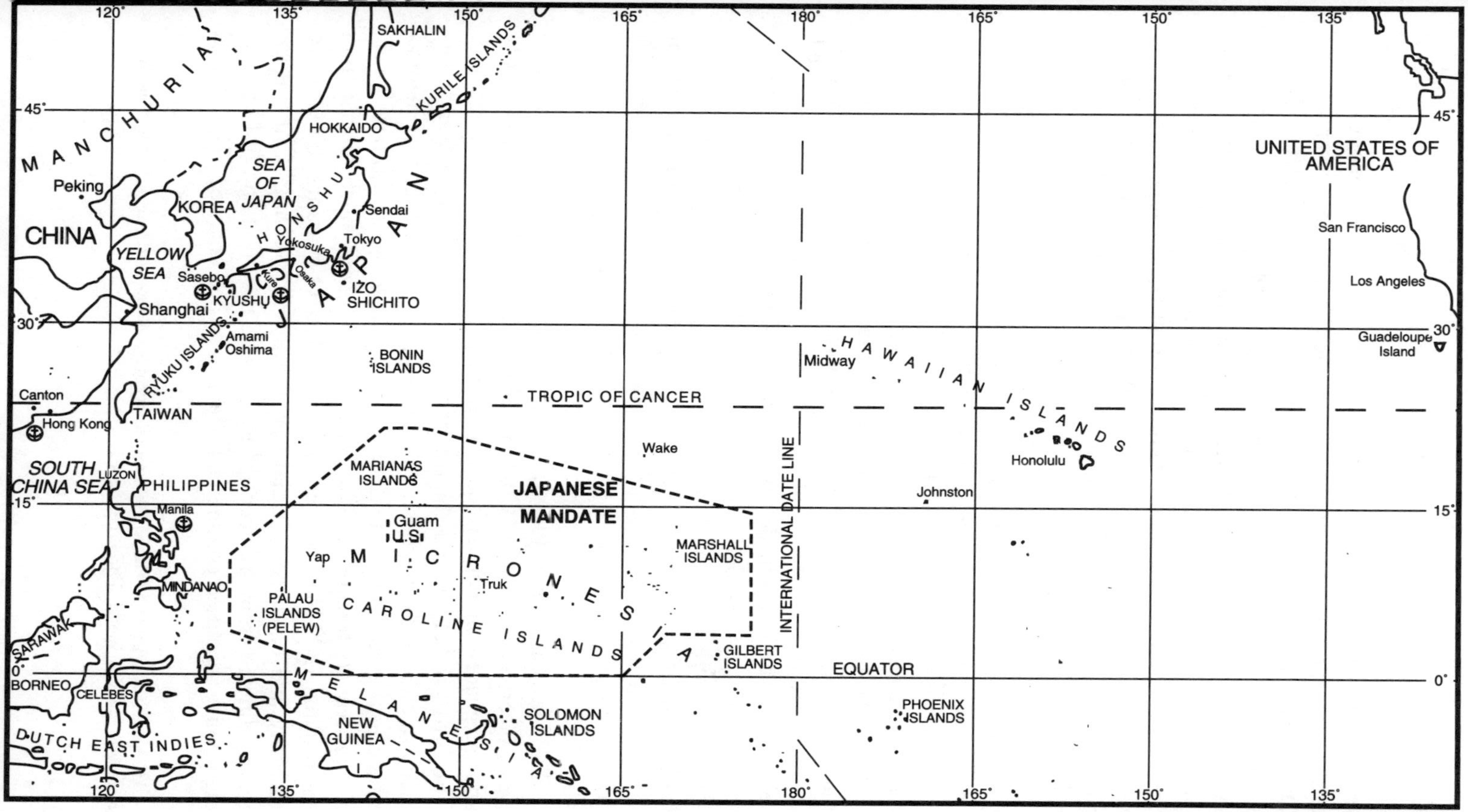

Fig. 2. The Pacific, 1922

Adapted from Dingman, Power in the Pacific

spheres. It was fear of this, coupled with pressure from American business groups for a more spirited policy in the Far East, that prompted the Open Door Notes of September 6, 1899. Alfred E. Hippisley, a British subject and member of the Chinese Imperial Maritime Customs Service, urged Secretary of State John Hay to take the lead in securing guarantees from each European power that interests already vested in open treaty ports would be protected and that equal commercial opportunity for commerce would be ensured by application of the Chinese treaty tariff, without discrimination, to all merchandise entering spheres of influence.

The original Open Door Notes, however, reflected a passive, negative response to public demands for a vigorous assertion of U.S. rights and interests in China. The notes did not call for destruction of spheres of influence or express concern for China's welfare. Rather, they proposed adherence to three principles: "non-interference with vested interests within the existing spheres of influence in China; uniform application of Chinese treaty tariffs to all ports within these spheres; non-discrimination regarding railroad charges and harbor dues in these spheres."[33] The notes made no reference to mining and railway concessions or to the problem of capital investment but assumed foreign spheres of influence and territorial concessions in China would continue to exist and even to expand. The notes requested endorsement only for equal commercial opportunity within each sphere, essentially accepting the impairment of China's territorial integrity as a fait accompli.

The Hay Circular of July 3, 1900, by contrast, advanced a startling new objective: to preserve Chinese territorial and administrative entity and safeguard commercial equality in all parts of the Chinese empire. The Boxer Rebellion and the use of it as a pretext by Russia and Germany to enlarge their spheres encouraged Hay to conclude that maintenance of the open door in China necessitated complete Chinese sovereignty over its territories. The July 3 circular went much further than the original 1899 Notes by suggesting a collective guarantee for Chinese integrity and equal commercial opportunity. "Preserving" Chinese integrity differed from "respecting" it. Though the chief end of U.S. foreign policy remained commercial, the means had changed. The United

---

33. Akira Iriye, *Across the Pacific: An Inner History of American–East Asian Relations* (New York: Harcourt, Brace & World, 1967), pp. 80–81.

States had at least nominally committed itself to halting violations of China's territorial and administrative integrity.

Theodore Roosevelt's China policy embraced no startling new initiatives. It did not promote the principles embodied in the second Open Door Notes but rather subverted Chinese interests to the greater cause of improving U.S.-Japanese relations. Roosevelt's policy culminated in the Root-Takahira Agreement of 1908. Though controversy surrounds the interpretation of this agreement, it appears that in return for Japan's pledge to respect the security of the Philippines, the United States conceded to Japan a free hand in Manchuria in recognition of the 1905 Treaty of Portsmouth, which had transferred Russian rights in Manchuria to Japan. The agreement did not prefix the phrase "integrity of China" with the word "territorial," and the phrase "existing status quo" implicitly undermined Chinese integrity and recognized Japanese political and economic influence in south Manchuria. As Griswold summarizes the agreement,

> The "existing status quo" included not only the important railway and mining rights, leaseholds and privileges in Manchuria transferred from Russia to Japan by the Portsmouth Treaty of 1905, but also Chinese recognition of that transfer by a special Sino-Japanese Treaty of 1905 [the Komura treaty], further recognition of Japan's special interests in Manchuria by the Franco-Japanese and Russo-Japanese Treaties of 1907, and last but not least, the principle that propinquity creates special interests so firmly established by the Anglo-Japanese Alliance Treaty of 1905.[34]

With Taft-Knox "dollar diplomacy," however, the United States embarked on a more aggressive and positive policy in China, using financial means for moral ends, helping China by challenging Japanese commercial domination in Manchuria. Investment would help China develop independently as a political unit and serve as an impediment to Japanese expansion in the Far East. Dollar diplomacy challenged Japanese financial supremacy in Manchuria and European financial monopolies in China proper, with the challenge to Japan clearly the boldest. The vanguards of dollar diplomacy attempted to undermine the monop-

34. Griswold, *Far Eastern Policy*, pp. 129–30.

olistic position of the south Manchurian railway by building a railway parallel to it, proposing the internationalization of all railways in Manchuria, and organizing an international consortium to finance commercial projects in Asia.

With the assumption of power by Wilson, moralistic diplomacy in China reached new heights, and China increasingly became the recipient of American sympathy. Yet the United States did not immediately launch a vigorous challenge to Japan's empire in Korea, Taiwan, and south Manchuria. Secretary of State William Jennings Bryan responded cautiously to the full text of Japan's Twenty-One Demands on China,[35] following the pattern of the Taft-Katsura and Root-Takahira agreements. The Taft-Katsura Agreement of 1905 and the Root-Takahira Agreement of 1908 demonstrated the passive nature of U.S. support for China in the face of Japan's continental drive. The former recognized Japan's dominant position in Korea in return for Japanese disavowal of any designs on the Philippines. The latter codified both governments' desires to maintain the status quo in the Pacific. Bryan's note of March 13, 1915 concluded that "while on principle and under the treaties of 1844, 1858, 1868, and 1903 with China the United States has ground on which to base objections to the Japanese [Twenty-One] 'demands' relative to Shantung, south Manchuria, and east Mongolia, nevertheless the United States frankly recognizes that territorial contiguity creates special relations between Japan and these districts."[36] In effect, the traditional balance of power in the Far East could still effectively inhibit Japanese expansion while permitting the United States to pursue its Asiatic policies with minimum force.

35. "The Twenty-one Demands were divided into five sections. Group one applied to Shantung, requiring that China recognize Japan's right to replace Germany in that area. Group two referred to south Manchuria and Eastern Inner Mongolia, and provided that the lease on Port Arthur and Darien should be extended from twenty-five to ninety-nine years. Group three dealt with control of the Hanyehp'ing Mining Company; group four demanded that China agree to the non-alienation of the entire China coast and group five made such extensive political demands that, if accepted, China would have been transformed into a Japanese protectorate." Roberta A. Dayer, *Bankers and Diplomats in China 1917–25* (London: Frank Cass, 1981), p. 40. For full text of the demands, see Sidney Osborne, *The Problem of Japan* (Amsterdam: C.L. van Langenhuysen, 1918), pp. 252–59. For a discussion of the Twenty-One Demands and their origins, see Griswold, *Far Eastern Policy*, pp. 186–89. The Wilson administration believed the Twenty-One Demands "would make China politically and in a military sense a protectorate of Japan and establish a Japanese monopoly in the commercial resources of China most requisite for military purposes." Iriye, *Across the Pacific*, p. 134.

36. Quoted in Griswold, *Far Eastern Policy*, p. 192.

Wilson's diplomacy had far-reaching implications for U.S. naval policy, however, because it placed the United States at odds with Japan and the European powers in China. To command respect for its China policy, the United States needed a foothold in the western Pacific from which to project naval power. The Philippines were perfectly situated for projecting power into the Far East to defend U.S. commercial interests in China. McKinley, however, had made a grave strategic mistake in 1899 by permitting the rest of Spain's island empire—the Carolines, Marianas, and Marshalls—to fall into the hands of Germany. For thousands of miles, the Marshalls, Marianas, and Carolines flanked U.S. lines of communication to the Far East via Guam and the Philippines and manifestly weakened the ability of the United States to protect interests and territories in the Far East and western Pacific. Transferring these islands from Spain to Germany in 1899 created no immediate threat because Germany's commitments in Europe precluded a concentration of naval power in the Pacific. By contrast, the advent of war in Europe destroyed the balances that had served the interests of U.S. foreign and naval policies in the Pacific. Japan's acquisition of Germany's Pacific islands during the war greatly imperiled U.S. insular possessions in the western Pacific and weakened U.S. diplomacy in the Far East.

Preoccupied with the war in Europe, the United States, like the other Allies, turned its back on the Far East, which served Japan's interests, the only power with a consistent wartime policy toward China. Lack of U.S. interest in investing in China also removed Western capital, leaving the Chinese little option but to borrow from Japan. This only strengthened Japan's financial monopoly and reinforced the political position of Japan at the Paris Peace Conference. When the Japanese arrived in Paris, they were armed with the Anglo-Japanese alliance, secret treaties with the Allies,[37] and the concession entailed in the 1917 Lansing-Ishii Agreement. With this agreement, the United States recognized that "territorial propinquity creates special relations between countries, and consequently, the Government of the United States recognizes that Japan has special interests in China, particularly in the part

---

37. In February 1917, as the price for Japanese aid against the German submarine threat in the Mediterranean, Britain agreed to support Japan's territorial claims at the peace conference. Britain would support Japanese claims to German rights in Shantung and to German Pacific island possessions north of the equator. Japan would support British claims south of that line.

to which her possessions are contiguous."[38] The Japanese, for their part, declared respect for the open door and the independence and territorial integrity of China. In addition, the Japanese had secured fresh commitments from China in the summer and autumn of 1918 beyond the Twenty-One Demands of 1915. China would transfer Kiaochow (Jiaozhou) and the German rights in Shantung to Japan, with the understanding that Japan would restore the Kiaochow leasehold yet retain and expand the former German economic privileges in the province.[39]

Wilson's offensive against Japan at Paris was fourfold: to bind Japanese capital investment in China to cooperative ordinances of a new four-power consortium; to participate in the Allied military intervention in Siberia in order to prevent Japan from detaching maritime provinces from Russian rule; to insist on the restoration of Shantung to China; and to codify in treaty form the principles of the U.S. Far Eastern policy, such as the open door and defense of China's territorial and administrative integrity, Wilsonian principles of nonaggression, and collective security and apply them to East Asia and the Pacific.[40] The Paris peace settlement succeeded only in prohibiting Japan from erecting fortifications or establishing military or naval bases on the former German islands, in theory protecting the United States's road across the Pacific. Yet Wilson failed to prevent the German islands or Yap from becoming Japanese mandates or to restore Shantung to China. Japanese occupation of these islands had grave strategic consequences.

In 1921, Hector Bywater, a British naval critic, described in detail those consequences. Japanese occupation, in effect, surrounded Guam with a cordon of potential strongholds and naval bases to be used in an emergency. Occupied Yap furnished an effective base for operations against the Guam-Manila line of communications. Even if Yap were not occupied, the Pelew islands and those islands to the south and east of Guam provided suitable havens for submarines and other naval vessels. In other words, "as long as these positions remained in the hands of a hostile Japan, an American fleet based on Guam would operate under difficulties comparable to those that would have confronted England's Grand Fleet in the late war if Germany had possessed a subma-

---

38. Ibid., pp. 213–20. This agreement lasted until April 14, 1923, when it was superseded by the Washington treaties.
39. Ibid., pp. 189–90; pp. 240–41.
40. Ibid., p. 223.

rine base in the Shetland islands at the threshold of Scapa Flow."[41] In addition, the Philippines, while perhaps indispensable in prosecuting a war against Japan, could become a liability. Wilson's acquiescence to Japan's occupation of the German islands had consequences comparable to McKinley's annexation of only part, rather than all or none, of Spain's Pacific empire, and to the failure of McKinley's successors to develop even one well-fortified naval base in the western Pacific. Nevertheless, Wilson vigorously asserted his new Far Eastern agenda, the chief aim no longer solely the economic one of securing equal commercial opportunity but the political objective of resisting Japanese aggression.

Wilson's postwar political and diplomatic assault included a building program that although driven by prewar naval policy, challenged Britain's traditional supremacy in the Atlantic and Japan's security in the western Pacific. The Great Preparedness Campaign of 1914–1915[42] and the German submarine threat prompted the Wilson administration to embark on an unprecedented armament program, designed to bring the U.S. Navy to equality with the most powerful navy of any nation by 1925. On August 29, 1916, Congress passed a naval building program without precedent in history, which was only temporarily suspended in 1918 to divert resources into antisubmarine craft production.[43]

Over time, the navy's building program, actual disposition of ships, and growing U.S. concern for large-scale shore developments on the western seaboard and in the Pacific reflected a strategic reorientation to the west. In 1919, the Wilson administration established a separate battle fleet in the Pacific, a radical departure from tradition. All the newest and most powerful battleships, including the battle cruisers of great speed and long cruising radius, would be stationed in the Pacific. By the end of 1919, the United States had a Pacific fleet of two hundred vessels with a total displacement of 800,000 tons, almost as formidable as the entire Imperial Navy then in commission. The 1920 estimates called for large cruisers with an endurance of more than 10,000 miles and submarines displacing 2,000 tons to be used as scouts or blockaders at great distance from home bases. These two recommendations were designed to meet strategic requirements in the Pacific. The

41. Hector C. Bywater, *Sea Power in the Pacific: A Study of the American-Japanese Naval Problem* (Boston: Houghton Mifflin, 1921), pp. 266–68.

42. Sprout and Sprout, *Rise of American Naval Power*, pp. 317–24.

43. See ibid., p. 340.

navy also planned to enlarge existing yards and develop additional stations on the west coast, to expand the naval base at Pearl Harbor, and to develop bases at Guam, Samoa, and in the Philippines. Clearly, U.S. naval policy was being formulated with an eye toward Japan, to support U.S. Far Eastern policies that were perceived at risk, given Japan's own recently authorized naval building program. As the U.S. Navy became more oriented toward the Pacific, the possibility of reconciling its building standard with that of the Imperial Navy became more difficult.

U.S. leaders had always operated under ideological and domestic political constraints.[44] The predisposition to avoid entangling alliances, the use of force, and the expenditure of funds to build advanced bases in the Pacific were severe obstacles to power projection into the Far East. The need to operate over great distances with no bases further exacerbated the problems of defending outlying commitments. All these factors made it more difficult for foreign policy and naval leaders to defend commitments to China and the Philippines. U.S. policy in the Far East was driven by economic considerations—securing equal commercial opportunity for Americans without demanding territorial concessions.[45] The policy of the United States was one of friendship and support to strengthen East Asia against a designing Europe and an expansionist Japan. In pursuing this "friendship" policy, the United States encouraged unification and a strong central government in China, but without interference or the use of military force. The American people would not sanction defense of interests in China by force, and Congress, it was firmly believed, would never appropriate funds for developing fixed defenses in Guam and the Philippines. Although the United States enjoyed remarkable security as a result of geographical isolation, naval growth, and the increasing complexities of naval technology,[46] it faced serious problems because of its exposed dependencies in the west-

44. See Robert Osgood, *Ideals and Self-Interest in American Foreign Policy: The Great Transformation of the Twentieth Century* (Chicago: University of Chicago Press, 1953).

45. For general background, see Selig Adler, *The Uncertain Giant 1921–1941: American Foreign Policy Between the Wars* (New York: Macmillan, 1965); Charles A. Beard, *American Foreign Policy in the Making, 1932–1940: A Study in Responsibilities* (New Haven: Yale University Press, 1946); Charles Neu, *The Troubled Encounter: The United States and Japan* (New York: John Wiley, 1975); and William Neumann, *America Encounters Japan: From Perry to MacArthur* (Baltimore: Johns Hopkins University Press, 1963).

46. Sprout and Sprout, *Toward a New Order*, p. 23. See Sprout and Sprout, *Rise of American Naval Power*, pp. 251–55, for a discussion of the technological difficulties facing a trans-Pacific aggressor against the continental United States in the opening years of the twentieth century.

ern Pacific. Advanced naval bases at Guam and the Philippines had yet to be developed because, in part, of the politics of naval-yard policy in Congress. Members of seaboard constituencies where navy yards and stations were located combined to support their claims for treasury funds, whereas overseas stations had no such representatives to advance their interests. The navy correctly anticipated it would be unable to adequately defend Far Eastern commitments. Therefore, at the Washington Conference, the U.S. delegation—Secretary of State Charles Evans Hughes; former Secretary of War, Secretary of State, and Senator Elihu Root; chairman of the Senate Foreign Relations Committee Henry Cabot Lodge, and its ranking minority member, Oscar W. Underwood—had to secure some diplomatic assurance that Japanese forces would desist from aggression in China and the western Pacific. Averse to any permanent political or economic alliance, President Harding would support only limited cooperation. Associations with other nations would be entered into only "for conference, for counsel . . . to recommend a way to approximate disarmament and relieve the crushing burden of military and naval establishments."[47] That any form of cooperation had to be consistent with a policy of avoiding entangling alliances was an ideological constraint under which the administration was forced to operate. The Washington Conference offered opportunities to orchestrate agreements more amenable to American predilections than formal alliances or the League Covenant.

The U.S. delegates were determined to secure cancellation of the Anglo-Japanese alliance, which they perceived as protecting and encouraging, rather than inhibiting, Japanese militarism. Of course the British argued that the alliance hindered Japanese aggression, but U.S. leaders insisted that it fostered Japanese activity in Asia, prevented the British from protesting, and actually furnished an incentive for Japanese aggression. The alliance could even be construed as designating Japan the policeman of East Asia, for each time it had been renewed, the Japanese made spectacular territorial gains. Moreover, they had actually secured a commitment from the British to come to the assistance of the Japanese if "unprovoked or aggressive action, wherever arising, . . . should involve [Japan] in a war in defense of its territorial rights or special interests."[48] Although the British might view their own activities

47. Buckley, *United States and the Washington Conference*, pp. 114–15.
48. The renewed Anglo-Japanese alliance of 1905 bound England, from 1905 until 1921, to

of acquiescence as "realistic acts of imperial protection," the United
States perceived these as "threats to China's territorial and administrative entity."[49] Furthermore, the alliance's insistence on "special interests" aroused U.S. suspicions, well founded or not, that the British and
Japanese might close the door in China.

Although U.S. civilian and naval authorities opposed Japanese expansionism, civilian leaders were even more passionately committed to
the goal of disarmament. A strong domestic disarmament movement
imposed significant constraints on political leaders. Popular pressure for
arms limitation developed rapidly in the winter of 1918–19, and by the
winter of 1920–21, a well-organized movement, directed by Senator
William E. Borah, chairman of the Foreign Relations Committee, had
emerged. Prior to December 1920, the "popular revolt against navalism" had been confined to congressional downscaling and rejection of
naval appropriations. But Borah's sponsorship of a joint congressional
resolution gave positive direction to the movement. In January 1921,
Borah requested that the Senate Naval Affairs Committee report on
suspending all naval construction for six months. The Harding administration resisted but in the end was defeated. The House ratified the
Borah amendment to the naval appropriation bill of June 30, 1921,
authorizing and requesting the president to call a conference on naval
limitation.[50] The strength of popular and congressional pressure was revealed in the almost complete disregard for professional naval opinion
by the civilian conference delegates, who were committed to reaching a
limitation agreement at whatever cost.[51] The navy believed that the
United States was in a position to extract maximum concessions while
conceding few to other conference delegates. However, much of the
navy's advice was ignored. The desire of naval leaders to complete their
program of ships under construction, in the belief that a two-to-one

---

come to the aid of Japan. In return for this concession, Japan agreed to defend British interests in
India. Buell, *Washington Conference*, pp. 112–13.

49. Buckley, *United States and the Washington Conference*, p. 27.

50. For a theoretical explanation of the influential role that popular pressures exert on U.S.
leaders, see Stephen D. Krasner, *Defending the National Interest* (Princeton: Princeton University
Press, 1978), pp. 54–90.

51. See Ernest Andrade, Jr., "United States Naval Policy in the Disarmament Era, 1921–1937"
(Ph.D. diss., Michigan State University, 1966), pp. 29–40, for the origins of the U.S. proposal
and the concessions made by the General Board, a professional advisory body that played a decisive policymaking role from 1900 until World War II, to meet the political goals of the State
Department. Buell offers an additional explanation for the policy of the U.S. delegation: the desire
to secure a foreign policy success for the Republicans who had prevented the United States from
joining the League. Buell, *Washington Conference*, p. 322.

superiority over Japan was necessary, was sacrificed to Hughes's "stop-now" proposal. Further, military opinion, strongly opposed to any proposal on the Pacific islands, was dismissed by State Department officials who viewed these islands as sources of tension and relics of naval expansion. The United States may have been better off after the conference if one assumes Congress would never have voted the necessary funds to support a postwar arms race or fortify bases in the Pacific. Paradoxically, the conference ended up serving rather than hindering Japanese designs in the Pacific and on the continent of Asia. Desiring disarmament, U.S. leaders acquiesced in Japanese demands to freeze the status quo of fortifications in the western Pacific, the price for the latter's acceptance of a reduced ratio in capital ships. As a result, it became increasingly difficult to challenge Japan's policies in the Far East.

In the immediate postwar years, domestic pressures coupled with fiscal constraints threatened to subvert attainment of a navy second to none. There is little doubt that the United States had the economic means to support a buildup to parity with Great Britain. Yet though there were very real differences between the United States and Britain, particularly over mercantile competition and freedom of the seas, the American people were not prepared to support competitive building against both the Grand Fleet and the Imperial Navy. Even traditional "big navy" advocates like Theodore Roosevelt opposed U.S. aspirations to naval parity with Great Britain, arguing that Britain's insular position and scattered empire justified possession of a navy larger than that of the United States. Increasingly, the Imperial Navy was perceived as the force best situated to threaten U.S. interests. Building down to parity with Great Britain by scrapping ships was more feasible than building up to parity. An arms limitation conference offered the opportunity to meet this naval objective within the constraints imposed by U.S. domestic politics and the competing strategic requirements confronting the U.S. Navy in the Atlantic and Pacific.

THE JAPANESE POSITION

Of the major powers in the Far East, only Japan had to manage an empire that was both continental and insular. Thus Japan had two sets of strategic requirements: defense of insular possessions against attack by sea and of continental interests against attack by land.[52] Integral to Japanese national defense, foreign policy, and security requirements at the turn of the century was the protective umbrella provided by the British Royal Navy. Japan emerged as an Asian power "based upon a strategic paradox: Japan became a major actor on the continent at a time when its naval security was absolutely dependent on the good will of the British fleet."[53] The Anglo-Japanese alliance provided the foundation for Japan's naval and continental policies. As such, the strategic requirements of these policies merged. Threats to Japan's Pacific status were perceived as threats to vital continental interests. Likewise, naval policies that the Japanese perceived as defending continental interests were frequently viewed as threatening interests of other Pacific powers.

In the mid-nineteenth century, while the occidental powers acquired privileged positions in China under the treaty port system, Japan claimed "special interests" in the area. From the Meiji Restoration up until Pearl Harbor, Japanese leaders perceived the opportunities for great-power status but lacked the capabilities. Controlled access to resources and markets, whether by territorial aggrandizement or colonialism, meant predominating in mainland Asia, and this remained an operating assumption of Japanese foreign policy throughout the post–World War I era. Korea and south Manchuria were designated as areas of prime strategic importance, and the "independence" of Korea—that no third country should be permitted to assert control over the "dagger at the heart of Japan"—was defined in the 1880s by the Meiji oligarchy as critical for the security of the home islands.

The Russo-Japanese War of 1904, while initially conceived to secure Japanese control over Korea, signified a "momentous redefinition of Japanese national interest," the "beginning of Japan's continentalism."[54] Transfer of Russian rights in south Manchuria—the Liaotung (Liaodong) leasehold—became as important an objective as control over Korea. Japanese leaders had long been infatuated with the vision of a

52. Crowley, *Japan's Quest for Autonomy*, p. 4. For general background, see Akira Iriye, "Imperialism in East Asia," in James B. Crowley, ed., *Modern East Asia: Essays in Interpretation* (New York: Harcourt, Brace & World, 1970), pp. 122–50; Akira Iriye, *Mutual Images: Essays in American-Japanese Relations* (Cambridge: Harvard University Press, 1975); Malcolm D. Kennedy, *The Problem of Japan* (London: Nisbet, 1935); Ian H. Nish, *Japanese Foreign Policy, 1869–1942* (London: Routledge & Kegan Paul, 1977); and Masamichi Royama, *Foreign Policy of Japan, 1914–1939* (Tokyo: Japanese Council, Institute of Pacific Relations, 1941).

53. Crowley, *Japan's Quest for Autonomy*, p. 4.

54. Iriye, *Across the Pacific*, p. 101.

continental empire. The alliance with Britain was vital to securing both Korea and south Manchuria, for it guaranteed British support and neutralized Russia's ally, France.

In the first decade of the twentieth century, Japanese ambitions in China were tacitly recognized by Great Britain and the United States. Foreign Secretary Sir Edward Grey viewed Japanese expansion on the continent as natural and convenient. As long as the Japanese emigrated to the Asian continent, they would leave the British empire in the Pacific alone. Theodore Roosevelt also viewed continental expansion as a check on Japanese Pacific ambitions and even encouraged Japan's continental policies short of complete domination of East Asia. Japanese predominance in Korea and south Manchuria was viewed as a minor redefinition of the status quo. It was even believed that Japan might provide order and stability in East Asia to the benefit of American commercial interests.[55]

Yet even though Japan was beginning to break into the great-power club, leaving its semicolonial status behind and establishing a colonial empire of its own, vestiges of inequality persisted. Japan, along with Russia, had been excluded from the international consortium set up in 1910 by the United States, France, Britain, and Germany to channel funds into China. Though Japan and Russia were excluded because they had no funds for investment, the consortium failed to acknowledge that they were the dominant commercial powers in Manchuria after 1905.[56] For the Japanese, who had never been accepted as an equal by the Western powers, the First World War provided an ideal opportunity to solidify influence on the Asian continent. The Japanese took bold action in China to prevent any postwar challenges to their influence. The Twenty-One Demands of 1915, which detached Manchuria and Mongolia from China, were only the beginning. By 1917, Japan had driven diplomatic bargains with the principal European allies, confirming Japanese succession to all German rights and possessions in the Pacific and Far East north of the equator. Through arms, diplomacy, and finance, Japan consolidated and extended its position in Shantung and south Manchuria. By 1918, China had consented to the perpetuation of Japanese rights in Manchuria and Inner Mongolia, to the transfer of German rights in Shantung to Japan, and to the formation of closer mili-

55. Ibid., p. 108.
56. Beasley, *Japanese Imperialism*, p. 34; Nish, *Alliance in Decline*, p. 17.

tary and economic ties between the two countries.[57] Yet Japan's political leaders also realized that postwar economic growth required expanding trade with the United States.

Trade between the United States and Japan had boomed during the war, and Japan for the first time emerged as a creditor nation.[58] With this economic orientation, Japanese political leaders advanced a policy of political and economic understanding with the West. Many prominent Japanese bureaucrats, businessmen, and politicians hoped to consolidate a framework of understanding with the United States. They viewed closer economic and political ties with the West as an effective way to protect Japanese interests and believed that if Japan guaranteed U.S. rights in China and demonstrated peaceful intentions, Washington would not feel obliged to assist China. The Lansing-Ishii Agreement of 1917 appeared to support this interpretation. Tokyo, however, continued to envision cooperation as an extension of the "imperialist diplomacy" of the prewar era with each power entitled to a loosely defined sphere of influence but recognizing the preserves of other imperialist powers. These twin objectives—preservation of spheres of influence and cooperation with the West—appeared in the diplomacy of Baron Kijuro Shidehara, the embryo of which was unveiled at the Washington Conference.

Akira Iriye distinguishes, in Japan, two perspectives on the value of cooperation with the West.[59] The economic approach supported trade and emigration to secure Japan's position in the world. The military/territorial approach supported direct control of overseas bases and resources. In the early phases of Japanese imperialism, these approaches coexisted. As Japanese industry grew, particularly during the First World War, priority was given to economic aims and to competing with rival powers, yet within an international framework to which all powers were willing to conform. This was the context in which Shidehara diplomacy flourished. Only with the international economic crisis of 1929–30 did Japan decisively reject the economic approach. Fearing

---

57. Iriye, *Across the Pacific*, p. 132; Griswold, *Far Eastern Policy*, pp. 240–41.

58. Iriye, *After Imperialism*, p. 9.

59. See Akira Iriye, *Pacific Estrangement: Japanese and American Expansion, 1897–1911* (Cambridge: Harvard University Press, 1972); "The Failure of Economic Expansionism: 1918–1931," in Bernard Silberman and Harry Harootunian, eds., *Japan in Crisis* (Princeton: Princeton University Press, 1974), pp. 237–69; and "The Failure of Military Expansionism," in James William Morley, ed., *Dilemmas of Growth in Prewar Japan* (Princeton: Princeton University Press, 1971), pp. 107–38.

exclusion from markets for its manufactures, from outlets for its surplus population, and from access to raw materials, Japan turned to military and territorial solutions, culminating in the drive to build the "Co-Prosperity Sphere."

Shidehara diplomacy advanced a broad commitment to economic development and became identified with three major policy prescriptions: disarmament, international cooperation, and noninterference in China. Despite a professed interest in China's self-determination, however, a hard core of territorial rights and interests remained sacrosanct. International cooperation was a means to support, not surrender, Japan's vital interests. Manchuria, in particular, must never be relinquished. Shidehara diplomacy informed Japanese foreign policy throughout the 1920s and reflected the consensus of the mainstream in the foreign ministry as early as the Washington Conference. Peaceful economic expansion was perceived as a way to maintain a unique position in Asia while cooperating with the United States to avoid economic isolation.[60] It is impossible to disentangle the Japanese drives for national security, great-power status, and access to resources and markets. Japan pursued these triple goals before World War I in the manner of other great powers, namely, by expanding and setting up colonial regimes. Joining the Western allies during World War I allowed the Japanese to make additional territorial gains cheaply, and the quest for greater control over the Asian mainland stimulated Japan's "invasion" of Siberia in 1918. In sum, though throughout the 1920s there existed a westernized parliamentary perspective in Japan, the drives for economic security and great-power status were never relinquished, and they strongly influenced Japanese policy and negotiating strategy at the interwar arms control conferences.[61]

Like its continental policy, Japan's naval policy reflected a confluence of strategic and economic requirements. As an island nation, Japan possessed no continental depth in which to retreat in the face of a powerful foe. Therefore, to protect the home islands, a battle fleet capable of meeting and destroying an enemy expeditionary force was deemed vital. A navy capable of supporting Japanese Far Eastern policies was also needed to ensure access to markets that were a matter of

60. Nish, *Alliance in Decline*, p. 280.

61. Sadao Asada, "Japan's Special Interests and the Washington Conference, 1921–1922," *American Historical Review* 67 (October 1961): 62–70.

life or death. Japan was an urbanized economy that purchased imported food and raw materials with exported manufactured goods. Inability to support its commercial interests in China could mean starvation. Even though Japanese and U.S. policies were designed to capture Far Eastern markets, the Japanese rejected the underlying assumption of the open door notes, namely, that no nation had a greater interest in Far Eastern trade than the United States. Statistics bear out the accuracy of Japan's assessment. Throughout the 1920s, the China market remained relatively unimportant to American businessmen. Between 1923 and 1931, U.S. exports to China averaged 3 percent of all U.S. exports and 18 percent of China's total imports. The United States, in fact, exported nearly twice as much to Japan as to China during this period because Japan was more economically developed, urbanized, and had more regular trading practices. During the same period, 22 percent of Japan's total exports went to China, furnishing 27 percent of China's total imports. Investments in China indicate an even greater disparity between Japan and the United States. Of the nearly $3.2 billion invested in China by all nations during the period, Japan could claim 35.1 percent of the total or 81.9 percent of its own total foreign investment, the United States only 6.1 percent of China's total or 1.3 percent of total U.S. investment abroad. As Gerald Wheeler puts it, when these figures are viewed in light of the fact that Japan did not attempt agricultural self-sufficiency in the 1920s, their importance increases.[62] Japan built a navy capable of supporting its Far Eastern policies. That navy was perceived by the United States as a threat to Guam and the Philippines.

Very early on, in 1907, Japan's "National Defense Policy" identified the United States as the "hypothetical" enemy.[63] The open door policy challenged Japanese interests in Korea and south Manchuria, and acquisition of the Philippines provided the United States with a potential naval base from which to undermine the security of the empire. The naval component of the 1907 policy identified two fundamental objec-

62. Gerald E. Wheeler, *Prelude to Pearl Harbor: The United States Navy and the Far East, 1921–1931* (Columbia: University of Missouri Press, 1963), pp. 28–29.

63. The term *hypothetical enemy* initially stood simply for a budgetary enemy. The United States served as the target of the navy's building plans and was utilized as such in contests with the army over budgetary appropriations. Sadao Asada, "The Japanese Navy and the United States," in Dorothy Borg and Shumpei Okamoto, eds., *Pearl Harbor as History: Japanese-American Relations, 1931–1941* (New York: Columbia University Press, 1973), p. 235.

tives: (1) preservation of naval superiority over the U.S. fleet in the western Pacific by following the "eight-eight" plan[64] and (2) maintenance of the cornerstone of Japan's continental and Pacific policies—the Anglo-Japanese alliance.

Opposition from the Wilson administration at Paris in 1919 on every major Pacific problem—Shantung, the German islands, the meaning of the open door policy—reinforced Japanese perceptions of hostility from the United States. Further, war had encouraged the U.S. Navy to expand enormously, transforming the United States into a great naval power. The Battle of Jutland led naval authorities in all countries to conclude that an attacking naval force needed at least a 40 percent superiority to assure victory.[65] For Japan, this meant that superiority over the U.S. fleet in the western Pacific required at least a 70 percent ratio to deny the United States this 40 percent advantage. Japan's naval general staff emphasized that "failure to obtain a 10:7 ratio would fatally compromise the naval security of the empire and force Japan to defer to an American definition of Japan's proper continental policies."[66]

In 1920, the Japanese faced several dilemmas. Their continental policies, supported by the wartime acquisition of former German possessions, had generated widespread resentment in the United States. The defeat of Germany had destroyed the prewar alliance system and a primary impetus for the Anglo-Japanese alliance. Britain seemed ready to renounce the alliance in the face of dominion pressures and a desire for collaboration with the United States. These developments exacerbated Japanese fears of political, economic, and strategic isolation. Growing insecurities, coupled with the postwar resumption in the United States of the 1916 naval building program, were powerful incentives for a renewed Japanese building program, and in 1920, Japan's parliament announced that by 1927 the Imperial Navy would have a fleet of eight super-dreadnought battleships and eight giant battle cruisers, all less than eight years old. Japan would have a total of twenty-five capital ships completed since 1913.[67]

64. The "eight-eight" plan called for the construction of eight battleships, eight battle cruisers, 27 light cruisers, 177 destroyers, and 64 submarines. If the empire augmented its fleet too rapidly and in the process stimulated fears in British naval circles, the 1907 plan recommended as an immediate goal the authorization of twelve capital ships, the "eight-four" program. Crowley, Japan's Quest for Autonomy, pp. 6–7.
65. Ibid., p. 25.
66. Ibid., p. 26.
67. Sprout and Sprout, Toward a New Order, p. 94.

According to Raymond Buell, "Japan had never been closer to realizing the dream of Yoshida Shoin for hegemony over Asia than in 1921."[68] Yoshida Shoin, a member of the Choshu clan that later controlled the army, called for the annexation of the Kurile Islands, Sakhalin, Kamchatka, Formosa, Korea, Manchuria, and part of eastern Siberia. The Japanese Army had succeeded in establishing political and economic ascendancy over Manchuria, Shantung, and parts of Siberia. In addition, as Roger Dingman points out, by the autumn of 1919, domestic pressures for arms expansion were mounting.[69] Only arms expansion could assure continued naval support for Prime Minister Hara Kei's cabinet. Admiral Kato Tomosaburo had been Hara's ally in the struggle with the army over retreat in Shantung and Siberia, and he deserved some reward. Expansion could also compensate the army for withdrawal from advanced positions on mainland Asia. Finally, arms expansion could expediently settle disruptive national defense issues, clearing the way to focus on pressing problems of economic stability. Yet refusing to accept President Harding's invitation to participate in an arms limitation conference would exacerbate fears in the West about Japanese ambitions. In addition, competing domestic claims on economic resources threatened to prevent the army from sustaining by force an Asiatic hegemony challenged by the combined resources of the United States and Great Britain, both of whose commitments in the Atlantic and Europe had eased enormously since the war. With increasing demands for spending on domestic programs, retrenchment in the military sphere was becoming imperative.[70]

In 1922, the Japanese perceived their nation as operating under severe economic constraints. As a regional power, they viewed their nation's livelihood as intimately dependent on maintaining a special relationship with the Asian mainland. As James Crowley summarizes the Japanese position, "The identification of national security and economic prosperity with a hegemonical position in East Asia became an article of faith for the Imperial government that was not compromised

68. Buell, *Washington Conference*, pp. 6–7, 149. Although Buell stresses the distinction between the military party and liberals in Japan, he also points out that the form of government in Japan enthroned the military party.

69. Roger Dingman, *Power in the Pacific: The Origin of Naval Arms Limitation, 1914–1922* (Chicago: University of Chicago Press, 1976), p. 129.

70. By 1921–22, naval expenditures comprised nearly one-third of governmental expenditure in Japan. Inflation was unabated. Recurrent strikes and labor disputes threatened to shatter industrial order. And in the spring of 1920, Japan plunged into a severe economic depression.

until the end of the Pacific War." In Crowley's assessment, Japanese imperialism was the rational manifestation of three convictions firmly held by military and civilian leaders alike: status as a world power required the capability to wage war against two strategic enemies—the Soviet Union and the United States; the ability to prevail against either was not possible within the limits of Japan's resources; to rectify this deficiency, it was necessary to impose a planned economy on Japan, destroy the Nationalist government of China, and to achieve hegemonical position in East Asia. Crowley disagrees that Japanese aggression resulted from "ultra-nationalism, political assassinations, military conspiracies, and factional disputes within the Imperial Army which enabled Japan's military leaders to seize political power and to launch the nation on a program of expansion."[71]

Buell advances a more sinister view of Japanese imperialism. He attributes the weakness of the Japanese liberal movement, and the fact that so many Japanese liberals were imperialists, to the propagation by militarist elements of the idea of biologic imperialism. Appealing to the instinct of self-preservation, establishing colonies was advanced as a matter of life or death, despite the fact that Japan depended for trade least on its colonies and most on the United States, Great Britain, and India.[72] Propaganda publicized acute population problems that were exacerbated by the prohibition of Japanese immigration to Western countries. Colonization was the logical remedy. Annexation, open or disguised, was necessary for colonization.[73] Dubbed the "Asiatic Monroe Doctrine," Japan's leaders asserted the right to dictate settlements in the Orient. Whether these beliefs reflected a doctrine of militarism, legitimate great power aspirations, or a reaction to Western intrusions into Japanese affairs[74] is of less consequence than the fact that by the time of the Washington Conference, an axiomatic belief in the need for exclusive rights on the Asian mainland had become part of the mindset of the Japanese leadership and populace.

Japan's leaders, therefore, agreed to participate in the Washington

71. Crowley, *Japan's Quest for Autonomy*, pp. xiv–xvii.
72. Buell, *Washington Conference*, pp. 328–68.
73. Ibid., p. 337.
74. The Triple Intervention of 1895, in which France, Germany, and Russia intervened and forced Japan to return the Liaotung Peninsula—the key tongue of land with the harbors of Port Arthur and Talien Bay—to China, had been tremendously humiliating and created a powerful incentive to ensure history would never repeat itself. Where other countries saw aggressive intent, the Japanese claimed pure defense and the quest for security.

Conference, but with the intent of using any cooperative arrangements that might result to assure, if not bolster, their own position on mainland Asia and in the western Pacific. One way or another, the Japanese delegation resolved to maintain the status quo in the western Pacific, prevent military intervention by any Western power in the Orient, and restrain Western diplomatic intervention in Japan's suzerainty in Asia. To prevent interference with what were perceived as their vital interests in the Orient, the Japanese delegates—Baron Kato Tomosaburo, minister of the navy; Prince Tokugawa Iesato, president of the House of Peers; Baron Kijuro Shidehara, Japanese ambassador to the United States; and Hanihara Masanao, vice-minister for foreign affairs—advanced the "Doctrine of Sole Concern" to exclude from the Conference disputes not affecting the treaty rights of third powers, placing disputes between the governments of Japan and China outside the Conference's purview. Likewise, the delegates advanced the "Doctrine of Accomplished Fact," which permitted discussion of future policies of foreign powers in Asia yet precluded challenges to positions already established. Japan would support general principles like the open door and preservation of the territorial integrity of states but refused to discuss established rights or questions that did not affect the participating powers as a whole.[75]

On the eve of the Washington Conference, the Japanese faced an impending arms race with the United States. Attempts to build up to a 70 percent ratio with the U.S. fleet very conceivably could encourage British building to safeguard the security of Australia and New Zealand. The worst scenario would be an Anglo-American alliance, capable of undermining the security of the home islands and empire. Fear of an Anglo-American combination impelled Japan's political and naval leaders to seek a diplomatic and naval accommodation with the United States that would, in one way or another, assure Japan's existing superiority in the western Pacific and preserve its Far Eastern interests.

THE FRENCH AND ITALIAN POSITIONS

France and Italy, the two other signatories to the Five Power treaty, had to be factored into British assessments of the naval balance, since

75. Buell, *Washington Conference*, pp. 240–41; Braisted, *United States Navy*, p. 569.

Britain's force structure had to be designed to operate simultaneously in the European and Pacific theaters. However, as continental powers first, French and Italian naval policies could not be divorced from the balance of land armaments or from the specter of renewed German aggression. The French were operating under a set of strategic constraints dictated by a continental conception of security. They refused to consider naval disarmament separately from land disarmament, since their security was as much threatened from land as from sea. The French also sought political guarantees on the continent as a quid pro quo for arms limitation.

Since 1919, the French perceived themselves as increasingly isolated on the Continent politically. In the postwar years, they were determined to reinforce and enhance what security they had achieved at Versailles. At Paris, Premier George Clemenceau relented in his demand for a buffer state along the Rhine in return for military guarantees from Great Britain and the United States. Subsequently, however, the Senate refused to enter the League or to ratify the Anglo-American-French alliance guaranteeing French frontiers. The British refused to guarantee France alone. For the French, the Washington Conference was an opportunity to enhance their strategic position in Europe. Believing the United States was committed to limiting both naval and land armaments, Premier Aristide Briand was prepared "to proclaim to the world that France, under these [present] circumstances, could not disarm."[76] The French, however, would reduce armaments in exchange for renewed military pledges from Great Britain and the United States.

The French viewed naval arms limitation as an attractive strategy to the degree that it could be manipulated to create a more favorable balance of power in Europe, preferably by securing political compensation for the French. The French needed to maintain a decisive superiority over any potential continental opponent, but were handicapped to the degree that their security was defined largely in terms of a German threat, whereas the immediate concerns of the three major naval powers were focused on the Pacific.

For the Italians, naval parity with the French, regardless of the absolute tonnage level, was the primary objective at Washington, and it would remain a cardinal goal of Italian policy throughout the decade. Although the demise of the Austro-Hungarian fleet consolidated Italy's position in the Adriatic, a long exposed coastline created vulnerabilities

76. Buell, *Washington Conference*, p. 203.

in the Mediterranean. The Italian delegates came to Washington to secure "parity with the strongest fleet of any of the Powers situated in the Mediterranean" or "to reduce their naval armaments to zero, if France [did] the same."[77] As these alternatives indicate, the Italians were more concerned with securing a level of naval tonnage for purposes of prestige rather than to meet some objective assessment of strategic requirements.

THE CHINESE POSITION

The Chinese could not prevent other delegations at the Washington Conference from making decisions about the future of China that were more in the interests of foreign powers than in the interests of the Chinese national government. Critically, the Chinese were operating under the severest economic and domestic political constraints. The national government in Peking was struggling to survive the triple challenge posed by a rival Canton government, bastions of warlord power throughout the country, and a multitude of foreign encroachments. The Chinese delegation came to Washington to secure tariff autonomy, the return of Shantung and Manchuria, cancellation of the Twenty-One Demands, and abolition of extraterritoriality. In essence, the Chinese were fighting to reclaim their sovereignty and believed their chances of securing these objectives—particularly vis-à-vis the Japanese—would be enhanced in a multilateral forum.

The Chinese wanted to regain administration of rates of customs, out of their control since 1842. Forced by foreign powers to charge no more than five percent on the value of goods leaving or entering the country, the Chinese were losing a valuable source of revenue, easy to collect, and instrumental for the creation of a strong central government. Though in theory the tariff schedule was to be adjusted to follow the rise and fall of actual prices, tariff revision had never occurred. By 1921, the Chinese authorities were receiving only 3.5 percent duty on imports. Lack of tariff autonomy increased dependence on foreign loans

---

77. See Richard Dean Burns and Donald Urquidi, *Disarmament in Perspective: An Analysis of Selected Arms Control and Disarmament Agreements Between the World Wars, 1919–1939*, vol. 3, *Limitation of Sea Power* (The U.S. Arms Control and Disarmament Agency, Contract No. ACDA/RS–55 III, July 1968), p. 26.

and prolonged foreign control. Flat duties prevented the taxation of luxuries more heavily than necessities, the protection of infant industries, and the negotiation of reciprocity agreements with other states. Finally, the *likin* transit tax, an internal tax on goods moving between different provinces, further undermined political order by providing a source of revenue for local military commanders.

The Chinese wanted to recover the former German leasehold of Kiaochow and economic control over Shantung. To the Chinese Shantung was part of China, and they rejected Japanese claims to it. The Chinese were determined to bring the Shantung issue before the conference as a whole to diminish the handicaps of negotiating with the Japanese directly and to secure a public repudiation of the Versailles Shantung Settlement.

Finally, the Chinese were committed to the repudiation of the Twenty-One Demands imposed on China when at peace with Japan. Though these demands had aroused moral indignation worldwide, the Japanese were committed to maintaining the supremacy in Manchuria the demands secured. The Chinese, in particular, wanted termination of the Port Arthur, Dairen, and the south Manchurian railway leases. A leasehold was unique among foreign rights because the foreign power gained complete political control over the territory concerned for the period of the lease. The Chinese did not even retain the right to govern their own subjects within the leasehold. Though the title to the territory remained with China, the actual exercise of sovereignty was vested with the foreign power.[78] Return of these leases would be a great boost to Chinese sovereignty and a significant setback for Japan.

TOWARD A NEW ORDER

A postwar order in the Far East had to address the domestic political, diplomatic, economic, and strategic concerns of the major powers if cooperation were to be robust. In addition to regional concerns, developments in the Far East had broader implications for relations in the Atlantic and on the continent of Europe. Japan had a set of regional demands and requirements that had to be reconciled with a newly

78. See Buell, *Washington Conference*, p. 267 n. 37.

emerging world order. Great Britain sought cooperation with the United States to facilitate transition from naval supremacy, at the same time that U.S. enmity with Britain's ally, Japan, was growing. The United States was attempting to alter the foundations of past international relations with its conception of a new world order.

A network of similar interests united the three great maritime powers in their efforts to forge a new framework of interaction. All were laboring under varying degrees of economic constraints and wanted to avoid the financial burden of an arms race. The memory of prewar naval races, coupled with economies weakened by war, created a similar interest in avoiding excessive monetary and resource outlays for armaments. Popular movements in all three countries shared this sentiment and demanded fiscal retrenchment. Furthermore, the United States, Great Britain, and Japan all shared a similar politico-ideological objective in checking the threat of Soviet Bolshevism in China. Finally, "China as an idea" created a common perception of the need for the China market. Though interests in China frequently conflicted, a common ground for negotiation emerged because Japan, the power with the greatest stake in China, viewed economic and political cooperation with the United States as the best means to protect its own continental interests.

World War I also left in its wake seemingly intractable conflicting agendas that had to be bridged if a stable postwar order were to emerge and be sustained in the Far East. Japanese possession of the former German Pacific islands jeopardized the Philippines and Guam and the demands of British imperial defense. The United States's naval program of 1916, though originally designed with Germany in mind, challenged British supremacy in the Atlantic and Japanese political and strategic interests in the Pacific. In December 1920, the U.S. Department of the Navy advanced a building program to lay down within three years an additional eighty-eight naval vessels. In March 1921, the British Admiralty announced a program to keep pace with the United States, to maintain at least a one-power standard. Although armed conflict between Great Britain and the United States was a remote contingency, growing discord threatened to jeopardize chances of cooperation in other areas. To defend its outlying Pacific possessions and Far Eastern policies, the U.S. Navy had to be able to blockade Japan and disrupt Japanese communications with mainland Asia. Such a navy would inevitably have sufficient strength to search out and defeat the Japanese fleet in its home waters. Although these challenges accelerated Japanese naval developments, at the same time they stimulated popular demand in Japan for naval limitation. The Japanese, however, would cooperate on naval limitation only if the United States accepted political and strategic terms calculated to ensure Tokyo's sphere of dominant interests in the western Pacific. In short, the United States would have to radically reorient its political and naval programs in the Pacific.[79]

In the postwar years, the British were determined to secure a naval agreement with the United States. Possession of the world's greatest navy had always been a symbol of power, prestige, and unity of the British empire; yet the British were no longer financially able to maintain even nominal equality with the U.S. Navy in open, unrestricted competition.[80] Further, British building might stimulate U.S. navalism, exacerbate U.S.-Japanese enmity, create a Japanese naval response, and ultimately threaten Britain's Pacific empire. Even if these naval contests were avoided, Anglo-American enmity would destroy what Britain perceived as the only firm foundation for a postwar order—Anglo-American entente.

A reorientation of British policy, however, risked alienating a loyal ally, Japan. The Anglo-Japanese alliance loomed as a huge obstacle to any tripartite cooperative arrangement. If the alliance were renewed in 1921, it would destroy hopes for naval limitation. U.S. leaders, for their part, saw the alliance as clear evidence of Britain's acquiescence to Japanese aggression and as sufficient justification to continue postwar naval expansion. If the alliance were abrogated, the Japanese might feel isolated and betrayed and perhaps refuse any role in a cooperative arrangement. The British also refused to relinquish the alliance as long as the United States pursued an intransigent naval program. In short, "the United States would not agree to limit its navy as long as the Anglo-Japanese alliance existed; Japan might well reject naval terms acceptable to the United States without the support which the alliance afforded; and Great Britain was reluctant to sacrifice its longstanding association with Japan for an uncertain naval agreement with the United States."[81]

79. See Herbert Feis, *The Road to Pearl Harbor: The Coming of the War Between the United States and Japan* (Princeton: Princeton University Press, 1950).

80. See Mary Klachko, "Anglo-American Naval Competition, 1918–1922" (Ph.D. diss., Columbia University, 1962).

81. Sprout and Sprout, *Toward a New Order*, pp. 128–29.

Finally, in the postwar years, the United States was working to create a new order in the Far East based on principles that had informed its own policies in prewar years: defense of Chinese territorial and administrative integrity and preservation of great-power economic interests by means of the open door. Obviously, these principles conflicted with the resolute premise of Japanese foreign policy in East Asia—that Japan had legitimate essential interests, particularly in Manchuria, and hegemony there was mandatory. Nevertheless, though the ends of Japanese and U.S. policy in the Far East conflicted, Japan's leaders recognized the advantages, at least in the near term, of cooperation with the West. Foreshadowing Japanese policy throughout the 1920s, the "older 'force' diplomacy, that stressed Japan's territorial control over strategic spots in China," was eclipsed by "an economic diplomacy giving the highest priority to the search for markets."[82] International solutions that could bring Japan closer to the West and to the greatest source of trading profits superseded national solutions to foreign policy issues. A postwar order had to exploit Japanese desires for economic interaction with the West.[83] At the same time, threats to perceived special interests in Asia risked bringing to power those political elements within Japan committed to national solutions.

82. Sidney DeVere Brown, "Shidehara Kijuro: The Diplomacy of the Yen," in Richard Dean Burns and Edward M. Bennett, eds., Diplomats in Crisis: United States–Chinese–Japanese Relations, 1919–1941 (Santa Barbara: American Bibliographical Center-Clio Press, 1974), p. 201.
83. As Morison reflects, "Looking backward, we can see that the only hope of preserving peace in the Pacific was to encourage and support the liberal elements in Japan responsible for [the Washington] agreements and concessions." Samuel Eliot Morison, History of United States Naval Operations in World War II, vol. 3, The Rising Sun in the Pacific, 1931–April 1942 (Boston: Little, Brown, 1957), p. 9.

3 Doctrine and Strategic Vision

CONVENTIONAL WISDOM POSITS a strong link between the characteristics of technologies that affect the military balance and the results of arms control negotiations, or arms control "outputs." Kruzel, for one, contends that "periods of great technological uncertainty are not conducive to the negotiation of meaningful arms limitations."[1] It has also become part of the arms control folklore that states agree to limit only weapons that are obsolete, or not critical in maintaining the balance of power or to shifts in the balance.[2] Both these assertions slight the influence of military doctrine on conceptions of security and strategic vision and on assessments of technology and the military balance. Evaluations of the military balance and assessments of the impact of technological developments on the balance, filtered through the lens of doctrine, affect the arms control process. The two assertions support the charge that our contemporary understanding of the arms control process has become technologically driven. Restraint, however, is not a product of weapons technology but of understandings and perceptions about the uses and limitations of weapons.

The decision of the three great maritime powers to limit battleships, coupled with the difficulties in imposing limits on submarines and air-

---

1. Joseph Kruzel, "From Rush-Bagot to START: The Lessons of Arms Control," *ORBIS* (Spring 1986): 195–99.

2. Berkowitz concludes that "the most irrelevant weapons (i.e., the oldest) are the easiest to control, and the most threatening weapons (i.e., those planned for the future) are the most difficult." *Calculated Risks*, p. 95.

power, may seem to evince that only obsolete technologies fall prey to the limits of arms control. In hindsight, one might argue that the role of the battleship had become significantly circumscribed, particularly with developments in airpower. In addition, as a developed weapon system, the battleship could not keep pace defensively with the offensive challenges posed by new technologies. Yet despite the claims of airpower advocates and the results of postwar bombing trials, naval leaders in Great Britain, the United States, and Japan still believed the battleship to be the greatest factor in naval strength and were convinced it would remain so for the foreseeable future. Airplanes and carriers were useful adjuncts in spotting and scouting roles but they had failed to undermine the dominant role of the capital ship. As Hedley Bull points out, "It would thus be quite wrong to conclude that the treaties merely sanctified a junking of useless vessels that would in any case have been carried out unilaterally."[3] At the Washington Conference, a shared belief among the leading maritime powers that the battleship was the main element in securing and maintaining command of the sea created a currency to assess relative naval strength, to reach agreements based on ratios of battleship tonnage, and to assess the impact of arms control on the attainment of national goals. Doctrine, for the Pacific powers, served as an important contributing factor to overlapping strategic visions.

In the interwar naval case, we have evidence concerning how technology affected the arms control process that contradicts conventional arms control wisdom. The conventional presumption is that technological change influences the military balance and then arms control outputs, or the products of the negotiating process:

technology > military balance > arms control outputs

Technological systems critical to the balance, or to shifts in the balance, will be very difficult to limit. Systems whose technological capacity has largely been exploited to the fullest, and which are thus less likely to be instrumental in shifting the balance, may be significantly limited. The interwar case demonstrates how doctrinal perceptions and

---

3. Hedley Bull, "Strategic Arms Limitation: The Precedent of the Washington and London Naval Treaties," in Morton A. Kaplan, ed., *SALT: Problems and Prospects* (Morristown, N.J.: General Learning Press, 1973), p. 40.

predispositions influence how technological change is perceived to affect the military balance, and these perceptions, rather than any objective quality about technology itself, are what affect arms control outputs:

technology > *doctrinal perceptions* > perceptions of the military
balance > arms control outputs

It is commonly argued that the submarine escaped limitation in 1922 because, as an innovative technology, its full military potential had yet to be exploited. In short, it was not ripe for limitation.[4] Even Bull points to "the failure of the naval treaties to impose restrictions on the [submarine and naval air power] comparable to those provided for the [battleship]" as an indication of the latter's obsolescence.[5] Although Japan and the United States recognized that the submarine could enhance their defensive superiority in important ways and did not rally behind the British initiative to abolish the weapon system entirely, they were, nevertheless, willing to establish quantitative limits. More important for the outcome, however, were the reasons the French opposed limits on submarines. France's military doctrine defined a large submarine force as critical to national security unless all types of weapons, rather than just naval forces alone, were limited, and unless France secured political guarantees in Europe.

A similar doctrinal argument explains why airpower limitations evolved as they did. Although carriers were in fact limited, though more permissively than battleships, as a surrogate for limiting aircraft directly,[6] most admirals in Great Britain, the United States, and Japan did not believe airpower significantly affected the balance of naval power. For the three maritime powers, revolutions in airpower were simply incorporated into doctrine to support the precept of battleship supremacy. Airpower assets escaped direct limitation, as well, because the French at the time possessed the largest air force in Europe, yet as an adjunct of their land power, refused to reduce their air force absent political guarantees from Britain or the United States. It was not simply the state of technology that determined the propensity of weapon sys-

---

4. Kruzel, "From Rush-Bagot to START," p. 199.
5. Bull, "Strategic Arms Limitation," p. 40.
6. The difficulty of limiting aircraft for military use without limiting its civilian uses also constrained airpower negotiations.

tems for limitation, but rather how different technologies and their limitations were perceived to enhance or to threaten security. These assessments, conditioned in large part by doctrine, defined the relationship between technology and arms control outputs. Doctrine influences how technology is perceived to affect security, regardless of hindsight that may disprove the validity of these perceptions and evaluations.

The Royal, U.S., and Imperial navies were dominated by conservative admirals whose shared doctrinal perspectives provided a foundation for naval arms limitation. Naval leaders in Great Britain, the United States, and Japan shared common assumptions about (1) the impact of naval technologies, (2) maritime doctrine and strategy, and (3) the lessons of World War I. They were convinced that the battleship was and would remain for the foreseeable future the backbone of the fleet. Although conceding that technological developments had circumscribed the battleship's radius of action, these admirals believed this development could be factored into ratios of battleship tonnage that would still reflect the balance of naval power. In addition, naval leaders in all three countries designed fleets to execute traditional maritime strategies aimed at securing and maintaining command of the sea. The lessons gleaned from World War I reinforced these shared doctrinal predispositions. The Washington treaties built on this shared belief in the primacy of the battleship and on the naval doctrine and strategies that supported it.

Two conclusions about the relationship between doctrine and arms control emerge from the interwar case. First, a shared doctrine may facilitate agreement on arms control and help transcend political differences, whereas incompatible or dissimilar doctrines may hinder arms control and even prevent the realization of mutual interests. The kinds of arms control provisions that serve the security interests of one state may be incompatible with those that serve the interests of another because of differences in doctrine, which provides the strategic rationale for the design, development, and deployment of military forces. British and French differences on submarine limitation provide an ideal illustration of how states with mutual security interests but different doctrines can develop force-structure preferences that constrain cooperation and arms control and may even exacerbate tensions between them. Furthermore, the British-French case suggests that military-based arms control can never surmount such obstacles, whereas political-based arms control strategies can. Arms control is easier when parties are able to agree on common measures of military capability from the outset, but it is not impossible when they cannot. Likewise, the ability to agree on common measures is no guarantee that arms control agreements will result.

The interwar arms control process mitigated tensions and enhanced security to the degree that the major naval powers shared a traditional maritime doctrine,[7] because shared doctrine reflected compatible definitions of security, or compatible strategic visions. The arms control process failed to enhance the security of those states with continental military doctrines. The Washington arms control process implied that orchestrating a balance of naval power alone would enhance security, but this made sense only for the three leading naval powers. These states were seriously threatened only by each other, and their security was enhanced by relative geographical isolation from one another. Continental conceptions of security, on the other hand, offered a more organic orientation toward military power and the arms control process. As a continental power, the French were reluctant to limit naval power alone and adamant against limiting naval assets by type, for this would compel them to develop a force structure based on maritime strategic assumptions rather than continental strategic assumptions.

A second conclusion about the relationship between doctrine and arms control drawn from the interwar experience is that compatible doctrines alone do not assure that states will identify arms control as playing the same role in enhancing security. Despite the same doctrinal orientation, the estimates of leaders in Japan and the United States about the arms control process diverged over time. Again, agreements to regulate military power cannot be separated from other, nonmilitary dimensions of security. Shared doctrine facilitates agreement on technical provisions, but not necessarily on the political context in which those provisions exist. By examining how consensus among the three leading naval powers facilitated agreement on arms control and how contrasting continental perceptions of security hindered efforts to forge a comprehensive system of arms control at the global level, we may be better able to correct for another bias in the arms control literature.

7. For general background, see H. P. Wilmott, *Empires in the Balance: Japanese and Allied Pacific Strategies to April 1942* (Annapolis: Naval Institute Press, 1982).

THE TRADITIONAL MARITIME CONSENSUS

In the years following World War I, a consensus existed that comprised beliefs about technology, doctrine, and the lessons of the First World War. Two critical perspectives on the state of technology in the post-war years shaped the views of influential naval leaders in Great Britain, the United States, and Japan. First, the battleship remained the back-bone of the fleet and represented the index of great power. A consensus on "battleship supremacy" prevailed among maritime nations, in part because of the low rate of technical change relative to the previous half century, in part because of vested organizational interests. Obsessive attachment to battleship supremacy predisposed naval leaders in all three countries to accept battleship ratios as the basis for calculating and limiting relative naval strength, and agreement on this standard of comparison skirted one potential obstacle to arms limitation. The second critical perspective about naval technology held that technological revolutions of previous decades had curtailed the battleship's freedom of action. Nevertheless, the belief in battleship supremacy was not discarded. Rather, the balance of naval power shifted to accommodate the battleship's newfound limitations. Regional centers of naval power emerged, and agreements on force ratios and base fortification were designed to preserve defensive superiority in respective spheres while curtailing the ability to bring the offensive to the enemy. The shift of greatest concern to the Washington treaty powers was that Japan had become undisputedly superior in the western Pacific.

Despite technological developments of the previous half century that had seriously restricted the cruising radius of the battleship, this vessel was still considered the capital ship[8] of the day and the index of naval power. Displacing a minimum of 10,000 tons and mounting 12-inch guns, the battleship represented "the hitting power of a navy in its most

---

8. The term "capital ship" was first used officially in the Washington Treaty of 1922. Prior to the Second World War, the battleship and battle cruiser were the core components of the strategic system of the day. As such, they were the ships others were designed to protect and support. With the technology of airpower, the aircraft carrier displaced the battleship as the capital ship and became the locus of fighting power of the navy. The terms "battleship" and "capital ship" were used interchangeably though they are not synonymous. The former refers to a temporary class of warship, the latter to "an abstract concept in a permanent philosophy of war." The battleship is a ship; the capital ship a role.

copious, compact, and durable form."[9] The battle fleet was designed to defeat the largest concentrated sea force of the enemy, to give and receive the heaviest blows possible to devise. Essentially a mobile, floating gun platform, the battleship remained the arbiter for command of the sea.

Despite professional faith in the battleship, advances in naval technology had circumscribed the battleship's radius of action and affected the tactics and strategy of naval warfare. The submarine, along with revolutions in steam propulsion, armor and ordnance, underwater warfare with the torpedo and mine, and the airplane, had far-reaching strategic and political consequences. They limited the range of the capital ship, decentralized naval power away from its European locus, and encouraged the rise of regional centers of naval power.

Steam increased the flexibility of battle fleet movement, but restricted the area in which fleets could operate in relative security. By introducing the problem of fuel supply, steam limited the range of fleets and enhanced the importance of bases abroad. "Without fuel, warships cannot move and without a secure and readily available source of supply, they dare not move."[10] Steam did augment the superior fleet's degree of control by increasing the probability of contact between fleets. Where chances for contact were enhanced, the superior fleet had the advantage, for it induced the inferior fleet to stay at home, reducing the threat value of a "fleet in being" strategy.[11] However, control had become isolated regionally, within range of one's bases.

Advances in ordnance increased the possibility of serious combat damage that would require extensive repairs. A fleet dare not venture too far from its repair bases unless it had overwhelming superiority to ensure the enemy would not engage. The need for proximity to repair bases further limited the battle fleet spatially, and the increasing size of

9. Bernard Brodie, A Guide to Naval Strategy (Princeton: Princeton University Press, 1944), p. 17.

10. Bernard Brodie, Sea Power in the Machine Age: Major Naval Inventions and Their Consequences on International Politics, 1814–1940 (Princeton: Princeton University Press, 1941), p. 111.

11. Traditional maritime strategists advocated securing command of the sea, with the underlying assumption that the superior fleet would prevail. What of the inferior fleet? The fleet-in-being strategy avoided battle with the superior fleet yet maintained maximum threat value. Although the strategy implied inferiority, whether local or general, it did not imply passivity. Even if one were unable to destroy an enemy fleet, one could still achieve a useful degree of command in an area, attack the enemy's trade or coasts, or deny the enemy, by harassment, the ability to enjoy the benefits of command. Brodie, Guide to Naval Strategy, p. 94 n. 1; Julian S. Corbett, Some Principles of Maritime Strategy, 2d ed. (London: Longmans, 1918), pp. 191–99.

battleships to sustain more armor for protection meant that many harbors and canals were rendered inadequate.

The submarine was developed initially to offset the defensive advantage heavy armor provided battleship superstructures. Though battleships were protected above the water, they were very vulnerable below its surface. The submarine further limited the radius of action of the battle fleet as the fleet was forced to resort to the defensive tactic of zigzagging at high speed, consequently expending more fuel. In addition, the submarine, along with the torpedo and mine, further exacerbated spatial limitation as capital ships became dependent on destroyer escorts whose range was inherently more limited. The battleship had once been a self-contained unit requiring no other vessels for its defense, but the submarine, torpedo, and mine altered the geography of naval warfare. With these developments, the battleship needed a protective screen of lesser craft to operate as a first line of defense against torpedo attack and as a smoke screen against enemy gunfire. These ancillary vessels, however, could operate only over shorter distances and in proximity to bases. The limited endurance of destroyers and their reduced cruising radius at high speeds seriously limited the extended action of the battle fleet. The range of a fleet ceased to be the range of its capital ships and became the range of its destroyers. Furthermore, the damage sustained by underwater explosion was far more debilitating than that inflicted on a ship's superstructure. A ship that sustained a torpedo hit would need extensive and timely repairs, and this required facilities that were few in number.[12] Again, action far from repair bases was taken at great risk, unless a fleet enjoyed overwhelming superiority.

The balance of naval power in the postwar years reflected these strategic realities. Great Britain formally surrendered global maritime supremacy, accepted battleship parity with the United States, and conceded to Japan control of the western Pacific. This shift in the balance of naval power entailed the devolution of political power in the Far East as well. Recognizing the limits technology had imposed on the battleship, yet still believing that the battleship was the most critical element to the balance of naval power, the Washington powers based force ratios on "total" battleship tonnage. Difficulties arose when the Anglo-

---

12. Brodie, *Guide to Naval Strategy*, p. 85.

Saxon powers were reluctant to sacrifice the political influence that their naval strength no longer afforded to them.

After battleship supremacy, the second component of the traditional maritime consensus subscribed to by conservative naval leaders was Mahanian maritime doctrine and strategies. Mahanian doctrine defined orientations toward arms control, influencing beliefs about what to limit, how to limit it, and how arms control could serve national security. Despite the tremendous losses sustained under Germany's unrestricted war on commerce, the primary mission of the fleet remained, in the Mahanian view, to secure "command of the sea."[13] Decision at sea, it was championed, would be decided as two fleets fired on one another, in parallel courses, and at great range. Arms limitation reflected these views about the use of naval force.

The classical or Mahanian school advanced a philosophy gleaned from the study of history. Classical theorists examined the rise of Britain's maritime empire and claimed to have discovered certain immutable principles of maritime strategy. Captain Alfred Mahan, the most popular proponent of the classical school, focused his analysis on the British Empire between 1660 and 1815.[14] An imperialist and mercantilist, Mahan argued that greatness and strength were products of wealth. Wealth derived from trade. Navies protected trade. Hence, sea power held the key to national greatness, and the advantages of sea power fell to those who secured command of the sea.[15] From his study of history,

13. Command of the sea is about the *use* of the sea, not its *possession*. Introduction to B. Mitchell Simpson III, ed., *The Development of Naval Thought: Essays by Herbert Rosinski* (Newport: Naval War College Press, 1977), p. xix.

14. See Alfred T. Mahan, *The Influence of Sea Power Upon History, 1660–1783* (Boston: Little, Brown, 1890); *Retrospect and Prospect: Studies in International Relations Naval and Political* (Boston: Little, Brown, 1903); and *The Interest of America in Sea Power, Present and Future* (Boston: Little, Brown, 1911).

15. "The thesis [of traditional maritime strategists] is that the interplay between the national productive base of the maritime system and the sea movement capacity of sea power systems steadily adds to national wealth and influence, and the end product is maritime dominance. . . . It requires organized protection. . . . *Sea force* (Navy) is a highly specialized sub-system geared primarily to the support and defense of sea-power. . . . [A]s the special uses that could be made of sea force came to be more fully appreciated, policy-makers tended to give a lower priority to the primary and original function of sea force—namely, the support and defense of sea power [or maritime communications]. The result in time was increasingly to equate the navy with the military elements of national power rather than to see it as a specialized sub-system of national maritime power. . . . In [Mahan's] view, a maritime power system was an integrated whole, working to forward a nation's position in the world." Quoted in B. Mitchell Simpson III, *War, Strategy, and Maritime Power* (New Brunswick: Rutgers University Press, 1977), pp. 105–6; my emphasis.

Mahan concluded that possession of the sea explained why Britain had never been defeated by a continental opponent.[16] Unlike land warfare, where inferior belligerents can hold their own against immensely superior odds, at sea the inferior are utterly helpless. The sea, he argued, is "indivisible." Control could only go to one side as a whole, or to the other. The most expedient way to win and maintain command was by prevailing in decisive battles. The battleship was the principal weapon. Control—the ability to use the sea for oneself while denying it to the enemy—could only be secured by the possession of a battle fleet. Mahan's writings were used to justify battleship construction in maritime states like the United States, Britain, and Japan and in the continental nations of France, Russia, and Italy as well.[17]

Mahan advanced equally immutable strategies and tactics of naval warfare. Commerce raiding represented the weakest form of naval warfare, an option of last resort. Mahan offered as proof the ineffectiveness of French commerce raiders against the British in the wars of Revolutionary and Napoleonic France. In contrast, the British experience, particularly the decisive battles fought by Nelson, demonstrated the superiority of Mahanian ideas. Recognizing the importance of fleet concentration, strategic location, and effective communication to coordinate effort, the British had achieved the ultimate goal of naval force: control of the seas.

Mahanian doctrine advanced particular strategies or "methods by which countries utilize sea force (or navy) to support sea power (or maritime communications) and to achieve desired objectives in peace and war."[18] The strategic objective of blue-water navies—those built around capital ships and designed for extended deployment over long periods of time—was to secure, maintain, deny, or contest command of the sea. Command of the sea was central to naval strategy because of the fundamental difference between war at sea and war on land. On

---

16. Herbert Rosinski, "Mahan and World War II," in Simpson, ed., *Development of Naval Thought*, p. 26. See also Michael Howard, *The British Way in Warfare* (London: Trinity Press, 1975).

17. Mahan's ideas were not new. He had merely advanced them at a time when the world was particularly receptive to them. For this reason, "Mahan's greatest significance is not as a strategist, or even as an historian, but as an historical actor." Geoffrey Till, *Maritime Strategy and the Nuclear Age* (London: Macmillan, 1982), p. 33. See also Margaret Tuttle Sprout, "Mahan: Evangelist of Sea Power," in Edward Meade Earle, ed., *Makers of Modern Strategy: Military Thought from Machiavelli to Hitler* (Princeton: Princeton University Press, 1941), pp. 415–45.

18. Simpson, *War, Strategy, and Maritime Power*, pp. 105–6.

land, a commander can establish a line of defense, but since "'the sea is all one' because no one part of it can be fenced off, fortified and defended by itself . . . effective protection of interests on or by the sea can only be assured by driving [the] opponent from the whole of it."[19] Command of the sea was designed to deal with the problem of defending the fleet, territorial possessions, and the most difficult of all, trade and shipping. Because merchantmen operate beyond national territory and are dispersed over the seas, they are extremely vulnerable to enemy raiders. More generally, at sea, there is no common frontier to establish contact with the enemy. Nor are there predictable lines for the opponent's advance. The attacker possesses unlimited opportunities to execute surprise attacks on far-flung commitments. Protection at sea requires elimination of the enemy from it altogether, by means of decisive battle or blockade.[20]

The decisive-battle school maintained that the defensive objective of sea control could be assured only through the offensive strategy of destroying the organized force afloat of the enemy. A naval battle, if it is decisive, will permit the victor to use the sea while denying its use to the enemy. What makes a battle decisive is not the damage inflicted, but the strategic consequences that flow from the battle. Admiral Sir Herbert Richmond summarized the orthodox concept of the value of the decisive battle as follows: "Concentration of our own units is no longer necessary. . . . Your defending force is multiplied, your powers of exercising pressure by blockade are increased. If the enemy possesses overseas bases, your powers of affording escorts to expeditions sent to capture them are increased. The dangers of invasion are removed and ships and men and material are set free for protection of trade, or attack upon trade."[21] The practical issues of how the battle was fought depended on the strategic circumstances and technology of the day. The principles of battle, however, never changed, the most important one being the principle of concentration: remaining as strong as possible at the decisive point.[22]

19. Herbert Rosinski, "Command of the Sea," in Simpson, ed., *Development of Naval Thought*, pp. 3–4.

20. Rosinski, "Mahan and World War II," pp. 23–24.

21. Richmond, "Evidence to the Cabinet Sub-Committee on Ship-Building" (January 5, 1921) Cab 16/37 Public Records Office, London, quoted in Till, *Maritime Strategy*, 91.

22. Alfred T. Mahan, *Naval Strategy: Compared and Contrasted with the Principles and Practice of Military Operations on Land* (Boston: Little, Brown, 1911), pp. 74–75. See also William E. Livezey, *Mahan on Sea Power* (Norman: University of Oklahoma Press, 1947). Corbett believed intel-

Decisive battles, however, were rarely fought because inferior fleets
took great pains to avoid major fleet encounters. Weaker opponents
possessed unlimited possibilities for evasion and in the end could withdraw into fortified ports. While relinquishing command, the weaker
opponent nevertheless prevents the superior fleet from decisively consolidating superiority. A more likely scenario was a sequence of engagements whose combined consequences proved decisive.

The Battle of Jutland, supposedly the great fleet encounter of the
First World War, exemplified the ambiguity of decisive battle. Though
Jutland was the only full-scale engagement of World War I, as Bernard
Brodie summarizes it, "The long range at which fire was exchanged and
the reluctance of Jellicoe to turn toward the enemy in pursuit caused it
to be indecisive."[23] World War I as a whole seemed to challenge the
contention that decisive battle was the sole or even the primary object
of navies. Rather, defense of shipping had assumed a higher priority and
securing command of the sea through decisive battle often conflicted
with the requirements of trade protection and amphibious operations.

More often than not, command of the sea came to rest on the power
of blockade, since inferior fleets generally evaded battle. Blockade was a
form of indirect trade protection, more feasible than the direct cover
provided by convoy. Offensively, blockade prevented needed supplies
from entering an enemy port. Defensively, it protected national interests of the blockading navy that were outside national boundaries and
could not be protected by ordinary defensive measures. Blockade also
ensured that one's forces would not be divided for convoy protection,
preserved the ability to concentrate in case of enemy attack, and made
defense of trade economically feasible.[24] Though inferior to destruction
of the enemy fleet, blockade did contain an inferior, yet potentially
dangerous, enemy and make use of the sea relatively secure.

The decisive-battle school prevailed after the war, despite the tendency by its enthusiasts to view decisive battle as an end in itself rather
than as a means to establish command. Battleship building programs
resumed as the development of sonar seemed to have reduced the threat
posed by the submarine. Defense of shipping was provided for only by a

---

ligent division was central to concentration. Julian S. Corbett, *The Campaign at Trafalgar*, vol. 1
(London: Longmans, 1919; reprint, New York: AMS Press, 1976), pp. 275–80; page references
are to the reprint edition.

23. Brodie, *Sea Power in the Machine Age*, p. 439.
24. Rosinski, "Command of the Sea," p. 7.

loose resolution at the Washington Conference forbidding the use of submarines as commerce raiders.

Consensus on the lessons of World War I reinforced these articles of faith about technology and doctrine. Postwar admirals in Great Britain, the United States, and Japan believed that command of the sea was a prerequisite for realizing the offensive and defensive ends of naval strategy. They conceded that command of the sea now required control below the surface as well as on it. Yet the antisubmarine campaign of World War I had proven, in their eyes conclusively enough, that control below the surface required indisputable command on it. And the battleship remained the decisive factor in exercising surface command.

Consensus on these lessons of World War I, however, had two contradictory effects. By reinforcing belief in the dominant role of the battleship, consensus fostered agreement on battleship limitation. Yet to the degree that the lessons of the war were learned incorrectly, obsession with battleship limitation blinded naval leaders to the need to limit other classes of ships. Indeed, submarine limitation was discussed extensively at Washington, and the failure to limit submarines quantitatively or qualitatively was not the result of leaders assuming that submarine limitation was unimportant.[25] Rather, French intransigence played a large role, as did Britain's refusal to enter into security guarantees on the Continent. If the lessons postwar leaders gleaned from the war in the Atlantic had been more balanced, perhaps they would have been willing to make more compromises to enhance French security, thereby paving the way for meaningful submarine limitation.

The experience of war stimulated a great deal of controversy in naval circles, yet a reaffirmation of conservative faith in the battleship and in the decisive fleet encounter prevailed. In Britain, the United States, and Japan, the ideas of Mahan continued, modified only minimally in response to technological changes. As Herbert Rosinski puts it, "Battle lines had become smaller, tactics more elastic, air power had changed the whole problem of reconnaissance; but the fundamental conception of basing naval strategy on the 'Command of the Sea,' if possible, by

25. For a succinct yet comprehensive treatment of the submarine deliberations at Washington, see Lawrence H. Douglas, "The Submarine and the Washington Conference of 1921," in Richard B. Lillich and John Norton Moore, eds., U.S. Naval War College International Law Studies, vol. 62, The Use of Force, Human Rights and General International Legal Issues (Newport: Naval War College Press, 1980), pp. 477–90.

the destruction of the enemy's main forces in battle, remained un-
shaken."[26]

The technical limitations of the submarine and the airplane explain
in part why these weapons were viewed primarily as reconnaissance adjuncts, not attack elements. Conceptual confusion that equated the
capital ship as a role with the battleship as a vessel contributed to the
assimilation of ambiguous data from wartime experience into prewar
views. Vested organizational interests, interservice rivalries, and competition for shrinking defense funds reinforced this conceptual ambiguity as the fate of the battleship became identified with the fate of the
navy as a whole. The predisposition toward Mahanian maritime doctrine reinforced perceptions shaped by the technical limitations of air
power and the submarine and by vested organizational interests. Not surprisingly, the lessons derived from World War I were biased, and these
lessons, in turn, reinforced the prevailing intellectual conservatism.

The Battle of Jutland, the only full-scale fleet encounter of the First
World War, could hardly be considered a decisive engagement. The
High Seas Fleet, under the leadership of Admiral Reinhard Scheer, met
up with Admiral David Beatty's battle cruisers on May 31, 1916.
Scheer punished Beatty's forces heavily before Admiral Sir John Jellicoe's main fleet arrived. A massed torpedo attack by Scheer's destroyers, however, forced the main British battle fleet to turn away, and
Scheer successfully returned home.[27] Jellicoe's "turn-away" order in the
face of German destroyers proved the battleship's vulnerability. Obsessed by the U-boat threat, in October 1916 Jellicoe ordered the
Grand Fleet not to venture into the southeastern quarter of the North
Sea, bounded by 55 degrees 30 minutes north, 4 degrees east, without
sufficient destroyer escorts. With the fleets in stalemate, the naval war
shifted from battle fleets in the North Sea to submarines in the Atlantic. By the end of the war, nearly eight million tons of merchant shipping had been lost to submarines. Without U.S. production of escort
vessels and reinstitution of the convoy system, Britain, in all proba-

26. Rosinski, "Mahan and World War II," p. 33. Only Castex theorized about the renewed use
of the submarine as a commerce raider. And Admiral William A. Moffett "led a group of American naval aviators outside the battleship navy to theorize that the fast carrier had replaced the
battleship as the backbone of blue-water navies." Clark G. Reynolds, *Command of the Sea: The
History and Strategy of Maritime Empires* (New York: William Morrow, 1974), p. 484.

27. Paul M. Kennedy, *The Rise and Fall of British Naval Mastery* (London: Macmillan, 1983), p.
246.

bility, would have met defeat. In hindsight, it is not surprising that in the postwar years junior naval powers seized on the submarine as a panacea to undermine British maritime superiority.[28]

The Royal Navy's obsession with the indecisive fleet encounter of May 1916 did produce some tactical innovations, such as the introduction of offensive destroyer tactics.[29] However, it also prolonged the life of the battle-fleet concept. Battle-fleet admirals argued that convoys, with weak surface escorts, had only been successful because the Royal Navy had retained surface command. According to Peter Padfield, "While the U-boat in its most devastating phase in the early summer of 1917 had seemed to overturn the classic Mahan doctrine, the *full* historic system of battle fleet command *and convoy* eventually proved more than a match for it."[30] Furthermore, not one battleship had been sunk during the war by a submarine.

In a similar vein, the General Board of the United States Navy claimed that German commerce raiders had succumbed to superior British force because the Grand Fleet, not the High Seas Fleet, had commanded the sea. They continued, "Throughout the war it was the Grand Fleet at Scapa Flow or thereabouts which controlled the movements of the enemy ships. It was the sea power vested and latent in the battleships which exercised the pressure upon the enemy which kept the sea routes open to the Allies and kept the German High Seas Fleet in its defended harbors until the morale of its personnel was sapped and the offensive power of that fleet was destroyed by inaction."[31] British

28. An interesting parallel can be made between the different lessons drawn from World War I and World War II by maritime and continental powers. "American naval tacticians and exercise planners spent the years after World War II reviewing the great carrier duels and fleet air actions in the Pacific, preparing to meet any potential adversaries in the same fashion and wipe them from the surface of the seas. The only other country that could match the U.S. Navy took home quite a different lesson from World War II. In the late 1940s, the Soviet Union assessed both the Battle of the Atlantic and the experimental weapons the Axis built. Since then, the Soviet Navy has built antiship missiles, ballistic rockets, and the greatest peacetime submarine fleet the world has ever known. . . . The United States continues planning fleet scenarios that call for three or four carrier battle groups to link up and wipe the opposing forces from 70% of the planet's surface . . . while the Soviets practice Okean series exercises to gain experience in worldwide interdiction of the sea lines of communication (SLOCs)—antishipping." Lieutenant Commander Sankey L. Blanton, "Learning the Wrong Lessons," *U.S. Naval Institute Proceedings* 113 (October 1987): pp. 178–79.

29. Roskill, *Naval Policy*, vol. 1, p. 533.

30. Peter Padfield, *The Battleship Era* (London: Rupert Hart-Davis, 1972), p. 246; see also David Henry, "British Submarine Policy, 1918–1939," in Bryan Ranft, ed., *Technical Change and British Naval Policy, 1860–1939* (New York: Holmes & Meier, 1977), pp. 80–107.

31. Quoted in Sprout and Sprout, *Toward a New Order*, p. 189.

surface command had protected the British Isles from invasion, prevented the use of the sea for German commerce, and succeeded in commercially blockading the Central Powers. Most important, command of the surface had ensured the success of the convoy system, thereby demonstrating that the battleship could deal with the submarine menace. Control of the surface, it was maintained, was necessary for control below the surface.

The converse of this argument produced a series of unlearned lessons. The British withdrew their close blockade in the North Sea because of the submarine threat, not because the High Seas Fleet was fulfilling the role Mahan had envisioned for the fleet-in-being. The submarine also virtually prevented surface engagements between capital ships in the North Sea. As Admiral Scheer, commander of the High Seas Fleet, admitted, "During the further progress of the submarine war (upon which, in my view, our whole naval policy will sooner or later be compelled to concentrate) the fleet will have to devote itself to the single task of bringing the submarines safely in and out of harbor."[32] Nevertheless, during the postwar years the British failed to study systematically the U-boat campaign of 1917–18. In fact, an indifferent attitude toward the role of convoy persisted, and the British did not carry out one merchant convoy exercise between 1919 and 1939. In Roskill's estimation, the reasons for not learning this critical lesson of the war were "obsession with fleet action, . . . belief that the Asdic [sonar] had mastered the submarine, . . . and the personal antipathy of many senior officers to convoy, which they regarded as a defensive measure and so one to be avoided by a service whose greatness (allegedly) lay in its readiness to assume the offensive in all and every circumstance."[33]

Even the most conservative battleship admirals admitted the submarine had forced changes in battleship design, tactics, and fleet organization. Battleships, thereafter, were constructed with external bulkheads and false outer hulls—or blisters—to absorb torpedo shocks, subdivided internally by watertight compartments, and designed for greater speeds. Naval strategists also recognized the tactical utility of protective destroyer escorts and advanced scouts. These developments, however,

32. Quoted in Kennedy, *Rise and Fall*, p. 250.
33. Roskill, *Naval Policy*, vol. 1, p. 536. See also Arthur Marder, "The Influence of History on Sea Power: The Royal Navy and the Lessons of 1914–1918," *Pacific Historical Review* 41 (November 1972): 421. See Williamson Murray, "Neither Navy Was Ready," *U.S. Naval Institute Proceedings* 107 (April 1981): 39–40.

only reinforced belief that the submarine would fail in its quest to drive the battleship from the sea. Obsessed with studying the Battle of Jutland, fleet admirals concluded that with heavier armor and enhanced speed, big guns and big ships would remain the decisive elements in sea power. The Japanese, as well, drew similar lessons from the British "victory" at Jutland.[34] The lessons of Jutland and the antisubmarine campaign dictated which weapons were critical to regulating the balance of naval power in 1922.

CONTINENTAL CONCEPTIONS OF SEA POWER

While Mahanian doctrine remained entrenched in Britain, the United States, and Japan, in Europe, emerging in opposition to the classical blue-water philosophy of maritime powers at the turn of the century was the doctrine associated with the French Navy's "Jeune Ecole." Whereas classical theorists derived immutable principles that, they argued, prevailed in any historical epoch, the Jeune Ecole advanced the theory that strategy varied with the material conditions of warfare. Historical truths were illusive because technological innovation could render weapons, like the battleship, and strategies, like command of the sea, obsolete.

For most of the European militaries, the navy remained a "stepchild of continental strategy."[35] Sea power played only a secondary role in the relations of the European states and was not the source of greatness Mahan claimed. Classical theories also failed to address the most critical naval problem of continental powers: how, with numerically inferior forces, to defeat a dominant maritime power. Continental theorists argued that technological solutions could compensate for inferior naval strength.

The torpedo boat was the first weapon to challenge the supremacy of the battleship and the classical tenets of doctrine and strategy on which battleship supremacy rested. Admiral Theophile Aube, leader of the Jeune Ecole, saw the torpedo boat as an inexpensive way for continen-

---

34. See Saburo Toyama, "Lessons From the Past," *U.S. Naval Institute Proceedings* 108 (September 1982): 62–69.

35. Theodore Ropp, "Continental Doctrines of Sea Power," in Earle, ed., *Makers of Modern Strategy*, p. 446.

tal navies to defeat superior maritime powers. Though the torpedo boat failed to drive the battleship from the sea, it seriously curtailed the battleship's freedom of action. The Jeune Ecole eventually embraced the submarine as the technological panacea of continental navies because of its tremendous strategic capabilities. Submarines could operate over extended periods of time in enemy waters, independent of supporting vessels, and unhindered by surface blockade. Submarines did possess serious drawbacks, such as limited battery capacity,[36] that increased vulnerability to destroyer attack by restricting the ability to dodge depth charges. Submarines were also plagued by poor vision. Yet despite these handicaps, the submarine retained a tremendous nuisance value. Defense of shipping against submarines absorbed resources far in excess of those required to launch a submarine offensive. In Brodie's estimation, defending against a submarine offensive involved "sending ships in convoys, which reduces the effectiveness of available shipping by at least 25 per cent; the wearisome, unending efforts of innumerable small naval craft and airplanes; the constant anxiety of the battle fleet commander and the marked restrictions placed upon his movements."[37] Only the most powerful industrial nations could neutralize a submarine threat without seriously weakening their war efforts. Even Britain was forced to rely on U.S. industrial capacity to wage the antisubmarine war against Germany. A submarine offensive could cause an adversary to disperse its forces, at the least preventing enjoyment of the benefits of command, at the most endangering strategic position. The challenge of the submarine was eloquently conveyed in a metaphor by Admiral Sir Reginald Bacon: "Imagine England and Scotland and Wales rolled flat, all hedges, towns, lakes, rivers removed until it was merely a sandy waste. One single rabbit in that vast area would be relatively the same in size as a submarine in the North Atlantic. Moreover, it would be a rabbit which could disappear under the sand in half a minute without leaving a track behind it."[38]

Continental thinkers advocated a maritime strategy of "guerre de course," or commerce warfare. To most effectively bring pressure to

36. "The limited space available in the submarine for propulsive machinery must be given over to a completely dual system—diesel engines for surface cruising and storage batteries with electric motors for submerged cruising." Brodie, *Guide to Naval Strategy*, p. 71.

37. Ibid., p. 75.

38. Admiral Sir Reginald Bacon, *The Life of John Rushworth Earl Jellicoe* (London: Cassell, 1936), p. 349.

bear on superior maritime powers, inferior navies must attack and inflict damage upon enemy shipping.[39] Inferior navies seeking command of the sea through decisive battle would undoubtedly meet "inevitable and rapid defeat, whereas by guerre de course it prolongs operations very considerably and knows that before going under it will do some damage."[40] Geoffrey Till adds that "apart from the physical destruction of intrinsically valuable cargoes, attacks on merchant shipping would push up marine insurance and freight costs. It might force its victim to cut back on certain commercial activities, allowing neutrals to take over his place and so injuring his long term trading prospects. Altogether, guerre de course would diminish the revenue and credit available for running the war."[41] The weaker side, therefore, can only counteract superior force by dispersing sporadic attacks on the latter's communications, forcing the stronger side to extend and strengthen its escorts, which increases the strain on its resources. A guerre de course strategy denies the enemy in part what the enemy has already denied one's own side completely: use of the sea in relative security. The immense losses inflicted by the German submarine campaign of the First World War provided evidence that "decision on the seas might go not to the belligerent with the stronger navy, but to the one least vulnerable to interrupted communications."[42] At the very least, guerre de course forced the enemy to expend resources for trade protection, whether for evasive routing, arming of merchantmen, or convoy-and-escort.

Despite these arguments, Mahanian strategists remained unconvinced. Guerre de course could never be as decisive or as successful as blockade for destroying an enemy's maritime commerce. Guerre de course possessed a nuisance value against which no command could ever be complete, yet could not provide the security of command and usually broke down before the superior strength of command. Mahanian believers maintained that only Britain's command of the sea had ensured success of the antisubmarine campaign against Germany in the war. Furthermore, a great sea power undoubtedly possessed such extensive maritime resources that guerre de course would be ineffective unless relentlessly pursued and supported by a great battle fleet. Orthodox

39. Corbett, *Some Principles of Maritime Strategy*, p. 236.
40. Fred T. Jane, *Heresies of Sea Power* (London: Longmans, 1906), p. 145.
41. Till, *Maritime Strategy*, p. 151.
42. Brodie, *Guide to Naval Strategy*, p. 139.

strategists clung to their faith, arguing that the master of the surface would always command the sea.

Shared doctrine among maritime powers created consensus on the type and method of limitation that was desirable in the Pacific but the doctrinal concerns of continental powers, coupled with new technologies like the submarine to support that doctrine, complicated British efforts to expand the regional arms control system to the global level and to meet the requirements for imperial defense. Similar doctrine makes agreement at least feasible. Competing doctrines render agreement partial at best. Junior naval powers rejected the traditional maritime predispositions of Great Britain, the United States, and Japan. French policy, in particular, rested on a curious mixture of maritime and continental doctrine. As a naval power superior to Italy, the French wanted to maintain their lead over Italy in surface combatants. Yet as an inferior naval power to Great Britain, the French displayed the enthusiasm of the then defunct Jeune Ecole school for submarines. The French continued to build battleships in the postwar years, but were more willing to accept that technological developments had undermined the role of the battleship. Consequently, they envisaged a postwar navy designed around the submarine and proceeded to build such a navy throughout the 1920s and 1930s.[43] Between 1922 and 1934, the French laid down 169 warships, 79 of which were submarines, almost 50 percent. By 1930, the French possessed 97,875 tons of submarines.

Furthermore, as a continental power, the French argued that all weapons were interdependent and that comprehensive limitation of all types of armed force was a prerequisite for naval limitation. In short, naval arms control had to proceed along with negotiations on land-based forces. If only naval limitation proved possible, the French subscribed to the method of global limitation: ceilings on total naval tonnage to permit maximum flexibility for transfer between categories of ships. Global limitation would preserve France's submarine force and reduce the need for a battleship building program that, for a junior maritime power, was of marginal utility. The French also continued to demand political guarantees as a prerequisite to disarmament. Naval limitation must be part of a general agreement limiting all armed forces.

43. William Gregory Perett, "French Naval Policy and Foreign Affairs, 1930–1939" (Ph.D. diss., Stanford University, 1977), p. 12.

Otherwise, Britain must offer guarantees of mutual assistance on the Continent.

French demands for the arms control process critically restricted the capacity of the treaty powers to extend the arms control system beyond an exclusively regional Pacific focus to a global one. The French had been deeply impressed by the helplessness of the High Seas Fleet during the war, remaining bottled up as it did in the North Sea, unable to break Britain's blockade. The submarine, by contrast, had achieved many unexpected successes. These two factors encouraged continental theorists to conclude that with new technologies, particularly airpower, command of the sea no longer remained the primary objective of naval strategy. Rather, naval warfare would revolve around the attack and defense of trade by means of convoy and cruiser warfare.

These beliefs informed French policy at the Washington Conference. In an article published in *La Revue Maritime* in January 1920, an official journal issued by the historical department of the Navy General Staff, Captain Raoul Castex, chief of staff to the Admiral of the Second Division in the Mediterranean and lecturer at the French Naval College, pronounced, "After many centuries of effort, thanks to the ingenuity of man, the instrument, the system, the martingale is at hand which will overthrow for good all the naval power of England."[44] The article hinted, according to the British, at France's approval of unrestricted submarine warfare. Although this particular passage was really a description of German reasoning, subsequent articles reinforced the view that Castex, an influential voice in the French Navy, saw the value of submarine warfare and advocated it.

Britain's orientation toward arms limitation reflected that of a maritime power whose naval arm dominated force structure. The British wanted total abolition of the submarine, but at a minimum, would accept limitation by category to strike a balance among fleets alone as fighting units. Though Britain and France had conflicts of interest, few at the time seriously believed they would go to war. British and French security requirements in Europe were compatible, since neither viewed the other as an imminent security threat. But their leaders failed to agree on the fundamentals of sea power and the role of sea power in national security. France refused to limit submarines, and this impelled the British in the years after the Conference to build craft to protect

44. Quoted in Buell, *Washington Conference*, p. 222.

commerce, which elicited a corresponding response from other naval powers. Though the British might concede battleship parity to the United States, they would never relinquish any degree of superiority to the French.

French general staff views, as suggested by Castex, coupled with continental predispositions that called for limitations to the ability to wage war, not just war at sea, constrained the talks in Washington. To the degree that the submarine could undermine the role of the battleship, failure to limit the submarine would undermine arms control agreements based upon the tenet of battleship supremacy. The struggle was no longer between two sea powers for the same objective, command of the sea, but between two diametrically opposed systems of naval strategy.[45] Since British naval policy in the Pacific was influenced by force levels in the Mediterranean, arms control in the Far East became hostage to European politics. France's negative success at Washington demonstrated that continental doctrines were firmly entrenched and that arms control would have to accommodate the requisites of both continental and maritime conceptions of security if it were to transcend its regional confines and move to a global level. French behavior, to a great degree shaped by continental conceptions of security, constrained qualitative and quantitative limitation at Washington, which demonstrates how asymmetries in doctrine can seriously restrict the scope of arms limitation.

MARITIME DOCTRINE AND AIRPOWER

For arms control in 1922, the impact of airpower on naval doctrine and the organizational rivalries over airpower's role operated less as obstructions than the traditional maritime consensus served as a facilitator. Nevertheless, it was undeniable that technological developments were constraining the role of the battleship. Offensive sea power was weakening. Blockade had become less effective. Airpower revolutionized reconnaissance. In response, however, Mahanian doctrine simply adjusted. Belief in the fundamental importance of command of the sea and the need for organized force endured, although the conditions of

45. Rosinski, "Mahan and World War II," p. 34.

modern naval strategy adapted to changing technical conditions. Rather than concede to airpower its revolutionary role, information about airpower was assimilated to support the doctrinal consensus of battleship supremacy.

After World War I, developments in airpower clearly challenged the supremacy of the battleship. In July 1921, the U.S. Navy initiated bombing trials that culminated in the sinking of the former German battleship *Ostfriesland*. The most controversial evidence was the damage from near misses, which produced a "water-hammer effect." The British were especially interested in these bombing tests. One communication to the Foreign Office reported, "The effects of the 2,000 lb bomb bursting along side the *Ostfriesland* . . . were so immediate and overwhelming as to render it immaterial whether these ships were possessed of 'watertight' integrity or not."[46] Nevertheless, the sinking of the *Ostfriesland* made no significant impact on strongly held convictions about the battleship. Blue-water sailors dismissed the evidence by pointing out that the *Ostfriesland* had been stationary, without a crew to make repairs, or anti-aircraft gunfire for defense. On the other hand, the pilots had selected optimum height, speed, and direction without interference. Finally, the *Ostfriesland* possessed no antibomb deck armor and was, therefore, obsolete.

Naval authorities predominantly, though by no means unanimously, concluded that airpower had far from rendered the battleship obsolete.[47] In the United States, conservative admirals stressed the limitations of the bombing tests and conceded only that battleship design had to be modified to incorporate improved anti-aircraft defenses. The General Board professed faith that defensive technologies would develop to offset offensive challenges. After all, as Padfield recites the logic,

---

46. Geoffrey Till, "Airpower and the Battleship in the 1920s," in Ranft, ed., *Technical Change and British Naval Policy*, p. 118.

47. Stephen Howarth, *The Fighting Ships of the Rising Sun: The Drama of the Imperial Japanese Navy, 1895–1945* (New York: Atheneum, 1983), pp. 146–47. Though the conservative view of battleship supremacy prevailed, opinion was by no means unanimous. In the United States, navy "radicals" included Admirals William S. Sims, William F. Fullam, Bradley Fiske, W. V. Pratt, and Harry E. Yarnell. In Great Britain, naval air enthusiasts included Admiral Sir Percy Scott and Rear-Admirals C. de Bartolome, S. S. Hall, and H. W. Richmond. For more detailed accounts of the aviation controversy, see Roskill, *Naval Policy*, vol. 1; Vincent Davis, *The Admirals Lobby* (Chapel Hill: University of North Carolina Press, 1967); Archibald D. Turnbull and Clifford L. Lord, *History of United States Naval Aviation* (New Haven: Yale University Press, 1949); and Padfield, *Battleship Era*.

There was good historical precedent: time and again the large gunned ship had been pronounced dead by enthusiasts for torpedoes and small, swift craft, and each time it had simply grown larger, mounted longer range and more rapid-firing guns and drawing a host of lesser craft to its protection and continued to wield supreme power at sea. If history were anything to go by this process would simply be repeated in the air age; the lesser craft would be fighter aircraft from a few aircraft carriers deployed with the far more numerous battle fleet.[48]

In 1921, the General Board declared that "concentration of power in attack was the fundamental basis of all war-like operations" and concentration of power in ships "that can deliver and receive the heaviest blows and that can overcome the strongest ships that may be brought against them will continue as long as navies exist."[49] In 1921, a group of high-ranking active Army and Navy officers reviewed the evidence from the bombing trials, partly in response to disarmament advocates who used the tests as grounds for declaring the battleship's obsolescence. They concluded in their "Report of the Joint Board on Results of Aviation and Ordinance Tests Held During June and July 1921" that "startling as the results unquestionably were and far-reaching as they may prove to be, it would not be the part of wisdom to draw too hasty conclusions or assert that battleships had thereby been eliminated."[50] In 1921, the secretary of the navy's annual report endorsed the findings of this Joint Board: the battleship remained the backbone of the fleet.

Firm belief in the dominant role of the battleship persisted despite additional bombing trials. In 1923 the *Virginia* and *New Jersey* were bombed and sunk, and in 1924 the new and as-yet-uncompleted *Washington*, the only modern battleship allocated to trials, was sunk. Difficulty in sinking the *Washington* strengthened the argument that properly defended battleships could survive the worst air attack. Airpower advocates maintained, however, that "the most important result of the whole series of tests was that every warship attacked with live bombs was sunk, and by bombs alone. . . . [I]t was thenceforth impossible to

---

48. Padfield, *Battleship Era*, p. 255.
49. Quoted in Sprout and Sprout, *Toward a New Order*, p. 188.
50. Reprinted in 67th Congress, 1st Session, *Congressional Record* Vol. 61, pp. 8622–8626.

argue that even the best protected warships were inviolate against such weapons."[51]

Nevertheless, in 1923, aviation appropriations were reduced at the General Board's obsessive insistence on building cruisers and improving the battle line's long-range hitting capacity by increasing the maximum elevation of the main battery guns on battleships. And in 1924–25, the Eberle Board continued to stress the limits of airpower and emphasize its auxiliary roles of fire control and scouting. As Harry H. Ransom sums up, "The Navy was willing to recognize the value of this new development in warfare, but not at the expense of the traditional weapons nor of basic alteration of traditional doctrine. The Navy was willing to add aircraft carriers to the fleet, but not at the expense of battleships, battle cruisers, or other craft that fit more neatly into the doctrinal pattern."[52] In 1934, the General Board told Secretary of the Navy Claude A. Swanson the "capital ship force is the backbone of the modern navy. . . . The basic strength of the surface fleet is in its heaviest vessels, under the protection of which its lighter craft may operate."[53] And as late as 1941, Captain W. D. Puleston, former head of the Office of Naval Intelligence, insisted that "the relative strengths of the opposing battle lines have been the determining factor in naval campaigns of the nineteenth and twentieth centuries. . . . The power of aviation is increasing, but events of the current war indicate that the strength of the battle line is still the decisive naval factor."[54]

Across the Atlantic, Great Britain's Post War Questions Committee concluded, "We do not consider that aircraft using any known form of weapon will render the capital ship obsolete until the capabilities of aircraft increase beyond anything that appears probable in the near future."[55] Airpower enthusiasts claimed that accuracy, destructive effectiveness, range, and carrying capacity of offensive aircraft were advancing. The battleship, on the other hand, was a developed weapon system whose defenses could never be improved sufficiently to offset the offensive advantages of airpower. Conservative admirals objected: since air-

51. Roskill, Naval Policy, vol. 1, p. 248.

52. Harry H. Ransom, "The Battleship Meets the Airplane," Military Affairs 23 (Spring 1959): 25.

53. Quoted in Stephen E. Pelz, Race to Pearl Harbor: The Failure of the Second London Naval Conference and the Onset of World War II (Cambridge: Harvard University Press, 1974), p. 88.

54. Ibid.

55. Till, "Airpower and the Battleship," p. 111.

craft could not reliably sink battleships, their role was ancillary to the weapon system that could, the battleship.[56] Attention was directed to aviation but only to determine how airpower could help the battle fleet attain its objective more efficiently.

At the same time, great efforts were made to improve anti-aircraft defenses.[57] Bombing trials against the *Baden* in 1921 (and subsequently the *Monarch* in 1924) proved ambiguous and only reinforced the belief that aircraft could not carry bombs whose damage exceeded that of a battleship's main armament shells. And despite the water-hammer effect of the *Ostfriesland* test, the Admiralty claimed that modern battleships with full anti-aircraft armament, better protection, better gunnery, room to maneuver, and screened with supporting ships and fighter aircraft could not be sunk.

The Admiralty's obsession had a variety of roots. In the first place, the burden of proof lay with the challengers, and inconclusive evidence only reconfirmed the status quo. Admiral Beatty argued, "In view of the wildly differing estimates of the future of submarines and aircraft and the nebulous data upon which hopes are based," the Admiralty could not follow a policy that "will substitute shadows" for a navy built around battleships.[58] Second, formation of the Royal Air Force reduced the number of airpower advocates in the higher echelons of the Royal Navy. Finally, as in Japan and the United States, the well-being of the battleship had become synonymous with the well-being of the navy. Admirals in all three countries feared that if another weapon, particularly from another service, proved superior to the battleship, the survival of traditional naval doctrine, strategy, force structure, and their very careers would be jeopardized. Embracing airpower might hurt the navy organizationally.

The Japanese, as well, continued to design their navy around the battleship. More important than the influence of Mahan or the lessons of Britain's wartime experience with the High Seas Fleet were the Im-

---

56. See Rolland A. Chaput, *Disarmament in British Foreign Policy* (London: G. Allen & Unwin, 1935), p. 88, for the "Statement of the First Lord Explanatory of the Naval Estimates for 1920–21."

57. "Development of an eight-barrelled multiple pom-pom was begun for use against torpedo-carrying aircraft. The anti-aircraft guns of battleships and cruisers were increased from the two 3-inch or so of the war years to four 4-inch guns, and new high-angled gun control systems were installed." Vice-Admiral Sir Arthur Hezlet, *Aircraft and Sea Power* (New York: Stein & Day, 1970), p. 111.

58. Till, "Airpower and the Battleship," p. 120.

perial Navy's own decisive naval victories over China in 1894 and Russia in 1904. In 1918, Admiral Kato Tomosaburo stated, "The more we study the lessons of the war, the stronger does our conviction grow that the last word in naval warfare rests with the big ship and the big gun."[59] In 1921, Japanese yards were building over 343,000 tons of warships but not one carrier. Naval strategists hardly dismissed the importance of carriers or airpower but, as in Britain and the United States, assigned them auxiliary roles: scouting before battle, spotting gunfire during action, harassing enemy fleets and bases at long range, and defending the battle line against air attacks. Throughout the 1920s and 1930s, despite technological advances in cruisers, destroyers, submarines, and torpedoes, the Japanese continued to place primary emphasis on improving the battleship and big gun. Armor was made heavier, and speed was increased, in line with lessons drawn from the Battle of Jutland. In Japan, a fixation with a main fleet encounter blinded conservative naval officers to the fact that technological innovations were rapidly transforming the conventional methods, and by extension the strategic concepts, of naval warfare. This dogma governed conservative naval thought throughout the 1930s, despite outspoken advocates of airpower like Admirals Yamamoto Isoroku and Inoue Shigemi.[60] Most significant, the centrality of the battleship in Japanese naval doctrine was typified by the design of the super-battleship *Yamato* as late as 1934, a vessel displacing 64,000 tons and mounting 18-inch guns.

In sum, blue-water admirals, who wielded overriding influence in all three countries, maintained that gunfire was still more accurate than aerial bombardment against *moving* ships, that the power of penetration of a gun's shell exceeded that of an aerial bomb's, and that a bomber could deliver only a few shots but a battleship's guns could continually be reloaded. In short, "the battleship [could] stand and slug it out until a decision [was] reached . . . and it [could] do that almost anywhere within its tremendous cruising radius and in almost any weather."[61]

Airpower threatened widely held beliefs about the nature of maritime strategy and naval warfare. The airplane was revolutionizing naval affairs, particularly through its ability to conduct reconnaissance. Visi-

---

59. Quoted in Howarth, *Fighting Ships of the Rising Sun*, p. 146; Sprout and Sprout, *Toward a New Order*, p. 188.

60. Asada, "The Japanese Navy and the United States," pp. 235–37. See also John Deare Potter, *Yamamoto: The Man Who Menaced America* (New York: Viking Press, 1979).

61. Brodie, *Guide to Naval Strategy*, pp. 33–36.

bility replaced the uncertainty about the opponent's dispositions and movements, the characteristic condition of naval warfare.[62] By carrying naval operations into a third dimension, the airplane also restricted the ability to secure surface command, for "the cubic area of the battlefield [becomes] so immense that command is hardly ever practicable."[63] Superiority in numbers did not secure control of the air the way superiority in surface squadrons yielded control of the sea, and the airplane was not limited by coastlines. It could operate as the advanced striking arm of sea power and penetrate deep into enemy territory.

In the eyes of the majority of postwar officers, however, airpower had not yet proved itself on the battlefield.[64] Despite debate that the airplane had undermined the supremacy of the battleship, the First World War had demonstrated that aerial power could strengthen the position of a surface fleet in important ways. The airplane could operate against the submarine, provide invaluable reconnaissance, and improve the accuracy of artillery fire. By performing the task of reconnaissance, the airplane could increase chances of engagement and effectiveness of blockade, enhancing the power of a superior fleet. Furthermore, the limited range of the airplane seemed to prevent airpower from superseding the surface fleet. Though the tests conducted in postwar years established that battleships could be sunk by aerial attack, the circumstances and cost required for success qualified results considerably.[65]

Overall confidence in the battleship was sustained, though the risks to the fleet had undeniably become greater. In 1922, the doctrine of battleship supremacy remained sufficiently entrenched to serve as the basis for arms limitation, despite vigorous aviation controversies in Great Britain and the United States immediately after the war. In the United States, the General Board recognized that airpower provided an important and valuable asset to fleet operations. Yet it refused to build up aviation at the expense of the capital ship program because embracing airpower might hurt the navy organizationally. General William "Billy" Mitchell, leader in the fight for a unified air service, argued that

62. Rosinski, "Mahan and World War II," p. 24. See also David Wragg, A History of Naval Aviation: Wings Over the Sea (New York: Arco, 1979).

63. Brodie, Sea Power in the Machine Age, p. 388.

64. For the exceptions, see Elting Morison, Admiral Sims and the Modern American Navy (Boston: Houghton Mifflin, 1942), and Rear Admiral William Sowden Sims, The Victory at Sea (New York: Doubleday, Page, 1921).

65. See Brodie, Sea Power in the Machine Age, pp. 401–3, for details of tests conducted by the United States and Britain between 1921 and 1936.

a unified air force would be more economical than separate army and navy air forces. Mitchell also used the General Board's pro-battleship predisposition to entice naval aviators to support his cause.

Like all who believed in the supremacy of airpower, Mitchell argued that command of the air was a necessary prerequisite for command of the sea. Moreover, he went a step further in projecting that the air battle would precede the advance of the fleet. At the time, most naval aviators viewed the air battle as taking place close to the battle line to keep the carrier within protection of the fleet's guns. Mitchell contended that carriers could execute an independent offensive thrust and bring the battle to the enemy's territory. Mitchell, however, refused to make the carrier the foundation block for strategic offensive operations, the means to project U.S. airpower overseas. This would be the domain of land-based air. The Canada-Greenland-Iceland route provided access to Europe. The Bering Strait offered a path to Japan. The longest overwater leg, 300 miles, fell within the range of bomber capacity.[66]

Naval aviators were attracted to Mitchell's vision, since he assigned the carrier its ultimate fighting role. In the field, aviators remained divided on the question of organizational control of aviation. Those attached to the Navy Department and most closely in touch with aviation, on the other hand, had become so discouraged that even a separate air force appeared at times a better solution.[67]

In the short-run, Mitchell argued, the navy would remain responsible for protecting maritime communications but even this would eventually become the province of the air force. The air force would soon constitute the nation's first line of defense, jeopardizing the navy's traditional role. In 1919, Mitchell went as far as to state to the House Military Affairs Committee that if he and his associates were "allowed to develop essential air weapons," they would "carry the war to such an extent . . . as almost to make navies useless on the surface of the water."[68] To preserve the navy's role and to maintain intraservice harmony, the Bureau of Aeronautics was created in 1921, despite the protests of other bureau chiefs who feared this would create "a fighting corps separate

66. Charles M. Melhorn, *Two-Block Fox: The Rise of the Aircraft Carrier, 1911–1929* (Annapolis: Naval Institute Press, 1974), p. 48.
67. Lieutenant Commander Albert C. Read, USN, quoted in Melhorn, *Two-Block Fox*, p. 57.
68. Quoted in Turnbull and Lord, *History of United States Naval Aviation*, p. 178.

and distinct from the line and would establish inequities in pay and rank between this corps and the rest of the Navy."[69]

In the United States, a reorientation of the navy's views toward the role of airpower in national defense developed. To prevent the formation of a unified air force, its advocates must be denied the support of naval aviators. This meant creating for these aviators an acceptable organizational structure within the Navy itself. With the creation of the Bureau of Aeronautics and the appointment of Rear Admiral William Moffett as its chief in August 1921, aviation received firm foundation within the U.S. Navy. This reorientation prevented advocates of a unified air force from undermining the navy's role as the first line of defense in the short run and reinforced the inclinations of battleship-minded admirals. Ultimately, however, airpower advocates received a legitimate channel through which to influence naval policy, doctrine, and strategy. In developments similar to those in the United States, the Japanese never unified their air forces, and "the Naval Air Service matured rapidly and successfully. . . . By the mid-1930s Japan had initiated her policy of expansion in the Far East and therefore embraced the carrier as an integral part of her military defenses."[70]

Across the Atlantic, the Smuts Committee, as early as July 1917, endorsed the creation of a unified air service and "postulated the adoption by it of a totally new strategy [strategic bombing]—independent from the strategy to which the land and sea forces were working."[71] The anticipated financial stringency of the postwar years coupled with pro-battleship forces firmly entrenched in the Admiralty and War Office meant that those departments would not divert a significant proportion of funds to the development of aviation. So the Smuts Committee and Prime Minister David Lloyd George recommended transfer of the Royal Navy Air Service to the unified Air Service. In August 1917, the Royal Air Force (RAF) was born. Two consequences flowed from this decision

69. Melhorn, *Two-Block Fox*, pp. 57–58. See also Clark G. Reynolds, "John H. Towers, the Morrow Board, and the Reform of the Navy's Aviation," *Military Affairs* 52 (April 1988): 78–84.

70. See Clark G. Reynolds, *The Fast Carriers: The Forging of an Air Navy* (New York: McGraw-Hill, 1968; reprint, Huntington, N.Y.: Robert E. Krieger, 1978), pp. 4–7, for the development of Japanese carrier aviation. In fact, as early as 1928, Admiral Yamamoto had predicted that "in the near future air power would become the mainstay of the navy"; page references are to the reprint edition. Asada, "The Japanese Navy and the United States," p. 237. See also James H. Belote and William M. Belote, *Titans of the Sea: The Development and Operations of Japanese and American Carrier Task Forces in World War II* (New York: Harper & Row, 1975).

71. Roskill, *Naval Policy*, vol. 1, p. 237.

that were critical for the future of aviation in the Royal Navy. First, the Royal Navy lost nearly all its officers who were experienced in, and enthusiastic about, naval aviation. Second, pressures for economy reduced the maritime component of the RAF to near extinction by 1919.

The Admiralty was seriously concerned that the Air Ministry wanted not only complete control over everything and everybody that flew but also over the navy's carriers. In March 1921, Air Marshall Hugh Trenchard circulated a paper to the Committee on Imperial Defense titled, "The Role of the Air Force in the System of Imperial Defense." Among other things, the document "named the defense of the British Isles against invasion—heretofore a cardinal responsibility of the Navy—as the principal responsibility of the RAF."[72] With the Singapore base in mind, Trenchard continued to advocate the use of air forces instead of heavy coast guns. Trenchard made bold claims for the role of airpower in the defense of Great Britain.[73] Once the RAF embraced strategic bombing in 1921 and the independent use of airpower, it disputed that airpower functioned merely as an auxiliary to other services. Trenchard even argued that the RAF could more economically carry out certain tasks historically the province of other services—the maintenance of order in the Middle East, coastal defense, and the protection of shipping in certain areas.[74]

The Admiralty did not oppose the development of naval aviation. At the end of the war, it had approved six aircraft or seaplane carriers for use with the fleet and the fitting of capital ships and cruisers for the operation of one or two aircraft.[75] However, the Admiralty considered the navy Britain's first line of defense, the battleship the backbone of the fleet, and the airplane an indispensable auxiliary for reconnaissance, fire control, and obtaining and disputing control of sea communications. The creation of the RAF organizationally removed airpower advocates from the Royal Navy, further consolidating the orthodox consensus within the navy's ranks. The independent status of the RAF eventually thrust strategic bombing[76] into the forefront, a strategy that

72. Ibid., p. 264.
73. Ferris, Men, Money, and Diplomacy, p. 69; Malcolm Smith, British Air Strategy Between the Wars (Oxford: Clarendon Press, 1984).
74. Roskill, Naval Policy, vol. 1, p. 264.
75. Ibid., p. 244.
76. See Edward Warner, "Douhet, Mitchell, Seversky: Theories of Air Warfare," in Earle, ed., Makers of Modern Strategy, pp. 485–503.

the Admiralty was unable to reconcile with the airpower needs of the Royal Navy. More than any other power, the Royal Navy was committed to the idea of battleship supremacy and to the belief that the battleship was the index of naval power. The upshot of these organizational rivalries was that an arms control system emerged because there was a general consensus about the types of weapons that were most crucial for naval power.

TECHNOLOGY, DOCTRINE, AND ARMS CONTROL

In postwar years, naval leaders in Great Britain, the United States, and Japan believed in the battleship as the index of naval power. Even though technological revolutions of the past half century had limited the offensive capabilities of the battleship, the balance of naval power merely shifted to accommodate these limitations. Regional centers of naval power arose in Japan and the United States. Recognition of the offensive limitations of the battleship by leaders in these three loci of naval power facilitated agreement on ratios to guarantee each defensive superiority in respective spheres.

Leaders of the postwar maritime states not only believed in battleship supremacy but also shared a philosophy about the role of sea power in national defense. They all subscribed to the tenets of Mahanian doctrine. These doctrinal predispositions, supported by organizational interests that tended to equate the well-being of the battleship with the well-being of the navy as a whole, shaped perceptions of wartime experience. Ambiguous information about the performance of new technologies during World War I was interpreted to support prewar views of battleship supremacy. Success of the antisubmarine campaign was attributed to the Royal Navy's ability to command the sea, and this was emphasized at the expense of the tremendous losses inflicted by submarine warfare. Similar conceptions of wartime experience reinforced compatible strategic beliefs and, hence, consensus on the type and method of arms limitation.

Arms control, it was argued, could enhance security (1) if each state maintained defensive superiority in its respective sphere, (2) if the ability to take the offensive were curtailed, and (3) if vital lines of maritime communication were maintained. The first two requirements were satis-

fied at Washington but the last was not. Shared doctrine, and agreement on a currency—the capital ship—for assessing relative power,
were critical for successfully negotiating arms control provisions in the
Pacific. However, disparate doctrines created obstacles to arms control
in Europe, significantly complicating Britain's ability to defend maritime communications. The threat to maritime communications represented by the submarine, and France's determination to use the submarine in a commerce-raiding strategy, constrained the degree to which a
purely maritime orientation toward naval arms control would enhance
international security.

Technological developments affected the strategic realities of all naval powers but the specific consequences for each varied. By increasing
the dependence of the battle fleet on its bases and narrowing its range
of action, steam, ordnance, and the submarine enhanced the defensive
position of states, such as Japan and the United States, separated by
wide oceans from their enemies. By measurably increasing the risk to a
fleet, air attack precluded use of a fleet or any major segment of it for
anything other than the most important strategic objective. These developments fostered the decentralization of naval power away from Europe and the rise of regional power centers. Japan and the United
States were able to assert hegemony in their respective spheres with
relative ease.

The submarine enhanced the defensive position of the United States
by deterring challenges in local waters. At the Washington Conference, the Americans, French, and Japanese argued that the submarine
was invaluable for coast and harbor defense. The special advisory committee to the U.S. delegation continued, "It will be impossible for our
fleet to protect two long coast lines properly at all times. Submarines
located at bases along both coasts will be useful as scouts and to attack
any enemy who should desire to make raids on exposed positions."[77]
Though it was also pointed out that the submarine could operate effectively as a commerce destroyer, this posed a relatively minor threat to a
self-sufficient U.S. wartime economy. The Japanese archipelagoes were
also well suited for submarine and aircraft havens, and the Japanese
viewed the submarine as "a relatively inexpensive and yet effective"

77. Quoted in Sprout and Sprout, *Toward a New Order*, p. 196.

defense for an insular nation."[78] Enemy surface squadrons would need overwhelming superiority to venture into Japanese waters.

These developments in subsurface and air technologies curtailed the ability to bring the offensive to the enemy. There was serious doubt that a surface fleet could successfully blockade an open coastline, let alone invade a hostile shore, given the menaces of minefields, submarines, and shore-based aircraft. In addition, a warship built for operation in home waters, by using less space for fuel and more for armor, could achieve superiority in resistance to one of equal age and tonnage designed to cruise in distant waters. This benefited the United States and Japan, though Japan's command in nearby waters could not prevent "commerce with regions other than China be[ing] cut off by an Anglo-American combination at points entirely beyond the range of the Japanese Fleet."[79] Hence, the concern of the Japanese about Anglo-American collusion that would become a major issue at the Washington Conference.

The development of marine mines, self-propelled torpedoes, submarines, and aircraft tremendously handicapped any power reliant on long, exposed lines of communication. For the first time, Great Britain was vulnerable, depending on its navy as a first line of defense, located only a short distance from continental Europe and possessing thousands of miles of sea lanes to protect. It was widely acknowledged that submarines and aircraft could inflict tremendous damage on a fleet's vulnerable transport and supply ships if operating far from repair bases. Most critical, the vulnerability of merchant vessels grew with the possibility of aerial attack. A shipping chain comprises many links, each vital to the life of a maritime nation like Great Britain. A battle fleet is of little use if shipping and shore facilities cannot be protected against raiding aircraft. Technological advances threatened the security of maritime communications, forcing Great Britain to rethink its strategy of global naval position.

The submarine, in particular, presented a menace to a nation dependent on overseas trade and geographically situated in narrow channel waters ideally suited for enemy submarine activity. World War I had provided evidence that decision on the seas might go not to the nation with the strongest fleet but to the one with uninterrupted lines of com-

78. Quoted in ibid.
79. Brodie, *Sea Power in the Machine Age*, pp. 122–23.

munication. In fact, commerce raiding by the Germans had nearly approximated a counterblockade. Strategic initiative, arguably, no longer rested with traditional command of the sea. As Sprout and Sprout put it, "The question was squarely raised whether such a 'streamlined' guerre de course might not ultimately supersede Mahan's classic doctrine of battle fleet supremacy so far as long-range operations upon the sea were concerned."[80] Both the submarine and airplane, alone and in combination with surface craft, undermined the strategic impregnability Great Britain had in the past secured from superior naval power and insular position.

By 1922, airpower was beginning to undermine the orthodox consensus on naval doctrine, strategy, and tactics. The submarine was championed as the panacea of continental navies, and the French refused to accept submarine limitations, unless linked to agreements on the military balance on the Continent. Technological considerations constrained the scope of arms control negotiations but not by creating a technological imperative, whereby new weapon systems were unlikely to be limited because their potential was unknown. Rather, technology constrained arms control by (1) challenging traditional maritime doctrine and requisites of security that were the rationales for battleship limitation by ratios, (2) by validating continental conceptions of security, and (3) by providing the tools to sustain continental strategies, placing at a disadvantage states, like Great Britain, that refused to come to terms with continental assumptions about naval power. As a result, significant agreements were reached only in areas where the doctrinal basis of security perceptions was compatible, namely, in the Pacific. In Europe, the Washington arms control agreements were divorced from political and doctrinal realities.

---

80. Sprout and Sprout, *Toward a New Order*, p. 42.

4 Arms Control as "Process"

BY TODAY'S STANDARDS the Washington treaty negotiations were an incredibly ambitious undertaking. They tackled a broad range of political, economic, and military issues in the Asia-Pacific region, the area of greatest global rivalry between the wars. The Washington treaty system, along with the Covenant of the League of Nations and the Locarno treaty of 1925, was part of an evolving postwar framework of international cooperation. The Washington component attempted to impose a global overlay of arms control as part of the process of constructing a new order. The statesmen who negotiated the Washington treaty system employed both political-based and military-based arms control strategies. The scope of the process in the Pacific reflected a political-based approach to arms control; the scope of the process in Europe a military-based approach. In the Pacific, the strategic visions of the great powers overlapped in two very crucial respects: on strategic doctrine, and on the need for stability in Asia through the gradual transformation of China into a modern state. Yet their interests diverged in other important ways. Bridging these conflicting agendas succeeded because of the nature of the arms control process. In Europe, the strategic visions of Britain and France clashed in critical ways, but a strong mutual interest in a stable Europe united these powers. The European states failed to transcend their differences, however, because of the nature of the arms control process.

Strategic vision—how nations define and understand security—influences the objectives and goals of the arms control process. Overlapping or compatible goals usually contribute to the initiation of the process. These so-called inputs to the process, however, do not predetermine the outcome of negotiations. The process itself is also an important ingredient influencing the course of events. The Washington treaty negotiations illustrate how political-based strategies bridged conflicting interests and national agendas in the Far East and reduced interstate tensions that all the Pacific powers perceived as dangerous and escalatory. In negotiating the Pacific balance of power, the delegates acknowledged that weapons themselves did not create conflict, but rather the political situation and perceptions of threat and conflict made armaments a contributing factor to instability. By confronting the underlying insecurities driving the arms race, political-based strategies reduced tensions in the Pacific arena. Negotiations among the European powers foundered as the relevant parties focused exclusively on regulating a military relationship in the manner of many Cold War arms control initiatives. Despite mutual interests, meaningful arms limitation proved elusive. The interwar experience illustrates the risk in the Cold War approach, for focusing exclusively on technical agreements may be counterproductive if, in the process, one oversimplifies the political dialogue. The Cold War assumption, that technical arms control agreements are more important for preserving peace than political understandings, proves inapplicable to more complex structures of conflict found in the pre–Cold War and post–Cold War worlds.

The Washington treaty experience reveals how arms control is a process, as well as an output of negotiations. From the process perspective, arms control is neither static, given, irrelevant, nor predetermined in its outcome. Rather, the policy process may reshape and transform the strategic visions and agendas of parties in important ways. Instead of assuming that the outputs of arms control negotiations merely manifest what countries are able to agree to at the outset, or that countries are not concerned about these issues and are therefore willing to enter into an agreement, we can unpack the black box of the interwar process to reveal that the process itself was a critical ingredient in the outcome and that shaping the process to effect more desirable outcomes was possible then and is possible now. The Washington treaty experience provides guidelines for making arms control a more effective tool in managing and reducing hostilities in the international system. For these reasons, it is as important to focus on the process of arms control as it is to focus on the initial structure of incentives that impel states to negotiate. Focusing on the policy process illustrates how arms control can alter the goals of the participants.

The major treaties concluded in 1922 at the Washington Naval Conference are in Table 5. Only the powers prominently involved in negotiating the treaties are identified. For example, France was included in the Four Power treaty to dispel accusations that the United States was entering an alliance, to assuage French pride, and to prevent the United States from being isolated should disputes arise that might pit long-standing allies, Britain and Japan, against it. France, however, was not a major player in negotiating the Four Power treaty. The treaties represent the decision "output" of the negotiating process. In this chapter I explore the relationship between the initial incentives for arms control, which influence but do not determine the outcome of the process, the strategies of arms control employed or the form of the process itself, and the output of the negotiating process or the provisions of the treaties. In Chapters 5 and 6 I analyze the relationship between the decision output of the negotiating process and the actual historical outcome, or the impact of the treaties on interstate relations over time.

Hindsight might suggest one interpretation of how well treaties enhanced state security but perceptions at the time provide a more accurate measure of how well each state believed its agendas were met. These perceptions, in turn, shaped treaty interpretation in subsequent years. Perceptions of how well compromises accommodated national agendas reveal how each state defined the requisites of its security and how well leaders believed the arms control process served their security

Table 5   Strategies of arms control in 1922

Interest Constellation	Arms Control Strategy	
	Military and Nonmilitary Means	Military Means Only
Resolution (Agendas aligned)	U.S. and Britain • Five Power treaty U.S., Britain, Japan • Four Power treaty 1	Britain and France • Submarine treaty 2
Contention (Agendas in dispute)	3 U.S. vs. Japan • Five Power treaty U.S. and Britain vs. Japan • Nine Power treaty	4

interests, directly or indirectly. In 1922, the interests accommodated and the arms control strategies implemented affected whether competition was managed and tension defused by the Washington treaties, and these provide the baseline for evolving perceptions of the utility of the treaty system over time.

At the opening session of the Washington Conference, U.S. Secretary of State Charles Evans Hughes elaborated his bold arms control initiative to restructure the global balance of naval power and to serve as a foundation for a new world order. Hughes proposed a ten-year naval holiday and four additional principles to guide naval limitation. All capital ship building programs, actual and projected, would be abandoned. Additional reductions would be achieved by scrapping older ships. Tonnage levels would be determined according to existing naval strength. Capital ship tonnage would be used as the index of naval power with a proportionate allowance of auxiliary craft prescribed. A capital ship was defined as a vessel of war, other than an aircraft carrier, that displaced more than 10,000 tons and mounted guns greater than 8-inch caliber. All vessels below these standards were classed as auxiliaries, or as ancillary combatants. With these procedures, sixty-six ships displacing a total of 1,878,043 tons were destined for scrapping. The navies of Great Britain, the United States, and Japan would then stand in the ratio of 6:5:3. This ratio would be maintained for ten years, and replacements could begin thereafter. No future capital ship could exceed 35,000 tons or mount guns in excess of 16-inch caliber. Replacement tonnage was limited to 500,000 tons for Great Britain and the United States, and 300,000 tons for Japan.[1]

Hughes's initiative set the stage for a series of bilateral and multilateral discussions (1) to establish the foundations of a new postwar order based on cooperation between the two superpowers of the interwar period, Great Britain and the United States; (2) to create a new

1. See Buckley, *United States and the Washington Conference*, pp. 71–72, and Andrade, "United States Naval Policy," pp. 27–29. The U.S. plan proposed fixing the capital ship ratio of 5:5:3 to all other classes of surface warships and submarines as well. Total replacement tonnage for aircraft carriers would be 80,000 for the United States and Great Britain and 48,000 for Japan; for cruisers and destroyers 450,000 and 270,000; for submarines 90,000 and 54,000. Replacement age for carriers would be twenty years, for cruisers seventeen years, for destroyers and submarines twelve years. Maximum gun caliber for replaced ancillary vessels would be 8-inch. In the end, carrier tonnage was revised upward, only qualitative limitations were placed on antisubmarine vessels (10,000-ton maximum displacement and 8-inch maximum gun caliber), and submarines were limited only by guidelines for their usage.

regional balance of power in the Pacific; (3) to orchestrate a series of political understandings in the Far East to support this new balance of naval power; and (4) to tie the European balance of naval power to the Pacific balance of naval power through ratios, thus establishing a new global balance of naval power. Four arenas of great-power interaction framed the Washington treaty negotiations: the Anglo-American global naval balance, and the naval balance and regional security in the Pacific, China, and Europe. Building on Anglo-American global parity, negotiations turned to the thorny issue of reconciling U.S.-Japanese force requirements in the Pacific. The Pacific powers then tackled a series of political understandings and compromises in the Far East to support the new military balance there. Finally, ratios were extended to embrace Europe in the new order.

ANGLO-AMERICAN PARITY

The Hughes proposal sought to codify Anglo-American parity, defuse any possibility of an arms race between the two, and establish a strong foundation for Anglo-American cooperation. Demands for fiscal retrenchment made parity through arms reduction, or by a build-down of naval strength, an attractive option for both Great Britain and the United States. For the British, the desire to maintain a navy at least equal to that of any other in the face of severe financial constraints created a strong incentive to accept Hughes's proposal. For the United States, the Hughes proposal would attain their goals of economy, disarmament, and parity in a manner acceptable to the British. Merely fixing the status quo might save money but would leave Britain superior to the United States. Completing authorized building programs would place the United States far ahead of Britain. The Five Power treaty codified a shared interest in a build-down to achieve battleship parity, and the transformation of this military relationship fortified Anglo-American partnership as the foundation of a new global order. Shared interest in parity facilitated agreement on capital ship tonnage and removed a major source of conflict between the two. An underlying political consensus that Anglo-American rivalry was counterproductive to the more desirable long-term goal of establishing a new order was solidified at Washington.

At the turn of the century, U.S. insistence on a fleet "second only to England's" assured a navy greater than Germany's, the most likely aggressor in the Western Hemisphere.[2] In 1916, the United States embarked upon an unprecedented building program with the goal a navy "second to none." The Navy Act of 1916 authorized construction of 156 new men-of-war, including 10 super-dreadnought battleships and 6 battle cruisers.[3] Though the initial impetus behind the 1916 building program was fear of a superior postwar German fleet, the General Board's call for a navy second to none survived as the "creed of American navalists throughout the 1920s,"[4] posing a serious challenge to Britain's traditional mastery of the seas. At the close of the First World War, the United States ranked second only to Great Britain. The Royal Navy had 42 capital ships in service and 4 under construction.[5] The U.S. Navy had 16 dreadnoughts ready for service, and 19 under construction, of which 16 were post-Jutland.[6]

Naval authorities declared, "Equality with the British Navy is the minimum standard acceptable to the United States,"[7] and Wilson supported this view, with the intent of coercing support for his peace program. Wilson, a great proponent of postwar naval expansion, envisaged the U.S. building program as a tool of moral suasion to mobilize international support for the League of Nations. An aggressive building program, he reasoned, would require Britain to respond in kind, a move, he believed, Britain would not undertake. The British would then be

2. Bywater, *Sea Power*, p. 36.

3. Ibid. In 1905, the British revolutionized naval design by laying down a vessel that carried ten of the heaviest naval guns then being made, 12-inch. With the "all-big-gun" dreadnought, battleships carried a primary armament of eight to fourteen identical large guns. The term *dreadnought* became a designation for all such capital ships. When guns larger than 12-inch were introduced, the term *super-dreadnought* was coined. Brodie, *Guide to Naval Strategy*, pp. 30–31.

4. Roskill, *Naval Policy*, vol. 1, p. 20.

5. These were the four *Hoods*, three of which were eventually canceled. Ordered before May 1916, they were subsequently recast to embody improvements, particularly in armor and surface protection, suggested by the Jutland experience.

6. The new post-Jutland capital ship evolved from the experience of the Battle of Jutland, May 31, 1916, the only major fleet action in the First World War. Post-Jutland vessels, sometimes designated "super-dreadnoughts," differed from their predecessors in important ways. They possessed guns of heavier caliber; massive armor protection to vital parts, including thick steel decks to resist projectiles fired at long range and descending at a steep angle; a more complete system of bulkheading, or subdivision, to localize the effects of underwater explosion; and, in some ships, external bulge protection. Hector Bywater, *Navies and Nations: A Review of Naval Developments Since the Great War* (London: Constable, 1927), p. 42.

7. Sprout and Sprout, *Toward a New Order*, pp. 61–62.

forced to support the League, and Wilson would introduce arms reduction based upon Anglo-American parity.[8]

The Unites States also required a navy sufficiently strong to protect
its merchant marine and enforce its own interpretation of freedom of
the seas, particularly given conflict with Britain over neutral rights during the war. Once at war, the United States had supported British
measures for controlling neutral sea trade; however, as a neutral, the
United States resented British measures to extend "Belligerent Rights."
These rights gave Britain the power to "intercept neutral merchant
ships and seize their cargoes in prize if they were contraband and destined for an enemy country."[9] Though Britain's objective was to tighten
the blockade of Germany, U.S. ships were inadvertently detained. After the war, a navy second to none was championed to secure the
United States's postwar maritime trade, welfare, and security.

Finally, impending crisis in the Far East underscored demands for a
vigorous naval program. By the end of 1919, U.S. naval plans were
being shaped increasingly to fight a war in the Pacific.[10] Though the
Royal Navy served as the official building standard for the U.S. Navy,
maintaining a superiority of at least five to three, preferably two to one,
over Japan's Imperial Navy became an influential, though unofficial,
building guideline.

On the other side of the Atlantic, the defeat of Germany forced the
British to reconsider their force requirements. The British wanted a
naval program sufficient to defend home and empire that would not
provoke a building competition with the United States or require huge
financial outlays. The Imperial Navy seemed little cause for concern,
for its size was negligible and the Anglo-Japanese alliance compensated
for Britain's naval inferiority in Far Eastern waters. More important,
Britain's economy, weakened by the war, would be hard pressed if
forced to engage in unrestricted competition with the United States.

At the end of the war, the British declared a naval holiday that
lasted nearly three years, canceling many unfinished ships, scrapping

8. A navy second to none would also provide the League with a naval police force. The League
required a fleet sufficiently powerful to overwhelm any particular member, or a single national
naval force equal in strength to that of any other. At least one navy had to attain equality with
the strongest naval power, Great Britain, and Wilson envisaged the United States in that role.

9. Roskill, *Naval Policy*, vol. 1, p. 21.

10. See Gerald E. Wheeler, "The United States Navy and the Japanese 'Enemy,' 1919–1931,"
Military Affairs 21 (Summer 1957): 61–74.

old and superfluous ones, and leisurely completing others left over from the war. The last capital ship to be laid down was the battle cruiser *Hood* in 1916. From 1917 until the autumn of 1921, British construction was limited to a single submarine. Though reduced to peacetime footing, the Royal Navy remained superior in tonnage and numbers to any other navy, nearly equal to all the remaining major fleets of the world combined. Superiority went unchallenged in European waters where in 1918, the next strongest navies, the French and Italian, possessed only six and five capital ships respectively.[11] The United States's 1916 building program and talk of a supplemental program in 1919, however, threatened to bring the United States to nominal equality in capital ships by 1924. On the eve of the Washington Conference, the United States and Japan had approximately thirty post-Jutland ships between them under construction or authorized, all due for completion in 1927. By 1921, the tonnage of U.S. capital ships built and building exceeded by nearly 50 percent the corresponding British total.[12] The United States, in reality, would be superior since, with the exception of one *Hood* completed and four authorized in 1921, all British ships would be of the pre-Jutland type. The relative strength of the Royal Navy would be less than mere numbers indicated.

Prior to the First World War, Britain's two-power standard had been applied strictly to other European powers. Defined as "ten per cent more than the strength of the next two European naval powers— France and Russia," the two-power standard was designed to guarantee supremacy in the Near East, the Mediterranean, the Red Sea, on the route to India, and in the south Pacific. The United States occasionally was included in the computation of the two-power standard, but only to justify a marked superiority over the High Seas Fleet. As First Lord of the Admiralty Winston Churchill explained in 1912, a strictly European standard would provide only a slight superiority over the German Navy so "it has become customary to extend the Two Power Standard so as to include the United States."[13] Officially, the British continued to shun competition with the United States, despite the Admiralty's persistence in considering the United States in its estimates of British naval strength. At the Imperial Conference of 1921, for the first time a

11. Chaput, *Disarmament*, p. 79 n. 2.
12. Bywater, *Navies and Nations*, p. 105.
13. Chaput, *Disarmament*, pp. 92–94.

one-power standard was formally adopted as the "Basis of Imperial Defense." It would last until the expiration of the naval limitation treaties
in 1936.[14] Though always the implicit minimum standard, formal adoption of the one-power standard affirmed Britain's decision to settle for
parity with, rather than striving for superiority over, the U.S. Navy.

Parity, however, proved to be an ambiguous concept. For the United
States, parity meant equal arms. For Great Britain, parity meant equal
security; asymmetries in strategic requirements and threat environment
could not be ignored. Given the demands of imperial defense, equal
arms—particularly in cruisers used to defend shipping—did not mean
equal security. Heavily dependent on global commerce and with a far-
flung empire to defend, the British distinguished battle fleet parity, or
offensive power parity, from parity in those vessels employed in the
defensive role of commerce protection.[15] The disparate nature of British
interests and the different circumstances facing Britain and the United
States meant that equality with the United States by matching type for
type would mean strategic superiority for the latter.

The United States needed to defend only its own coastlines and Pacific possessions. It could rely on internal lines of communication, faced
no potential threat in the western hemisphere, and had only one area
of significant commitment outside its hemisphere, namely, its Far Eastern concerns: the China trade and the Philippines. It could afford to
concentrate on the Japanese threat, whereas the Royal Navy, with an
empire scattered over the globe, had to be divided into different squadrons to maintain a naval presence in all seas. Christopher Hall summarizes that "Britain had to consider the likely actions of France, Italy,
Germany, and Soviet Russia and coordinate the actions of far-flung
dominions. Naval detachments were permanently stationed in the West
Indies, South Atlantic, Indian Ocean, Persian Gulf, and South Pacific.
Further, Britain could never fully concentrate its fleet, and mobility
between theaters did not exist as it did for the United States with the
Panama Canal."[16]

14. Roskill, Naval Policy, vol. 1, p. 21.
15. A similar dispute plagued Franco-Italian attempts at parity throughout the interwar years.
Like the British, the French argued that relative strength should reflect national needs. "Pointing
to their Atlantic seaboard, Mediterranean coast, Far Eastern possessions, and North African territories, French leaders believed that parity would mean either local inferiority or a denuded empire." Burns and Urquidi, Disarmament in Perspective, vol. 3, p. 156.
16. Hall, Britain, America, and Arms Control, p. 202.

The British did not fear cruiser parity with the U.S. Navy because they anticipated war with the United States. Rather, any quota of cruiser tonnage adequate for U.S. needs would be inadequate for British needs. The U.S. proposal at Washington calculated cruiser tonnage in terms of fleet requirements alone. The British, however, needed cruisers not only to defend the sea approaches to the British Isles and imperial outposts, but also to guard the vast ocean stretches in between, over which passed the raw materials vital to the life of Great Britain. These cruiser requirements were *in addition* to those assigned to the battle fleet. The United States, with its immense and varied internal resources, needed fewer cruisers.

The Anglo-Saxon powers agreed to parity in battleship tonnage and codified their commitment to a new order based on cooperation between them, but parity in cruiser strength proved more elusive because of the disparate definitions of security between a self-sufficient island nation and a commerce-dependent maritime empire. The debate over equal arms and equal security captured how asymmetries in strategic requirements supported different force structures and created technical obstacles to parity in ancillary categories. At this point in the process, absence of a technical solution reconciling British requirements for "light" cruisers (smaller craft operating within relative proximity to any one of Britain's numerous bases) with U.S. demands for "heavy" cruisers (those suited for operations over the vast expanses of the Pacific) precluded the full realization of mutual interests.[17] As a result, the Washington Five Power treaty contained a "cruiser loophole," that was, however, to prove of relatively little concern for Anglo-American relations because of the underlying political consensus that supported agreement on naval parity. However, the failure of the arms control process in Europe to build a political consensus between Great Britain and France engendered a contentious debate over submarine and cruiser requirements. Interestingly, the French made a similar argument to the British about equal arms and equal security, but to no avail.

17. Cruisers are classified as "light" or "heavy" not based on displacement but on the caliber of primary armament, six to fifteen identical medium-caliber guns. Light cruisers carry guns under 6.1 caliber. Heavy cruisers mount guns from 6.1 to 8-inch caliber.

U.S.-JAPANESE FORCE REQUIREMENTS

Though both Japan and the United States were receptive to arms limitation for reasons of economy, their strategic interests in the Far East and their arms control objectives clashed. Pursuing a strategy of political-based arms control permitted the United States and Japan to shift their arms control objectives in important ways. The Japanese surrendered a fundamental tenet of their national defense policy, 70 percent of U.S. naval strength. The United States agreed to base restrictions in the western Pacific. These compromises, more than simple negotiating tactics, proved possible only because of broader understandings enshrined in the Four and Nine Power treaties.

The Japanese came to Washington committed to securing a ratio of 70 percent of U.S. naval tonnage. A 70 percent ratio represented the Imperial Navy's long-standing consensus on its minimum security requirement; yet it was surrendered. Militarily, the 70 percent ratio was "predicated on the strategy of attrition and interceptive operations against the American fleet."[18] Japanese war plans called for an assault on the Philippines to eliminate local U.S. forces and secure mastery of the western Pacific; attrition tactics to reduce the U.S. fleet an additional 30 percent on its transpacific passage; and, finally, a decisive encounter with the weakened U.S. fleet. Politically, the 70 percent ratio symbolized Japanese naval hegemony in the western Pacific and, if accepted by the West, a commitment to respect and maintain this status quo. To the degree that arms control codified a 70 percent ratio, discouraged Western intervention, and bolstered Japan's position in the Far East, the Japanese were prepared to accept it.

U.S. naval authorities in Washington advised their delegates to demand a 2:1 ratio over Japanese forces. Civilian leaders in the United States, believing the navy's position too extreme, revised their demands downward to a 10:6 ratio. Had the United States been interested only in defending the continental United States, they would have been able to accept parity with Japanese forces. However, the U.S. Navy required a force level sufficient to project power into the western Pacific to defend the Philippines and commitments to China. Since the greatest potential threat to U.S. interests in the Far East was from Japan, force levels were calculated to give the U.S. Navy a sufficient superiority

18. Asada, "Japanese Admirals," p. 149.

over local Japanese forces. U.S. civilian leaders, because they faced a lack of popular resolve to use force to defend China and a lack of congressional support for developing fixed defenses in Guam and the Philippines, were determined to explore cooperative arrangements with Japan as an alternative way to protect Far Eastern assets.

The interesting story at Washington was how the arms control process permitted the United States and Japan to regulate and begin to moderate fundamentally conflicting strategic agendas in the Far East. Significant concessions were required to bridge the gap between U.S. objectives and Japanese objectives in the Pacific, and to reach a preliminary three-power naval accord.[19] The United States wanted the capability to project superior power into the western Pacific, to take any war into Japanese home waters. The Japanese wanted to prevent Western intrusion into their sphere of influence. The Japanese ultimately accepted the inferior capital ship ratio of only 60 percent advanced by Hughes, and the United States made two concessions in return. It agreed not to fortify bases in the western Pacific and conceded a minor adjustment in super-dreadnought strength that permitted the Japanese to retain the *Mutsu*, a vessel of symbolic value to the Japanese people. These were significant compromises, the first steps in reconciling foreign policy objectives.

Admiral Baron Kato Tomosaburo, leader of the Japanese delegation, raised the major objection to the Hughes proposal. Reiterating the Imperial Navy's long-standing position, Kato demanded a ratio of 70 percent of U.S. capital ship tonnage for Japan rather than Hughes's proposed 60 percent. As Kato explained, guidelines were laid out in Japan's 1907 Imperial National Defense Policy, stipulating that "a 70 per cent naval ratio vis-à-vis the United States was Japan's minimum defense requirement."[20] The policy officially sanctioned the eight-eight plan—designed to give Japan by 1927 a fleet of eight super-dreadnought battleships and eight battle cruisers, two laid down per year, all less than eight years old. According to Hector Bywater, a contemporary naval expert and commentator, completion of Japan's eight-eight program would extinguish the U.S. primacy in dreadnought tonnage

---

19. Once the "Big Three" had reached an accommodation, the French and Italians would be brought into the negotiations to extend the Pacific naval balance to embrace the European theater.

20. Asada, "Japanese Admirals," pp. 147–48.

unless further new construction were undertaken in the interim. To maintain a lead, the United States would have had to make a continuous effort, keeping ahead of Japan not merely in the number of ships but in the individual power of ships, extending stockyard and base resources to keep pace with ever growing fleet requirements, increasing personnel establishment year by year, and making larger and larger financial provision for construction and maintenance.[21]

Full budgetary approval for the eight-eight plan was attained in 1920.

A 70 percent ratio, "sufficient to defend but insufficient to attack," had become a firmly established consensus within the Imperial Navy by the time of the Washington Conference, growing into "an axiomatic conviction, even an obsession, that dominated Japanese naval policy, strategic planning, and building programs throughout the 1920s, and indeed up to Pearl Harbor."[22] Still, the Japanese defined their strategic requirements regionally. Japan possessed no naval stations outside local waters and only during the First World War, at the request of the Allies, did Japan conduct naval operations beyond the Yellow Sea, Sea of Japan, and western Pacific. The Japanese were prepared to fight only a limited war, adapted to their circumscribed forces. Local naval superiority could then be exploited to achieve limited territorial objectives.[23]

In postwar years, a consensus developed in Japan on the lessons of the First World War as Japanese leaders came to recognize the need for economic self-sufficiency to prevail in a protracted conflict.[24] In an era of "total war," the decisive contest would be one of national power, and Japan was burdened with significant disadvantages, two of which being poverty in steel and poverty in oil. However, with the eight-eight plan, added to five older dreadnoughts and four battle cruisers, Japan would possess a total of twenty-five capital ships completed since 1913. An accelerated naval program giving Japan a fleet at least equal, if not superior, to that of the United States in the Pacific would permit the Japanese to maintain the strategic status quo and defend their trade and vital economic interests, despite U.S. naval construction.

21. Bywater, *Navies and Nations*, p. 114.
22. Asada, "Japanese Admirals," pp. 147–48.
23. See Herbert Rosinski, "The Strategy of Japan," in Simpson, ed., *Development of Naval Thought*, pp. 102–20.
24. Dingman, *Power in the Pacific*, p. 125.

By July 1921, a special committee on naval limitation had drafted a resolution stating that "the Navy does not persist in the construction of the 'eight-eight fleet' as long as it can maintain a balance with Britain and the United States." Retreat from an earlier position that declared any reduction below the eight-eight plan as "absolutely unbearable" was modified in light of fiscal and domestic policy pressures. However, the resolution also stated that "the Empire absolutely requires a naval ratio of 70 per cent or above vis-à-vis the American Navy. . . . There can be no room whatsoever for compromise on this."[25] The Japanese perceived their Far Eastern agenda, for them an issue of vital rather than peripheral interest, as seriously threatened by the U.S. postwar building program.

Moving toward an acceptable military balance was a multistage process that ultimately had to be integrated with a series of political concessions. In the first phase, Japan and the United States argued over technical definitions of "existing strength" as the basis of the ratio compromise. The U.S. delegates advocated assessment of strength based on dreadnoughts built *and building*.[26] Since the major portion of Japan's program—four battleships and four battle cruisers—remained on paper, this would draw the Japanese ratio closer to 50 percent. The United States, by contrast, had already laid the keels of every capital ship in the 1916 program. Inclusion of ships under construction would permit the United States to reap at least some benefit from the $300,000,000 already sunk into the postwar building program, since all vessels under construction, even those as much as 90 percent complete, would be scrapped under the Hughes proposal. The Japanese delegates argued existing strength should be determined by counting only ships *already completed*, thereby raising their ratio to 70 percent. Beside the fact that a 70 percent ratio had been the minimum defense requirement since 1907, Kato faced strong opposition to the 60 percent ratio, not from the highest naval circles but from civilians on the Diplomatic Advisory Council, an interparty organ not connected to the Foreign Ministry but designed to give party voice to various foreign policy issues, and from certain officers in the Imperial Navy. Kato feared the disarmament proposal as it stood would mean a deathblow to Japan's naval profession because the historic rivalry between the army and navy virtually assured

25. Asada, "Japanese Admirals," p. 149.
26. Buell, *Washington Conference*, pp. 156–57.

that an increase in the power of the army clique would follow. The proposal probably would ensure Kato's demise as well.

The Japanese also included the super-dreadnought *Mutsu*, according to the U.S. delegation only 98 percent complete, in their tonnage of completed vessels. This gave the Japanese a ratio of 70 percent. The Japanese people had developed a sentimental attachment for the *Mutsu* and by designating it complete, it would be preserved under the U.S. proposal.[27] The Japanese were determined to retain the *Mutsu*. Since the system of capital ship ratios depended mainly on the allocation of post-Jutland tonnage, the *Mutsu* demand had important consequences for it left Japan with twice as many post-Jutland capital ships as the United States and Great Britain. The original Hughes proposal allowed Japan to retain the *Nagato*, a super-dreadnought completed in early 1921. The United States would retain one super-dreadnought, the *Maryland*; Great Britain would retain the *Hood*, displacing 41,200 tons. In total, three super-dreadnoughts would be retained, one for each power. Retention by the Japanese of the *Mutsu* would give the Imperial Navy twice as many state-of-the-art ships as the navies of the United States and Great Britain. To offset this difference, the Japanese offered to sacrifice the *Settsu*. This was an unacceptable solution because the *Settsu*, an older ship completed in 1912, displaced only 21,420 tons and mounted 12-inch guns. The *Mutsu*, by comparison, was one of the most powerful vessels afloat. It displaced 33,800 tons, had a speed of 23.5 knots per hour, two knots more than the *Maryland*, and mounted 16-inch guns.[28]

In the first phase of compromise, the Japanese were permitted to retain the *Mutsu*, and the gain was offset by corresponding increases in U.S. and British strength. The United States and Britain were to build up to treaty strength to maintain the 5:5:3 ratio, leaving them each three super-dreadnoughts to Japan's two. The United States would complete two battleships of the West Virginia class, the *Colorado* and *Washington*.[29] Both, 80 to 90 percent complete, were originally designated to be scrapped. Britain was permitted to build two of the four super-*Hoods* authorized in August 1921. Since the *Mutsu* was virtually completed, whereas the two ships of the British super-Hood-class were

27. The *Mutsu* had been built by the donations of school children. See Buell, *Washington Conference*, p. 159.
28. Ibid., pp. 159–60.
29. Later, *West Virginia* was substituted for *Washington*.

scarcely started, "Japan forced the British people to expend some $80,000,000 in the construction of two additional ships, all in the interest of disarmament."[30]

The second phase of compromise among military assets was an agreement to freeze all naval base fortifications in the western Pacific. For the Japanese, this represented the first in a series of political concessions to secure recognition of their sphere of hegemony in Asia, a process that would culminate with the Four and Nine Power treaties. Admiral Kato suggested he might be willing to abandon insistence on a 10:7 ratio if Britain and the United States halted all construction of naval bases in the western Pacific. This nonfortification "clause" had serious consequences for the balance of naval and political power in the western Pacific and East Asia.

Given the importance of the base factor for their strategic requirements, the Japanese delegation had carefully considered its position on fortifications prior to the conference. In anticipation of the disarmament conference, the Japanese had even accelerated the naval works in progress at several island bases, including the Bonins and Amami-Oshima. An acceptable ratio of strength vis-à-vis the U.S. Navy, however, hinged predominantly on the status of U.S. bases in Guam and Manila. From the lessons of World War I, the Japanese calculated that at a distance of 4,500 miles, the United States would need a fleet at least 40 percent superior to the Imperial Navy to challenge Japan in home waters. A ratio of 10:7 would give the U.S. Navy 43 percent superiority. Modernized bases in the western Pacific meant the Imperial Navy would need a ratio of tonnage greater than 7:10. The Japanese were particularly concerned because Congress had appropriated funds to modernize and improve projected bases at Guam and Manila for forward-based operations, even though the funds Congress had appropriated would probably have sufficed to cover only preliminary operations.

The Japanese delegation believed that if they accepted the tonnage levels in the Hughes proposal coupled with fortified bases in Guam and the Philippines, the probability of a U.S. attack on Japan could become a reality. Given that the United States possessed no such developed facilities *at the time* of the conference, the Japanese demanded a halt to further fortifications as a quid pro quo for accepting Washington's proposed ratio in capital ship tonnage. Kato also believed this provision

30. Buell, *Washington Conference*, p. 161.

would save face for the Japanese government in the eyes of its domestic audience, given Japan's concession to the 10:6 ratio in capital ships.[31] Without such bases, an attacking navy would require a two- to three-fold superiority over the Imperial Navy, at least a 10:5 ratio, to maintain communications with a home base, which for the U.S. Navy was 4,500 miles away. Otherwise, "an American fleet would only be forty . . . or fifty percent effective in operations in Far Eastern waters."[32]

Across the Pacific, U.S. naval authorities calculated that a war in Japanese waters without nearby repair bases required a ratio of at least 5:3 (66 percent superiority) or a ratio of 2:1 preferably (100 percent superiority). The Imperial Navy's concentration in regional waters, U.S. naval leaders argued, meant Japan's naval strength was relatively greater than numbers suggested.

> When two navies are in close proximity such as the British and the German, or British and French, their relative strength may be roughly determined by the usual method of counting up tons, guns, and men since each could confront the other practically in full force. This method of comparison, however, is misleading when applied to naval power in the Far East for while Japan could bring her entire strength to bear at any point within the northwest Pacific, no other country could apply more than a fraction of its fleet in those waters without proper base facilities, which at present do not exist. Relatively, therefore, the Japanese Navy is very much *stronger* than a mere computation of its ships and men would suggest.[33]

U.S. naval leaders actually wanted a 2:1 ratio without any restrictions

31. Buckley, *United States and the Washington Conference*, p. 100.

32. Buell, *Washington Conference*, p. 164. "For any attack on Japan, as matters now stand, the enemy must be in possession of a fleet about three times as powerful as that of the defense, because no other country has a fully equipped modern naval base and arsenal in the Eastern Pacific capable of docking two or three of the largest battleships simultaneously; or of removing guns one hundred tons in weight; or of manufacturing wholesale supplies of heavy caliber ammunition; or, lastly, of storing the millions of tons of oil fuel required by a twentieth century fleet in war. Without such a base in easy reach, a large proportion of the attacking fleet—probably a third—must constantly be at some distance from the theater of operations; while the force actually on the spot must always be twice as strong as the defense if any effective watch or blockade is to be possible. No Power exists at present in a position to undertake such a task." Vice-Admiral G. A. Ballard, C.B., *The Influence of the Sea on the Political History of Japan* (London: John Murray, 1921), p. 291.

33. Bywater, *Navies and Nations*, p. 220.

on fortifications. Well-equipped fleet stations in the western Pacific were critical for the defense of Far Eastern commitments, not to mention for offensive operations.

The Hughes proposal dealt only with capital ships, excluding reference to other elements of naval power. Whether this omission was due to the opposition of naval authorities to negotiations regarding bases or to the failure of the civilian delegates to fully appreciate the connection is unclear. Arguably, the proposal divorced the issue of ship building from that of base fortification, since it was doubtful the American people would pay to develop facilities capable of supporting operations in China or the Philippines. In 1922, U.S. bases in the Pacific were not yet properly equipped for the repair and maintenance of ships, least of all capable of supplying the needs of a great fleet. A large dry dock at Pearl Harbor had opened in 1919 but remained incapable of accommodating a large number of vessels. Three bases in the Philippines and Guam were neither equipped nor defended. The U.S. delegation hoped to stabilize the balance of naval power through battleship ratios alone, whereas the Japanese demanded the battleship ratio and base issues be linked. From the Japanese perspective, "bases were as necessary as ships, and if the interests of peace demanded a drastic reduction in ship tonnage, it followed logically that naval bases should also be restricted."[34]

Acquiescing to Japan's demand to link fortification of bases with capital ship tonnage restrictions demonstrated the value U.S. civilian leaders attached to arms limitation. The United States sacrificed any possibility—assuming the will existed—of physically enforcing the open door in China and defending the Philippines from attack. The U.S. delegates willingly surrendered a large degree of independence in the western Pacific for absolute security in the eastern Pacific.[35] Thereafter, U.S. and Japanese battle fleets would be separated by a vast ocean that could not, under the circumstances, be traversed in war conditions. The three great naval powers had also taken the first step in

34. Ibid., p. 126.
35. In the words of Elihu Root, the delegates "had started with the proposition that the United States would not be sufficiently interested in the Open Door or the preservation of Chinese integrity to go to war about them, and . . . Japan realized this probably better than the average American did, and that our naval program was very doubtful any way, because of the very strong opposition in this country to the immense expense involved. Therefore the first point in their minds was that we were not throwing away any weapon with which we could threaten Japan." Braisted, *United States Navy in the Pacific*, p. 595.

creating exclusive spheres in the Pacific: the United States in the east, Japan in the west, Great Britain in the south.

By January 1922, nearly a month and a half after the initial decision to freeze fortifications, the signatories agreed on a definition of "fortifications and naval bases in the Pacific region." The Hawaiian Islands, Alaska, the Panama Canal Zone, and the islands adjacent to the coasts of the United States, were excluded. Hence, the United States sacrificed the right to build new bases at Manila and Guam. The British agreed to the status quo in Hong Kong and to other insular possessions in the Pacific Ocean, east of 110 degrees east longitude. Those adjacent to the coasts of Canada, Australia, and New Zealand were excluded. Japan agreed to the status quo in the Kuriles, the Bonins, Amami-Oshima, the Loochoo Islands, Formosa, and the Pescadores. The islands of Japan proper were excluded. All agreed as well to the status quo of possessions acquired in the Pacific in the future.[36] In the end, Singapore became the only base from which an attack could possibly be launched against Japan. Singapore was distant enough to make attack improbable by either the United States or Great Britain operating *alone* with only a 5:3 superiority. A *combined* Anglo-American force, however, would create a sufficient margin of superiority to offset the disadvantage of distance. If the Anglo-Saxon fleets could be arrayed in combination against the Imperial Navy, the capital ship compromise would collapse because the ratios were calculated to preserve defensive superiority of each fleet *alone*. Firm in their resolve to prevent anything from jeopardizing their control of the sea approaches to China and the home islands, the Japanese demanded assurances that the British and U.S. fleets would not operate together against the Imperial Navy.

As long as the Anglo-Japanese alliance existed, the possibility of a joint Anglo-American naval operation against Japan was remote. The U.S. delegation, however, was committed to dissolution of the alliance and a restructuring of political obligations in China. The technical compromises reached in the Five Power treaty, provisions necessary to diffuse a U.S.-Japanese arms competition, now became conditional on a political accommodation that would dissolve the Anglo-Japanese

36. Buell, *Washington Conference*, pp. 165–69. In the case of Japan, the islands were of great strategic importance, particularly the Bonins and Amami-Oshima located closer to Japan proper than Hawaii to the United States. Yet many were already well defended, and the agreement did not prohibit "such repair and replacement of worn-out weapons and equipment as is customary in naval and military establishments in time of peace." Bywater, *Navies and Nations*, p. 128.

alliance and prevent any possibility of an Anglo-American offensive against Japan.

MODUS VIVENDI IN THE PACIFIC

The Four Power treaty, a political understanding, grounded the military arrangements of the Five Power treaty. The Four Power treaty was designed to protect the Pacific interests of Great Britain, the United States, Japan, and France without resort to alliance, force, or the combination of any two nations against a third. The British recognized the necessity of abrogating the Anglo-Japanese alliance. Nevertheless, they needed to protect their imperial dominions in a manner that would not alienate the United States or Japan, and that would not require huge financial outlays. The United States demanded cancellation of the Anglo-Japanese alliance yet refused to enter into any agreement resembling an alliance or entailing the commitments associated with one.[37] The Japanese would not accept the capital ship ratio of 5:5:3 as long as nothing prevented an Anglo-American combination against the Imperial Navy. The Four Power treaty became the quid pro quo for Japanese acceptance of dissolution of the Anglo-Japanese alliance.[38]

With the Four Power treaty, "the British Empire, France, the United States, and Japan . . . promise[d] to respect the rights of each in their insular possessions and insular dominions in the region of the Pacific Ocean." Hughes included France to ensure the United States would not be isolated should disputes arise, given that Britain and Japan had been allies for twenty years. Hughes also hoped to dispel accusations that the United States had simply joined the Anglo-Japanese alliance. Finally, French pride, hurt by exclusion from previous negotiations, could use some soothing. Critically for Japan, this treaty created obstacles to the joint intervention of Britain and the United States in the Orient. The U.S. delegation accepted the Four Power treaty because it supplanted a two-power defensive alliance calling for the use of force with a broad agreement in which the United States did not assume heavy obliga-

---

37. Hughes had declared "that this Government could enter into no alliance nor make any commitment to the use of arms or which would impose any sort of obligation as to its decisions in future contingencies." Buell, *Washington Conference*, p. 176.

38. See Fry, "The North Atlantic Triangle," pp. 46–64.

tions, but promised only to attempt to settle disputes arising in the Pacific by diplomacy or conference. Both methods had long been employed in U.S. foreign relations.[39] The Four Power treaty was in essence a nonaggression pact. It provided for the security of outlying possessions that Britain and the United States were either unable or unwilling to expend resources to protect.

The Four Power treaty, coupled with the nonfortification clause of the Five Power treaty, created powerful impediments to U.S. power projection into the western Pacific, since the treaty enshrined a pledge not to use force against Japan and not to intervene jointly in the Orient.[40] Challenges to Japanese policies in the Far East were virtually neutralized. Japan's inferior capital ship ratio had been more than adequately offset by the Four Power treaty. The nonfortification clause of the Five Power treaty made it impossible for either Britain or the United States acting *alone* to forcibly intervene in the Orient. The Four Power treaty prevented Great Britain and the United States from *combining* their fleets. The Four Power treaty reinforced elements of the Five Power treaty and "as long as these treaties were adhered to, Japan was absolutely supreme in the western Pacific and over Asia."[41] Moreover, the spirit of the Four Power treaty, by establishing a modus vivendi in the Far East whereby the signatories agreed to respect the rights of one another in their respective spheres, limited the degree of diplomatic pressure Britian and the United States could bring to bear against Japan.

By a strategy of political-based arms control, the Washington powers capitalized on their overlapping interests to structure a political compromise that reinforced and facilitated agreement on the technical provisions of the Five Power treaty. The treaty process succeeded in bridg-

39. Buckley, *United States and the Washington Conference*, p. 144.

40. Buell states, "I do not know whether the American delegation realized the exact import of the Four Power Treaty or not. Certainly the fact that it constitutes a pledge of non-intervention in the Orient was not brought out in the debates on the Treaty. Nevertheless, it is difficult to see how the conclusion can be avoided that in the future the United States will be forced to follow this policy, so much desired by Japan." However, the U.S. delegates—Hughes, Lodge, and Underwood—all denied the existence of any secret understanding with Great Britain in relation to the Four Power Treaty, which had created "such a basis of sympathy . . . between Great Britain and the United States that both sides assume that in all future emergencies they can both count on having the very closest cooperation." Buell, *Washington Conference*, pp. 182–84.

41. Ibid., p. 200. Even though Buell was writing in 1922, his conclusions are consistent with those of present-day scholars. Nonetheless, at the time, many Japanese believed they had suffered a serious defeat at the hands of Britain and the United States.

ing what initially appeared to be incompatible arms control objectives. For different though compatible reasons, Japan, the United States, and Britain desired an arrangement to protect respective rights and serve respective agendas, to prohibit the combination of any two against a third, and to prevent the formation of alliances and the use of force in the Pacific. The Japanese wanted to prevent an Anglo-American combination that could threaten their interests in the Far East. The United States was committed to dissolution of the Anglo-Japanese alliance, a mechanism that facilitated Anglo-Japanese alignment to the detriment of U.S. interests and had become a major source of tension in Anglo-American and American-Japanese relations. Such an alliance, the United States feared, would continue to protect Japanese imperialism as it had in the past, and would constitute tacit recognition of Japanese special interests in China and Siberia. The United States also refused to be party to any arrangement that smacked of an alliance or sanctified the use of force. The British were wrestling with the problem of imperial defense, similar to the situation facing the United States in Guam and the Philippines: the defense of far-flung territories with insufficient resources. Britain recognized that demanding an alliance to protect its interests would alienate the United States. Conversely, deserting Japan would directly jeopardize British economic interests in China, threaten dominion security, and require a greater military presence in the Far East than the British were prepared to sustain. The Four Power treaty served these diverse, yet converging, interests and provided the foundation for a security system in the Far East, built by a strategy of political-based arms control. Absent the political compromises embodied in the Four Power treaty, the Five Power treaty in all probability would never have been implemented.

POLITICAL COMPROMISES IN CHINA

The Nine Power treaty was the final piece in the Far Eastern puzzle and brings to light the full scope of issues the arms control system had to address in order to reduce tensions and displace competition with cooperation. Bruce Berkowitz, in his treatment of interwar arms control, writes that "along with the naval treaty, the delegates negotiated two other agreements. One of these was a treaty regarding trade with

China. The other was an agreement on fortifications on the Pacific islands. Although neither of these agreements really had anything to do with limiting arms, they were closely tied to the naval treaty itself."[42] The historical record suggests that these "other" agreements were, in fact, critical to arms control and to the successful negotiation of naval limitations. In this crucial respect, the Four Power treaty and the Nine Power treaty had something in common. However, whereas the Four Power treaty codified the convergence of interests among the treaty powers, the Nine Power treaty only bridged the conflicting interests of the major Far Eastern powers. For this reason, the weaker Nine Power treaty required the concerted attention of the signatories to cultivate and nurture the nascent cooperation it represented.

The U.S. delegation came to the Washington Conference with few concrete plans for China, yet U.S. interest there, particularly in Shantung, dated back to Wilson's platform at Versailles. Wilson was determined to restore to China the German rights in Shantung that had devolved to Japan after World War I. After World War I, Shantung became a highly politicized topic in the United States. On September 11, 1919, then-Senator Harding denounced the Shantung Settlement of the Versailles Treaty granting the former German rights in China to Japan as the "rape of the first great democracy of the Orient." Reiterating these Wilsonian sentiments in his presidential campaign, Harding recommitted the United States to the restoration of Chinese sovereignty, integrity, and independence.

The Japanese would never be satisfied with an arrangement that jeopardized what they perceived as their special interests on the mainland. They were, however, willing to make limited face-saving concessions in Shantung. Anticipating these concessions from the outset, the Japanese presented them as quid pro quos for concessions in areas they considered far more vital: Manchuria and Siberia. The Japanese refused to settle on Shantung until assurances were granted regarding Manchuria and Siberia. Japan's demands for retention of the leases of Kiaochow, Port Arthur, and Dairen received support when the British refused to surrender Kowloon, claiming it necessary for the defense of Hong Kong. In the end, the Japanese made a series of concessions in Manchuria that were more apparent than real and in return insisted on

---

42. Berkowitz, *Calculated Risks*, p. 36.

"the sacred validity of treaties exerted under duress" to solidify control of Manchuria until expiration of the lease in 1997.[43]

The future disposition of Shantung revolved around the property held by individual Japanese in Tsingtao, taken from the Chinese and Germans during the war, and control of the Shantung (Tsingtao-Tsinan) Railroad that delivered control of the entire province. The Japanese eventually permitted the Chinese to buy back the railroad over a period of five years, but retained extensive commercial interests in Shantung because the vested rights of Japanese in Tsingtao were left undisturbed. China failed to regain economic control over Shantung, and the Japanese made only negligible sacrifices to appease the United States.

Both the United States and Japan had an interest in resolving differences in China as part and parcel of the arms control process. The Japanese were unwilling to relinquish real control to China, but the United States was satisfied with a compromise arrangement providing China symbolic rights as an important first step toward strengthening China. The Shantung arrangement between Japan and China imposed no significant costs on either the Japanese or the United States, and succeeded in bridging divergent goals. Yet U.S. desire to reach an arms limitation agreement based on capital ship ratios had the unintended consequence of further solidifying Japanese hegemony in the Far East. Domestic pressures in the United States made settlement of Shantung a necessity, and lack of U.S. interest in Manchuria made accommodation possible. British interests, likewise, served Japanese objectives. More concerned with economic than political matters, the British conceded Manchuria to Japan in return for the safety of British interests in Shantung. For the British also, the price for Shantung was willingly paid: the loss of Manchuria.

The other critical outstanding issue regarding China involved the broader question of international cooperation there and became enshrined in the Nine Power treaty. The American people were committed to an open door policy in China but reluctant to go to war over Japanese aggression. Cognizant of these constraints, the U.S. delegation never seriously challenged *existing* concessions in China, but did want assurances that the Japanese would work to stabilize and

---

43. See Buell, *Washington Conference*, pp. 272–73, for details of Japanese concessions.

strengthen China, and that no power would further expand at the expense of China.

The Root Principles were adopted by nine powers—the United States, Belgium, the British Empire, France, Italy, Japan, the Netherlands, Portugal, and China—to provide guidelines for *future* policy in China, omitting references to vested rights. The Japanese, along with the other signatories, agreed to respect the principle of equal commercial opportunity in China and to provide the environment for the development of a stable government. This commitment, however, did not shift the status quo or affect Japan's special interests, in large part because no means for enforcing the open door, either through the publication of private contracts or the development of institutional machinery to settle disputes arising out of the open door principles, were developed. Since no power offered to surrender existing railway control rights, unification under Chinese authority never occurred. The Chinese failed as well to secure tariff autonomy. As Buell puts it, "China could not take the first steps toward creation of a strong central government, able to suppress military governors supported in part by Japanese funds and the likin tax, without an increase in revenue."[44] Tariff autonomy would not threaten the vested rights of foreign powers but only permit the Chinese, by increasing taxes on imports, to prevent the dumping of manufactures in China, to secure independence from foreign loans, and to develop domestic industry. Yet the economic interests of Western powers, coupled with Japanese opposition, defeated tariff autonomy.

In the end, the Chinese secured a tariff increase insufficient for their needs. The Japanese retained economic control over Shantung through the vested rights of nationals in Tsingtao even though Japanese troops were evacuated by the end of 1922. Manchuria remained firmly under Japanese control. The Nine Power treaty, while not acknowledging Japan's special interests in the Orient, in practice failed to undermine Japanese influence or to enhance Chinese sovereignty. The treaty, an agreement on general principles of behavior to be pursued in the future, preserved the status quo and great-power position in China, though establishing a regime of cooperation to assist in gradually transforming the country. The Nine Power treaty was an important first step, but

---

44. Ibid., pp. 252–53.

only that; the system remained weakest in China, where conflicting agendas tended to be masked rather than confronted and managed.[45]

The Nine Power treaty demonstrates that despite conflicting interests, limited cooperation may emerge. The United States was committed to a strong and independent China. The Japanese were determined to maintain their special relationship with mainland Asia as it had been codified in a plethora of treaties negotiated with the Chinese and other treaty powers since 1905. The Nine Power treaty, by outlining general principles of behavior, left sufficient latitude and ambiguity to satisfy the signatories. The Nine Power treaty was a relatively cost-free political compromise that facilitated technical agreements on arms limitation. In many ways, the Nine Power treaty resembles the Basic Principles Agreement negotiated between the United States and the Soviet Union as part of the first Strategic Arms Limitation Talks. Both established broad boundaries of a political status quo to avoid dangerous extremes. But the Nine Power treaty, like the Basic Principles Agreement, was "a contractual arrangement of a very loose and general character, the specifics of which remained to be filled in over time."[46] As George Breslauer describes the Basic Principles Agreement, because it did not define more concretely the rules of competition, it "contained the seeds of disillusionment. For unless both sides proceeded to explore, separately and collaboratively, the operational meaning of these abstractions and their applicability to concrete situations, those principles would create either cynicism or false expectations of harmony in a world of competitive global powers."[47] Strengthening the Nine Power treaty demanded translating abstractions into concrete choices, as well as working toward a shared conception of a future vision for China. Movement down this path was not unfeasible, given Japan's internationalist foreign policy orientation throughout the 1920s, desires for economic cooperation with the West, and commitment to disarmament and international cooperation.[48] But future events in China, coupled

45. Iriye makes the interesting argument that the revolt against the Washington system in China "paradoxically, may be viewed as evidence that the system had steadily become strengthened; those opposed to it would have to resort to drastic measures to undermine it." Akira Iriye, *The Origins of the Second World War in Asia and the Pacific* (London: Longman, 1987), pp. 4–5.

46. Alexander L. George, "Detente: The Search for a Constructive Relationship," in Alexander L. George, ed., *Managing U.S.-Soviet Rivalry: Problems of Crisis Prevention* (Boulder: Westview Press, 1983), p. 23.

47. Breslauer, "Why Detente Failed," p. 322.

48. Iriye makes the most persuasive argument for the strength of the Nine Power treaty and the

with worldwide economic depression, proved too difficult to surmount. The Anglo-Saxon powers were never able to appreciate the impact of the Nationalist unification of China on Japanese threat perceptions.

THE EUROPEAN BALANCE

The British and the French shared an interest in enhancing mutual security in Europe. The French feared most the specter of renewed German aggression and wanted to create a more favorable balance of power in Europe by obtaining political guarantees from the British. At a minimum, the French were determined to maintain superiority over the combined strengths of the German and Italian fleets, the "G + I" thesis, "to ensure that the French fleet could defeat the German and Italian navies singlehandedly,"[49] and to secure the transmediterranean routes for the transit of wartime reinforcements from the African colonies. The French were willing to enter into naval arms limitation to achieve these ends.

British strategic requirements called for superiority over the combined fleets of Japan and France and denial to any preponderant military power control of the ports of the Low Countries because the deltas of the Scheldt, the Meuse, and the Rhine offered excellent base locations for submarine attacks on British commerce.[50] In the abstract, the French security concerns laid out above posed no serious obstacle to Britain's pursuit of a one- or two-power Standard—parity with the United States or superiority over the combined fleets of the next two greatest fleets, Japan and France. The British, however, were operating under severe economic constraints, making the dual pursuit of a battleship program, to keep pace with the United States, and a cruiser program, in response to France's submarine program, impossible. From the British perspective, a favorable balance of power in Europe meant reducing the maritime strength of its rivals. Britain was concerned with security at sea, fearing most from France a submarine threat. France, on the other hand, was concerned with comprehensive security, on land as

---

forces in Japan that were committed to the Washington Treaty system well into the 1930s. Iriye, *Origins of the Second World War*, pp. 1–29.

49. Perett, "French Naval Policy," p. 22.

50. Chaput, *Disarmament*, pp. 31–32.

well as at sea, and would only moderate its submarine program if provided political guarantees in Europe.

Hughes proposed that France's existing dreadnought tonnage, 164,000, rounded up to 175,000, be the baseline for its capital ship ratio, and Italy's also. The French delegation, however, wanted ten capital ships, displacing a total of 350,000 tons. The French argued that had they not been forced to suspend naval construction during the war, by 1921 they would have possessed a fleet of twenty-eight capital ships displacing 700,000 tons. Since the "Big Three" had launched a great number of battleships and cruisers during the war, the proportionate strength of the French Navy was artificially low. France possessed the second largest colonial empire and maintenance of maritime communications required protection of three sea frontiers: the Mediterranean, Atlantic, and North Sea. "Ten capital ships were necessary to guard the communications of France with her colonies and to protect her 60,000,000 subjects there."[51] The United States considered its offer a windfall for the French. Based on existing strength, Britain and the United States exceeded France by a ratio of 6:1. If French tonnage, 164,500 tons of capital ships in 1921, was reduced in proportion to that of the three major powers, the French would be left with 136,500 tons. Accepting the offer in the U.S. proposal of 175,000 tons would lower the ratio to 3:1, the very ratio that existed in 1914. Hence, the French would not suffer from wartime inactivity. Rather, they were being offered the opportunity to economize while doubling their relative strength.[52] Bywater argues that French intransigence on battleship restriction had less to do with limitation per se, since French strategists had previously denounced the capital ship as an anachronism. Instead, the French rejected the presumption of naval equality between their own and the Italian fleets, for at no earlier period had Italian sea power approached the French standard.[53]

Conceding French demands would leave France with ten post-Jutland vessels compared to Britain's three. Other naval powers would be inclined to build to offset this imbalance, thereby undermining the entire arms limitation enterprise. Briand eventually agreed to the 1.75 ratio in capital ships but added that "so far as defensive ships [were] concerned

51. Buell, *Washington Conference*, p. 213.
52. Buckley, *United States and the Washington Conference*, p. 110.
53. Bywater, *Navies and Nations*, p. 232.

(light cruisers, torpedo boats, and submarines), it would be impossible for the French Government . . . to accept reductions corresponding to those which we accept for capital ships."[54] The French insisted on no less than 330,000 tons of lighter surface craft of which 90,000 tons would be in submarines. At the time of the Conference, the French possessed between 30,000 and 40,000 tons of submarines built, building, and projected. On the grounds that a weak surface fleet and vulnerable coastlines and sea communications made a powerful fleet of submarines necessary for self-defense, the French demanded at least a doubling, at most a tripling of their submarine tonnage.[55]

The British were adamant about abolishing the submarine, a patently "un-British" weapon that had become a symbol of "organized barbarism and brutality" because the submarine, "by its very nature, could not be used with effect against merchant shipping unless it ignored the laws of prize and other established rules of warfare."[56] The British, however, failed to obtain the support of any other delegation for their radical proposal of complete abolition. The U.S. Navy, for one, regarded the submarine as a positive military asset that could delay Japanese operations against U.S. insular possessions. In fact, the Hughes proposal actually provided for substantial increases in existing submarine fleets. According to U.S. estimates, in 1921 the United States possessed 95,000 tons built and building, Great Britain 82,500 tons, and Japan 31,500 tons. Britain and the United States would be allotted 90,000 tons; Japan 54,000 tons, permitting the British to build 7,500 tons and the Japanese over 20,000 tons.[57]

Failure to limit submarines precluded any significant restrictions on antisubmarine craft, a role performed by cruisers. Since the strategic requirements of the British Empire called for a large fleet of cruisers, the

54. Buell, *Washington Conference*, p. 214.

55. Bywater, *Navies and Nations*, p. 129.

56. Ibid., p. 132. Prize rules refer to the international laws governing the conduct of commerce warfare formulated at the Hague between 1899 and 1907. Commerce raiders were to stop and search merchant ships before seizing and destroying contraband. However, a submarine was too vulnerable when surfaced and, given its small size, was unable to either take a prize into port or to disembark passengers and crew before sinking the vessel. Furthermore, belligerent resort to arming merchant vessels, flying neutral flags on them, and disguising auxiliaries as merchantmen left submarine commanders no choice but to sink victims on sight without warning. Otherwise, the role of commerce destroyer would have to be abandoned. Before 1914, submarines were not even perceived as commerce raiders because they were clearly incapable of obeying these international laws. The unrestricted submarine warfare of World War I changed perceptions and expectations.

57. Sprout and Sprout, *Toward a New Order*, p. 192.

British had opposed parity with the United States in the cruiser category from the beginning. The empire's complete dependence on seaborne commerce necessitated proportionately more cruisers than any other power to protect trade routes. The British had always interpreted the one-power standard to mean "parity with the strongest *plus* what cruisers are absolutely necessary to protect trade and communications."[58] The Lloyd George Government defined parity as "parity in battle fleets, not in auxiliary vessels and commerce protecting craft," and the Admiralty contended that "the Navy should be maintained in sufficient strength to ensure the safety of the British Empire and its sea communications as against any other Power." The one-power standard meant "more than mere parity; it was parity or anything over, that the maintenance of security and sea communications might require."[59]

France's submarine program only enhanced British fears about cruiser limitation. The war had demonstrated that destroyers and patrol boats provided effective protection against submarine attacks on merchant shipping; yet these ancillary surface craft, in turn, required protection from interference by enemy surface vessels. Cruisers, the guardian vessels, were important antisubmarine vessels, and the British wanted sufficient numbers to maintain maritime communications. French demands for a huge submarine fleet even if for "defensive" purposes exacerbated British fears.

Bywater argues that no rational person really imagined that destruction of British commerce was the sole purpose of the French submarine fleet; however, a great deal of antagonism plagued Anglo-French relations. Interests had clashed in Paris in 1919 on nearly every European issue, and a belief that Britain had deserted France after the war had become an assumption of French diplomacy. Events at Washington, particularly Britain's attitude toward French security concerns, did little to dispel tensions. Balfour's instructions as he understood them were to

> induce the French to agree to a very small battle fleet so as to leave us free to accept American proposals without modification. Having persuaded them to deprive themselves of their form of naval defense I am to persuade them that they really require no submarines because a war between France and En-

58. Chaput, *Disarmament*, p. 138.
59. Ibid., p. 95.

gland is unthinkable. This task being successfully accomplished, I am then to ask them to reduce the number of their aircraft seeing that we cannot sleep securely in our beds lest in a war with France, London should be burned to the ground."[60]

Bywater continues that the British believed in times of war, states used whatever devices necessary, regardless of peacetime pledges to respect the laws of humanity. And whereas the Germans had begun the war with only thirty submarines, at the time of the Washington Conference, the French possessed forty and were demanding more. Finally, extracts from Captain Castex's study on submarine warfare were raised during the conference. Although the British did not assume that Castex spoke for all French naval opinion, his views undoubtedly carried weight. "Castex not only condoned the sinking of merchant vessels and liners with their crews, passengers, and cargo, but claimed with pride that these very methods had been advocated by French naval strategists many years before the war."[61] To make matters worse, many British suspected the French were using their submarine program as a form of blackmail to secure from Britain a political guarantee against a resurgent German threat. French definitions of security contributed to the failure to limit the size and total tonnage of submarines.[62]

Though the submarine escaped both abolition and restriction, rules were drawn up for the conduct of warfare on merchant shipping. A treaty relating to the use of submarines reaffirmed that submarines were not under any circumstances exempt from the rule of "visit and search" before seizure of a merchant ship, a rule that had long been applicable to surface warships. This appeased the British somewhat but the French never ratified the submarine treaty, refusing to force their submarines to observe the traditional rules governing visit, search, and capture at sea as long as enemies retained the right to arm merchant ships.

Differences between British and French doctrine and strategic vision

60. Telegram from Arthur James Balfour to the Foreign Office, November 24, 1921, CAB 4/7-288 B, Public Record Office, London. See also Donald S. Birn, "Open Diplomacy at the Washington Conference of 1921–1922: The British and French Experience," *Comparative Studies in Society and History* 12 (July 1970): 297–319.

61. Bywater, *Navies and Nations*, pp. 132–33. See Buell, *Washington Conference*, pp. 231–32, for discussion of the Castex article. Despite misquoting Castex's article at the Conference, Buell concludes that Castex did approve of unlimited submarine warfare.

62. See Douglas, "The Submarine and the Washington Conference of 1921"; Dorothy T. Groeling, "Submarines, Disarmament, and Naval Warfare" (Ph.D. diss., Columbia University, 1950).

created obstacles to arms limitation, despite their mutual security interests in Europe. The force requirements of France's continental doctrine
threatened the lifelines of a maritime nation like Great Britain. Though
neither the British nor French viewed the other as an enemy, and although no one seriously believed Britain and France would go to war,
practical measures to enhance mutual security could not be devised so
long as concessions were confined to technical issues exclusively. The
British were determined to reach a compromise on the military balance
alone, but the French demanded an explicit political understanding.
Absent some sort of political assurance against a resurgent Germany,
the French agreed to limit battleships only and refused to accept limits
on submarines, the panacea of inferior naval powers and the centerpiece of the French navy. For Great Britain, a power with thousands of
miles of maritime communications, it was precisely the submarine that
posed the greatest threat in European waters. From this clash between
continental and maritime conceptions of security, the most that could
be achieved was an agreement, never even ratified by the French, establishing guidelines for submarine operations.

The submarine issue directly interjected European politics into calculations of tonnage levels in the Far East and created insurmountable
obstacles to the quantitative limitation of cruisers and destroyers. To
prevent the building of vessels that were capital ships in all but name,
these ancillary antisubmarine craft were restricted only qualitatively to
10,000 tons displacement and guns of 8-inch caliber, limits considerably above the prevailing standard for cruisers.[63] It is doubtful whether
Japan or the United States would have agreed to abolition of the submarine. Nevertheless, failing to quantitatively limit submarines and antisubmarine craft created loopholes to be exploited by navies intent
upon pursuing their national agendas within the confines of the arms
control system.

---

63. Bywater argues that this was a loophole introduced into the U.S. proposal, by naval experts,
to permit the construction of large cruisers for operation over the vast expanses of the Pacific.
Greater cruising endurance combined with the speed of scouting vessels required greater displacement. Harold and Margaret Sprout offer an additional reason: the desire by the United States to
match the largest British cruisers, the Hawkins-class of nearly 10,000 tons. See Sprout and Sprout,
Toward a New Order, pp. 209–10.

SECURITY PERCEPTIONS

The three Pacific naval powers—Great Britain, the United States, and Japan—recognized that economic constraints in the postwar years coupled with demands for fiscal retrenchment had increased the degree of mutual dependence on one another for realizing security interests. But how well did the Washington treaties meet the security requirements of the signatories? The answer to this question requires examining post-Conference perceptions, since actors act on their perceptions of fulfilled or unfulfilled expectations.

British civilian leaders viewed the Washington arrangement as the lesser of two evils, since open rivalry with the United States, according to Lloyd George, would have been potentially a more dangerous decision than that made in August 1914. The Cabinet agreed that the prospect of an arms race with the United States was "ghastly, horrible, and unthinkable,"[64] and these assessments were reinforced by pressures from the Dominions for resolution of Anglo-American differences, from the electorate for peace, and from the Treasury for retrenchment in defense spending. British popular opinion, viewing competition with the United States as futile, bowed to the inevitable and welcomed the new atmosphere of stability.

There was, however, a body of opinion in Britain, represented by Admiral Sir Rosslyn Wester-Wemyss, former First Sea Lord, sympathetic with Admiralty concerns. Wester-Wemyss was outraged at the surrender of naval supremacy, "the cornerstone of British statecraft for more than three hundred years."[65] Britain's maritime tradition reflected the essence of national identity. For the first time in centuries, the Royal Navy was settling for parity instead of mastery. The capital ship, source of strength and backbone of the shipbuilding industry, was severely limited, whereas the submarine, greatest menace to the Royal Navy, escaped all limitation. International treaties rather than considerations of defense were determining naval posture. No longer would "Britannia rule the waves," and with this loss of authority went loss of prestige. "Great Britain had won the late war on the sea only to lose it

---

64. Kennedy, *Rise and Fall*, p. 277.
65. Sprout and Sprout, *Toward a New Order*, p. 260.

at the conference table—truly a paradoxical result of the greatest victory in history."[66]

Wester-Wemyss contended that although France and Japan had also suffered from the conference, the United States had gained everything it desired. "They have rid themselves of a vast and ruinous shipbuilding program without giving up the object for which it was projected; they have secured a general ratio of naval strength which leaves them free from anxiety in all quarters; and they have attained an equality with the first naval Power with a minimum of effort."[67] Finally, the Anglo-Japanese alliance, based upon mutual interests and relative capacities, had been replaced by a system dependent upon the incalculable shifts and whims of U.S. democracy.[68] The United States's history of isolationism, anglophobia, and anti-imperialist sentiment cast further doubts on the durability of the Washington settlement.

In the United States, the administration viewed the conference as a success, a foreign policy victory for the Republicans over the intransigent Senator Borah. A commitment to disarmament created a strong incentive for curtailing an impending naval building competition, and laying the foundation for a new world order was worth compromising the need to secure the Philippines and the open door, particularly given weak domestic support for maintaining commitments abroad. The treaties, considered "as a whole," contributed to "the establishment of conditions in which peaceful security [would] take the place of competitive preparation for war."[69] Overall, popular response was enthusiastic with dissenting opinions very much in the minority. "The public and Congress saw the treaty itself as proof that the underlying tensions in the Pacific had been eliminated, and naval construction was seriously restricted."[70] Congressmen apparently were not persuaded by the arguments that U.S. naval strength had brought the Japanese to the negotiating table and that preparedness was as much a factor in controlling tension as arms reduction.

Though opponents argued the Four Power treaty was an alliance in

66. Ibid., p. 261.

67. Ibid., pp. 261–62.

68. Max Beloff, *Imperial Sunset: Britain's Liberal Empire, 1897–1921*, vol. 1 (New York: Knopf, 1970), p. 342.

69. Sprout and Sprout, *Toward a New Order*, p. 255.

70. Norman Friedman, *U.S. Battleships: An Illustrated Design History* (Annapolis: Naval Institute Press, 1985), p. 183.

disguise, the treaties were eventually ratified with the Four Power treaty subject to the reservation that "under the terms of this treaty there is no commitment to armed force, no alliance, no obligation to join in any defense."[71] Still, pro-League Wilsonian Democrats continued to criticize the administration for failing to limit land armaments or assume responsibility for stability in Europe. As long as France remained obsessed with a sense of insecurity, they argued, peace would be illusory.

The U.S. Navy, like its foreign counterparts, viewed the conference results less enthusiastically. A consensus prevailed that the Japanese had achieved all their objectives: preventing fortification of Guam and the Philippines; consolidating a hold in the Far East; and checking U.S. interference there.[72] The nonfortification clause left the United States the only naval power without a well-equipped base in the western Pacific and nullified the margin of strength over Japan symbolized by the 5:3 ratio. In short, the ability to wage war successfully against Japan had disappeared. Finally, parity with Great Britain was a myth, for capital ship tonnage was not the only index of naval power. On indices of personnel and materiel, Britain retained superiority. The statement of official navy opinion, reported from the General Board to the secretary of the navy, concluded that the ability of the United States to defend interests or enforce policies in the western Pacific had been seriously diminished by the Washington treaties.

Captain D. W. Knox's *Eclipse of American Sea Power*, the "classic statement of American Service opinion on the Washington Conference,"[73] argued that the United States emerged the loser, having abandoned the ability to defend its interests and the opportunity to achieve real parity with Britain. Great Britain had gained "on every count," from the new code of submarine warfare, the removal of the threat of U.S. naval supremacy, and the opportunity to construct two new battleships that would help maintain industrial preparedness. Further, despite a ratio of equality with the United States, "preponderance in cruisers, merchant marine, and a worldwide system of naval bases and cables" made British naval power the most effective in the world. Japan, according to Knox, had secured the greatest gains of all. The na-

71. *Treaties and Resolutions of the Conference on the Limitation of Armament as Ratified by the United States Senate* (New York: Federal Trade Information Service, 1922), p. 30.
72. See Andrade, "United States Naval Policy," pp. 74–75.
73. Sprout and Sprout, *Toward a New Order*, pp. 264–66. Knox's book was published in 1922 by the *Army and Naval Journal*.

val treaty had halted a defense program that was consuming nearly half of Japan's total revenue while achieving what that program had been designed to deliver: prevention of U.S. interference with Japan's Asian policy.

U.S. naval opinion did not unanimously oppose the treaties. Admiral William V. Pratt, the treaties' most vocal proponent, argued that the Five Power treaty had reduced international tensions and restored a climate of peace. Further, the 5:3 ratio, the nonfortification clause, and the scrapping of the 1916 building program were not so disastrous, since lack of funds would have prevented completion of construction programs anyway. Since the U.S. Navy would be financially constrained, the United States had achieved a coup, restricting its competitors by bargaining away a "paper navy" that in all likelihood would never have become a reality.[74] The General Board, according to Pratt, had failed to acknowledge that given doubts that Congress would vote the necessary funds to complete ships and fortifications, the losses incurred from the Washington treaties were of potential, not actual, power.

In Japan, nationalistic newspapers claimed the empire had merely gained a "breathing space in naval competition" at the expense of its destiny in the Far East. Japan had suffered the equivalent of defeat in war while the Americans and British had won great victories. Popular opinion, however, welcomed the diversion of funds from armaments to domestic programs, and commercial interests were enthusiastic over prospects for improved trade with the United States. Some civilian leaders, including Prime Minister Takahashi Korekio fervently endorsed the treaties as a step toward peace, whereas civilian obstructionists in the Diplomatic Advisory Council firmly denounced the 60 percent ratio. The Council argued that Japan had sacrificed the Anglo-Japanese alliance in return for a dangerously inferior ratio of naval strength and paralysis in the Far East. The Privy Council approved the Five Power treaty but only with great difficulty and with accompanying reprimands to the delegates for acquiescing to an inferior ratio.

The compromises that permitted Japan to acquiesce in an inferior capital ship ratio produced unquestionable benefits for the Imperial Navy. One could confidently say the Japanese were in a better position to realize their goals in the Far East after the Conference than before it. Not only had they secured hegemony in China and the Pacific but by

74. Andrade, "United States Naval Policy," p. 76.

participating at all, they had affirmed to the world a commitment to the spirit of internationalism and cooperation and could enjoy the benefits of economic relations with the West rather than the costs of isolation that a nationalist and militarist diplomacy would invite. Nevertheless, the 60 percent capital ship ratio also symbolized defeat. The Washington compromises began to polarize domestic politics in Japan, laying the seeds of conflict between civilians and professionals, and between factions within the navy. Though much of the Japanese agenda had met with success, a perception of inferiority, sustained by the 60 percent ratio, always loomed in the background, to be exploited later by anti-internationalists committed to overthrowing the Washington system.

The most significant domestic repercussion of the treaty negotiations emerged in the beginnings of a schism in naval opinion in Japan. Kato Tomosaburo, chief delegate at Washington, succeeded in building a consensus among top naval leaders in Tokyo around the 60 percent ratio. In Sadao Asada's estimation,

> It was Kato Tomosaburo's political and organizational leadership, ably assisted by his subordinates in Tokyo, that cut through domestic tangles and contained opposition in naval circles to conclude the Five Power Treaty. The most significant feature of [this] process [was] the remarkable extent to which Navy Minister Kato ignored and bypassed the naval bureaucracy in arriving at his decision and winning Tokyo's approval for it. His success in freeing himself from the constraints of "bureaucratic politics" was nearly complete.[75]

At a meeting of the Supreme Military Council, highest advisory organ to the throne on military affairs, even Fleet-Admiral Togo Heihachiro, hero of the Battle of Japan Sea, endorsed Kato Tomosaburo's decision. Yet strong opposition arose, spearheaded by Kato Kanji, a young admiral whose influence was rising with his appointment to the Naval General Staff in May 1922. Although Kato Tamosaburo was able to squelch Kato Kanji's opposition at Washington, the latter never became reconciled to the inferior ratio. The day the ratio was "imposed," Kato Kanji declared, "As far as I am concerned, war with America starts now. We

75. Asada, "Japanese Admirals," p. 157.

will take revenge on her. We will!"[76] Kato Kanji's reservations found support among civilian obstructionists in the Diplomatic Advisory Council, whereas those in high naval circles remained sympathetic to Kato Tomosaburo.

These dynamics within the Imperial Navy reveal that the decision to accept an inferior ratio had been an extremely delicate one. It was in no small part due to the personality of Kato Tomosaburo. Cognizant of this precarious equilibrium, he labored to reform civil-military relations by creating a system of civilian navy ministers on the British pattern and to subordinate the Naval General Staff to the Navy Ministry. His efforts failed, and his death in 1923 removed a major obstacle to ascendance within the navy of forces in Kato Kanji's camp.

For the Japanese, arms limitation did not extinguish the competitive thrust of their foreign policy.[77] However, Japan did abide by the treaties, though they interpreted them more "narrowly," honorably faithful to their "letter," whereas Britain and the United States acted also to preserve their "spirit." Treaty evasion occurred in all countries but the Americans and British used capital ship ratios as guidelines for ancillary craft construction, whereas the Japanese built with no intention of accepting a 40 percent inferiority in other classes of ships. Nevertheless, in 1922, the Washington treaties and the tenets of Shidehara's economic diplomacy that justified a pro-Western orientation enjoyed a great deal of support in Japan. It would take the events of the next decade—the Nationalist unification of China, worldwide economic crisis, and developments at the London Naval Conference of 1930—to shift the balance of forces in Japan.

In France, civilian leaders, popular opinion, and naval authorities viewed the conference as a betrayal of French national interest. Only on the submarine issue had the French delegation prevailed. Demands for security guarantees in Europe had been dismissed, and the French had been portrayed by the British as aggressors, imperialists, and conference obstructionists. In a tremendous blow to their prestige, the French were forced to accept parity with the Italians. Italy would become superior in the Mediterranean, simply because France was unable to concentrate forces there at the expense of its defense requirements elsewhere. Furthermore, by creating parity between these two European powers, a

76. Quoted in ibid., p. 158.
77. Crowley, *Japan's Quest for Autonomy*, pp. xiv–xvii.

great victory for the Italians, the Washington treaties actually introduced a situation of naval competition that had never before existed. The French perceived only one route to security: building in unregulated areas, a decision that further fueled British accusations of French aggressiveness and spurred building programs in ancillary categories.

For the most part, popular and immediate financial pressures in all states were assuaged, although it should be noted that although in the short term, arms limitation freed up funds for domestic programs, arms limitation harmed shipbuilding industries and contributed to depressed economies in the interwar years. Civilian leaders in every country except France appeared satisfied. Even though civilian opposition existed in Japan, the party in power firmly supported Kato Tomosaburo's decisions at Washington. In contrast, naval authorities expressed disappointment. That professional demands were sacrificed is not surprising, given the conscious decision by civilian leaders to pursue broader goals at Washington and relegate naval experts to technical committees.[78] Given overall professional dissatisfaction, naval authorities in all states worked to redress perceived unfavorable balances, irrespective of initial arms control goals. The French considered parity with the Italians unacceptable and embarked on a major building program in unregulated vessels in post-Conference years. The Japanese devised innovative technologies, tactics, and strategies to compensate for an inferior capital ship ratio. U.S. experimentation with carrier tactics and strategies proceeded in an effort to improve forward-based operations and overcome the constraints imposed by the nonfortification clause of the Five Power treaty. Finally, the British perceived threats in French demands for submarines and U.S. demands for heavy cruisers and felt compelled to build 10,000-ton cruisers, which were largely superfluous to their strategic requirements.

Over time, the Washington treaty system began to exacerbate security concerns in Japan. Despite the fact that interests had been bridged, mutual security conceptions between the Japanese and the Anglo-Saxon powers failed to mature. This turn of events, however, was not a foregone conclusion at the outset, but developed with shifts in the internal and external constraints facing the treaty powers and with how the system evolved in response to those shifts. In 1922, competition would have been far more vehement without the Washington treaties.

---

78. Sprout and Sprout, *Toward a New Order*, pp. 134–35.

STRATEGIES OF ARMS CONTROL

It has been argued that "so long as the demand for weapons remains, arms control will not control arms, but will simply alter the pattern in which nations acquire them."[79] Such an argument "black-boxes" the arms control process and slights how that process may be shaped to influence and reorient perceptions of power, interest, and status among states. The ability of the Washington treaty system to manage competition by serving the respective interlocking interests and expectations of its members was affected by the types of interests served and the arms control strategies pursued. Cooperation emerged from different interest dyads—similar, convergent, and conflicting—and although confined to agreements on the military balance in Europe, was linked to political understandings in the Pacific and, at the global level, between Great Britain and the United States. To the degree that the arms control process ignored differences in strategic vision, which occurred to differing degrees in both the Far East and Europe, cooperation was susceptible to competitive pressures.[80]

By referring to Table 5, which summarizes the output of the Washington Conference into three of four cells, organized by interest constellation and arms control strategy, we can draw certain conclusions at this stage. By comparing cells 1 and 2, in which agendas were similar but different arms control strategies were followed, we see that when doctrinal definitions of security are incompatible, military means alone are likely to be insufficient to build an agreement because it is precisely the military requisites of security that are the subject of dispute. Under these circumstances, political understandings may provide a more productive avenue to bind signatories and to build cooperative agreements. The proximate cause in the failure to limit the submarine either qualitatively or quantitatively was the difficulty in reconciling the different imperatives of British and French military doctrines. Without drawing on areas of political consensus, extremely polarized negotiating positions—total abolition of the submarine versus unrestricted building—

---

79. Berkowitz, *Calculated Risks*, p. 28.

80. Philip Kerr argues that arms control was successful when political understandings were reached and unsuccessful when a political basis of agreement was absent. See preface to Hugh Latimer, *Naval Disarmament: A Brief Record from the Washington Conference to Date* (London: The Royal Institute of International Affairs, 1930), pp. v–vii.

limited compromise and opened the way for post-Conference building in ancillary categories by all the Washington powers.

Failure to link agreements on capital ships with those on ancillary vessels, which was due to the absence of any type of political guarantee for the French, made the European dimensions of the treaty system less robust. In addition, because Great Britain was the linchpin between the European and Pacific balances, developments in Europe spilled over to the naval balance in the Pacific. As a result, the submarine treaty diminished the impact of battleship ratios codified in the Five Power treaty. This occurred because a failure to curtail submarine development reduced the chances of limiting cruisers and destroyers, vessels used to protect merchant shipping from submarine attack. As technological developments in ancillary weapon systems proceeded, battleship ratios failed to reflect the true balance of naval power in post-Conference years.

By comparing cells 1 and 3 of Table 5, in which the same arms control strategy—linking nonmilitary with military understandings—was employed but in which agendas were aligned in one case and in dispute in another, we see how political-based arms control strategies may reduce tensions and bridge even contentious agendas in the short run. A comparison of cells 2 and 3 further reinforces the potential power of political-based arms control strategies. This can be contrasted with Anglo-American and Japanese agendas in China and the Pacific at the London Conference of 1930, in which contention was addressed by military means alone or by a cell-4 type scenario. However, agendas in dispute, such as in cell 3, must be resolved or brought into alignment over time if the treaty system is to evolve, be durable, and continue to enhance mutual security. The Washington treaty system crumbled first at its weakest points, cells 2 and 3. Naval competition reemerged in submarine and cruiser categories, and by 1926, cooperation in China based on the guidelines laid out in the Washington treaties had practically ceased.

At the global level, the Washington arms control system could contribute to world order only as long as the British perceived the Pacific as the critical arena of conflict. Absence of a German threat between 1919 and 1933, traditionally the central strategic problem in Europe, permitted the British to focus on relations with the United States and Japan in the Pacific and made the Washington system possible. In the words of the Admiralty, "with the disappearance of Germany as a naval power, the western Pacific has become the area to which all eyes are turned."[81] Once British threat perceptions shifted to the Continent, the treaty system lost a great deal of its utility because the European component of the system was not strengthened and Germany was not brought into the system in a meaningful way.

The Washington treaty process continued to face both internal and external pressures. Pressures may find relief within a treaty system if the system can evolve. Conversely, if the system cannot, pressures may compel leaders to seek relief outside the treaty system. We have explored the negotiating process in 1922, examined the products of that process, and identified military and political components of agreement. In 1922, areas of dispute over military content persisted in the European arena, and areas of political dispute remained in the Pacific arena. Several conclusions emerge at this stage in the treaty process:

1. Doctrine is an important component of strategic vision, indicating how a state defines its security. Doctrinal differences that support contrasting strategic preferences and force structures may impede arms control despite mutual political interests.

2. Conflicting political agendas may be bridged by political-based arms control strategies, demonstrating how arms control objectives and elements of strategic visions evolve and shift. The case of Japan illustrates this process. Some elements of Japan's competitive foreign policy agenda were modified; others were not. On the positive side, the treaty process validated Shidehara's economic diplomacy, demonstrated the value of cooperation with the West, and evinced that security in the Far East could be attained multilaterally. Collapse of faith in the Washington process was largely a function of unforeseen pressures and international developments that were not predetermined at the outset.

3. Military professionals can be expected to redress perceived unfavorable balances by exploiting the system from within and by pressing for the system to evolve in response to changing threat perceptions. How the system evolves in response to shifting threat perceptions, just as how the system is created, is a process of forging both political and military understandings that respond to disparate strategic visions.

81. Roskill, *Naval Policy*, vol. 1, p. 354.

5 Perverse Effects of the Policy Process

ARMS CONTROL TREATIES may redirect military strategies and programs in ways very difficult to anticipate during the negotiation stages of an arms control process. The "rechanneling" argument, or the balloon effect, hypothesizes that arms control has no fundamental impact on the competitive process it seeks to dampen, but simply redirects military competition into areas that have escaped regulation by interstate agreement.[1] However, arms control may dampen competition and at the same time stimulate forces external to the process, like technology, or create avenues, through loopholes and ambiguities, that invite circumvention. After all, it is only natural in an arms control environment for nations to substitute legal methods and weapons for tasks formerly dealt with by now prohibited methods and weapons.[2] Technological innovations, loopholes, and ambiguities create opportunities, and as Schelling and Halperin cogently summarize, "Any agreement is bound to have loopholes, and the loopholes may tend to discriminate in favor of one side or the other. Whether or not exploiting loopholes

1. This is not the same as arguing that arms control accelerates defense spending. Defense spending may or may not rise because of rechanneling. See Sean M. Lynn-Jones, "Lulling and Stimulating Effects of Arms Control," in Albert Carnesale and Richard N. Haass, eds., *Superpower Arms Control: Setting the Record Straight* (Cambridge, Mass.: Ballinger, 1987), pp. 223–73; Graham T. Allison and Frederic A. Morris, "Armaments and Arms Control: Exploring the Determinants of Military Weapons," *Daedalus* 104 (Summer 1975): 101; Roger Zane George, "The Economics of Arms Control," *International Security* 3 (Winter 1978–79): 123; and Kruzel, "From Rush-Bagot to START," pp. 207–8.

2. Schelling and Halperin, *Strategy and Arms Control*, pp. 69–70.

is an abuse of the system is bound to be a matter of judgement, and may become a matter of subsequent negotiation. What has to be recognized is that 'abuse' will usually be a matter of intent, rather than simply a matter of actions."[3] The naval limitation agreements of 1922 reveal how limiting selective weapon systems may create opportunities to exploit and circumvent treaty restrictions and may have the perverse effect of redirecting the arms competition. In short, the policy process may produce consequences that no one intended.[4] Those consequences may be perceived as positive or negative, but ultimately that is a matter of perception, judgment, and worldview, and arms control should not be pronounced irrelevant simply because redirection occurs. Nor should redirection per se be taken as evidence of bad faith on the part of signatories.

The redirection of military strategies and programs that occurred in the wake of the Washington treaties was driven by three different, yet interdependent, forces. First, redirection emerged as an unintended consequence of treaty provisions. For example, because the treaties freed up the hulls of large battle cruisers for conversion to carriers, the advantages of the large carrier, previously viewed as an inefficient allocation of aviation assets, could be exploited with unforeseen results. It can be argued that the treaties played a pivotal role in altering U.S. incentives for large carriers. Treaty provisions also altered British incentives for large cruisers. Although these vessels were of little strategic value, given Britain's global network of fueling and repair bases, other naval powers were using the cruiser loophole to build very large cruisers. Since heavy cruisers possess combat advantages over light cruisers, the British began producing these larger "treaty" cruisers as well. Redirection may initially be benign, yet ultimately lead to the development of new weapons, tactics, and strategies that are perceived as threats to another state's security. These developments may reinforce suspicions of ulterior motives, compel other states to respond in kind, and exacerbate international tensions. In this way, arms control may inadvertently fuel interstate rivalry.

Rechanneling may also be driven by technological and bureaucratic imperatives not necessarily connected to the arms control process and

---

3. Ibid., pp. 131–32.

4. For a general treatment of the perverse effects of policy processes, see Raymond Boudon, *The Unintended Consequences of Social Action* (London: Macmillan, 1982).

which defy political control.[5] Technology is dynamic and unpredictable; and since it is virtually impossible to separate military technology from its civilian counterpart, this method of unintentional redirection of military programs is difficult to prevent.[6] The Washington treaties encouraged weapons designers to develop more efficient designs and more advanced technologies to stay within battleship weight restrictions, developments that were later exploited in modernization programs. Even if arms control treaties do not stimulate a search for new technologies, they may accelerate tendencies in weapons procurement, development, and employment that have their genesis in the personnel and politics of pre-treaty days.

Finally, to the degree that rechanneling between the wars was intentional, it represented the attempts of military professionals to execute their strategies as effectively as possible given the constraints posed by the arms control system, not insincerity in their commitment to the treaty process. For example, the Imperial Navy, determined to compensate for the constraints battleship limits placed on their military strategy, refined the attrition stage in their war plan and built a force structure to execute it. The French were committed to developing the submarine as the centerpiece of their naval strategy. The United States built large cruisers to retain some power projection capability across the Pacific. These examples of intentional redirection resulted as military leaders sought to reduce vulnerabilities created when the constraints of arms control raised concerns about the ability to protect and defend national interests.

The context of redirection between the wars was shaped by three sets of circumstances: (1) asymmetries in political agendas, such as that between the United States and Japan; (2) asymmetries in military doctrine, such as that between Great Britain and France; (3) asymmetries in threat environment and strategic preference, such as that between Great Britain and the United States (see Table 6). These asymmetries influenced perceptions and judgments about whether rechanneling evinced abuse of the treaty system. To some extent, every signatory pushed the limits and at times transgressed the bounds of the treaties.

5. George, "The Economics of Arms Control," p. 123; Berkowitz, *Calculated Risks*, pp. 90–135.
6. See Berkowitz, *Calculated Risks*, for a discussion of the difficulties of controlling technology and how arms control can stimulate technological development.

Table 6   Patterns of rechanneling

Context of Redirection	Intentional Redirection	Unintentional Redirection
Asymmetries in political agendas (U.S. vs. Japan)	Japan: submarines and destroyer tactics	U.S.: large carriers
Asymmetries in doctrine (G.B. vs. France)	France: submarines	Britain: cruisers
Asymmetries in threat environment (G.B. vs. U.S.)	U.S.: large cruisers	Britain: large cruisers

Yet throughout the 1920s at least, the behavior of the treaty powers, overall, remained within tolerable limits.

TECHNOLOGICAL INNOVATION

In an arms control system, the development of new technologies or innovations in existing technologies may be sought and/or exploited to meet strategic requirements, given the constraints created by arms control. Although these developments may not be attributed exclusively to the arms control treaties, they demonstrate that technological innovation was often an unintentional by-product of treaty provisions, yet later exploited to compensate for arms control limitations.

In 1922, naval architects were designing battleships displacing between 42,000 and 49,000 tons, mounting a primary armament of eight to twelve 15- or 16-inch guns, with a speed of 20 to 25 knots. As requirements for firepower, protection, and mobility naturally rose, the minimum displacement necessary to satisfy those requirements increased, and the tendency was for battleships to grow in size. As Norman Friedman describes it, "The history of battleships is a history of growth despite cost."[7] With the Five Power treaty, for the first time standard displacement was curtailed,[8] but the development of aerial and

7. Norman Friedman, *Battleship Design and Development, 1905–1945* (New York: Mayflower Books, 1978), p. 39.

8. The Washington treaties defined standard displacement as "the displacement of the ship complete, fully manned, engined, and equipped ready for sea, including all armament and ammunition, equipment, outfit, provisions and fresh water for crew, miscellaneous stores and implements of every description that are intended to be carried in war, *but without fuel or reserve feed water on board.*" Displacement is given in English tons (1 ton = 2240 pounds). "Treaty for the

underwater weapon systems, and fire control for long ranges, remained unconstrained. These treaty provisions meant that future battleships would require greater horizontal and underwater protection, protective features that added substantial weight, within a reduced standard displacement.[9] An upper limit of 35,000 tons riveted the attention of naval engineers on weight-saving devices to accommodate the best set of performance characteristics within a restricted displacement, promoting the development of more efficient warship design and technology. "Throughout the period that the Washington Treaty remained in force, no consideration influenced warship design (more) in those countries which adhered strictly to its terms than the need to save weight."[10]

Processes initiated to save weight in accordance with treaty restrictions resulted in the development of weapons of superior strength and accuracy, in efforts to incorporate these new developments into existing ship designs, and ultimately to battleships with enhanced combat effectiveness. Weight-saving requirements encouraged experimentation with new shipbuilding materials. Because the treaties allowed the British to build the *Nelson* and *Rodney*, the first battleships built under treaty restrictions, the British were the first to experiment with weight-saving techniques for protection and structure that eventually became characteristic of all treaty battleships. The British introduced "D steel,"[11] an alloy 30 percent stronger than the steel used in previous ships, and this substantially reduced the weight of the hull. By 1927, experimentation with new alloys and processes led to the production of "all-steel" guns that were stronger, lighter, and less likely to droop with use. From this point on, the Royal Navy manufactured all-steel guns exclusively. Experiments in large caliber gun development, accelerating with developments in steel alloy, led eventually to the introduction of a new type of cordite propellant charge with superior ballistic accuracy. Finally, de-

Limitation of Armament," 1922, II.4. This definition was adopted to reduce the disparity between navies (like that of the United States) that needed long-range vessels and those (like Italy's) that required only a short-range capacity.

9. Friedman, *U.S. Battleships*, p. 209.

10. Roskill, *Naval Policy*, vol. 1, p. 332.

11. See Eric Lacroix, "The Development of the 'A Class' Cruisers in the Imperial Japanese Navy," Part 4, *Warship International* 18: 1 (1981): 75 n. 56; Berkowitz, *Calculated Risks*, p. 44; and Alan Raven and John Roberts, *British Battleships of World War II* (Annapolis: Naval Institute Press, 1976), pp. 160–61.

velopments in cordite explosives spurred experimentation in protection and stimulated capital ship modernization programs in the 1930s.[12]

Another very important outgrowth of the Five Power treaty was that modern capital ships became available for weapons tests. The lessons from these tests—that future battleships should have triple bottoms and that existing deck armor was inadequate—were incorporated into post-treaty building and modernization programs.[13] The big three maritime powers continued to pursue battleship innovation because their leaders were convinced that the battleship was, and would remain for the foreseeable future, the backbone of the fleet. Construction of fast, well-protected battleships proceeded within the confines of the Washington treaty system, gradually rendering the battle lines of the world obsolete. The battleships built in post-treaty years succeeded in merging the speed of the battle cruiser with the power and protection of the battleship. Because of technological advances, the trade-off between high speed and improved protection and firepower diminished. Post-treaty battle fleets were more flexible, and each battleship was relatively more powerful, possessing better gun platform stability and considerably improved fire-control systems. Paradoxically, greater cost and larger crews combined to make the loss of such ships a national disaster. In all, these new battleships "represented the culmination of a long trend in capital-ship design" that had proceeded in spite of and because of the Washington treaties.[14] Some have even gone so far as to argue that "the Washington Naval Treaty, despite the ten-year naval 'holiday' it enforced, altered the course of capital-ship design and exerted the most profound influence on battleship technology since the *Dreadnought*."[15]

Carrier design and development had its genesis in the experiences of World War I.[16] The General Board of the United States Navy, though a conservative, pro-battleship advisory body, recognized the value of carrier development as early as 1919, but strict budgetary constraints impeded carrier authorizations. Throughout the 1920s, carriers were few

---

12. See Raven and Roberts, *British Battleships*, pp. 160–65.

13. Friedman, *U.S. Battleships*, p. 186.

14. William H. Garzke, Jr., and Robert O. Dulin, Jr., *Battleships: Axis and Neutral Battleships in World War II* (Annapolis: Naval Institute Press, 1985), pp. 12–13.

15. Ibid., p. 5.

16. For background on carrier development, see Norman Polmar, *Aircraft Carriers: A Graphic History of Carrier Aviation and Its Influence on World Events* (London: Macdonald, 1969); Geoffrey Till, *Air Power and the Royal Navy, 1914–1945* (London: Jane's, 1979); Belote and Belote, *Titans of the Sea*; and Norman Friedman, *Carrier Air Power* (Annapolis: Naval Institute Press, 1981).

in number and mostly experimental. Even in the 1930s, the development of the carrier paralleled battleship modernization, in large part due to the technical limitations of carrier aircraft, which only reinforced the pro-battleship sentiment of many admirals until after the battles of the Coral Sea and Midway. In the United States, carrier development evolved through war games conducted at the Naval War College and through the full-scale fleet exercises of the 1930s. Although the personalities and politics involved were critical to the process,[17] the naval limitation treaties influenced carrier development in three important ways.

First, the constraints of the Washington treaties created an important incentive for carrier development in the United States. After the First World War, U.S. naval planners confronted a new dimension in naval warfare in the airplane and the paradox of defending Far Eastern commitments with inadequate power projection capabilities. Although carriers were limited at Washington, no limits were placed on land-based air forces. Yet by restricting the fortification of insular possessions in the western Pacific, the Five Power treaty denied the U.S. Navy the advanced fleet bases necessary to operate land-based aircraft in the western Pacific. The Japanese Navy, unlike its Western counterparts, was able to make extensive use of its long-range land-based bombers by operating them from the island chains mandated to Japan at the end of World War I.[18] Fleet aviation, centered on the carrier concept, offered a way for the United States to remedy this deficiency within treaty constraints. As Charles Melhorn puts it, in the 1920s "the U.S. Navy made prodigious strides in developing its fleet aviation, and by 1929 led all other powers in this category. It would not be difficult then to draw the conclusion that there was a deliberate and calculated effort on the part of the U.S. Navy in the interwar years to resolve its problems through the medium of this new weapons system."[19]

Second, the Washington treaty limits on total and maximum unit tonnage imposed strict choices on naval designers. Restrictions on carrier displacement made it impossible for designers to provide sufficient flight-deck armor to repel dive-bomb attacks. When dive-bombing was

17. See Stephen Peter Rosen, "New Ways of War: Understanding Military Innovation," *International Security* 13 (Summer 1988): 134–68.

18. Friedman, *Carrier Air Power*, p. 53.

19. Melhorn, *Two-Block Fox*, p. 5; see also Roskill, *Naval Policy*, vol. 1, pp. 58, 530, on the U.S. lead in fleet aviation.

introduced in the mid-1920s,[20] aircraft, for the first time, could reliably hit rapidly maneuvering targets like warships. Dive-bombers, however, were unable to generate sufficient diving speed for their bombs to penetrate thick deck armor and destroy capital ships, though they could wreck and disable a carrier's flight deck.[21] An upper displacement of 23,000 tons permitted a reasonable level of underwater and hull protection, but protecting the ship's airplane operating facilities proved infeasible.[22] This was one important consideration in the evolution of carrier tactics and in the decision to detach the carrier from the battle fleet and adopt a doctrine of preemptively destroying the enemy carrier. Carriers initially operated close to the battle fleet in reconnaissance and spotting roles, controlling the air over gunnery engagements. A series of major fleet exercises in the late 1920s and early 1930s revealed the ease of spotting the battle fleet from the air, demonstrating the ease of destroying any carrier operating with the battle fleet. U.S. carrier doctrine, therefore, called for the carrier to operate independently as long as opposing carriers were a threat.[23] The U.S. Navy and the Japanese Imperial Navy were in the forefront in detaching carriers for independent operations. Both, however, remained preoccupied with carrier vulnerability. According to Till, this explains why the U.S. Navy did not develop carrier task forces in the 1930s, and why as late as 1942 the U.S. Navy "still held that carriers should act independently, to evade the enemy, and that even as many as two carriers in company represented a great risk."[24] The Japanese and British appear to have been readier to operate carriers in company. Along with these tactical developments, speed became a highly valued characteristic for protection against the fast 10,000-ton treaty cruisers that could harm any carrier operating independently. "The threat of numerous heavy cruisers would continue to be a factor in carrier design through the early part of World War II."[25]

Third, and perhaps most important, the treaties freed up the hulls of large battle cruisers for conversion to carriers. The Washington Confer-

20. On developments in dive-bombing, see Melhorn, *Two-Block Fox*, pp. 110–11, and Pelz, *Race to Pearl Harbor*, pp. 30–31.

21. Norman Friedman, *U.S. Aircraft Carriers: An Illustrated Design History* (Annapolis: Naval Institute Press, 1983), pp. 8, 11.

22. Ibid., p. 66.

23. Operating carriers in groups required developing the means for carriers to protect themselves against surprise air attack. Ibid., p. 8.

24. Till, *Air Power and the Royal Navy*, pp. 165–66.

25. Friedman, *U.S. Aircraft Carriers*, p. 62.

ence led directly to the second generation of aircraft carriers, seven vessels that were the products of capital ship conversion.[26] In the early 1920s, aircraft made minimal demands on flight deck space and carriers displacing as little as 10,000 tons could operate effectively. In the United States, however, the first two fleet carriers were the *Lexington* and *Saratoga*, two very large and very fast vessels, whose size and inherent capability were "fixed by the battle-cruiser origins of their hulls."[27] Plans for ships of much the size and speed of these large carriers had evolved prior to the Washington Conference but given the pro-battleship disposition of the navy, the chances were slim that they would have been built. At the time, it remained unclear whether these converted battle cruisers represented the best possible investment in tonnage given treaty limits, and tremendous debate ensued over the relative merits of large and small carriers. Equating flight-deck area with airplane operating capacity, the U.S. Navy determined that many small carriers would yield a larger total flightdeck area than a few large carriers so that "the smaller the individual carriers, the larger their total operating capacity."[28] In 1926, the *Lexington* and *Saratoga* remained under construction, precluding an operational comparison of large and small carriers. So when the Bureau of Construction and Repair proposed building a 13,000-ton carrier, five such permissible under the Washington treaties, the General Board approved the *Ranger* in an effort to achieve "the smallest effective carrier, which under the Treaty could be built in the largest numbers and so support the largest possible seaborne naval air force."[29] Operations with the *Ranger*, along with the smaller converted collier *Langley*, soon demonstrated the severe limits imposed by a small flight deck. The *Ranger* proved wholly ineffective during World War II.[30]

Initially, U.S. naval designers regretted the immense size of the converted carriers, vessels far larger than necessary to accommodate the small air groups anticipated in the near future. Their size also dramati-

26. The first generation of carriers were those outfitted between 1917 and the mid-1920s. They were, for the most part, converted cruisers, merchant ships, and auxiliaries. Only Britain's *Hermes* and Japan's *Hosho* were specifically laid as aircraft carriers. Polmar, *Aircraft Carriers*, p. 51.

27. Friedman, *U.S. Aircraft Carriers*, p. 7.

28. Friedman, *Carrier Air Power*, pp. 9–10.

29. Ibid., p. 39.

30. Friedman, *U.S. Aircraft Carriers*, pp. 44–66; Melhorn, *Two-Block Fox*, pp. 108–9. Treaty limits still diverted attention to carriers below 10,000 tons that were not carriers by treaty definition, particularly in the Japanese Navy where the overall treaty limit was virtually consumed by the converted capital ship hulls.

cally reduced the total number of carriers that could be built within total displacement limitations. Yet once in service, the large carriers exhibited such unsuspected advantages as their ability to operate in nearly all types of weather and deploy large air strikes from a single deck load. Large hulls also imposed less restrictions on individual aircraft characteristics and aircraft development and turned out to be readily adaptable to rapidly evolving aircraft and amenable to considerable technical growth over the entire interwar period.[31] Their tremendous size permitted experimentation with new carrier tactics that heralded changes in the role of the U.S. Fleet between the wars.[32]

In sum, "by the accident of the existence of suitable hulls for conversion, the United States, Great Britain, and Japan each obtained two rather large carriers, and at least the U.S. and Japanese navies began to experiment with the type of mass carrier attacks which proved so successful during World War II."[33] From exercises with the Lexington and Saratoga, the U.S. Navy learned the value of large air groups, and this created a consensus on building large carriers in the future. The large carriers also proved to be substantially faster than the rest of the battle line, inclining them to operate independently with a screen of heavy cruisers. These tactics were explored in 1929 during Fleet Problem IX, and the concept of the independent carrier task force—built around a single carrier screened by heavy cruisers—became well established by the early 1930s.[34] As in the United States, the advent of very fast, powerful carriers, a direct product of the Washington treaties, strongly influenced Japanese tactical doctrine and aircraft design. Because of the large carrier's ability to strike at very long range, the Japanese emphasized range in aircraft specifications during the 1930s.[35]

FORCE-STRUCTURE CHANGE

The failure to limit ancillary warships (cruisers, destroyers, and submarines) at Washington created an avenue for postwar building. Between

31. Friedman, *Carrier Air Power*, p. 39.
32. Friedman, *U.S. Aircraft Carriers*, p. 7.
33. Friedman, *Carrier Air Power*, p. 9.
34. Ibid., p. 39.
35. Ibid., p. 54.

1922 and 1929, France had twenty-one submarines completed and forty-seven building, Italy eighteen completed and fourteen building, Japan eighteen completed and seven building, Great Britain seven completed and sixteen building, and the United States one completed and five building. In the cruiser category between 1922 and 1927, Britain had eleven built and building, Japan twelve, and the United States, constrained by domestic pressures, only two. In 1928, however, Congress passed a bill for construction of fifteen cruisers and in 1929, the cruiser bill became law. Qualitatively, the maximum limit set for cruisers at Washington, as in the battleship class, eventually became a minimum standard for post-Conference cruisers.[36] Accounts of the interwar naval accords frequently refer to an "auxiliary arms race" that developed after the Washington Conference established qualitative and quantitative limits on battleship construction. Roskill argues that arms limitation stimulated interest in a new, larger class of cruisers and that 10,000 tons, rather than being an upper limit actually became a standard for new cruiser construction. Friedman claims that by limiting the number of battleships, the large 8-inch gun cruiser became a kind of "junior capital ship."[37] Emphasis on the construction of ancillary warships did occur after the Washington Naval Conference, but the process was complex, varied from state to state depending on strategic requirements and domestic political constraints, and was more often than not driven by the need to round out postwar fleets. The perception persisted in all the treaty states, however, that a renewed arms race was under way.

Treaty restrictions exerted the greatest practical effect on the U.S. Navy, since its extensive power projection requirements were severely hampered by a dearth of fortified bases. The Washington treaties actually created an opportunity for the United States to do what naval force planners had been advocating since the days of Theodore Roosevelt, namely, correct critical deficiencies in ancillary categories. The cruiser program received first priority in order to round out an unbalanced fleet as well as to keep pace with cruiser construction in other post-treaty navies. Although the British had an undisputed lead in cruisers in the postwar years, by 1926 it appeared as if the Japanese were attempting to compensate for capital ship inferiority with cruiser construction. Given

36. Chaput, *Disarmament*, pp. 145–47.
37. Norman Friedman, *U.S. Cruisers: An Illustrated Design History* (Annapolis: Naval Institute Press, 1984), p. 111.

these pressures and the General Board's belief in Mahan's concept of the decisive fleet encounter, quantity production of 8-inch, 10,000-ton cruisers received top priority in the U.S. Navy. The General Board was convinced that "successful transit to the western Pacific would avail nothing if the fleet, when it arrived, was not properly constituted to fight. . . . There was no such thing as a swift battle cruiser in the U.S. Navy, whereas Japan had four. Some form of offsetting speed and gun-power was absolutely necessary for the climactic fleet encounter that would pit type against type, and where loss of balance in fleet composition could be fatal."[38] Domestic politics, however, continued to constrain U.S. building programs. Congress successfully obstructed cruiser construction for nearly a decade. When negotiations at the 1927 Geneva Conference collapsed, the U.S. Navy requested twenty-five 10,000-ton cruisers to match Japan's, nine flotilla leaders, thirty-two submarines, and five aircraft carriers. This program was scaled back to fifteen cruisers and one carrier, and Congress did not pass the "Fifteen Cruiser" bill until March 1928.[39] No cruisers were built until 1929.

The Washington treaties, by restricting base fortifications, emphasized a need for vessels with a long cruising radius. Only by increasing displacement was it possible to provide stable gun platforms and adequate storage facilities for food, fuel, and living quarters on long cruises.[40] Coupled with a traditional emphasis on firepower, U.S. cruisers were by nature "heavy" cruisers. The qualitative cruiser limits set at Washington—10,000 tons displacement and 8-inch maximum armament—became the minimum requirements of the U.S. Navy for strategic reasons as well as for their designation as treaty limits. U.S. naval authorities, however, maintained that

> the 10,000-ton cruiser . . . is an outcome of the insistence of Great Britain at the time of the Washington Conference on the retention of her Hawkins-class, which approached this tonnage and had 7.5″ guns. Our nearest gun being the 8″, we agreed on 10,000-ton 8″ gun ships as the maximum for this category. There was probably no study made by our Navy, at the time, of the results of these limitations. Afterwards, when General Board hearings were held preliminarily to designing and building the

38. Melhorn, Two-Block Fox, p. 108.

39. Robin Higham, Armed Forces in Peacetime: Britain, 1918–1940, A Case Study (Hamden, Conn.: Archon Books, 1962), p. 130.

40. Andrade, "United States Naval Policy," p. 86.

first of our new cruisers, Nos. 24 and 25, the natural decision was reached to utilize the maximum tonnage and caliber of guns.[41]

Friedman adds that the cruiser fleet the United States took into World War II "was designed at least as much to fit treaty restrictions as to fit any concept of naval tactics." He offers the example of the 6-inch cruisers, the Brooklyns. According to Friedman, there would never have been any had there not been a London Naval Treaty of 1930. The treaty limited the Japanese to twelve 8-inch cruisers, which had all been built by 1931. So Japan's naval general staff authorized the design and construction of the "B" class, or 6-inch gun cruisers of the Mogami class and Tone class.[42] The Mogami light cruiser diverged from all previous designs and incorporated electric welding and light alloys to save a maximum amount of weight. Designed to fight heavy cruisers, the Mogami was armored like a heavy cruiser to withstand 8-inch shells and its 6-inch triple turrets could be rapidly replaced with twin 8-inch turrets in wartime.[43] This in fact happened in 1939.[44] The Mogami was superior to any British or U.S. light cruiser and nearly equal to the Royal Navy's County-class heavy cruisers. In response to this heavy "light cruiser," the British laid the Southampton-class light cruisers, the United States, the Brooklyn-class.[45] The U.S. Navy quite suddenly was "obligated to build 6-in-gun cruisers, whether or not it considered them of optimum use in a military sense."[46]

In Japan, the building of ancillary warships proceeded at an increased pace after the conference. In February and March of 1922, the Japanese authorized the construction of eighteen vessels not limited by the treaty "to compensate for the halting of construction of capital ships . . . and to maintain activity in the shipyards."[47] Between 1922 and 1930, the

41. Memorandum, 26 January 1930, Comment on Tentative Plan [of the American Delegation] of 27 January 1930, Department of the Navy, Records of the General Board of the Navy, Study No. 438-1, National Archives, Washington, D.C.
42. Lacroix, "A Class Cruisers," Part 4, p. 75.
43. Eric Lacroix, "The Development of the 'A Class' Cruisers in the Imperial Japanese Navy," Part 5, Warship International 18:4 (1981): 323.
44. Anthony Preston, Cruisers (London: Bison Books, 1980), p. 117.
45. Ibid., pp. 109–10; Friedman, U.S. Cruisers, pp. 194–200, 217; Alan Raven and John Roberts, British Cruisers of World War II (Annapolis: Naval Institute Press, 1980), p. 172.
46. Friedman, U.S. Cruisers, pp. 5, 183.
47. Eric Lacroix, "The Development of the 'A Class' Cruisers in the Imperial Japanese Navy," Part 2, Warship International 16:1 (1979): 42.

Japanese had authorized and building twenty-one cruisers[48] and by December 1929, they had completed four 7,100-ton cruisers mounting six 8-inch guns and almost completed eight 10,000-ton cruisers mounting ten 8-inch guns. Since the U.S. cruiser program was still largely on paper, the disparity between the actual relative strength of the Japanese and U.S. fleets and the relative strength set up by the ratio system at Washington had increased dramatically.

The Japanese also made important strides in the technological development of heavy cruisers, governed by building guidelines officially laid down on February 3, 1923. This "Second Change of Policy" was a response to the "restrictions of the Washington Treaty, American shipbuilding policy and the differences between Japan and America over the extension of military bases in the Pacific."[49] Accordingly, future fleet strength required 9 battleships, 3 carriers, 40 cruisers, and 70 submarines. This policy was altered on June 3, 1936, only after Japan had denounced the Washington treaty and refused to sign the second London Naval Treaty in January 1936. The "Third Change of Policy" envisioned, by 1945, a fleet strength of 12 battleships, 10 carriers, 20 "A class" cruisers, 8 "B class" cruisers, 13 squadron leaders, 96 destroyers, and 70 submarines.

The Royal Navy, with an undisputed lead in cruiser strength at the end of World War I, had to maintain this superiority to defend both imperial lines of communication and European interests. The British could not afford to let the French build submarines without responding with antitorpedo craft, and France would only accept limits on submarine forces as part of a general disarmament settlement limiting land forces as well. Defining commerce protecting vessels—6-inch cruisers—as those over and above battle fleet needs, the British wanted "exception to the principles laid down in regard to cruisers for which the geographical position of the British Empire created a particular need not relative to or dependent upon the naval armaments of other Powers."[50]

While the British had one eye on a potentially destabilizing Franco-British building competition, they were simultaneously committed to "battle fleet parity" with the United States, or equality in the 8-inch

---

48. Robert A. Hoover, *Arms Control: The Interwar Naval Limitation Agreements* (Denver: University of Denver Monograph Series in World Affairs, 1980), p. 69.

49. Hans Lengerer, "Akagi and Kaga," Part 1, *Warship* 24 (October 1982): 127–28.

50. Chaput, *Disarmament*, p. 157.

offensive cruiser type used to establish command of the sea. The British wanted freedom to build in response to the submarine programs of non-European states that in wartime could threaten imperial dominions and lines of communication and were prepared to concede to the United States, in return, equality in 6-inch cruisers. The U.S. Navy, however, refused to expend scarce resources building cruisers for which it had no use. Although small cruisers with a reduced cruising radius were sufficient for the Royal Navy with its network of global fueling and repair bases, the U.S. Navy required larger 8-inch cruisers for extended fleet operations in the Pacific.

The cruiser controversy continued to be a major source of tension throughout the 1920s. At the 1927 Geneva Disarmament Conference, Britain, demanding cruiser limitation by category, clashed with the United States, which demanded limitation by total tonnage with each free to choose which type of cruisers to build within a given global tonnage. In the end, failure to limit cruisers at Washington left the British no choice but to build 10,000-ton cruisers to keep pace with other navies, since heavy cruisers usually prevailed in confrontations with light cruisers. The relative defensive capability of 8-inch and 6-inch gun cruisers, assuming the same armor, became a function of the vulnerability of each to opposing guns. A large part of each ship was vulnerable to 6-inch gunfire, whereas a small part was fairly well protected against 6-inch gunfire but not against 8-inch gunfire. Even for these parts, however, the vulnerability of the two calibers approached equality at long ranges, though the range of the 8-inch gun exceeded that of the 6-inch gun.[51] By 1924, the British had announced a program for fifty-two cruisers, eight of the type that "under the Washington Treaty, has become the standard type adopted by all great naval Powers, namely, vessels of 10,000 tons armed with 8-inch guns."[52] To maintain superiority over other navies and reach a total of seventy modern cruisers, the Royal Navy further called for the construction of seventeen 10,000-ton cruisers (the Kent class). The 1924–25 Building Program was to include eight of these but with the assumption of power

51. For operations involving encounters with hostile destroyers, the 6-inch gun ship was superior to the 8-inch gun ship, as the rate of fire of the former was nearly three times that of the latter. Record of the General Board of the [U.S.] Navy, Study No. 438-1 (Serial No. 1427-2) LDB, pp. 5–6. See also Friedman, *U.S. Cruisers*, pp. 3–4, 112, 166.

52. First Lord of the Admiralty Amery, quoted in Chaput, *Disarmament*, p. 149 n. 2; Higham, *Armed Forces in Peacetime*, p. 127.

by Labor in 1924, the planned program of eight ships was scaled down to five. In 1927, the Admiralty proceeded again with designs for 8-inch, 10,000-ton cruisers, specifically to match Japanese building in this category.[53]

For the French, concentration on ancillary warship construction was consistent with a pre-Conference building policy that rejected the doctrine of battleship supremacy. Because the Washington Conference reinforced the futility of relying on British and U.S. security guarantees in Europe,[54] the French steadily built submarines and cruisers to match the combined totals of the Italian and German fleets. Coupled with the humiliation suffered by being relegated to a status of parity with the Italians, the treaties created and reaffirmed French incentives for accelerated post-Conference construction of light surface vessels. Not surprisingly, French building stimulated Italian desires to maintain parity. Between 1922 and 1935, the Italians laid down 138,900 tons of cruisers, the French 143,250 tons. By 1935, each had seven 10,000-ton treaty cruisers.[55]

EXPLOITATION OF LOOPHOLES AND AMBIGUITIES

Loopholes and ambiguous treaty provisions are a natural consequence of the process of treaty drafting, for negotiators cannot be expected to possess the foresight or technical expertise to anticipate the many ways a treaty can be evaded. Honest differences in interpretation may reflect different notions of security or different strategic doctrines. Signatories may only be able to agree on wording so vague that it invites circumvention. Or, in some cases, signatories may purposely write ambiguities or loopholes into treaties with the intent of exploiting them later. For example, the London Naval Treaty of 1930 created a category of small surface ships between 600 and 2,000 tons mounting guns of up to 6.1-inch caliber, absent torpedo tubes, and incapable of exceeding 20 knots. Admiral Pratt, head of the U.S. delegation, conceded that he

53. Raven and Roberts, *British Cruisers*, pp. 109–10, 130.

54. The Locarno Pact, or Treaty of Mutual Guarantee, concluded in 1925, guaranteed the inviolability of the Rhine boundary. However, the French were dissatisfied with the vagueness of Britain's obligations, and the agreement failed to curtail France's building program.

55. Burns and Urquidi, *Disarmament in Perspective*, vol. 3, pp. 158–64.

envisioned this unlimited gunboat or sloop category as a way to over-come restrictions on total cruiser and destroyer tonnage. Pratt even pushed for the higher speed of 20 knots rather than 18 knots to render these vessels suitable for operations with the 20-knot U.S. battle line. "Pratt justified two knots on the ground that ships of that speed were required by the Coast Guard to hunt down rumrunners. Without them the Coast Guard would have to use scarce destroyer tonnage, as it was then doing. It is clear from a 1932 General Board hearing that this explanation was an excuse, a means of evading a treaty restriction Pratt considered excessive."[56]

Ambiguities

Ambiguities in treaty provisions may result from asymmetries in force structure, threat environment, or strategic preference. All three en-hance the difficulty of defining a "currency" or "unit of account"—"a measure of the things that the treaty actually limits which is both tech-nically feasible to monitor and politically acceptable."[57] For example, the Washington treaties failed to reconcile British requirements for light cruisers with U.S. demands for heavy cruisers. The Pacific outlook of the United States failed to take into account British difficulties in Europe, while the British exploited asymmetries in bases by demanding symmetrical arms reduction. The Royal Navy could expect to operate within hundreds of miles of its bases in the event of a Pacific war. The U.S. Navy would have to cross far greater distances simply to engage, and recross them for refueling and repair. As one member of the Gen-eral Board observed, "in effect, bases equal more ships."[58]

"Parity" is an inherently ambiguous measure of comparison for stabi-lizing an arms competition, and it in fact implies rivalry. "It means that neither country is to have a bigger navy than the other; but it also means that each country must have a navy as large as the other."[59] Although the system of naval ratios established at Washington was based fundamentally on Anglo-American parity, it was not clear

56. Friedman, *U.S. Cruisers*, p. 167.
57. Berkowitz, *Calculated Risks*, p. 50.
58. Friedman, *U.S. Battleships*, pp. 210–11.
59. Quoted in Chaput, *Disarmament*, p. 165, from Lord Grey of Falladon in a letter to the [London] *Times*, August 11, 1927.

whether "parity" meant equal arms or equal security. Britain's one-power standard reflected this ambiguity, defining battle fleet requirements as relative and commerce protection requirements as absolute. Because the United States regarded even defensive needs as relative and refused to limit cruisers by type, the Royal Navy felt pressured to keep pace with the United States in 8-inch cruisers, even though British strategic requirements were better served by 6-inch cruisers. Britain and the United States did not disagree on the principle of parity, but they failed to find a method to apply the principle to different circumstances and needs. From the British perspective, the issue was only exacerbated by the building programs of the French and Italians. By establishing parity between the navies of France and Italy, the Washington treaties gave form and substance to a competition that had not formerly existed, and failure to limit ancillary warships at Washington left both free to concentrate on building torpedo craft, a very real threat to British lines of communication.

Ratios were also an ambiguous measure of relative strength. An outgrowth of the materialist school of the late nineteenth century and First World War,[60] ratio systems focused on instruments rather than on policy and strategy. They were based on the "doubtful presumption that any nation would withdraw all its forces from all areas to attack one opponent." Ratio systems failed to factor in differences in national defensive needs and avoided such important questions as, "What is the political situation armaments must meet, who are the enemies and allies, and under what conditions, and who will in the circumstances be allies, and who will be neutrals?"[61] Finally, the effectiveness of tonnage ratios was questionable when new alloys were being introduced that permitted significant reductions in weight without corresponding reductions in capability.

Different interpretations may result from differing yet equally valid expectations, as well as from ambiguous treaty provisions. Hughes's proposal at Washington assumed the 5:5:3 ratio in capital ships would be extended to all categories of vessels. The "extension principle" made sense given the United States's economic and domestic political con-

60. See "Offense and Defense: The Historical and Materiel Schools," in Bernard Semmel, *Liberalism and Naval Strategy: Ideology, Interest, and Sea Power During the Pax Britannica* (Boston: Allen & Unwin, 1986), pp. 134–51.

61. Norman Angell, "Why the Disarmament Deadlock?" *The Nineteenth Century and After* 116 (July 1934): 16–28; quoted in Higham, *Armed Forces in Peacetime*, pp. 118–19.

straints. It was an assumption, however, that Japanese naval planners did not share. In post-Conference years, Congress and the American public came to view the Washington treaties themselves as evidence that political competition had been defused. The Japanese were also faithful, but more narrowly to the letter of the treaties. The Japanese took advantage of the fact that no quantitative limits were placed on ancillary warship construction to concentrate building in those categories. As a result, "instead of the 10:7 treaty ratio of U.S. to Japanese naval forces, Japan enjoyed at least equality, if not superiority" between the wars.[62] In 1934, the president of the Naval War College estimated the cruiser ratio between the United States and Japan "in tonnage only 4:3 . . . and in numbers 1:1, both fleets possessing thirty-seven cruisers."[63] Variant interpretations and expectations undermined in fact the principle of the ratio system established at Washington.

The Modernization Loophole

Military programs were redirected in post-Conference years toward improving the fighting quality of existing vessels. The Washington treaties permitted a certain amount of battleship modernization, such as the installation of anti-aircraft defenses and blisters or bulges, streamlined cofferdam structures built outside the original hull to keep torpedo explosions away from the vitals of the ship. The British had bargained to prohibit alteration in battleship main armament. Since they had modernized their own battleships by elevating guns for greater range, the Royal Navy wanted to prevent others from doing the same. The British also disputed the legality of substituting oil for coal fuel. By narrowly interpreting the battleship modernization clause, the Royal Navy hoped the arms control system would preserve British existing superiority over its U.S. counterpart without a costly modernization program.

During the 1920s, however, the U.S. Navy stretched the modernization clause to its limits in order to secure qualitative parity with British capital ships. The U.S. Navy embarked on a major battle fleet modernization program and upgraded its forces in a manner wholly distinct

62. Robin Ranger, "Learning from the Naval Arms Control Experience," *Washington Quarterly* 10 (Summer 1987): 50–51.

63. Friedman, *U.S. Cruisers*, p. 218.

from its British and Japanese counterparts. By 1929, the U.S. battle fleet was qualitatively superior to the Grand Fleet. U.S. guns outranged their British counterparts. The U.S. Navy was prepared to fight at greater distances due to the use of spotter aircraft. Finally, all U.S. battleships had been converted from coal to oil.

The Washington treaties were designed to reduce navies to defensive forces by reducing fighting capability. The success of this effort rested in part on the limited ability of coal fired ships to operate far from home bases. Oil, however, significantly increased the operating radius of ships, and this could undermine the defensive balance established by battleship ratios. Despite British protests, the United States converted its battleships from coal to oil, thereby enhancing speed and increased cruising range from 7,500 miles to as much as 12,000 miles if oil were stored in the blisters.[64]

The General Board justified these conversions by ruling in 1922 that the word "blister" had been used to "limit changes outside the hull" and this did not preclude changes internal to the hull if such changes decreased vulnerability to air and underwater attack. "Almost any internal modification could be justified in this manner," such as replacement of boilers or conversion to oil burning.[65] In addition, U.S. naval leaders pointed out differences between the French and English versions of the treaties. "The French idea versus the English idea carried with it the implication that the protection was not only external through 'bulge', but could be internal through the word 'caissons'. This was a very natural implication on [the French] part because of their system of torpedo protection." Given that the "French version . . . used terms of French naval architecture of long standing, . . . [it] therefore instead of being the weaker version . . . is perhaps for that reason a stronger version than the British."[66]

Although the U.S. Navy would not reach actual parity with the Royal Navy until 1942, the Grand Fleet would still have a decisive advantage because after Jutland, the British had modernized their battleships by adding blisters and deck armor, increasing gun elevation,

---

64. George T. Davis, *A Navy Second to None: The Development of Modern American Naval Policy* (New York: Harcourt, Brace, 1940), p. 313.

65. Friedman, *U.S. Battleships*, p. 189.

66. Correspondence of July 2, 1925, and July 14, 1925, Subject File 1906–1935, Box 4, Jones Papers (Rear Admiral Hilary P. Jones), Library of Congress, Manuscript Division, Naval Historical Foundation Collection, Washington, D.C.

and improving fire control. At 20 degrees elevation, British guns had longer range, greater penetrating power at medium ranges, and hence, the Royal Navy could fight at extreme distances more effectively.[67] A Naval War College study recommended the U.S. Navy install heavier deck protection on battleships and increase the maximum elevation of the main battery to 30 degrees. The British protested, claiming elevation of the main battery a violation of the "reconstruction clause" forbidding "alterations in side armor, in calibre, number or general type of mounting of main armament."[68] Elevation would require extensive alterations in gun mountings and turrets, constituting an alteration in general armament. The United States, however, countered that reconstruction included improvement in fire control. Increased gun elevation, to take advantage of new fire controls, was therefore permissible, and the United States increased the maximum elevation of the main battery guns on their battleships from 15 to 30 degrees. The British interpreted the reconstruction clause narrowly to maintain an existing military advantage without embarking on a major modernization program. The United States interpreted the clause loosely to escape being locked into a position of inferiority.

Finally, in one of the most flagrant treaty violations of the 1920s, the United States exploited the battleship modernization clause to enhance carrier power. The Five Power treaty permitted the conversion of battle cruisers, destined to be scrapped, into aircraft carriers. The upper limit of new carriers had been established at 27,000 tons, though carriers converted from existing capital ship tonnage were permitted to displace up to 33,000 tons. Once converted, however, battle cruiser carriers displaced 36,000 tons, down from their original battle cruiser displacement of 43,500 tons. The modernization clause for existing capital ships permitted the addition of up to 3,000 tons in protection—deck armor and blisters. The United States argued that this clause should also apply to capital ships converted to carriers. Hence, the *Lexington* and *Saratoga*, the first two U.S. fleet carriers, were officially listed as displacing 33,000 tons, though in fact they displaced 35,689 and 35,544 tons.

67. Andrade, "United States Naval Policy," p. 94. On the gun elevation issue, also see Bywater, *Navies and Nations*, pp. 164–71, and Davis, *A Navy Second To None*, pp. 311–32.
68. "Treaties for the Limitation of Armament," 1922, II 3.1(d).

The Carrier Loophole

Prior to the Washington Conference, naval bureaucracies had been concentrating their energies on developing more powerful battleships to enhance combat effectiveness. Afterward, attention was redirected to the development of ancillary vessels and airpower because the treaties stimulated not only assessment of new weapons but reassessment of tactics and strategy for the use of all naval weapons. For the United States, the nonfortification clause of the Five Power treaty prevented the use of bases in the western Pacific. The carrier, however, could facilitate the projection of power even without island bases and revolutionize the offensive capabilities of navies operating over vast ocean expanses. For the Japanese, the carrier could compensate for an unfavorable balance in capital ship tonnage. Primitive aircraft carriers had emerged during the First World War. From then on, carrier design developed rapidly with several carriers in service abroad and others projected or under construction by 1921. Though carrier development was still in the experimental stages, the first ship designed as a carrier was completed in 1922. Although under ordinary circumstances the battleship admirals dominating every navy would never have chosen the carrier over the battleship, the potentialities of airpower coupled with capital ship limitations created incentives for the development of aircraft carriers and the use of airpower for offensive as well as defensive tasks.

Indirectly, aircraft were limited at Washington through restrictions placed on carriers. The original U.S. proposal extended the 5:5:3 ratio to carriers with total replacement tonnage restrictions of 80,000 tons for the United States and Britain, 48,000 for Japan, and 28,000 for France and Italy. These were revised upward to new tonnage restrictions of 135,000, 81,000, and 60,000 tons. These new totals cleared the way for acceptance of a 27,000-ton restriction on individual carriers, which had initially been rejected because it confined each navy to so few carriers. The final ratio was a close approximation to the capital ship formula: 5:5:3:2:2, with all carriers in service or under construction classed as experimental and not included in total tonnage restrictions. The U.S. delegation, however, anticipated congressional opposition to funding. Every naval building program since 1918 submitted by the General Board to Congress had included one or more carriers, and none had been authorized. On advice from the Navy Department, the U.S. delegation proposed a "carrier conversion" clause for the Washington treaty to permit them to convert two battle cruisers, destined to be scrapped, into carriers. The proposal was accepted, and other delegations seized the opportunity to press for minor concessions.[69]

One loophole not exploited to the degree it might have been was the building of carriers below the minimum displacement specified. The Washington treaties defined an aircraft carrier as "a vessel of war in excess of 10,000 tons standard displacement, designed for the specific and exclusive purpose of carrying aircraft." Individual carrier tonnage was limited to 27,000 tons with total carrier tonnage for each signatory also restricted. Although at the time it was not deemed feasible to construct a carrier of 10,000 tons or less, this loophole encouraged some experimentation with light fleet carriers. As early as 1919, the Japanese had already laid the *Hosho*, which displaced 7,470 tons, demonstrating the possibility of the light carrier concept. Under treaty and budget constraints, the *Ryujo*, at 8,000 tons, was laid in 1929 and launched in 1931.[70] Designed with the intent of evading treaty limitations on carrier tonnage, the *Ryujo* was designed with only one hanger deck. It proved to be an inefficient fighting unit, however, because carriers require a minimum number of aircraft not feasible within the design limitations of the *Ryujo*. An extra hangar deck was eventually added, increasing displacement to 10,600 tons.

The U.S. Navy began exploring the light carrier concept as early as 1920 with the flight-deck cruiser, or a flight-deck built on a cruiser, included in cruiser tonnage, and as a result, not regulated by Washington carrier limits. In the early 1930s, the flight-deck cruiser was viewed as a way to increase the number of aircraft at sea by circumventing treaty limits.[71] Though the General Board wanted cruisers and would not approve their completion as light carriers, by 1927 the Board and the navy as a whole began to appreciate the value of naval aviation. To no small degree, this was due to the U.S. lead in what appeared to be the most effective aerial antiship weapon, the dive-bomber.[72] The Bu-

69. The British wanted to increase the antitorpedo protection of certain ships with blisters or artificial hulls. The French and Italians wanted to increase the size of battleship guns to 16-inch. The British and Japanese also reserved the right to make their own carrier conversions. Melhorn, *Two-Block Fox*, pp. 84–85.

70. Polmar, *Aircraft Carriers*, p. 68.

71. Friedman, *U.S. Cruisers*, p. 174.

72. The dive-bomber had the agility of a fighter, could deliver more high explosive with greater accuracy than the torpedo plane, and its compactness—two-thirds the dimensions of current bomber models—meant that it could lift an equal bomb load in half the deck space.

reau of Aeronautics began pressing for a carrier whose upper limit was 14,000 tons, and in 1927, the General Board recommended five 13,800-ton flush deck carriers. It was a short step to see the light carrier as a means to nullify the effect of Article XIX of the Five Power treaty—which froze the status quo of fortifications and naval bases in the western Pacific—and redress the United States's unfavorable balance.[73] By the 1930s, however, the evolution of carrier doctrine shifted attention away from the light carrier. Large carriers, with greater speed and protection, were more suitable for offensive operations. By contrast, unprotected light carriers, such as the *Ranger*, seemed useful only in the battle line.[74] A potential loophole went largely unexploited because no one ever did build a truly successful fast fleet carrier under 10,000 tons.

Merchant Conversion Programs

According to Article XIV of the Five Power treaty, "No preparations shall be made in merchant ships in time of peace for the installation of warlike armaments for the purpose of converting such ships into vessels of war, other than the necessary stiffening of decks for the mounting of guns not exceeding 6 inch calibre." No objections were raised regarding violation of this clause though the principle embodied in this provision was clearly transgressed between the wars. The U.S. war plan "OR-ANGE" against Japan called for *rapid mobilization to compensate for treaty limits* on base facilities and the anticipated loss of the Philippines early in a war.[75] An expanded carrier force was instrumental to success but would be unavailable at the onset of war. New hulls took on average three years to build, and as late as 1929, the U.S. Navy had only three carriers. A merchant conversion program could rapidly augment offensive capability and compensate for a deficiency in the number of carriers. Covert preparation ensued, and as early as 1923, naval authorities

73. Commander Bruce G. Leighton, USN, led the fight in the Bureau of Aeronautics for the carrier of less than 10,000 tons. This type of ship "would have the immediate result of removing all restrictions, real or implied, on total carrier tonnage so far as existing treaty limitations are concerned, and hence all restrictions upon effective air power at sea. . . . If in the end air power becomes a preponderant factor in sea power the ultimate result would be almost completely to nullify any influence which the Limitation Treaty of 1921 may have had in restricting competition in naval armament." Quoted in Melhorn, *Two-Block Fox*, p. 112.

74. Friedman, *U.S. Aircraft Carriers*, pp. 79–89.

75. Ibid., 119–31.

were assessing "the extent to which non-naval hulls could be adapted to make up for prewar treaty (and budget) limitations"[76] and were drafting plans for converting merchant hulls for a variety of naval missions, particularly convoy escort. Lack of fast merchant ships in the U.S. Merchant Marine presented the major obstacle to rapid conversion, along with an absence of funds to design ships expressly suitable for conversion. Only after 1929 were several fast liners built at all, and it was not until 1939 that a 25-knot liner was designed specifically for the purpose of rapid conversion to a carrier. Prewar planning experience facilitated large-scale wartime conversions and gave the U.S. Navy an indispensable base on which to build during wartime.

The British Admiralty proceeded with its merchant conversion plans in the 1930s, primarily interested in expanding the number of inexpensive trade protection carriers to defend against surface raiders and submarines. In 1934, the Royal Navy developed plans to fit a variety of vessels of 14,000 to 20,000 tons and 15 to 20 knots with a hangar, elevator, and landing deck. By 1935, the Admiralty had identified the requirements for merchant ships suitable for conversion to trade protection carriers.[77]

For the Japanese, merchant conversions presented an opportunity to compensate for industrial inferiority. By the early 1930s, the Imperial Navy had built to the maximum permissible carrier tonnage and embarked on a program of "shadow" carrier construction. The Japanese began laying support vessels with provisions in their designs for rapid conversion to light fleet carriers in time of war.[78] The most spectacular conversions were two 24-knot liners, planned in 1936, laid down in 1939, subsidized by the navy, and incorporating naval features from the outset. According to Friedman, "The two ships were designed specifically for conversion, naval design requirements including a greater height between decks, a stronger main deck, the more extensive wiring that a liner would require, better subdivision, and a longitudinal bulkhead in the engine spaces. The liner design also made provision for later construction of hangars, installation of elevators, and extra fuel and avgas tanks."[79] In addition, "the liners were designed to accommodate 18 dive- and 18 torpedo-bombers, as well as 12 fighters, with a

76. Ibid., p. 119.
77. Ibid., 129–30.
78. See Anthony J. Watts and Brian G. Gordon, *The Imperial Japanese Navy* (London: MacDonald, 1971), pp. 184–87, and Friedman, *U.S. Aircraft Carriers*, pp. 130–31.
79. Friedman, *U.S. Aircraft Carriers*, pp. 130–31.

total of ten more aircraft in reserve (2 dive- and 5 torpedo-bombers, and 3 fighters)."[80] These liners became the fleet carriers *Hiyo* and *Junyo*. The balance of the shadow program produced fast light carriers including the *Zuiho* and *Shoho*, two former submarine support ships that received destroyer machinery to increase their speed to 29 knots; the somewhat larger *Ryujo*; and the ex-seaplane tenders *Chitose* and *Chiyoda*.[81] As in the U.S. and Royal navies, merchant ships in the Imperial Navy were converted into escort carriers for antisubmarine warfare.[82]

The Japanese also passed a Ship Improvement Law in 1932, the primary impetus to create a new merchant fleet for commercial reasons— for Japanese steamship companies to assume the trade between East Asia and the Atlantic coast of the United States. Certain firms, however, had intimate relations with the Japanese Navy, and at least two very swift tank ships were built at the direct request of the Imperial Navy. Despite the commercial genesis of the new fleet of Pacific merchantmen, the ships had remarkable strategic value. As Norman Davis, Roosevelt's chief disarmament negotiator, remarked, "Faced with the possibility of extensive fleet action remote from bases, the Japanese Navy found that its fuel and supply ships could not keep up with the fleet. An identical situation, incidentally, faces the American Navy. The difference is that the Japanese Navy now has available cargo ships of large tank capacity which can keep up with the fleet."[83] This subsidized construction program provided for the construction of passenger liners and cargo ships for conversion into merchant cruisers for transport and convoy duty.

CHEATING

Cheating is the most direct method of treaty circumvention, an expedient way to gain a significant, decisive advantage over one's opponent. It is relatively difficult to conceal warship construction. Only a limited

80. Friedman, *Carrier Air Power*, pp. 56–57.

81. Ibid., p. 57; see also Polmar, *Aircraft Carriers*, pp. 132–34.

82. Friedman, *Carrier Air Power*, p. 57.

83. "The Strategical Value of Japan's New Merchant Fleet," August 14, 1934, Norman H. Davis Papers, London Naval Conference, Naval Memos March–October 1934, Box 35, Library of Congress, Manuscript Division, Washington, D.C.

number of shipyards exist, making monitoring a relatively easy task. Aerial reconnaissance can detect shipyard activity as well as the size of armament. The potential for security breaches escalates with the thousands of designers, subcontractors, and workmen needed for construction. Displacement, however, can be disguised with relative ease. As Barton Whaley describes it,

> The tonnage of a ship can be estimated closely from its dimensions—length, beam, and draft—taken together with certain (easy) assumptions about its type and (more difficult) estimates of thickness and/or weight of its armor. Length and beam are easily verified by aerial photography, and unusual variations are immediate cause for suspicion. However, draft and armor thickness need to be verified by either physical inspection or by access to plans or specifications. Consequently, most cases of tonnage deception involve either draft or armor.[84]

During the interwar years, all major naval powers built vessels exceeding displacement limits, though rampant violations did not begin until the 1930s. Design modifications during construction often resulted in increases in displacement, a natural consequence of the ship construction process.[85] Hence, minor deviations between projected and actual displacement, up to five percent, did not necessarily indicate intentional treaty violation.

In the case of Japanese excesses in the heavy cruiser category in the 1920s, there is reason to believe these were not intentional. The overweight condition of the Takao-class heavy cruisers—the *Maya* and *Chokai* displacing 14,129 tons and the *Takao* and *Atago* 12,986 tons— had a variety of deleterious consequences. "The additional displacement reduced the freeboard, the seaworthiness, the reserve buoyancy, the longitudinal strength, the maxim speed and the radius of action at

---

84. Barton Whaley, *Covert German Rearmament, 1919–1939: Deception and Misperception* (Frederick, Md.: University Publications of America, 1984), p. 87.

85. See Friedman, *Battleship Design and Development*, pp. 154–64, for an explanation of the design process. Friedman notes that frequently "[d]isplacements are too small or they are improperly labelled. For example, the Italian Navy used a displacement which refers to an empty ship [so that water in the boilers and ammunition were not included]. For a time just after World War II, *Jane's* listed this as the *standard* displacement, so that the *Vittorio Venetos* came out at about 38,000 rather than 41,000 tons. Weight breakdowns of Italian ships often refer to this displacement, which makes them misleading."

the effective 2/3 trial displacement."[86] The Italians, on the other hand, ran trials without ammunition and, in the case of the heavy cruiser *Gorizia* in 1931, without gun mountings installed, and failed to inform foreign navies of these "unrealistic conditions." Italy's heavy cruisers, built in the early 1930s, exceeded treaty limits by 15 percent.[87]

By the 1930s, however, all navies were transgressing the Washington treaty limits on capital ship displacement. In 1934, Italy's battleships *Littorio* and *Vittorio* each displaced 41,500 tons, exceeding limits by 18 percent. France's *Richelieu* laid in 1935 exceeded displacement limits by 8 percent; Britain's *King George V* in 1936 was in excess by 5 percent. The Japanese abrogated the treaties in 1934 but began planning the super-battleship *Yamato* in 1930. The *Yamato* exceeded announced displacement by almost 95 percent and mounted 18-inch rather than the announced 16-inch guns. In addition, the first three ships of the Yamato-class were built behind sisal curtains to prevent any photographing of even the base hulls.[88] Despite cheating on precise displacement, the treaties kept the naval powers close to specified limits until 1936.

INNOVATION IN STRATEGY AND TACTICS

Innovation in strategy and tactics often proceeded in step with technological development in an effort to retain the capability to execute military strategies under the Washington treaty constraints. The treaties attempted to create defensive superiority by limiting the major agents of offensive power—the battleship and big gun—and by establishing a ratio system that allowed sufficient forces for defensive missions but inadequate levels for offensive operations. Nevertheless, naval strategists and designers devised ways to reassert offensive superiority.[89]

86. Eric Lacroix, "The Development of the 'A Class' Cruisers in the Imperial Japanese Navy," Part 3, *Warship International* 16:4 (1979): 341.

87. Preston, *Cruisers*, pp. 80, 99–101.

88. Anthony Preston, *An Illustrated History of the Navies of World War II* (London: Bison Books, 1976), p. 152.

89. Jervis examines the impact of the offensive/defensive balance on the outbreak of war, identifies the destabilizing consequences of offensive superiority, and supports limits on offensive armaments to reduce the likelihood of war. The interwar naval case demonstrates how limiting a critical offensive system can stimulate the development of new offensive weapons and innovative tactics and strategies for their use. For example, to strengthen their defensive capacity, the Japa-

For Britain, the United States, and Japan, desires for offensive superiority were rooted in shared conceptions of the navy's role in securing
national interests. Most of the admirals were proponents of the classical
school of naval thought, were committed to a blue-water navy, and
pursued strategies to acquire and maintain command of the sea.[90] With
limitations placed on the battleship and big gun—the traditional means
of prevailing in decisive battle and securing command of the sea—efforts accelerated to find new ways to perform old missions. One result
was tactical and strategic innovation.

The Imperial Navy's Attrition Strategy

The Imperial Navy, like the Grand Fleet, had to defend the home
islands and maintain lines of communication with the empire. The Japanese were determined to maintain defensive-deterrent superiority in
the western Pacific.[91] Japanese war plans were designed around a decisive fleet engagement with the U.S. Navy in the western Pacific. Prevailing in a decisive battle required at least equality with the enemy,
yet the Washington treaties limited the Imperial Navy to 60 percent of
U.S. battleship strength. The treaties also reduced offensive battleship
strength without regulating technological improvement, and the U.S.
Navy had taken advantage of this loophole to launch a major battleship
modernization program. U.S. conversion from coal to oil threatened
the defensive balance in the Pacific created at Washington, because
although coal-fired ships could not operate far from home bases, oil-
fired ships, which had a significantly augmented cruising radius, could.
To reduce U.S. naval strength and offset the deficiencies created by the

---

nese devised offensive tactics that required offensive weapons. Attempting to limit forces based on
offensive and defensive criteria may lead to unintended and destabilizing consequences, given the
evolution of weapons, tactics, and strategy. Robert Jervis, "Cooperation Under the Security Dilemma," *World Politics* 30 (January 1978): 167–214.

90. Despite the claims of some scholars such as Alexander Kiralfly, "Japanese Naval Strategy,"
in Earle, ed., *Makers of Modern Strategy*, pp. 457–84, the Imperial Navy was not a mere adjunct of
land power. Although Japanese aspirations were regional rather than global, the navy, like other
blue-water navies of the period, was deeply influenced by the writings of U.S. Captain Alfred
Thayer Mahan and his emphasis on the decisive fleet engagement. More of Mahan's works were
translated into Japanese than into any other language. Hoover, *Arms Control*, p. 63.

91. On the defensive nature of Japan's strategy, see Reynolds, *The Fast Carriers*, p. 10.

inferior battleship ratio, the Imperial Navy planned to wage an "attrition" campaign against the dominant U.S. fleet.

In the mid-1920s, the Japanese introduced and refined the attrition
stage in their plan for war with the United States. In the first phase of
battle, the Japanese would attack and capture U.S. bases in the western
Pacific, quickly defeating local U.S. military power. To recapture these
possessions, the United States would be forced to make a lengthy voy-
age across the Pacific. In the second stage, the Japanese would employ
attrition tactics to wear down the U.S. fleet as it crossed the Pacific. In
the final stage, the Imperial Navy would ambush the U.S. fleet. As
Robert Hoover describes this stage of the Japanese war plan, "Superior
in number but fatigued from the crossing and tactically outmaneuvered,
the American navy, without supporting naval bases, would be decisively defeated."[92]

To execute the attrition tactics in the second stage of Japan's war
plan, the Japanese built high-speed submarines with greater range and
more reliable torpedoes to offset the blisters added to defend U.S. battleships. By the mid-1920s, Japan had more ocean-going submarines
built or under construction than any other power, with a higher average
speed and cruising radius than their British and U.S. counterparts.[93]
The J1 cruiser submarine, an entirely new design, could cruise the Pacific and Indian Oceans without supporting vessels. In trials, it successfully steamed 25,000 miles carrying provisions for sixty days at sea.[94]
In 1932, the Japanese laid the J2 with improved diesel engines that
increased horsepower and raised surface speed. To mitigate scouting
problems, the J2 was fitted with a catapult and designed to carry a
seaplane. The 2,000-ton J2 could speed faster than the U.S. fleet and,
with a cruising range of 20,000 miles, could easily reach the California
coast.

Admiral Suetsugu Nobumasa, while commander of the First Submarine Squadron in 1923–25, began experimenting with submarine tactics. As commander in chief of the Combined Fleet by 1933, he refined

92. Hoover, *Arms Control*, p. 64.

93. Bywater, *Navies and Nations*, pp. 215–16. The Germans introduced the technology of
oceangoing submarines as early as 1913, and throughout the interwar period, this technology was
distributed to the other major naval powers. With the exception of the Japanese Navy, whose
special operational requirements demanded large submarines, most navies preferred smaller, more
maneuverable types. See Karl Lautenschlager, "The Submarine in Naval Warfare, 1901–2001,"
International Security 2 (Winter 1986–87): 94–140.

94. Watts and Gordon, *Imperial Japanese Navy*, pp. 318–19.

his "strategy of interceptive operations." Repeated submarine attacks would gradually reduce U.S. fleet strength by 30 percent in its trans-pacific passage. A decisive fleet engagement in the western Pacific would then finish off the enemy. "The combat mission assigned to the submarine—a major role in the early stage of interceptive operations to the important auxiliary role in the main fleet engagement—was a unique feature of Japanese strategy."[95] In yearly maneuvers, submarine commanders perfected the tactics and strategy of submarine warfare. They improved reconnaissance for locating and tracking the U.S. fleet and "concentration tactics for submarine warfare as their forces made the transition from reconnaissance to attrition attacks in packs against American screens and battleships."[96]

The Imperial Navy's attrition strategy depended on lighter craft successfully damaging the enemy's capital ships. Therefore, Japanese heavy cruisers and destroyers had to be able to fight against the enemy battle line. It was extremely difficult, however, for a light craft to approach within torpedo range of a capital ship without suffering serious damage. To overcome this obstacle, and in response to similar activity in Britain, the Japanese resumed development of oxygen-propelled torpedoes. Experiments culminated in the long-range, high-speed Type 93 torpedo that was fueled by compressed oxygen and kerosene and left a scarcely visible wake when running toward its target.[97] At 39 knots, it could range twenty-four miles; at 49 knots, twelve miles. The 93 carried an extremely powerful warhead, twice the strength of earlier torpedoes. "The long range of this new weapon meant that Japan's destroyers and cruisers could choose their distance and carry out their night torpedo attacks in relative safety."[98]

Massive torpedo attacks launched at night coupled with innovative night tactics for destroyers would create sufficient confusion to give the Japanese a tactical advantage in the decisive engagement stage of operations. As Eric Lacroix explains, "The fitting of a heavy torpedo armament in the 'A' Class Cruisers occurred under pressure of the Naval General Staff, which, after the signature of the Washington Treaty, emphasized the importance of night combat and torpedo attacks (this

95. Asada, "Japanese Navy and the United States," p. 235; see Pelz, Race to Pearl Harbor, pp. 34–39, for a detailed account of Japan's war plan with the United States in the Pacific.
96. Hoover, Arms Control, p. 65.
97. See Lacroix, "A Class Cruisers," Part 5, p. 364 n. 76.
98. Pelz, Race to Pearl Harbor, p. 31.

concept also led to the development of the 'Special Type' destroyers of the *Fubuki* class) to compensate for the limitation of the battleline force."[99] The long-range Type 93 torpedo and Yamato-class battleships—with their superior range—would enhance the Imperial Navy's decisive advantage in the final stages of battle. Japanese carrier tactics also emphasized attack with torpedoes. According to General Minoru Genda, this tactical philosophy was a direct outgrowth of the Washington treaties. "Since we could build to only 60 per cent of the levels allowed the major powers, we were forced to compensate by developing our capabilities with the torpedo, submarine warfare, and other supplementary areas."[100] The Japanese developed a range of weapons to execute their attrition strategy, a strategy devised to achieve Japanese victory in a decisive fleet engagement with the U.S. Navy in the western Pacific.

Submarine and destroyer tactics became key components of the Imperial Navy's attrition strategy. Only in the 1930s were aircraft incorporated into the strategy as a forward arm of operations. Although aircraft were employed in a new role, not strictly for reconnaissance, they operated primarily from bases in the Mandates against the screening cruisers of the battle fleet since battleships were still believed to be immune to aircraft attack.

The U.S. Navy's War Plan ORANGE

The strategic dilemma confronting the U.S. Navy in the post-Conference years was how to operate in the western Pacific in defense of Far Eastern commitments without fortified bases. The army-navy ORANGE plan called for a fleet advance across the Pacific to relieve local forces holding Guam and the Philippines. By 1924, naval planners already recognized the inability of the U.S. fleet to reach the Philippines in less than six weeks. By that time, local resistance would have collapsed. Developments in offensive technology, such as submarines and

99. Lacroix, "A Class Cruisers," Part 2, p. 54. For more details on night torpedo attacks and battle tactics in the second and third stages of the attrition strategy, see Lacroix, "A Class Cruisers," Part 5, pp. 337, 365 n. 79.

100. General Minoru Genda, "Evolution of Aircraft Carrier Tactics of the Imperial Japanese Navy," in Paul Stillwell, ed., *Air Raid: Pearl Harbor! Recollections of a Day of Infamy* (Annapolis: Naval Institute Press, 1981), p. 23.

land-based aircraft, their incorporation into Japan's attrition strategy, and the steadily deteriorating condition of U.S. fortifications forced U.S. naval planners to abandon reliance on a relief column.

Since the U.S. Navy would be unable to mobilize sufficient battle fleet strength in time to prevent the invasion of the critical base at Manila, defeat of Japan would require a strong naval aviation component. "An air offensive was essential since [ORANGE] did not envisage anything approaching the logistical or manpower buildup necessary for an invasion of Japan."[101] In short, the carrier appeared the only way to achieve air superiority once the Philippines were lost.[102] Revised ORANGE called for step-by-step movement across the Pacific, taking the Mandates on the way to recapturing the Philippines. The Philippines would then be reestablished as the chief base of operations against Japan. In war games during the interwar period, the U.S. Navy studied the tactical and strategic problems of long-range logistics, fueling at sea, convoy defense, amphibious landings, and offensive carrier operations.[103] The fleet was rounded out for long-range logistics, scouting, and screening. Long cruising radius became a mandatory characteristic for all future vessels. Despite appropriation difficulties, by the late 1920s, the U.S. Navy was a much more balanced fleet.

For the United States, the carrier could facilitate power projection into the western Pacific. Carrier tactics and doctrine continued to evolve as war games against the Panama Canal with the Lexington and Saratoga in 1929 demonstrated the degree to which carrier power could augment the offensive capability of the fleet. The qualities of these converted large carriers, as they participated in the critical naval exercises of the early 1930s, became major factors in the evolution of tactical carrier doctrine. Advances in tactics and strategy precipitated more comprehensive changes in battle fleet offensive doctrine.

Battleships and big guns, the primary offensive weapons, had been limited by treaty. Older, less valuable battleships had been scrapped, increasing the perceived risk of using the few valuable battleships in

101. Friedman, U.S. Aircraft Carriers, p. 120.

102. The success of carrier airpower was hardly a foregone conclusion. The carrier did enhance reconnaissance capabilities and increase the offensive capability of the battle fleet by facilitating the destruction of targets deep inland. However, Friedman argues that the carrier successes of World War II surprised naval planners. Improvements in land-based aircraft accelerated rapidly in the late 1930s, and land-based aircraft could outrange their carrier counterparts since performance of the latter was limited by carrier flight decks. Friedman, U.S. Aircraft Carriers, p. 13.

103. Hoover, Arms Control, p. 74.

fleet operations. Finally, the inability to fortify bases seriously restricted the traditional offensive mission of the battleship. The strategic dilemma created by the Washington treaties, coupled with the "accident" of large converted battle cruiser hulls, contributed to the evolution of carrier doctrine, strategy, and tactics. The net result was a shift to a weapon system that had escaped extensive limitation at Washington.

DESTABILIZING CONSEQUENCES OF REDIRECTION

In the wake of the Washington Conference, military programs in all treaty states were redirected to some extent. Such an unintended and perverse consequence of the policy process does not by necessity preclude the reduction of tensions, and practical leaders should recognize that a certain amount of rechanneling naturally results from the arms control process. In certain cases, however, redirection unintentionally undermined the defensive balance of naval power the treaties had attempted to codify. Developments in carrier technology, doctrine, and tactics and battleship modernization programs provide the clearest examples. Exploiting loopholes and ambiguous treaty provisions; devising innovative technologies, tactics, and strategies; or changing force structure to compensate for weaknesses created by arms control agreements are not necessarily acts of bad faith. Whether redirection represents an abuse of the arms control system is a matter of intent on the part of the potential violator and also of judgment on the part of those adversely affected by the purported violation. Redirection may be intentional without being insincere. Hence, the destabilizing impact of redirection is linked to the context within which that activity occurs, or to such background factors as asymmetries in political agendas, doctrines, and threat environments noted at the outset, coupled with emerging domestic, regional, and international developments shaping the security environment of the treaty powers. Both these background and foreground forces influence perceptions and judgments about the meaning and implications of rechanneling.

Mutual suspicion accompanied arms limitation in the interwar years—U.S. suspicion of illegal Japanese fortifications in the Mandates; Japanese and British suspicion of the U.S. battleship modernization program; British and U.S. suspicion about each other's interpretations of parity and the legality of battleship modernization. Those suspicions became more acute as political tensions in other foreign policy arenas intensified and as redirection itself produced offensive weapons and strategies. For example, the Japanese devised "offensive" tactics and strategies to reassert "defensive" superiority in the western Pacific. A strategy perceived by the Japanese as defensive raised U.S. suspicions about Japanese intentions in the Far East. In this instance, Japanese behavior "reinforced naval and political rivalry between the two and added to the American Navy's commitment to develop a warfighting capability within the constraints of the treaty regime."[104]

The ambiguity of parity was probably the greatest source of tension in Anglo-American relations in the interwar years, although the establishment of Franco-Italian parity created a rationale for competition between two navies that had never before built in response to each other. The ratio system actually gave form and substance to a "global" naval competition. The British built in response to the French in Europe and the Japanese in the Pacific, and this meant that French and Japanese building programs could indirectly affect one another. In certain ways, the global arms control system may have unintentionally broadened the scope of naval competition in the international system.

There will always be differences of opinion over whether abuses mean that treaty provisions are being exploited for purposes outside and contradictory to the agreement, or whether they simply represent attempts to maximize military effectiveness within the constraints created by arms control. The critical variables become (1) the perceptions and expectations of the participants about what types of behavior should evolve from the agreements; (2) what role arms control is perceived to play in enhancing state security; and (3) whether those perceptions of the role of arms control, which are strongly influenced by international and domestic political realities, are compatible.

104. Ibid., p. 66.

6 System Maintenance: Coping with Nationalism, Economic Crisis, and Great-Power Resurgence

DURING THE LIFE OF the Washington treaty system, the Far East was racked by nationalist violence, civil war, and economic crisis, and Europe was confronted by the rebirth of German power. These external challenges to the arms control system were beyond the scope of the treaty powers to anticipate, let alone control. Yet the arms control process did provide levers of influence, primarily by linking political and military understandings in order to enhance mutual security. The treaty powers, however, ended up resorting to military-based arms control strategies, which exacerbated, rather than mollified, the impact of situational factors, such as worldwide depression and revolution in China, on the threat perceptions of states. Far from being an epiphenomenon, the arms control process itself influenced interstate relations through the mechanisms by which it responded to the emerging and evolving internal and external pressures that faced the treaty powers. Those mechanisms may be thought of as strategies of treaty maintenance.

Maintaining a security system involves something more than "consolidating" it, or dealing with loopholes, ambiguities, and differences in interpretation in the existing security arrangements. Yet maintenance involves something less than "adapting" the security system or changing the system's principles and norms to infuse the system with new political content. Although the more popular and restricted definition of maintenance equates it with compliance,[1] maintenance may be more

1. Keohane, *After Hegemony*, pp. 98–100; Charles S. Floweree, "On Tending Arms Control Agreements," *Washington Quarterly* 13 (Winter 1990): 199–214.

usefully described as a process of adapting rules (or the specific prescription and proscriptions for action) and procedures (or the prevailing
practices for making and implementing collective choice) in response to
shifting security problems, evolving foreign policy objectives, and
emerging technological developments.[2] Different rules and procedures
may be consistent with a single set of principles. Between the wars,
those principles—arms control; security without resort to collusion, alliance, or force; and preservation of the open door to and the integrity
of China—were codified in the Washington treaties.

A close analysis of the Washington treaty system reveals how maintaining a security system in many respects may be a greater challenge
than creating one. System formation may be comparatively easy, because it does not require participants to reach a consensus on longer-
term objectives guiding the security order. Maintenance, on the other
hand, does require the development of a consensus that may extend
well beyond initial negotiated provisions. By Condoleezza Rice's estimation in her reading of the Strategic Arms Limitation (SALT) regime of
the Cold War period, "the maintenance and furthering of a limited
regime is difficult in the absence of broader political cooperation."[3]
Ironically, in the interwar years, the treaty powers struggled to extend
the technical provisions of the security order without nurturing the political consensus necessary for maintaining the system. In effect, the
pursuit of military-based strategies of arms control crippled the treaty
system in the long run, because only by linking political and military
means could the treaty powers hope to bridge conflicting political
agendas in the Far East and meet the maritime and continental requisites of security in Europe.

From the late 1920s through the mid-1930s, five strategies were implemented at times by intention, at times by neglect, to maintain a
security system challenged by nationalism, civil war, economic crisis,
and great power resurgence. They "delinked" technical arms control
from economic and political developments in the Far East; split the
political from the military components of security in the Far East and

2. For a discussion of norms, principles, rules, and procedures in the context of regimes, see
Stephen D. Krasner, "Structural Causes and Regime Consequences," in Stephen D. Krasner, ed.,
International Regimes (Ithaca: Cornell University Press, 1983), p. 2.

3. Condoleezza Rice, "SALT and the Search for a Security Regime," in Alexander L. George
et al., *U.S.-Soviet Security Cooperation: Achievements, Failures, Lessons* (New York: Oxford University Press, 1988), p. 303.

Europe at the London Naval Conference of 1930; incorporated escape and escalator clauses into arms control treaties; attempted to negotiate a nonaggression pact with Japan; and sought to bring the "reconstituted" great power, Germany, into the arms control component alone of the security system. With the exception of the attempted nonaggression pact with Japan, all the other maintenance strategies shared a common deficiency: they were pursued in a manner fundamentally inconsistent with a political-based approach to the arms control process. In an effort to preserve and extend the technical or military dimensions of agreement, the Washington powers neglected a host of more profound threats to security emerging in the Far East and Europe, thus slighting the broader political consensus necessary for managing the conflict, competition, and pressures that were developing within and among the treaty powers.

SYSTEM CHALLENGES

Nationalism, Civil War, and Economic Crisis

The Washington treaty powers believed that successful arms control in the Pacific required political understandings regarding China. The Nine Power treaty was designed, at least nominally, as a substitute for all prior statements and agreements concerning China. The signatories condemned spheres of influence; endorsed equal opportunity for the commerce and industry of all nations throughout China; and agreed to respect the sovereignty, independence, and territorial and administrative integrity of China. These abstract principles guiding behavior in China reflected the conviction that progress in arms limitation required marked improvement in political relations throughout the Pacific. As the decade progressed, however, the political situation in China changed so radically that the Nine Power treaty became obsolete as a meaningful basis for stability. Revolutionary nationalism spread throughout China, and the Nine Power treaty failed to adapt to the newly emerging challenges confronting Great Britain, the United States, and Japan in the Far East.

In the early 1920s, the treaty powers worked to maintain peaceful economic relations with one another inside and outside China, even while renewed naval competition reared its head. Delinkage became an important strategy for system maintenance, implemented early on, because it divorced limited competition in the naval arena from economic cooperation. Japan and the United States, in particular, succeeded in sustaining peaceful bilateral economic relations, while preparing for war against each other in the Pacific. The Japanese military never abandoned the idea of a future conflict with the United States, and despite Japan's adherence to the Washington system, such a conflict remained a basic assumption of both the army's and navy's defense policies. Across the Pacific, naval planners continued refining war plans against Japan that had first been prepared after the 1904 Russo-Japanese War. In 1924, U.S. naval planners revised ORANGE, and this remained basic strategy until 1938. Yet in Iriye's estimation, "In both Tokyo and Washington, . . . the primacy of economic over military policy was clearly asserted during the first half of the 1920s."[4] By the mid-1920s, however, economic cooperation in China began to falter as well, making delinkage again necessary, but this time to isolate tensions in China from the arms control arena in preparation for the London Naval Conference of 1930.[5]

The Washington Conference may have marked the demise of imperialist diplomacy in the Far East, but it did not eradicate conflicts of interest there. In 1922, the treaty powers differed in their approaches to assisting China's central government with stabilizing its economic base and extending authority over China proper. The Peking government desperately needed funds to implement programs of reconstruction and to consolidate its central authority. Loans, however, might be wasted if the government were too weak to use them constructively. Sir Victor Wellesley, an influential force in British Far Eastern policy between the wars and deputy under-secretary of state for foreign affairs from 1925 to 1936, summarized the British perspective as follows: "Until all the leakages are stopped, which implies a comprehensive reorganization of China's financial and fiscal system, to place the Chinese Government in funds is like pouring water into a bottomless tank."[6] China was al-

---

4. Iriye, *After Imperialism*, pp. 36–37.

5. For background, see James William Christopher, *Conflict in the Far East: American Diplomacy in China from 1928–1933* (Leiden: E. J. Brill, 1950).

6. Louis, *British Strategy*, p. 142.

ready heavily in debt, and future credit depended on honoring past obligations. The only feasible securities on which to base new loans were additional customs duties, but these had yet to be granted. The Washington customs treaty stipulated that a tariff conference should be called three months after the Nine Power treaty was ratified by all signatories. Yet the French delayed ratification until 1925, because, according to Iriye, of a "petty squabble over the Boxer indemnity issue," thereby preventing the convening of such a conference to strengthen the central government in Peking.[7]

The Washington customs treaty advanced a formula for tariff revision—a 2.5 percent tariff increase on ordinary dutiable articles and a 5 percent surtax on luxuries—ostensibly designed to support the emergence of a strong stable China. The formula, however, required China to meet certain obligations. Reasoning that instability was too pervasive in China to warrant any radical change in the status of foreigners and their activities, the treaty powers refused to take risks to stabilize China's internal situation until the Chinese demonstrated an ability to protect foreigners and foreign property. In effect, this meant a stable Chinese government must precede treaty revision. Only then would the Washington powers actively assist the Chinese. The treaty powers withheld the assistance that could have stabilized China, facilitated a new order in the Far East, and guaranteed a peaceful environment for economic interaction. They failed to implement any measures to enhance the stability of China or create a sound government that could revise prior unequal treaties gradually and peacefully. Even the Root Resolutions, which obliged the signatories to provide the fullest opportunity for China to develop and maintain an effective and stable government, fell short of restoring tariff and jurisdictional autonomy. The unequal treaties, which granted privileges to foreign nationals not reciprocally granted to the Chinese, remained intact. Extraterritorial rights removed foreign citizens and their property from the jurisdiction of the Chinese government and permitted these residents to claim exemption from Chinese taxes. By undercutting China's financial independence, lack of tariff autonomy undercut China's political independence.[8]

7. Iriye, *After Imperialism*, p. 33.
8. See Ann Trotter, *Britain and East Asia, 1933–1937* (London: Cambridge University Press, 1975), p. 14.

Between 1922 and 1925, the treaty powers searched for limited ways to stabilize political and economic conditions in China. In October 1920, banking groups in the United Kingdom, Japan, France, and the United States had agreed to a consortium procedure whereby all were to share equally in loans made for the purpose of providing China with the capital necessary for development.[9] The United States and Britain were prepared to assist the Chinese with such a consortium loan, but the Japanese vetoed the initiative, refusing to extend further credit until the Chinese had moved toward debt consolidation on previous unsecured loans. The consortium failed to make any loans by 1933. Active cooperation proved elusive as the treaty powers struggled unsuccessfully to define rules and procedures to support the principles underlying the Washington treaty system. Meanwhile, Soviet diplomacy began to organize opposition to the Washington powers. By working to unite all anti-imperialist forces in China, the Comintern encouraged the emergence of a broad-based antiforeign movement. In January 1924, the Kuomintang congress in Canton formalized an alliance with the Chinese communists, and two months later, the Soviets scored a triumph in the North by signing an agreement with the rival Peking government. The Soviets also preempted the Washington powers by renouncing extraterritoriality and special rights and privileges in China. The greatest outgrowth of the Soviet initiative, however, was the identification of anti-imperialism as the immediate goal for China and the unification of all Chinese on the necessity for treaty revision. No Chinese government could be stable thereafter unless it could guarantee treaty revision. The Soviet initiative inverted the Washington formula—a stable Chinese government must precede treaty revision—by making treaty revision a prerequisite for stability, thereby undermining any chances for cooperation based on the Nine Power treaty.

From 1925 to 1926, the Washington powers attempted again to forge a cooperative strategy at the Peking Tariff Conference.[10] Convening on October 26, 1925, the tariff conference represented the sole attempt at collective action in China among the Washington powers after the Washington Conference. By this time, however, it was futile to expect to appease Chinese nationalism with the methods advanced in 1922.

9. See ibid., p. 62.
10. For more details on the Tariff Conference, see Borg, *American Policy and the Chinese Revolution*, pp. 95–121.

The treaty powers would have to adapt to the tides of antiforeignism encouraged by the Kuomintang and to the demands of every Chinese faction for the dismantling of informal empire. Though meeting to forge a joint response to Chinese demands for treaty revision, positions on treaty revision became entangled with a host of other issues: positions on revolutionary nationalism, the struggle between the Kuomintang and rival warlord factions, tensions between noninterference in China—in the "spirit of Washington"—and support for moderate elements within the Kuomintang.

The British were prepared to deal comprehensively and liberally with the Chinese to gradually establish tariff autonomy in return for guarantees of commercial rights. The British were even prepared to go beyond the Washington formula and consider unilaterally granting a tariff increase of up to 12.5 percent, provided the internal tax system in China, the *likin*, was abolished.[11] The U.S. delegation came to the Peking Conference willing to discuss extraterritoriality as well as treaty revision. They were prepared to grant unconditionally the 2.5 percent surtax stipulated at Washington, and to consider a maximum rate of 12.5 percent if the *likin* were abolished. At the same time, they were prepared to act independently of the other Washington powers and enter into bilateral relations with the Chinese, dispensing with the Washington formula of joint action in China. The Japanese were opposed to a uniform surtax since this would place Japanese imports in competition with native Chinese products. Tariff autonomy, if it were granted, must occur in stages. For example, treaties to determine the taxes on specified articles could be negotiated between China and each of the foreign powers. This would prevent a drastic and indiscriminate change in Chinese tariff rates, which was important to Japan because, as Dorothy Borg points out, Japanese exports, being cheaper in quality than those of other nations, were more likely to be affected by higher duties and by the competition Chinese manufactures might offer if adequately protected.[12] In short, as Iriye summarizes, "The Japanese would consent to

11. "Likin is defined narrowly by the British as the levy of tolls on merchandise in transit. . . . '[T]he likin stations all over China are innumerable, and the charges, delays, arbitrariness and other vexations constitute a heavy incubus on trade.' In a broader sense, likin embraced consumption and other taxes and comprised many forms of internal taxation on foreign and domestic trade. . . . Without the cessation of likin, the Foreign Office saw little point in proceeding to discuss such issues as tariff autonomy and debt consolidation." Louis, *British Strategy*, p. 148.

12. Borg, *American Policy and the Chinese Revolution*, p. 99.

a change in the economic order of the Far East only if the change insured against the loss of China as a market for Japanese goods and capital."[13] Finally, the Japanese feared China would begin borrowing on the increased revenue before redeeming existing debts. In the end, the Japanese conceded to granting the Washington surtax increases of 2.5 percent for ordinary and 5 percent for luxury goods, provided a counter-vailing excise on native produce was levied, and some arrangement was reached to ensure debt consolidation.

The Peking Tariff Conference was interrupted by renewed civil war and the fall of the Tuan regime in Peking in April 1926. An immediate levying of additional customs duties, though it may have bolstered the Tuan regime, was rejected as support for a particular warring faction and a violation of the principle of noninterference. Instead, the Washington powers began formulating unilateral policies to cope with threats to interests posed by civil war in China. The Japanese, realizing the futility of negotiating a multilateral tariff agreement, focused on securing reciprocal arrangements and debt consolidation to protect their trade in China. The British began leaning toward a rapprochement with the Kuomintang government in Canton in an effort to resolve the boycott that had developed in the aftermath of the Shanghai incident of May 30, 1925. The incident had its genesis in labor disputes in the Japanese mills at Shanghai. In response to mob demonstrations, police-men fired on a crowd, killing seven Chinese and inciting demonstra-tions, strikes, and boycotts throughout North, Central, and South China. Though directed against all foreigners, the Japanese and British became the object of antiforeign hostility because Japanese mills had been the locus of conflict and because the police in Shanghai were under British command. With Hong Kong trade down 40 percent and exports to China down 25 percent, the British abandoned their support for abolishing the *likin*.[14] The United States refused to deal with any one faction, and this prevented their granting the Washington surtaxes. As it developed, the Washington powers failed to cooperate, to assist a nonrevolutionary China, and to fulfill the provisions of the Washing-ton customs treaty. At most, the powers agreed to restore tariff auton-

13. Iriye, *After Imperialism*, p. 68.
14. For more details, see Borg, *American Policy and the Chinese Revolution*, pp. 20–46, and Iriye, *After Imperialism*, pp. 59–62, 82.

omy to China by 1929 and to separate tariff autonomy from the *likin* issue.

The Peking Tariff Conference represented a failure of the Washington formula to evolve and adapt to changes in China and to the challenges these changes posed for the treaty powers. The Washington agreements on principles of conduct in China were tailored toward the redefinition of relations among the treaty powers—to the renunciation of particularistic policies and the prewar diplomacy of imperialism—not toward the peaceful management of change in China. No mechanisms were devised to deal with developments within China, and these internal factors posed the greatest obstacles to success at Peking. The treaty powers were not negotiating with a united China, but merely with a Chinese government in Peking. No assurance of stability or permanence existed because power remained divided among rival warlord factions. And though all factions demanded treaty revision, there was no consensus on how to achieve it. The Peking warlords favored a tariff conference, rival warlords opposed it, and the Kuomintang in Canton believed the conference was only a tactic of the Peking government to consolidate power against the revolutionaries. The tariff conference underscored as well that the principles embodied in the Nine Power and Washington customs treaties were the least common denominators for the pursuit of what were in effect divergent long-term interests. Agreement on process did not translate into a consensus or compromise on policy objectives. And although reaching agreement does not require a consensus on the objectives a treaty serves, a convergence of agendas is necessary for treaty maintenance over the long term. For the Washington powers, however, no shared conception of a future vision for China ever evolved. To the degree that any convergence developed, it proved more superficial than real, for the powers were willing to give up very little at the outset to effect treaty revision.[15] The sentiments of Sir Victor Wellesley of Britain's Foreign Office, Far Eastern Department, captures the thinking that resulted in policies of inaction. In Wellesley's view, this was the only logical path for Britain. "From whatever angle I approach the problem I always come back to the conclusion that the really right policy is to let China work out her own salvation, at any

---

15. Japan did agree to restore Kiaochow to China, Britain promised to restore Weihaiwei, and foreign postal agencies were abolished. Iriye, *After Imperialism*, p. 21.

rate, up to a point."[16] Any discussion of China's rehabilitation would only stir up an international hornet's nest because of the divergent and conflicting aims of the great powers in Asia. Yet while the treaty powers waited passively for the emergence of the "necessary" conditions to implement the Washington formula, China's civil war altered the political and strategic context in the Far East and the perceived benefits of cooperation—even in the arms control arena for the Japanese.

By 1926, the Washington powers had abandoned cooperative strategies in China. With the launching of the Nationalist Northern Expedition in 1926—the Kuomintang's drive to unify China—and the anti-foreign protests of 1927 in Hankow and Nanking, assaults on foreigners became the slogan of national unification. The Kuomintang called for a common front against imperialism to secure mass support. With this, the domestic struggle for power in China, and the platform of Nationalism, became the principal factors determining the treaty powers' policies in China. The Nine Power formula had failed as a stimulus for political organization. In Iriye's estimation, this may have been because the treaty, while it symbolized an abandonment of unilateralism, exclusivity, and particularism for multinational cooperation and consultation, was gradualist, reformist, and evolutionary, not radical or revolutionary. And wholesale transformation of Asian international relations was precisely what the Communist International and an increasing number of Chinese Nationalists were demanding.[17] Nor did the Washington formula take into account Chinese aspirations, and this was particularly irritating, as Ann Trotter points out: "The contention that, by the Nine Power Treaty, China was being offered an opportunity to set her house in order, with its implications that powers other than China were best qualified to judge the nature of China's house-keeping requirements and the standard which this house-keeping must reach before treaty rights could be relinquished, was insulting to the Chinese nationalists."[18]

The year 1926 represented a watershed, by Borg's estimation, with Chinese governments in the North and South imposing measures in defiance of the treaty system, with the administration in Peking launching a systematic denunciation of the unequal treaties, and with the

16. Quoted in Louis, *British Strategy*, p. 144.
17. Iriye, *Origins of the Second World War*, pp. 2–3.
18. Trotter, *Britain and East Asia*, p. 14.

privileges, interests, and lives of foreigners endangered by civil war.[19] In that year, the Washington powers resorted to unilateral postures to serve their respective interests. In December, the British published their "Christmas message," declaring they had "abandon[ed] the idea that the economic and political development of China can be secured under foreign tutelage" and "disclaim[ing] any intention of forcing foreign control upon an unwilling China."[20] The British realized they had to relinquish significant portions of their treaty rights to safeguard important economic interests. Settlements like Shanghai, in particular, were crucial for British trade. Aside from conducting nearly all the foreign business of China, trade flourished there despite civil war because banks continued to function and foreign nationals were protected under systems of municipal government.[21] To halt the anti–Hong Kong boycott, the British relinquished Hankow to the Kuomintang in the first of many concessions. In return for safeguards at Shanghai, the British accepted minor infringements of their treaty rights—handing over concessions and abolishing extraterritoriality in the interior.[22] Yet these concessions consistently fell short of the Kuomintang's radical demands.

Britain was aware of the need to deal with the Nationalists, but the United States would negotiate only with a central Chinese authority, which at the time did not exist. Only in 1928 did the United States begin to negotiate with the Nationalist government in Nanking. In January 1927, Secretary of State Frank B. Kellogg announced the willingness of the U.S. government to negotiate a new treaty on tariffs and extraterritoriality with any delegation representing both the regime in Canton and the factions in the North, reiterating standard U.S. policy. Kellogg also declared publicly his willingness "to act on behalf of the United States alone if it was impossible to secure co-operation from the other Powers."[23] Kellogg hoped that the United States would be perceived as a friend and shielded from the brunt of antiforeign activity.

The Japanese, unlike their U.S. and British counterparts, were aware early on of rifts within the Kuomintang and of the existence of a core of moderates. However, the Japanese were reluctant to interfere in an unpredictable situation and were hesitant to use force even to protect

---

19. Borg, *American Policy and the Chinese Revolution*, p. 420.
20. Quoted in ibid., p. 421.
21. Louis, *British Strategy*, p. 158.
22. Ibid., p. 164.
23. Borg, *American Policy and the Chinese Revolution*, p. 422.

their own nationals for fear of provoking a radical reaction. Force, however, was an option if the Chinese attempted to unilaterally impose the Washington surtaxes in Manchuria and Mongolia.[24] At the Eastern Conference of 1927, Prime Minister Tanaka Giichi advanced a China policy that had much in common with the spirit of Shidehara diplomacy. Conceding the probability of a united China, Tanaka declared Japan's readiness to cooperate with other powers to endorse legitimate Chinese aspirations, to implement decisive actions if Japanese lives or property were endangered, and to vigorously act to defuse anti-Japanese movements on the mainland. However, Tanaka's policy was oriented toward "Manchuria first," in contrast to Shidehara's "China first" policy. Shidehara considered trade with China more important than Manchuria and believed Japan had "no rights nor interests whatsoever in Manchuria except those which belonged to the South Manchurian Railway." Tanaka, by contrast, "not only considered Manchuria-Mongolia as a separate entity from China proper but also thought that Japan had a 'special position' there . . . and a special 'duty and responsibility' as 'Lord of East Asia' to maintain peace and order in that region."[25] If unrest spread to Manchuria and Mongolia and jeopardized Japan's special position and interests there, the government, according to Tanaka, must "be prepared to combat this menace, regardless of where the danger may originate."[26]

The Tanaka cabinet drew a clear distinction between policy in Manchuria and Mongolia and policy in China proper. It was determined to exclude the Kuomintang from the former and made this objective the cornerstone of Japanese continental policy. By the winter of 1926–27,

---

24. In Japan, it was difficult to think of Manchuria without thinking of Japan's "visible and invisible rights and interests in Manchuria and Mongolia. The visible rights were those guaranteed by treaties, including the agreements of 1915. They included the lease of Kwantung Territory, the management of the South Manchuria railway, the right to station troops along the railway, and various other rights to engage in mining, farming, and business activities in specified areas of Manchuria and Inner Mongolia. There were also 'invisible' rights which resulted from Japan's peculiar relations with Manchuria—the war against Russia in which 'one hundred thousand soldiers' blood' was spilled, the investment of more than one billion dollars to turn Manchuria into an industrially developed region, and Japan's 'right of survival' which required that the 'untouched treasures' of Manchuria and Mongolia be made available for Japanese use. For the military, Manchuria meant the Kwantung Army and its strategic location facing Soviet Russia." Iriye, *After Imperialism*, pp. 111–12.

25. Nobuya Bamba, *Japanese Diplomacy in a Dilemma: New Light on Japan's China Policy, 1924–1929* (Vancouver: University of British Columbia Press, 1972), pp. 300–301.

26. Quoted in Crowley, *Japan's Quest for Autonomy*, p. 32.

the Japanese began unilaterally supporting Chiang Kai-shek's antiradical faction of the Kuomintang in an effort to forge a Sino-Japanese understanding based on coexistence, co-prosperity, and cooperation "as Japan defined it." The Japanese insisted that preservation of their essential rights in Manchuria was integral to any arrangement with the Chinese. The Chinese, however, were committed to complete diplomatic sovereignty. The Manchurian question would doom "any attempt by Japan to create a new order of Sino-Japanese understanding by other than forceful means."[27]

Though different, the unilateral strategies of the treaty powers initially proved compatible. The British accepted minor infringements of treaty rights in return for safeguards at Shanghai. The United States declared a willingness to negotiate alone, but only with a central Chinese authority. The Japanese began supporting Chiang Kai-shek, yet remained committed to excluding Kuomintang influence from Manchuria and Mongolia. Unilateral strategies coexisted peacefully up until 1932 when the Shanghai crisis destroyed any hopes of settling the Manchurian problem without creating a major rift between Japan and the Anglo-Saxon powers. According to James Crowley, "No [Japanese] premier, following the rancor generated by the Shanghai hostilities, could anticipate support for a policy which would confirm the 'principle' of Chinese sovereignty in Manchuria."[28] Sino-Japanese conflict spread to Shanghai in January 1932, directly threatening British trade and industry. The crisis precipitated a major shift in British opinion, because Japanese movements into Shanghai might be interpreted as a prelude to controlling all of China. In short, the anti-Japanese boycott was not illegal, and it represented China's sole weapon against foreign powers. Yet the Japanese responded brutally, bombing civilians, burning bridges, and killing large numbers of noncombatants.

In retrospect, the unification of China by 1928 made it impossible for Tokyo to stand by passively as nationalism and civil war threatened Japanese interests in Manchuria. Influential civilian and military leaders, even factions within the "total war" clique of the Army, continued to stress that action in Manchuria need not antagonize the United States or any other power, and that Nationalist rule in the

27. Iriye, *After Imperialism*, p. 160.

28. Louis, *British Strategy*, p. 187; Crowley, *Japan's Quest for Autonomy*, p. 168. See also Christopher Thorne, "The Shanghai Crisis of 1932: The Basis of British Policy," *American Historical Review* 75 (October 1970): 1616–39.

south was acceptable so long as rights in Manchuria were protected. These officers recognized the importance of at least cordial relations with the West to achieve economic self-sufficiency and wage total war successfully. Other factions within the Japanese military, however, assumed the inevitability of conflict between Japan and the United States and asserted the need for a predominant position in Manchuria, based on more than simply treaty rights, to ensure success in total war.[29] The total war officers were interested first and foremost in achieving self-sufficiency for Japan, and this required comprehensive domestic reorganization, as well as territorial expansion. All the total war officers believed that the development of Manchuria was necessary to give the empire the economic capacity to wage war with the United States. However, some, like Lieutenant Colonel Nagata Tetsuzan, advocated delayed military action on the continent, since war would only jeopardize progress toward self-sufficiency. Others, like Lieutenant Colonel Ishiwara Kanji, argued that development of Manchuria could not be achieved under any Chinese leader and called for immediate action to seize the territory. It was the unilateral action of this second faction that precipitated the occupation of Manchuria on September 18, 1931.

Britain and the United States were torn between support for China's quest for sovereignty and a desire not to isolate the Japanese. The British wanted to reconcile an accommodation with the Nationalists to protect British economic interests in China with a sympathetic posture for Japan's dilemma in Manchuria. As W. Roger Louis aptly puts it, "To the British Manchuria was, to use the recurrent analogy, a sort of Asian Alsace-Lorraine, a problem defying a straightforward or satisfactory solution. . . . On the whole British sympathies lay with Japan, perhaps above all because of the power of analogy. In the words of . . . Ambassador [to Japan] Sir John Tilley: Japan 'estimates the importance of Manchuria to herself as Great Britain does that of Ireland or Egypt.' "[30] Both the United States and Japan had an interest in preserving peaceful economic relations with each other. Japan was the United States's biggest customer in Asia and the recipient of millions of dollars worth of loans. Japan's Minseito party supported cooperation with the West in

29. Chihiro Hosoya, "Retrogression in Japan's Foreign Policy Decision-Making Process," in James William Morley, ed., *Dilemmas of Growth in Prewar Japan* (Princeton: Princeton University Press, 1971), pp. 81–106; Akira Iriye, "Failure of Military Expansionism," in Morley, ed., *Dilemmas of Growth*, pp. 107–38.

30. Louis, *British Strategy*, pp. 174–75.

China and a cautious China policy, because U.S. financial assistance was considered indispensable for the economic development of Manchuria. Yet while Japanese civilian leaders were deemphasizing Sino-Japanese co-prosperity, the military was championing co-prosperity as the strategy to attain imperial self-sufficiency. By 1929, Lieutenant Colonel Ishiwara Kanji and his army supporters began imposing their vision of a comprehensive global strategy on Japanese foreign policy.[31] They advocated strong action in China to prepare for the next war, which would require the mobilization of the total resources of the nation. "Japanese unilateral action in China . . . was for them . . . merely a first step, in the direction of creating a self-sufficient empire capable of waging such warfare."[32]

Ishiwara Kanji's view achieved increased saliency as the world economic crisis undermined Prime Minister Shidehara's economic diplomacy of cooperation with the West. Political and military considerations displaced the primacy of an economic policy that had called for peaceful coexistence among the Washington powers in China. Throughout the 1920s, though each power at times had pursued different economic policies in China, these policies were consistent in that they were directed toward the attainment of certain broader economic objectives: increased trade and investment, nondiscrimination, and economic stability in a nonrevolutionary China. However, depression in the Far East significantly altered the economic reality facing Japan.

Many Japanese wished to preserve economic ties with the West. Peaceful bilateral economic relations were critical for a Japan that had become integrated into the world economy "in a way that made necessary a substantial degree of cooperation with Britain and America, not only in East Asia: the United States was Japan's chief silk market; British India supplied cotton and pig-iron for Japanese industry."[33] Depression undercut the foundations of Japan's economic diplomacy by radically transforming trade patterns. The Japanese were unable to retain their preeminent place in U.S. and Chinese trade. The decline in U.S. income and U.S. commodity prices contracted the U.S. market for Japanese goods. Silk, the most important import from Japan and a major foreign exchange earner, fell in price by 25 percent. Between 1929

31. Mark R. Peattie, *Ishiwara Kanji and Japan's Confrontation with the West* (Princeton: Princeton University Press, 1975).

32. Iriye, *After Imperialism*, p. 261.

33. Beasley, *Japanese Imperialism*, p. 173.

and 1930, Japanese exports to the United States declined by 40 percent. Enactment of the Smoot-Hawley tariff in June 1930 raised import duties on Japanese goods on average by 23 percent, while U.S. exports to Japan declined by 30 percent between 1929 and 1930, and by another 20 percent between 1930 and 1931. The China market also contracted for all countries whose currencies were based on gold. According to Iriye, "Between 1929 and 1931 American exports to China declined by 30 percent, and Japanese exports by 50 percent. . . . Japanese export trade suffered a greater decline, and in 1931 Japan was replaced by the United States as the biggest supplier of goods to China."[34] The collapse of the U.S. market, decline in trade with China, and the failure of the United States and Britain to respond to renewed Japanese overtures for cooperation in the Far East[35] removed any rationale for Japan's economic diplomacy.

In addition, an acute controversy in Japan surrounding the ratification of the London Naval Treaty of 1930 united critics of the government's cooperative policies. The London Treaty created acute and widespread political turmoil in Japan.[36] Japanese naval policy in 1930, like that of 1922, called for defensive superiority in the western Pacific. This translated into supremacy over the U.S. fleet in Japanese home waters. By 1930, the Japanese perceived escalating threats to their national security from Nationalist forces in China. They demanded more cruisers to supplement their fleet in Chinese waters and insisted that the 10:6 cruiser ratio by itself was inadequate for their local security requirements. The Washington treaties had recognized the legitimacy of defensive superiority in respective spheres, and the Japanese sought reconfirmation in 1930 by demanding 70 percent of U.S. heavy cruiser strength. The United States, however, demanded extension of the 10:6 capital ship ratio, codified in the 1922 Five Power treaty, to the cruiser class. The U.S. position was perceived by the Japanese as a challenge to their hegemony in the western Pacific and to a principle that had been validated at Washington eight years earlier based on understandings regarding Shantung, Manchuria, and the status of base fortifications in the Pacific. To the Japanese, the Western powers had failed to reconfirm the legitimacy of Japanese defensive superiority in the west-

34. Iriye, *After Imperialism*, p. 279.

35. Ibid., pp. 242–43.

36. See Baron Kumao Harada, *Fragile Victory: The 1930 London Treaty Issue*, trans. Thomas Francis Mayer-Oakes (Detroit: Wayne State University Press, 1968).

ern Pacific. Japanese perceptions were not far afield. U.S. naval leaders recognized that a 10:7 ratio would guarantee U.S. supremacy in the eastern Pacific and Japanese supremacy in the western Pacific. However, they wanted a ratio that would, should war occur, permit the U.S. Navy to take the war into Japanese home waters.

With an upcoming general election, Japan's commitment to a 10:7 ratio in the cruiser class became a highly publicized and politically charged issue. The compromises Japan's representatives conceded to at the London Conference precipitated a constitutional crisis. With the Reed-Matsudaira compromise,[37] the Japanese accepted a 10:6 ratio in heavy cruisers while the United States was authorized to build to a total of eighteen such ships. The United States agreed to defer construction of the sixteenth until 1934, the seventeenth until 1935, and the eighteenth until 1936. The Japanese would build no heavy cruisers during the life of the treaty, but would retain the twelve they already possessed. Thus, the Japanese accepted the 10:6 ratio in principle, while actually securing a de facto 10:7 ratio until 1936. Yet this compromise precipitated a major political crisis in Japan because the 10:6 ratio was perceived as a challenge to Japanese hegemony in the western Pacific. In addition, the Japanese agreed to refrain from building any heavy cruisers and were granted only 50,768 tons of new construction. By contrast, the United States was authorized to build fourteen heavy cruisers for a total of 346,811 tons of new shipping.[38] The Japanese had agreed to stop active construction of heavy cruisers and to accept inferiority to the United States's "potential" program. The Minseito party platform of fiscal austerity, arms reduction, a moderate China policy, and cooperation with the West was contingent on Japanese hegemony in the western Pacific. The collapse of one pillar brought the whole facade crashing down.

The Hamaguchi cabinet argued that though they had compromised the 10:7 ratio "in principle," in reality Japan had secured that ratio until 1936 since the United States would not lay the keels of the last three vessels until 1934. Furthermore, any deficiencies could be minimized by technological improvements and by increases in the naval air force. To override objections of the Naval General Staff, Prime Minister Hamaguchi Osachi engaged in delicate backstage political maneu-

---

37. O'Connor, *Perilous Equilibrium*, pp. 76–83.
38. Crowley, *Japan's Quest for Autonomy*, p. 55.

vering, effectively ignoring the professional advice of the navy on a
critical matter of national security. This incited a national controversy
over the interpretation of Article XI of the Meiji Constitution on the
"right of supreme command." Article XI entrusted the right of supreme
command to the general staffs, and they, as a result, held responsibility
for national security policy.[39] Admiral Kato Kanji, chief of staff of the
Imperial Navy, declared that according to the constitution, the Naval
General Board was "the instrument by which the Emperor alone exercised his prerogative of determining the size of the Navy."[40] The civilians had violated this prerogative by making naval policy without con-
sulting the Naval General Staff. The liberal Hamaguchi government
responded that the Cabinet was responsible for affairs of state. Because
political and economic considerations were involved in addition to
questions of naval policy, the Cabinet possessed the constitutional
power to accept the Reed-Matsudaira compromise without approval of
the Naval Board. As Hall concludes, the critical question became
"whether the Cabinet had the right to determine the size of the Japanese Navy."[41] The struggle over ratification boiled down to a conflict
between the military and civilian branches of government over authority and responsibility. As Raymond O'Connor summarizes the dispute,
"The navy held that its administration was delegated by the Emperor
directly to the chief of the naval general staff, and that naval authorities alone, under the Emperor, could determine the strength of the
fleet. The civilian statesmen, navy spokesmen contended, had exceeded their powers in executing a treaty that applied restrictions which
those responsible could not accept."[42] Nor was the military alone in its
opposition to the policies of Hamaguchi and Shidehara. The opposition
party, the Seiyukai, demanding maintenance of Japan's privileged position in Manchuria, was far less wedded to international cooperation
and naval disarmament to meet this continental agenda and eagerly
seized the opportunity to depose the Minseito cabinet.

---

39. See ibid., pp. 66–74, and James B. Crowley, "A New Deal for Japan: One Road to Pearl
Harbor," in James B. Crowley, ed., Modern East Asia: Essays in Interpretation (New York: Harcourt, Brace & World, 1970), p. 243.
40. Hall, Britain, America, and Arms Control, p. 108.
41. Ibid.
42. O'Connor, Perilous Equilibrium, p. 118.

The civilians prevailed in Japan, but not without a price. Following treaty ratification, the Supreme War Council approved a supplemental naval budget, prepared by the Naval General Staff alone, to offset the deficiencies created by the London Naval Treaty. In a dangerous precedent, neither the finance ministry, the naval ministry, nor the premier were consulted in budget formation. The London Naval Treaty controversy effectively weakened civilian control and undermined those leaders committed to arms limitation. On November 14, 1930, Hamaguchi was shot by a youth claiming the prime minister had violated the right of supreme command. He died shortly thereafter.

A shift in cabinet politics, coupled with a shift in public opinion, rapidly undermined the basis of Shidehara diplomacy. In 1930, military critics of the London Treaty united with critics of the Minseito cabinet's economic policies. Given this broad-based domestic pressure, the Tokyo government concluded that any retreat in China would lead to its downfall. Only exacerbating the government's problems, the Nationalist government in China, having determined its strength depended upon a strong posture against Japan, announced its intent to unilaterally abrogate all unequal treaties by January 1932.

In retrospect, attempts to isolate differences over economic priorities in China from arms control considerations by extending force limitation provisions at the 1930 London Naval Conference without addressing the changes that had occurred in China were doomed once Japan's economic and military policies became reunited in a philosophy of "total war." War would be a contest of national power, particularly economic power. In theory, success in total war demanded cultivation of a "special" relationship with China. After World War I, Japan's Imperial Army concluded that Germany's defeat had more to do with economic vulnerability to the Allied blockade than inferior military tactics or strategy. As Michael A. Barnhart describes this position:

> It appeared that the great powers of the twentieth century would have to have more than military prowess. They would have to be self-sufficient, capable of waging 'total war' without reliance on materials or equipment from outside their borders. If the Japanese Empire was to retain its international status . . . some means of achieving autarky had to be found. . . . First, the Empire would have to grow to include territory which held re-

sources necessary for war-making. Second, Japan would have to construct a modern industrial base.[43]

Hence, economic cooperation with the West in China and success in total war were ultimately incompatible. In practical terms, as the growth of nationalism in China threatened to undermine the traditional policies of Japan in Manchuria and Inner Mongolia, efforts to secure the requisites for a self-sufficient wartime economy became impossible to reconcile with the Washington formula for cooperation in the Far East and nonintervention in Chinese domestic politics. By 1930 in Japan, economic relations with the West, policies in China and Manchuria, and naval policy in the wake of the London Treaty controversy were relinked. Japan's invasion of Manchuria in 1931 was the culmination of a process that demonstrated the difficulties of delinking intrinsically related security issues. As Iriye summarizes, it was unrealistic to expect that

> the nation's economic interests should and could be promoted in all directions, that problems of a non-economic nature could be handled individually, and consequently that there was no need to develop a comprehensive foreign policy. Independent action in China, understanding with the West outside China, indifference to the military implications of Soviet and Chinese radicalism, unwillingness to relate the naval rivalry with the United States to the question of overall Japanese-American relations— all were . . . [untenable assumptions of Japan's economic diplomacy].[44]

Up until 1930, civilian leaders consciously shielded arms control from turmoil in China by divorcing developments in the two arenas. This delinkage, however, was artificial, and once military and economic policy were reunited in Japan, there was no firm foundation for a political accommodation in the Far East to sustain even minimal arms control.

By 1931, Japanese priorities had shifted from the primacy of coexistence with the West toward the primacy of Asian relations. "Co-prosperity, signifying an exclusive and unequal economic partnership be-

43. Barnhart, "Japan's Economic Security," p. 107.
44. Iriye, *After Imperialism*, p. 301.

tween China and Japan, became the slogan of the decade."[45] Against a
background of worldwide economic depression, Japanese exports to and
imports from Taiwan and Korea rose between 1929 and 1930. It seemed
that "foreign trade had resisted the depression best . . . where Japan
exercised political authority,"[46] and it was a short leap to conclude that
benefits would flow from a similar relationship with Manchuria, less a
"special interest" now and more an issue of "national survival."

That the Manchurian incident—the occupation of Mukden by Japanese troops on September 18–19, 1931—occurred at the nucleus of the
south Manchurian railway system was not surprising.[47] Hegemony in
Manchuria had been predominantly an issue of railway construction,[48]
and the Chinese were undermining the exclusive operation of the
South Manchurian Railway by building lines parallel to it. The Manchurian incident, however, was less the critical turning point in Sino-
Japanese and Japanese-Western relations folklore claims and more the
culmination of a process. As Crowley puts it,

> A virulent anti-Japanese movement in China and Manchuria,
> the growing capabilities of the Soviet Maritime Army, and the
> political turmoil provoked by the London Naval Treaty [had]
> generated in the officer corps a pervasive disaffection toward the
> policies of Baron Shidehara. Factional disputes, new concepts of
> warfare, new estimates of the significance of Manchuria, and the
> security problems posed by Chinese nationalism and the Soviet
> Army undammed in army circles a torrent of discontent with
> the government's foreign and fiscal policies, and ultimately im-
> pelled the Mukden incident in September 1931.[49]

45. Beasley, *Japanese Imperialism*, p. 175.
46. Ibid., p. 190.
47. Sadako Ogata, *Defiance in Manchuria: The Making of Japanese Foreign Policy, 1931–1932*
(Berkeley and Los Angeles: University of California Press, 1964); Takehiko Yoshihashi, *Conspiracy
at Mukden: The Rise of the Japanese Military* (New Haven: Yale University Press, 1963).
48. See Louis, *British Strategy*, pp. 175–76, for details.
49. Crowley, *Japan's Quest for Autonomy*, p. 82. On the threat from the Soviet Union, Crowley
notes that the five-year economic programs had greatly augmented the strength of the Red Army
in the maritime provinces, and that a vastly improved Red Army on Manchurian borders was a
legitimate concern to Japan's General Staff. By 1931, the operations division of the general staff
was convinced of the historical inevitability of Soviet-Japanese conflict and advocated direct military action in Manchuria. Ibid., pp. 83, 111.

Western opinion did not unanimously condemn Japanese actions un-til conflict spread to Shanghai in January 1932, directly threatening British trade and industry.[50] In response to Japan's seizure of North Manchuria and the creation of "independent" Manchukuo, the League of Nations voted to create a new administrative arrangement for Man-churia that would protect Japan's special rights, yet "be consistent with the principle of Chinese sovereignty over Manchuria."[51] In response, Japan withdrew from the League of Nations in March 1933. Concilia-tion with the Kuomintang and cooperation with Britain and the United States had become policies of the past.[52]

The Reconstitution of German Power

By 1928, the French were becoming increasingly concerned about Ger-many's emerging naval posture. Germany, a formidable adversary of the past, was well along the road to reconstituting its military prowess. De-fense Minister Wilhelm Groner and Naval Commander-in-Chief Admi-ral Erich Raeder had begun replacing obsolete capital ships retained under the provisions of the Versailles Treaty.[53] In March, a Commission of Control was created, consisting of the army and navy chiefs, a per-manent official of the Finance Ministry, and the president of the treas-ury, symbolizing acceptance by the government of full responsibility for naval rearmament. In November, Germany's Socialist leaders agreed to support construction of the first pocket battleship, *Panzerkreuzer A*,[54] rather than risk the fall of the government and the emergence of a more conservative cabinet. Finally, the naval budgets of 1928–29 and 1929–30 indicated an accelerated pace in Germany's replacement programs.

50. Thorne, "Shanghai Crisis," pp. 1616–39.

51. Crowley, *Japan's Quest for Autonomy*, p. 186.

52. See James William Morley, ed., *The Fateful Choice: Japan's Advance into Southeast Asia, 1939–1941*, Japan's Road to the Pacific War Series (New York: Columbia University Press, 1980).

53. See Robin Rudoff, "Influence of the German Navy on the British Search for Naval Arms Control, 1928–1935" (Ph.D. diss., Tulane University, 1964), pp. 32, 34, 36, 40.

54. During construction until the official launching ceremony, this first pocket battleship was to be referred to as *Panzerkreuzer 'A'*, signifying it was the first of its type, and also as *Ersatz Preussen*, indicating that it was replacing the old battleship *Preussen*. On May 19, 1931, this pocket battle-ship was launched and renamed the *Deutschland*.

These developments stimulated a response in France and signaled the failure of Britain's policy of "disarmament by example."[55] Germany's pocket battleship was called a "miracle in naval architecture," a "perfect commerce-raider as plainly as anything that the Kaiser ever built."[56] Britain's leading naval annual claimed that Germany had used "mechanical ingenuity to overcome limitations without violation of the letter of the Versailles restrictions."[57] The German Navy had been limited at Paris to six battleships displacing no more than 10,000 tons each, six light cruisers, twelve destroyers, twelve torpedo boats, and no submarines. However, since no limitations were placed on budgetary expenditure, the Germans spent tremendous resources and built highly efficient commerce raiders or "pocket battleships." The Deutschland-class units were more powerful than any cruiser and faster than any battleship. Innovative weight-saving technologies—the use of high-strength steels, improved armor, electric arc welding rather than riveting hulls—freed up tonnage for armament and speed.[58] The pocket battleship threatened to undermine the Washington treaty system in two ways. First, it created the possibility of Franco-German naval rivalry, which would probably involve Italy. Since France had already increased its naval expenditures, German building was having an indirect effect on British policy. As noted earlier, the Washington treaty system was premised on the fact that absence of the traditional central European threat freed up Britain to focus on the Pacific. That premise was rapidly becoming as obsolete as an arms limitation system that excluded Germany. Second,

55. The downward spiral of British naval appropriations began in 1922. As late as 1929, the British decided to suspend part of their 1929 naval program and cancel completely construction of three ships in order to demonstrate a commitment to arms reduction. In defense of this policy of "unilateral disarmament," designed to reduce Britain's fleet while maintaining its leading position, First Lord Alexander in April 1931 stated that "Britain was prepared to go further still, if other nations reciprocated." Quoted in Rudoff, *Influence of the German Navy*, p. 103.

56. Lord Robert Vansittart, permanent under-secretary in the British Foreign Office from 1929 to 1938, quoted in ibid., pp. 54–55.

57. *Brassey's Naval Annual* (London, 1929), p. 41. For a complete treatment of German evasion of the Versailles Treaty, see Whaley, *Covert German Rearmament*; Michael Mihalka, *German Strategic Deception in the 1930s* (N-1557-NA) (Santa Monica: The RAND Corporation, July 1980); and Roskill, *Naval Policy*, vol. 1., pp. 440–41.

58. "On a nominal standard displacement of 10,000 tons (actually 11,700 tons as completed) [German designers] managed to mount two triple 11-inch gun turrets and by adopting for the first time an all-diesel power plant they could provide a staggering 10,000 miles' endurance. Although the speed was only 26 knots and the armour no thicker than the best-protected heavy cruisers, the combination of heavy gunpower, a fair turn of speed and high endurance seemed to be an ideal combination for a commerce raider." Preston, *Cruisers*, pp. 104–6.

and more directly, the existence of a vessel that could outshoot any vessel that could catch it and outrun any vessel that could outshoot it threatened to undermine the balance of naval power established by the Washington treaties by rendering obsolete the 10,000-ton treaty cruisers, which because of the limits placed on battleships, had become a kind of "junior capital ship."[59]

In 1930, the Washington powers reconvened for the first time outside the forum of the League Preparatory Commission to consolidate the security system created at Washington by extending limitations to ancillary categories of combatants (cruisers, destroyers, and submarines). Three years earlier, under pressure from Congress, President Coolidge had issued invitations for a naval conference in Geneva under the auspices of the League Preparatory Commission. The Geneva Disarmament Conference convened in June 1927 as a Three-Power Conference; the French and Italians protested the exclusion of land and air armaments from discussion by sending only observers. The conference ended on August 4 without an agreement.[60] At London in 1930, the French and Italians participated, though they were unable to agree with Washington, London, and Tokyo on a treaty limiting ancillary vessels. According to O'Connor, "The five power treaty was a victim of Italian pride, French fears, British caution, and American isolation."[61]

The first London Naval Treaty, signed on April 22, 1930, consolidated the Washington treaty system in two ways: by limiting all categories of warships of the three great powers, quantitatively in all classes and qualitatively in each class and, by blocking a major loophole in the Washington Five Power treaty, namely, the failure to place quantitative restrictions on ancillary combatants. The treaty limited cruiser, de-

59. Friedman, *U.S. Cruisers*, p. 111.

60. Hall cites a variety of reasons for the failure to reach any agreement: the central cruiser question between the United States and Great Britain; the lack of preliminary diplomatic consultation among the participants; the control exercised by admirals over their civilian counterparts in the Technical Committee; and the lack of publicity the proceedings received because they were conducted in secrecy. Hall, *Britain, America, and Arms Control*, pp. 37–58.

61. As O'Connor explains, "To avoid loss of prestige, the arrogant Mussolini felt that he could not accept less than parity with France. Tardieu and Briand could not grant parity to Italy because of public opinion and the dual threat of Germany in the Channel and the North Sea and Italy in the Mediterranean. MacDonald was prevented from furnishing France with adequate safeguards by public opinion and an adamant domestic political opposition. In effect, Britain was afraid of being drawn into a Continental war as she had been in 1914; France was afraid that she might not be. In any event, British guarantees would only have effected a reduction in the size of the French naval demands, not an acceptance of parity with Italy." O'Connor, *Perilous Equilibrium*, p. 103.

stroyer, and submarine tonnage totals of the United States, the British Commonwealth, and Japan and permitted a proportionate increase in these categories should national security be affected by the naval construction of a nonsignatory. All five powers (the Big Three plus France and Italy) agreed to a moratorium on new capital ship construction until 1936, to limits on individual submarine displacement, and to the exemption of certain noncombatant classes of naval vessels from limitation.

Yet the London Naval Treaty represented an important shift in the prevailing practices of the Washington treaty system for reaching arms control agreements. First, concessions were confined to ships alone, with no explicit linkages made between arms control and the resolution of political problems. The signatories simply endorsed the Kellogg-Briand Pact of 1928, also known as the Pact of Paris, as the political basis for arms limitation. Indeed, the London Conference invitations stated that the Kellogg-Briand Pact was "the starting point of any agreement" and the basis for naval limitation.[62] The pact condemned and renounced the use of force as an instrument of national policy unless for defense, and the signatories agreed to resolve peacefully any conflicts among themselves. The pact, however, did not guarantee security or provide any machinery for the resolution of disputes. It represented a very weak political foundation to sustain arms control. Whereas the Washington treaties had been premised on the idea that arms limitation in the absence of the political resolution of tension could not promote stability, political agreement was replaced at London by vague references to the pact. No serious consideration was given to events in China. French pleas for enhanced security in Europe were left unanswered. The overriding consideration was to advance arms limitation, despite the political sources of conflict in Europe and Asia. The London process reflected a military-based approach to arms control.

Suspecting isolationist sentiment in Britain, the French had come to London seeking a regional pact for the Mediterranean along the lines of the Four Power treaty. The French argued that "programs of disarmament could not be based alone upon such unimplemented declarations of good will such as the Kellogg Pact,"[63] which contained no provisions

---

62. Hall, *Britain, America, and Arms Control*, pp. 67, 80.

63. Although the British opposed a Mediterranean Pact that would commit them to guaranteeing France's security, some mention was made that the United States "was contemplating a cautious advance in the direction of implementing the Kellogg Pact by suggesting a general consulta-

for enforcement and which created no "political arrangements in which the loss of diplomatic bargaining power to France and Italy from a reduction of their naval force would be offset by some corresponding advantage."[64] In 1922, the signatories had come to an accommodation in China that permitted the peaceful coexistence of their economic policies in the Far East. Likewise, the Four Power treaty established a modus vivendi in the Pacific by creating spheres of influence and by pledging the parties to confer should disputes arise over the Pacific islands. Though the political agreements reached at Washington may have had weaknesses and ambiguities, there was an assumption that political arrangements and assurances were as important to international security as force limits. At London, no attempt was made to relate the political and military components of security. France continued to demand specific political guarantees as a necessary prerequisite to disarmament, whereas the United States and Britain maintained that the Kellogg-Briand Pact was a satisfactory basis for disarmament.[65] As a result of the failure to meet France's political demands for security, a five-power naval agreement was superseded by a three-power agreement at London, demonstrating the second way the London Treaty marked a shift in the prevailing Washington practices for arms control. The procedures for implementing collective choice were modified to maintain the Far Eastern component of the arms control system, despite failure to appease French demands in Europe.

In a third shift from Washington practices, the British Empire, facing possible unrestrained growth in Continental navies, inserted escape or escalator clauses into the London Naval Treaty that "made the treaty limits purely conditional, for it reserved to Great Britain the right to exceed the tonnage totals agreed upon [in Part III of the treaty regarding cruisers] should they become insufficient to ensure her two power standard."[66] The escalator clause provided an avenue for preserving British supremacy in the Mediterranean in the face of French and Italian ancillary construction. Article 21 permitted corresponding increases in

---

tive treaty." In the end, the United States proved unwilling and unable to make such a commitment. Hall, *Britain, America, and Arms Control*, pp. 83–84. "The assurances that France needed could come only from England, but Tardieu and Briand felt that they must come via the United States." O'Connor, *Perilous Equilibrium*, p. 101.

64. Chaput, *Disarmament*, p. 194.

65. O'Connor, *Perilous Equilibrium*, p. 91.

66. Merze Tate, *The United States and Armaments* (Cambridge: Harvard University Press, 1948), p. 180.

tonnage if the security of a signatory were threatened by the new construction of any power not a party to Part III of the Treaty (namely, France and Italy). The British were able to agree to limit ancillary craft despite France's large submarine tonnage, but provisions were made for the eventual defection of Great Britain if the European situation required it. Limitations were accepted "only so long as they so permitted the British Navy to maintain its supremacy in European, Indian, and South Pacific waters."[67]

Increases in Germany's naval budget in February 1930 and the authorization of funds for a second pocket battleship in April 1930 ultimately stimulated a cycle of Franco-German naval competition. In November 1930, proposals were advanced to complete three pocket battleships and lay down a fourth, along with seventeen other smaller vessels between 1931 and 1936. Though all this construction fell within the limits of the Versailles restrictions,[68] the French were not consoled. To neutralize the threat posed by the pocket battleships, the French began to construct a "pocket battleship chaser," a 23,000-ton battle cruiser to outrun *and* outshoot the pocket battleships. Their efforts ultimately produced the *Dunkerque*, launched in 1935,[69] and spurred the Italians to lay their first treaty battleships in 1934, the *Vittorio* and *Littorio*.[70] When the Reichstag appropriated funds for a second pocket battleship in March 1931, the French announced their decision to start replacing overage capital ships in 1935. The British had planned to delay replacements until 1936. In essence, the pocket battleship made Germany a major factor in the global balance of naval power, even though its navy was still constrained by the Versailles Treaty.

German rearmament had precluded a Franco-Italian naval agreement that, the British hoped, might be eventually negotiated to bring these two under the restrictions of the 1930 London Treaty. Germany had become the key to any future naval understanding, and German demands for equality of status to rearm, rejected fervently by the French, impelled the British to negotiate with Germany in order to contain a European arms race.

67. Chaput, *Disarmament*, p. 202.
68. Rudoff, "Influence of the German Navy," pp. 89–90.
69. Preston, *Cruisers*, p. 107.
70. "These ships established a new standard of speed, about 30 knots, which had been made possible by engineering developments originally tested in the treaty cruisers of the 1920s." Friedman, *U.S. Battleships*, pp. 223–24. See also Preston, *Cruisers*, pp. 99–101.

The British first attempted to bring Germany into the balance of naval power at the Geneva Disarmament Conference of 1932. The Germans, with a 1932–33 military budget that included allocations for a third pocket battleship, demanded equality in armaments and were willing to accept either the disarmament of other states or German rearmament. Germany's apparent willingness to disarm, provided others reciprocated, was well received, but the British rejected out of hand Germany's call for abolition of all capital ships in excess of 10,000 tons. The Geneva Conference failed to produce an agreement, and in October 1933, the Germans withdrew, protesting that the principle of equality had not been granted. Shortly thereafter, the Germans gave notice of their intention to withdraw from the League of Nations, and Hitler ordered Raeder to build two 26,000-ton battleships, a size forbidden by the Versailles Treaty.

As the linchpin between the Pacific and European naval balances, the British could focus their attention on the Pacific arena only as long as Germany remained bound by the Versailles Treaty restrictions.[71] Only with a negligible German fleet would the French and Italians accept inferior naval status. Germany's withdrawal from the League of Nations rendered the Washington and London treaties inadequate for regulating the balance of naval power in the Pacific and worldwide and confronted the British with the impossible task of matching the combined rearmament efforts of the Germans and Japanese. To meet defense requirements in European and Pacific waters, but through arms limitation rather than by invoking the escalator clause of the London Naval Treaty, the British pursued two strategies. First, they began courting the Japanese to secure a rapprochement, in the form of a bilateral nonaggression pact, that would lighten the burden of imperial defense in the Pacific. Second, given France's determination to preserve naval superiority over Germany and refusal to grant Germany "equality of status" to rearm, the British attempted to regulate German rearmament by negotiating the Anglo-German Naval Treaty of 1935.

In 1932, Sino-Japanese conflict at Shanghai had revealed the incapacity of the Royal Navy to defend Singapore, the "impregnable door to the eastern empire." Although the Ten Year Rule[72] was abandoned in

71. See F. S. Northedge, *Freedom and Necessity in British Foreign Policy* (London: C. Tinling, 1972).

72. The Ten Year Rule, adopted in August 1919, assumed Britain would not be engaged in any great war during the next ten years. With this assumption came drastic cuts in defense spending.

1933, Britain had dropped below the one-power standard, and developments in the European theater raised grave doubts about the sufficiency of even the one-power standard for the future. Despite a resurgent Germany, Japan was perceived as a more immediate threat to British interests worldwide. In October 1933, the Committee of Imperial Defense (CID), Britain's highest defense directorate, initiated a review of imperial defense policy. Among other things, the Chiefs of Staff Subcommittee concluded that protecting possessions and interests in the Far East was the first of Britain's defense requirements, followed by European commitments and the defense of India.[73] The Admiralty called for a fleet sufficient to meet the Imperial Navy at any moment—at least three battleships, twenty more cruisers, and sufficient merchant cruisers to match Japan's ships of the line and Germany's commerce raiders[74]— but the Treasury preferred a political understanding to neutralize Japan. Chancellor of the Exchequer Neville Chamberlain argued that "if it proved possible to improve relations with Japan, it might be possible to reduce the far east in order of priority and so concentrate Britain's limited resources on defense spending in Europe."[75] Accommodation with Japan became an increasingly attractive option, and the Treasury took the lead in advocating political appeasement to eliminate the Far East from defense calculations altogether. Sir Warren Fisher, permanent secretary of the exchequer, believed Britain had only enough strength to deal with Germany and that political accommodation with Japan was vital. To improve relations with Japan, Fisher argued it might be necessary "to cut Britain off from the United States, and the London Naval Conference [of 1935] might prove 'the parting of the ways.'"[76] In 1933, however, an accommodation with Tokyo appeared rather remote, given Japan's accelerated naval program and determination to seek parity at London in 1935. Japan's admirals had initiated a major drive for increased arms spending, and in late September 1933, Navy Minister Osumi Mineo requested the cabinet adopt a new naval policy before the next disarmament conference, based on either a large increase in its naval ratio or even full equality. With the Roosevelt administration's passage of the National Industrial Recovery Act in July 1933, authorizing funds for thirty-two warships totaling 126,000 tons to bring the

73. Trotter, *Britain and East Asia*, p. 36.
74. Pelz, *Race to Pearl Harbor*, p. 103.
75. Trotter, *Britain and East Asia*, p. 37.
76. Quoted in Pelz, *Race to Pearl Harbor*, p. 105.

U.S. Navy up to London Treaty limits, Osumi threatened to resign and bring down the cabinet unless his demands for a larger naval budget were met. The military's share of the budget rose from 36 to 45 percent.[77]

In March 1934, before the full cabinet, Chamberlain recommended a bilateral nonaggression pact with Japan, and if necessary to this end, detachment from the United States at the upcoming second London Naval Conference. Foreign Secretary Sir John Simon outlined the pros and cons of such a pact. On the positive side, the pact would reassure Tokyo that Britain would not ally with the United States against Japan and could moderate Japanese naval demands. On the negative side, the pact might be perceived by the Chinese, the Soviets, and the League of Nations as British acquiescence to Japanese policies in the Far East.[78] Wary of such a pact, Simon suggested it might be more useful if linked to the upcoming naval negotiations to induce the Japanese to accept a lower ratio. Accommodation with Japan, though requiring splitting with the United States, would permit Britain to concentrate on the German threat while keeping defense expenditures down. Simon and the Foreign Office, however, remained doubtful that the Japanese would forgo demands for naval parity at London. The Japanese had never been content with a 60 percent ratio. And although Japan had built to treaty strength and the United States had not, which gave Japan 80 percent of total U.S. tonnage, in the spring of 1934, the Vinson-Trammel Bill was passed, authorizing the president to bring the U.S. Navy up to treaty limits. Threatened with the loss of its 80 percent ratio, the Japanese were sure to oppose naval limitation unless granted parity with the Anglo-Saxon powers. China was a potential lever for bargaining with Japan to improve relations, stabilize political and economic conditions in China,[79] and maintain the treaty system given

77. See ibid., p. 19.
78. Trotter, *Britain and East Asia*, p. 43.
79. The most notable effort was the Leith-Ross mission of September 1935, an effort to cooperate with Japan to restabilize Chinese affairs by providing economic assistance. A loan would be extended to China to bring order to the financial chaos created by the United States's silver purchase policy. In return for the aid, the Chinese hopefully would extend de facto recognition to Manchukuo. The Leith-Ross scheme attempted to salvage cooperative diplomacy and was based on the assumptions that Japan had not entirely left and did not intend to leave the system and that China and the other powers would accept the new status quo. As in Europe, the British were willing to come to terms with Japanese (and German and Italian) revisionism, provided it remained within bounds. Japan, however, preferred to strengthen its bilateral ties with China to stabilize their relations. Iriye, *Origins of the Second World War*, pp. 31–32. See also Trotter, *Britain and East Asia*, pp. 148–67, on the Leith-Ross mission.

shifting security requirements in Europe. The risks, however, were high—alienation of the United States, the Soviet Union, and China. Yet since Britain's National government faced elections in 1935 or 1936, making sizable spending on armaments politically untenable, the Japanese threat, it was determined, should be met by conciliation, not confrontation.

The Foreign Office, in an effort to save the Washington system from complete disintegration, was prepared to grant Japan equality in "status," with certain increases in naval strength to assuage demands for parity at the second London Naval Conference. The Admiralty countered that if the Japanese refused to accept the existing ratio, Britain should opt to freely build to meet the situation. Chamberlain, by contrast, recommended an arrangement with Japan over China—the only area of contention between the two countries—in the event the conference broke down. Chamberlain saw Japan's position in China as the major obstacle to improved Anglo-Japanese relations and believed that a solution to commercial disputes—in essence relinking cooperation in China with arms control along the lines of the political-based approach to arms control—might create an atmosphere conducive to improved relations in the naval arena. Whereas the Admiralty believed that a fleet in the Far East was a necessary deterrent to Japanese aggression, the Treasury advocated accommodation with Japan as the best means for defending Far Eastern interests. According to Sir Warren Fisher, basing war preparations primarily on Japan was pointless, for the risk of disaster lay nearer home. Even the most optimistic estimates revealed Britain could not fight both Japan and the strongest European power. Hence, "Britain had everything to gain and nothing to lose by effecting a genuine and lasting reconciliation with Japan." Fisher supported "detachment from the United States, a thorough and lasting accommodation with Japan and the indication to Germany that Britain was prepared to concentrate maximum force in Europe."[80]

The British continued to view China as the locus of Anglo-Japanese tensions and hoped to use China as a lever to persuade the Japanese to agree to the existing naval ratios. While anticipating Japan's rejection of the existing ratios, the British nevertheless hoped, by assuring Japan a role in any economic reconstruction scheme in China, to preserve the principles of the Washington treaty system. Accommodation in the Far

80. Trotter, *Britain and East Asia*, p. 56.

East was becoming all the more attractive given France's rejection, in April 1934, of a revised disarmament agreement to include Germany.

The British came to the pre–London Conference negotiations in June 1934 hoping to secure a rapprochement with Japan and an increase in the Royal Navy's cruiser strength. The United States opposed both objectives. The British wanted to increase their cruiser ratio over the 1930 London Treaty limits. Demanding fifteen 10,000-ton heavy cruisers and forty-five light cruisers in 1929, the British had settled for fifteen and thirty-five respectively in 1930, leaving themselves, they believed, in an untenable position. Dispatching a fleet sufficient to meet Japan in the Far East and protect maritime communications meant leaving a fleet in European waters inferior to the strongest European power. Since half of Britain's cruiser force was assigned to the fleet, insufficient numbers remained to patrol the Atlantic and Pacific sea lanes. Ability to meet requirements in the Pacific, Atlantic, and Mediterranean were jeopardized further by Germany's pocket battleships, for one was a match for three of Britain's light cruisers, and by an unfortified Singapore base that constrained fleet operations in the Pacific.[81] With Hitler demanding naval equality with France, the British could not tolerate Japan's demands for an increased ratio. In essence, "Hitler's rise in the West meant rigidity of the ratios of naval strength in the East."[82]

To neutralize the fast surface raiders the Japanese had been building steadily throughout the 1920s and which the Germans had nearly "perfected" in their pocket battleships, the British now demanded a total of seventy light cruisers, or twenty-five new cruisers—120,000 tons of additional light cruisers—and the abolition of heavy cruiser construction. The Admiralty planned on retaining 50,000 tons of overage cruisers to yield an end strength of 70 cruisers. They estimated that in war, it would be possible to convert seventy-eight fast merchantmen. If the United States objected, the British were prepared to reduce their demands to a total of sixty cruisers, still an increase of ten over the 1930 London limits. The United States was unyielding: a 20 percent reduction in overall tonnage and maintenance of existing treaty limits. By late July 1934, the British agreed to an increase of only 70,000 tons

81. The decision to fortify Singapore was finally made in 1933, ensuring that the British would be able to send a fleet there by 1938.
82. Pelz, *Race to Pearl Harbor*, p. 113.

rather than 120,000 tons of light cruisers originally demanded, but in the eyes of Britain's ministers, U.S. obstinacy had enhanced the attractiveness of a rapprochement with Japan.

In October 1934, the British first broached the idea of a nonaggression pact with Japan to keep the latter in the treaty system. British Foreign Secretary Simon offered the Japanese equality of prestige in exchange for Japanese guarantees of Western interests in East Asia. Having established Japanese prestige and security, the three Pacific naval powers would then enter into a "secret gentleman's agreement" to regulate naval construction by establishing qualitative building limits and procedures for communicating yearly outlines of building programs. Dubbed the "middle course," British leaders were willing to settle for qualitative restrictions and a system for registering new construction.[83] In the Admiralty's assessment, naval competition was less about numbers of ships constructed than about the development of new designs. Hoping for broader naval limits, if the choice were between nothing and something, "qualitative limits would be worth something."[84] A nonaggression pact, based on equality of prestige, was perceived as a way to help Japanese moderates save face, while assuaging pro-navy elements. Though quantitative limits would not be explicit, the British assumed construction plans could be regulated by the Washington and London 1930 ratios.

British assumptions about the impact such an agreement, based on an equality in status declaration and a voluntary declaration of tonnage levels, would have in Japan were fatally flawed. Earlier that summer, Admiral Osumi Mineo, a strong supporter of the fleet faction, had been appointed minister of the navy. According to Trotter, the notion of helping moderate elements save face and overcoming extremist elements opposed to a naval treaty was built on false premises, for the moderate treaty group was incapable of revival by 1934, and the cabinet concurred that the naval treaties and the ratio must go. "The concept of a Japanese navy divided between extremists and moderates offered British negotiators some hope, but represented a misinterpretation of the situation."[85] And even though the newly formed government was

83. "Brief Analysis of Middle Course," Norman H. Davis Papers, London Naval Conference, Miscellaneous Memos, October–December 1934, Box 36, Library of Congress, Manuscript Division, Washington, D.C.

84. Burns and Urquidi, *Disarmament in Perspective*, vol. 3, p. 224.

85. Trotter, *Britain and East Asia*, pp. 96, 98.

headed by the moderate Admiral Okada Keisuke, the naval program published in July revealed little willingness to compromise on demands for equality to arm and for a common upper limit of overall tonnage within which each nation would be free to select independently which weapons to develop.

The Japanese argued that since the Washington Conference, technological developments had substantially increased the range of warships and enhanced the offense over the defense. To reestablish superiority of the defense, the Japanese proposed lowering the overall tonnage limit as much as possible and drastically reducing or abolishing offensive weapons such as battleships, aircraft carriers, and heavy cruisers. The British countered that these demands failed to consider the worldwide responsibilities of an imperial power and would grant disproportionate latitude to lesser powers. The United States also refused to accept any compromise on existing ratios, unless building programs were embodied in a contractual form (meaning an agreement to exchange information on building plans), a further limit on freedom and flexibility that the Japanese rejected.

Finally, the Japanese refused to link naval matters to policies in China along the lines of the Washington principles. The Japanese, instead, proposed a modified Washington system. International cooperation must proceed from the premise that Japan had primacy in Chinese affairs. The Japanese refused to cooperate with other countries or the League to help China along the road to economic recovery and fiscal reform.[86] Given this developing consensus in Japan on policy toward China, Britain's strategy began to take on an aura of complete unreality. In Japan, a committee of high-ranking army, navy, and Foreign Office officials met from June to December 1934 and agreed on a new initiative toward China: "First, Japan would secure East Asian peace by leading a cooperative system composed of Japan, China and Manchuria; second, Japan would expand its economic rights in North China. . . . [M]oreover, by positive diplomacy and by economic measures, [Japan] would by all means eliminate aid to China from foreign countries."[87] Rather than a nonaggression pact, Japanese ambassador to Great Britain Matsudaira Tsuneo called for a reaffirmation of the Four Power

86. Iriye, *Origins of the Second World War*, pp. 22–23.
87. Pelz, *Race to Pearl Harbor*, pp. 51–52.

treaty. This, however, appeared a weak reed on which to lean the security and stability of China.

In a final quest for compromise, the British suggested that if the Japanese agreed at least to abide by the qualitative limits of the treaty system, the Anglo-Saxon powers would continue to refrain from fortifying their bases in the Far East. The Japanese, however, refused to budge from their minimal demands—parity, coupled with drastic reductions in overall naval tonnage. Further, they rejected the notion of exchanging building plans as an indirect method of preserving the Washington and London ratios.

On December 29, 1934, the Japanese gave formal notification, as prescribed by the London treaty, of their intent to abrogate the Washington treaties and withdraw from the system in 1936. The British continued to hope the 1935 London Conference might provide an opportunity to at least negotiate actual construction programs. Minister of Foreign Affairs Hirota Koki had suggested that denunciation of the treaties might assuage Japan's big navy advocates, intimating that in 1935, the Japanese might be more flexible. The British had been conducting bilateral discussions with the French since July 1934 on the European naval balance. After the Japanese abrogation, the British accelerated conversations with the French, Italians, and Germans to reach a resolution of the European situation before the upcoming London Conference. The Foreign Office believed that with the Pacific powers in deadlock, any advances made in European negotiations, even if based only on qualitative limits and not ratios, would strengthen Britain's hand at London.

Japan's basic naval strategy had remained remarkably consistent throughout the treaty years: maintaining defensive superiority in the western Pacific and prevailing against any aggressor there in a decisive fleet encounter. By the mid-1930s, several elements had changed, and these obstructed British attempts to accommodate the new strategic realities of the 1930s. First, the Japanese perceived that technological innovations had yielded decisive advantage to the attacking force, thereby jeopardizing their ability to preserve command of the western Pacific. Navy Minister Osumi cited improvements in cruising range, speed, gun power, armor, communications, and surveillance capacity.[88] These technological developments, coupled with changes in Japan's

88. Ibid., pp. 149–50.

threat environment—the strengthening of western bases at Singapore and Hawaii, the growth of Soviet naval and air assets in the Far East, and the emergence of China's air force[89]—undermined support for a ratio system that had always faced serious opposition within certain naval circles. By withdrawing from the treaty system, the Naval General Staff claimed, Japan would be free to pursue a more economical strategy of building only those vessels suited for its particular national requirements.

Second, by 1934, the Japanese had construction plans ready for a post-treaty battleship mounting 18-inch guns, the Yamato-Musashi-type. Uproar in the wake of the 1930 London Treaty was mollified only by assurances to Japan's naval chiefs that quantitative restriction did not necessarily mean qualitative limitation. With the signing of the treaty, the naval budget was augmented to modernize existing warships and construct new, improved vessels, ultimately leading to the Yamato class. Commander Ishikawa Shingo claimed that with a five-year head start on the United States, "at one bound [the mammoth battleships would] raise our [capital ship] strength from the present ratio of 60 percent of U.S. strength to a position of absolute supremacy."[90] The *Yamato* combined the virtues of battleship and battle cruiser. With a standard displacement of 64,000 tons, it could withstand 18-inch shells above the waterline, was protected with a three-foot bulge and three separate hull layers against torpedoes, could speed at thirty knots, and cruise 8,000 miles.[91] The belief was that the *Yamato*'s "speed would allow its commander to choose the occasion for action, and its armor and

89. "Before 1934, the League of Nations and the United States had been providing some technical and financial assistance to China. In early 1934, the Western nations also began to give military aid to the Nationalists. A German military mission undertook to reorganize the Chinese army, and Americans and Italians began to train the fledgling Chinese air force." Ibid., p. 21.

90. Quoted in Asada, "Japanese Navy and the United States," p. 242.

91. The 18-inch triple turrets could be replaced with 20-inch twin turrets once the U.S. Navy began constructing battleships with 18-inch guns. The design innovations of the super-battleship included indirect protection by a large number of watertight compartments, electric welding in place of standard riveting, diesel drive, and exchangeable 18-inch and 20-inch guns through a common cartridge and shell transport system. See Hans Lengerer, "The Japanese Super Battleship Strategy," Parts 1–3, *Warship* 25 (January 1983): 30–39; 26 (April 1983): 88–96; and 27 (July 1983): 161–69. The super-battleship strategy was designed to give the Imperial Navy supremacy in gun power for ten years. The 18-inch gun, although only two inches larger in caliber than standard main armament, could hurl a projectile 30 percent more powerful on impact. Pelz, *Race to Pearl Harbor*, p. 32.

armament would make it invincible."[92] The super-battleship strategy reflected a consensus in Japan that there was "no alternative but to aim for qualitative advantage if they were to stay on level terms, should the treaties terminate, or Japan withdraw from the Treaty."[93]

The third development that obstructed British efforts to accommodate changing strategic realities in the Pacific within the confines of the treaty system was the transformation within the Imperial Navy after the London Naval Treaty controversy. This controversy diminished the roles of the Navy Ministry and moderate pro-treaty elements within the navy. Asada provides a sophisticated analysis of the groupings of officers in the naval leadership, and their influence on policymaking and institutional change. He identifies three overlapping groups: the administrative group versus the command group; the supporters of the Washington treaty system versus its enemies; the Anglo-American faction versus the German faction. Asada argues that the influence of men such as Kato Kanji and Admirals Suetsugu, Takahashi, Osumi, and Nagano—representatives of the command group, enemies of the Washington treaty system, and members of the German faction—facilitated "the eclipse of Japan's naval leadership, the supremacy of the naval high command, the idée fixe of the inevitability of war with the United States, the demise of the Washington-London treaty system and the reopening of the armaments race, [and] the beginnings of the southward expansion."[94] In 1932, Vice-Chief of the Naval General Staff Takahashi informed Navy Minister Osumi that Chief of the Naval General Staff Prince Fushimi Hiroyasu would resign unless the Naval General Staff was restructured along the lines of the army. To stem a political crisis, in September 1933 the right of command of naval forces in peacetime was transferred to the chief of the Naval General Staff, establishing the supremacy of the General Staff over the Navy Ministry. In addition, over the course of 1933–34, the "Osumi purge" systematically retired or placed on reserve leaders of the "treaty faction," thereby fatally weakening moderate elements within the navy.

Finally, a power shift occurred within Japan's foreign policy community. In May 1933, the Naval General Staff created the post of "staff officer A," charged with "formulating national policy and maintaining a

92. Pelz, Race to Pearl Harbor, p. 32.
93. Lengerer, "Super Battleship Strategy," Part 1, p. 31.
94. See Asada, "Japanese Navy and the United States," pp. 225–59.

close liaison with the officials of the Army General Staff, the Army Ministry, and to a lesser extent the Foreign Ministry."[95] By establishing direct and independent contact with these other branches of the government and bypassing the Navy Ministry, the Naval General Staff began to assume a more assertive role in foreign policy.

In essence, the Japan of 1934 was very different from that of 1930. Civilian leaders feared that failure to withdraw from the treaty system would produce an internal political crisis, and Admiral Kato Kanji claimed that if Japan did not demand parity, naval leaders might lose control over their young officers. With the Osumi purge, moderate voices within the navy were eliminated, and the revised rules of the Naval General Staff gave that body exclusive right to determine fleet strength. Fearing that another controversy over naval limitation would re-create the domestic violence that had occurred after ratification of the 1930 London Naval Treaty, withdrawal from the treaty system seemed the only path to preserving domestic tranquility.

Failing to secure a nonaggression pact with the Japanese in 1934 in an indirect attempt to maintain supremacy in European waters through arrangements in the Pacific, the British embarked on a direct strategy to maintain supremacy: reaching agreement with Germany to, at the very least, *regulate* German rearmament. The issue was what level of German armament would not threaten established relationships of naval power and would not require Britain to engage in a costly rearmament program. Hitler denied any intent to challenge British naval supremacy. Perhaps to ensure British neutrality toward Germany's ambitions and to divide Britain from France, Hitler was prepared to limit the size of the German Navy, but at a level that would entail some rearmament. The British were making modest moves toward rearmament. The 1933 Naval Estimates showed an increase of 3,093,700 pounds over the 50,476,300 pounds of 1932 and provided for the construction of four cruisers and nine destroyers. Although only a modest increase, the 1933 estimates reversed the trend of reductions begun in 1921.[96] Nevertheless, popular sentiment still favored negotiated resolutions, even if this meant accepting some German rearmament. Given a choice between regulated, or secret and unlimited, rearmament in Germany, the British opted for the former.

95. Ibid., p. 232.
96. See Rudoff, "Influence of the German Navy," p. 179.

The German budget of March 1934 revealed rearmament plans for all military forces. Despite denials in April 1934, the Germans were planning ships of 20,000 to 25,000 tons (the French had begun plans for construction of a second *Dunkerque* battle cruiser). Foreign Minister Konstantin von Neurath expressed Germany's willingness to limit its fleet to between one-third and one-half of Britain's, whereas Hitler, in the meantime, gave permission for the secret increase in size of guns and armament on two battleships under construction, the *Scharnhorst* and *Gneisenau*. On June 30, 1934, the third pocket battleship, the *Admiral Graf Spee*, was launched, and that same day, the French approved a new naval construction program.

In July 1934, the British and French met to discuss European naval ratios.[97] Despite French opposition to any increase in German naval strength, the British were determined to pursue bilateral talks with the Germans, particularly in light of Germany's decision in August 1934 to begin constructing submarines, a weapon totally forbidden by the Versailles treaty and perceived as a direct challenge to Britain's position on the seas. By February 1935, the Anglo-French Arms Declaration—a symbol of renewed Anglo-French solidarity in the face of the new Continental threat—was concluded. The agreement formally acknowledged the end of the Versailles treaty and acquiesced to German rearmament. One month later, the Germans openly repudiated the disarmament clauses of the Versailles treaty, proclaimed the freedom to rearm based on "equality of rights," and reintroduced compulsory military service.

Bilateral negotiations between the British and Germans began on June 4, 1935.[98] The German delegates were under strict instructions to discuss only the 35:100 ratio, which would bring the German Navy to 35 percent of Britain's fleet strength, not details of future building plans. The British accepted the ratio, privately estimating they could tolerate a German Navy up to 50 percent as large as the Royal Navy. Then on June 6, the Germans requested the right to build to parity with Britain in submarines. Assuming that German submarine production could not be halted, that sonar had neutralized the submarine threat, and that Britain's own small submarine force would impose a

97. See Perrett, "French Naval Policy," pp. 125–53.
98. Charles Bloch, "Great Britain, German Rearmament, and the Naval Agreement of 1935," in Hans M. Gatzke, ed., *European Diplomacy Between Two Wars, 1919–1939* (Chicago: Quadrangle Books, 1972), pp. 125–51.

low limit on Germany, the British conceded. In return, the Germans agreed voluntarily to limit their submarine construction to 45 percent of Britain's for the present. The 35:100 ratio gave Germany near parity with France and Italy, provided these two remained bound by the Washington limits. From the British perspective, the agreement left the Royal Navy decisively superior to the German Fleet in European waters and halted the naval rivalry between France, Italy, and Germany. If Japan could be brought back into the ratio system, the combined fleets of France and Britain could meet a German Navy in European waters and leave the Royal Navy sufficiently strong to defend imperial interests in the Pacific.

The Anglo-German Naval agreement ended clandestine German rearmament and extended proportional ratios to each class of ship.[99] Increases in the proportion of Germany's submarine arm would be balanced by decreases in other classes. Most important for the British, the agreement preserved the principle of arms limitation established at Washington, though the procedure had changed from one of reducing armament to one of regulating rearmament.

SYSTEM MAINTENANCE

The Washington treaty system faced challenges to its political and military provisions. The treaty powers devised a variety of responses (Table 7). To maintain the system in the face of the Nationalist drive to unify China and economic crisis in the Far East with their attendant impacts on Japanese foreign and military policies, the signatories pursued a strategy of delinkage. In addition, for a limited time, they replaced cooperative economic strategies with unilateral though compatible strategies to defend and advance their respective economic interests in China. To maintain the system in the face of German rearmament, the signatories employed four strategies. First, they separated European political considerations from military ones at the London Naval Conference of 1930. This permitted the Pacific powers to consolidate the arms control system among themselves, despite failure to limit French and

99. D. C. Watt, "The Anglo-German Naval Agreement of 1935," *Journal of Modern History* 28 (June 1956): 155–75.

Table 7   System maintenance

Challenge	Strategies of Maintenance

Nationalism, civil war, and economic crisis in Far East	(1) Delinkage
	    (a) Economic relations from arms control
	    (b) Arms control from politics in China at 1930
	        London Conference
	        (i) Concessions confined to ships alone
	        (ii) Reed-Matsudaira compromise

Reconstitution of German power in Europe	(2) Separation of political from military concerns at 1930 London Conference
	    (a) 3-power accord replaces 5-power accord
	    (b) Kellogg-Briand Pact
	(3) Escape clauses
	(4) Attempted nonaggression pact with Japan
	(5) Anglo-German naval agreement of 1935

Italian ancillary construction. A three-power agreement, rather than a five-power agreement, endorsing the Kellogg-Briand Pact as the political basis for arms limitation, represented a shift in rules for implementing collective decisions. Second, the British introduced escape clauses into the arms control treaty. Third, the British attempted, but failed, to negotiate a nonaggression pact with Japan to free up British forces for the European theater. Finally, the British brought the reconstituted great power Germany into the system to maintain the principle of arms control, but by regulating rearmament, instead of reducing or limiting armament (Table 7).

Strategies in the Far East

Delinkage was used throughout the 1920s, at first to preserve economic cooperation despite renewed competition in the naval arena, subsequently to isolate the collapse of cooperation in China from arms control and to ensure the extension of arms limitation at the London Conference of 1930. Initially, delinkage succeeded because of how cooperation unraveled in China. Though the Washington powers abandoned the Nine Power treaty formula and began to pursue unilateral strategies, these unilateral strategies were not mutually incompatible. Unilateral policies could coexist as long as no power threatened the

critical national interests of any other. As Iriye points out, the decision
to pursue unilateral initiatives

> did not result in an immediate antagonism among the Washing-
> ton powers. Herein lies the essential difference between the pre-
> war diplomacy of imperialism and that of the mid-1920s. . . . In
> the 1920s, . . . it was not felt that a Washington Conference
> power's unilateral action in China would necessarily lead to a
> clash with others. . . . While Japan, the United States, and
> Britain lost interest in cooperative policy and began looking for
> separate arrangements with China, these governments contin-
> ued to view each other in friendly terms.[100]

Eventually, events revealed the artificial nature of delinkage, and it
collapsed on two fronts. First, delinkage collapsed because of domestic
developments in Japan over the London Naval Treaty controversy. The
proponents of Foreign Minister Shidehara's diplomacy—who advocated
cooperation with the West, arms limitation, and a moderate China
policy—had negotiated a treaty that ignited political unrest in Japan by
challenging the principle of Japanese naval hegemony in the western
Pacific. Events in China by the end of the 1920s had convinced many
Japanese that it was no longer feasible to protect their rights and interests on the mainland by cooperating with the West. Cooperation made
sense only so long as China remained weak. The prospect of a strong,
united China demanded a vigorous policy that would ultimately conflict
with the open door principle and would inevitably be unilateral, since
the Anglo-Saxon powers had "outlawed" the use of force under the
Kellogg Pact. Shidehara diplomacy collapsed once it became evident
that friendship with the United States, arms limitation, and the safety
of Japanese continental interests could not be harmonized into a cred-
ible foreign policy. By 1929, nationalist forces in Japan were openly
questioning the utility of a China policy that precluded the use of force.
The London Naval Treaty united the critics of the Hamaguchi government's China and arms control policies and, by linking these critics,
relinked policies that had been artificially delinked throughout the
1920s.

100. Iriye, *After Imperialism*, pp. 87–88.

Delinkage also collapsed because it was an untenable strategy for managing chaos in China. To many Japanese, it had become clear that "the principles of armament reduction and the denial of force as an instrument of national policy were incompatible with the particular military, political, and economic ingredients brewing in the Manchurian cauldron."[101] Chinese nationalism and a growing Soviet threat jeopardized the economic and security interests of Japan directly. Only the Japanese feared Soviet rearmament early on and simultaneously faced a nationalist movement that directly threatened their major colonial and semicolonial investments.[102] The Washington Conference had linked the economic, political, and strategic interests of the three major Far Eastern powers, but at London in 1930, deliberations were confined to naval affairs alone. To the Japanese, this deliberate delinkage appeared inconsistent with "the peculiarities of the Asian scene, which, if only because of the activities of the Soviet Union, could not be handled in terms of disarmament."[103] In short, it had become completely unrealistic, by 1930, to expect that peace in Asia could be effected by arms limitation or by "abolishing war" along the lines of the Kellogg-Briand Pact. National security in Asia required a military arrangement other than cooperation in arms limitation. "Only if the Anglo-American nations recognized this fact . . . could Japan and the Occidental countries cooperate in the quest for peace and stability in Asia."[104] It was no longer possible to pursue arms control given the chaos in China, or to strengthen the naval component of the Washington system without addressing the realities of the Far East. The Japanese, therefore, began to formulate a military policy to defeat the Red Army, exert their will in China, and secure the home islands from the U.S. naval threat.[105] Chinese nationalism and the growing power of the Soviet Union relinked Far Eastern and naval policies. The Japanese recognized this earlier than the other Washington powers, since these events, of regional interest to the Anglo-Saxon powers, were of more vital national interest to the Japanese.

---

101. Crowley, "A New Deal for Japan," p. 242.

102. Only Japan had continental possessions in Northeast Asia (Korea) and semicolonial rights in China (South Manchuria) that were critical for its overseas investments. Ibid., p. 240.

103. Shigemitsu Mamoru, ambassador to the Soviet Union and later foreign minister, quoted in Crowley, *Japan's Quest for Autonomy*, p. 189.

104. Ibid., p. 190.

105. Ibid.

In retrospect, the Washington powers failed to adapt to a rapidly changing situation in China, particularly to the Nationalist drive to unify China, because their long-term objectives remained fundamentally at odds. British and U.S. long-term goals were convergent in theory. British policy in China was an outgrowth of a global strategy to create and sustain political stability so that free trade could flourish. The United States wanted a China free from foreign control, partly as a bulwark against Japanese imperial designs, but just as much as an end in itself. British interests in stability were compatible in principle with U.S. desires to promote a united and prosperous China. Though Britain and the United States agreed on the desirability of a stable, unified China, in practice conflict did arise over short-term goals. British support for the Kuomintang diverged from the U.S. policy of withholding assistance until a central Chinese authority had emerged. And Ian Nish points to serious Anglo-American dissension at the Peking Tariff Conference of 1925 and differences over the Nanking incidents of 1927 and subsequent tariff concessions. In his estimation, "Anglo-American cooperation could not be relied on in east Asian affairs and there was no guarantee that the two would join together to keep Japanese influence in check."[106]

Nevertheless, by comparison, Japanese long-term interests in China conflicted far more fundamentally with the interests of both Britain and the United States than either Anglo-Saxon nation did with the other. The open door principle, endorsed by the Nine Power treaty, tacitly rejected the legitimacy of Japan's special interests in Manchuria and Mongolia. Japanese diplomacy, however, was designed to protect rights and interests on the mainland, whether that meant cooperation with the West or unilateral action. Between 1922 and 1926, Foreign Minister Shidehara sought to promote economic development by supporting the open door, Chinese territorial integrity, and nonintervention in China's civil war. His long-term goal, however, was to secure China as Japan's export market, a policy at variance with free trade and the open door. By 1927, Prime Minister Tanaka's policy of economic development was deemphasizing trade expansion with China proper and turning to a "Manchuria first" policy—extending and developing Japanese rights and interests in Manchuria at the expense of cooperation with

---

106. Ian Nish, "Japan in Britain's View of the International System, 1919–1937," in Ian Nish, ed., *Anglo-Japanese Alienation, 1919–1952* (Cambridge: Cambridge University Press, 1982), p. 36.

the West. The dual commitment to preserve Japanese interests in treaty ports and to maintain dominance in Manchuria, also created conflicts with the Anglo-Saxon policy of uniting China. Though there were differences of opinion within Japan over whether to let Manchuria fall under Kuomintang control, provided, of course, Japanese economic interests were safeguarded, the Japanese welcomed unification of China under a moderate Nationalist regime if it could enhance stability and facilitate trade with China. However, when the Nationalist drive threatened to undermine Japanese hegemony in Manchuria and Mongolia, support for unification was subordinated to the goal of keeping the Kuomintang out. A strategy of divide-and-conquer would serve Japanese interests better than supporting Nationalist aspirations for unity, particularly since unification would curtail Japan's ability to manipulate affairs in North China and Manchuria by playing warlord factions off against one another.

The Nationalist drive to unify China polarized civilian and military thinking in Japan and increased the obstacles to cooperation with the West. Japanese opinion was united in the belief that stable political conditions in Manchuria were imperative, and it was becoming ever more difficult to separate Japanese policy in Manchuria from its position on the civil war.[107] Once a "Manchuria first" policy became firmly entrenched, it took precedence over establishing a stable government in China proper. Furthermore, once the Nationalists became the only prospect for stability in China proper, it not only became impossible for the Japanese to support them, but actually incumbent on the Japanese to oppose the Kuomintang's drive for complete diplomatic sovereignty. Support for the Nationalists to create stability in China proper could no longer be reconciled with support for Chang Tso-lin, Manchurian warlord and leader of the "anti-Kuomintang," to protect Japanese rights in Manchuria. The unification of Manchuria and China in December 1928 channeled Japanese policy into a course at odds with the principles of the Washington treaty system.

107. There were divisions among civilians, and between civilians and the military, on "whether Japan's rights should be considered genuine economic rights without political implications, [thereby permitting any faction to control Manchuria, even the Kuomintang, as long as Japan's economic rights were preserved] or whether [Japan's rights] should be linked with China's civil war to induce Chang [Tso-lin] to accept them in return for Japanese favors." Iriye, *After Imperialism*, p. 167.

Strategies in Europe

Though the London Naval Treaty of 1930 extended the arms control system among the Pacific powers, it did little to curtail competitive armament in Europe. The vulnerability of European nations from both land and sea created obstacles to naval limitation. The French argued for restricting all weapons rather than just one arm of a nation's defense forces, particularly since naval weapons are not the most important component of a continental power's armed forces. Defining naval needs as absolute rather than relative in the Statut Naval of 1924, the French demanded 800,000 tons of vessels at London in 1930, a level unacceptable to the British, who were committed to retaining a two-power standard in European waters at parity levels agreed to with the United States. The French also demanded security guarantees in the form of a mutual assistance pact as the price for limiting their fleet. Only the United States and Great Britain were capable of providing the French with such guarantees, yet neither was willing to oblige. Instead, the Kellogg-Briand Pact was advanced as the basis for arms limitation at London. No attempt was made to relate the political and military dimensions of security. As a result, a three-power system of regional limitation in the Pacific replaced a five-power system of global naval limitation with an escalator clause written into the treaty to permit Britain, the United States, and Japan to respond to the building programs of the French and Italians. In contrast, Article 21 of the Washington Five Power treaty had called for the contracting powers to meet in conference to amend the treaty by mutual agreement if the national security requirements of any signatory were affected by change in circumstance. Treaty compliance imposed more stringent constraints in 1922 than in 1930. The use of escalator clauses for treaty maintenance was a short-term strategy that changed the rules of compliance in order to further the security system, despite the evolving security problems facing the French. Both strategies, separating political and military considerations and employing escape clauses, entailed shifting rules and procedures to preserve the principle of arms limitation and maintain the security system, despite German rearmament.

These strategies of treaty maintenance devised at London in 1930, however, were only short-term fixes. A political consensus in Europe to support arms limitation never emerged. In effect, tensions in the European arena were no closer to being resolved in 1930 than they had been in 1922, and probably much farther away as Germany challenged the balance of power in Europe and the balance of naval power globally. The Washington treaties had assumed a negligible German fleet. The unilateral abrogation of the Versailles restrictions rendered the Washington and London treaties inadequate for regulating rearmament, let alone for sustaining or enhancing arms limitation or reduction. A resurgent German threat demanded strategies beyond those short-term fixes devised at London to maintain the principles of the treaty system.

By the early 1930s, the British were acutely aware of threats to the European and Asiatic poles of the empire. In the Far East, the situation in China was deteriorating rapidly, Japan was preparing to abrogate the Washington treaties, and the Soviet Union was actively strengthening its defenses in Asia and the Pacific. With events in Europe taking on a dynamic of their own, the British found themselves at the center of this turmoil. Unable to match the combined rearmament efforts of the Germans and Japanese, the British adopted two strategies to meet defense requirements in European and Pacific waters. Both strategies were designed to maintain imperial security through arms limitation, rather than by invoking the escalator clause of the London Naval Treaty.[108] First, the British courted the Japanese, but ultimately failed in their attempt to secure a bilateral nonaggression pact to relieve the burdens of imperial defense in the Pacific. Second, given France's determination to preserve naval superiority over Germany and refusal to grant Germany equality of status to rearm, the British attempted to regulate German rearmament. Convinced that "the only safety for the Continent lay in bringing Germany back into the concert of powers and that Britain was the only hope of carrying out such a project successfully,"[109] the British negotiated the Anglo-German naval agreement of 1935. The principle of arms control would be preserved by regulating the pace of German rearmament.

Regulating German rearmament was again, however, only a stopgap measure for system maintenance. The British wanted to limit the Ger-

108. See C. C. Bright, "Britain's Search for Security, 1930–1936: The Diplomacy of Naval Disarmament and Imperial Defense" (Ph.D. diss., Yale University, 1970), and James Herzog, *Closing the Open Door: Anglo-Japanese Diplomatic Negotiations, 1936–1941* (Annapolis: Naval Institute Press, 1973).

109. U.S. Delegate to Geneva Hugh Wilson to the Secretary of State, March 21, 1935, quoted in Rudoff, "Influence of the German Navy," p. 233. For general background, see Margaret George, *The Warped Vision: British Foreign Policy, 1933–1939* (Pittsburgh: University of Pittsburgh Press, 1965).

man Navy to a level that would preserve Anglo-American parity, Britain's two-power standard in European waters, and the empire's defensive position in the Pacific. Japan, however, had announced, in December 1934, its decision to abrogate the Washington Naval Treaty in one year. And the Anglo-German agreement skirted, once again, the more profound political problems in Europe that had always stunted the arms control process. First, though sharing mutual security interests in Europe, the British and French differed over which policies toward Germany would enhance stability on the Continent. France wanted a weak Germany; Britain wanted an economically recovered Germany. Second, neither Great Britain nor the United States was prepared to grant the French a mutual assistance guarantee. With Japan outside the treaty system and German rearmament preventing the Royal Navy from diverting sufficient resources to meet threats from extra-European powers, Britain would have to rearm.

ARMS CONTROL AS "PROCESS" IN THE 1930s

As Table 8 shows, the arms control agreements of the 1930s fall across cells 3 and 4, all under the military-based strategy column. Arms control strategies were entirely military based, not political based.

Table 8   Strategies of arms control in the 1930s

Interest Constellation	Arms Control Strategy	
	Military and Nonmilitary Means	Military Means Only
Resolution (Agendas aligned)	1	2 Britain and France • London, 1930
Contention (Agendas in dispute)	3	4 U.S. vs. Japan • London treaty, 1930 Britain vs. Germany • Anglo-German naval agreement, 1935

The first London Conference separated the political and military dimensions of security in Europe, as the process had done in Washington in 1922, and for the first time, in the Far East as well. The primary reason an arms control package was nonetheless reached in the Pacific was due largely to the political risks accepted by Japan's delegates when they accepted the Reed-Matsudaira compromise. The compromise, however, precipitated a political crisis in Japan, ultimately contributing to Japan's defection from the treaty system. In Europe, the Kellogg-Briand Pact was substituted for a real political accommodation on the Continent, and French obstinacy was hardly surprising. The Anglo-German naval agreement, again, delivered only a technical arrangement to regulate force levels and never addressed political motivations driving rearmament. In all probability, it had little chance of influencing German actions, given the absolute nature of Germany's ambitions. However, the case of Germany per se is not sufficient to undermine the argument that a political-based approach to arms control is more effective than a military-based approach for enhancing security. Hitlers are more the exception than the rule, just as worldwide depression, another exception, should not negate arguments about the dynamics of the arms control process in general.

Only by linking political means with military means could the Washington treaty system have evolved to bridge differing political agendas in the Pacific and different doctrinal conceptions of security in Europe. Only a political-based approach to arms control would have acknowledged what the Japanese understood to be boiling in the Manchurian cauldron and what the French saw to be simmering in Europe. In both cases, purely technical adjustments of the military balance oversimplified a complex political dialogue and exacerbated perceptions of insecurity.

7 Lessons

I HAVE STUDIED an important arms control process that predates the Cold War in order to question the traditional functions and utility of arms control that are inextricably bound up with the Cold War structure of conflict and to critique the prevailing notions of arms control that form the Cold War "orthodoxy." I argue that contemporary theorists miss many important aspects of the dynamics of the arms control process because they focus almost exclusively on the behavior of the superpowers and on the consequences of the nuclear dimension for arms control. I criticize the arms control orthodoxy that has prevailed more or less intact since the 1960s for being technologically driven and for assuming that the state of technology can determine the results of an arms control process by dictating which weapons state leaders will be willing to limit or by presuming that there is a hard-and-fast relationship between technological change, the military balance, and incentives for arms control. Because they are obsessed with stability in the military balance and with "the technicalities of a very narrowly and apolitically defined condition identified as 'stable deterrence,'"[1] I fault

---

1. Colin S. Gray, "The Arms Race Is About Politics," *Foreign Policy* 9 (Winter 1972–73): 123. Fairbanks takes to task the apolitical nature of the term *arms race*, in comparison to the more normal and political notion of rivalry between nations. "'Race' differs from 'rivalry' in pointing to the absurdity of the process . . . because there is no object beyond the competition itself." Charles H. Fairbanks, Jr., "Arms Races: The Metaphor and the Facts," *The National Interest* 1 (Fall 1985): 77. See also Colin Gray, *The Soviet-American Arms Race* (London: D. C. Heath, 1976), pp. 12–33.

Cold War arms control scholars for their reluctance to deal with the multidimensional and subjective qualities of security as a meaningful part of the arms control process that is more than symbolic. In sum, I reject Cold War strategies of arms control for being apolitical, not in terms of their domestic context or negotiating objectives, but in terms of the methods by which they seek to tackle what are, at heart, political problems.

We must reorient how we think about arms control, most critically by understanding arms control not just as an outcome of negotiations, shaped and predetermined by a set of stable preferences brought to the negotiating table but also as a politically relevant process that itself can transform the strategic visions and preferences of the participants. Cold War arms control theory shares with neoclassical economic approaches a static view of process: preferences are specified in advance as givens, and are seen as interacting automatically, like a market, to produce an outcome.[2] This approach resembles David Easton's analysis of politics in terms of the inputs and outputs of the policymaking process.[3] Agreements manifest national interests and may be deduced from the preferences with which actors enter negotiations. This economic orientation neglects the social and communicative side of the policy process and how the process of negotiating may modify and alter preferences and interests. Only by engaging in detailed studies of the policy process may we begin to capture the "suasive" element in negotiations.[4]

The Washington treaty system of 1922–1936 was an important precursor to the contemporary post–Cold War arms control environment; this is especially clear when we reflect on its multilateral and regional qualities. So, unlike those who may believe that the present period of radical political transition means arms control's day has passed and that the enterprise has been overtaken by events, I consider arms control as relevant as ever. Only the way we have become accustomed to thinking about the arms control process, the so-called Cold War orthodoxy, has become irrelevant.

    2. Mancur Olson, Jr., and Richard Zechauser, "An Economic Theory of Alliances," in Bruce M. Russett, ed., *Economic Theories of International Politics* (Chicago: Markham, 1966), especially p. 44.
    3. David Easton, *A Systems Analysis of Political Life* (New York: John Wiley, 1965).
    4. Robert D. Putnam, "Diplomacy and Domestic Politics: The Logic of Two-Level Games," *International Organization* 42 (Summer 1988): 454–55; James A. Caporaso "Global Political Economy," in Ada A. Finifter, ed., *Political Science: State of the Discipline* (Washington, D.C.: American Political Science Association, 1993), pp. 451–81.

With the post–Cold War era upon us, the challenges of restructuring political, economic, and military relationships at the global level, and in regional arenas like Europe and the Middle East, appear daunting. Although positive trends seem to contradict those who predict a return to the turmoil of the 1930s,[5] prognostications that a fully functioning collective security system will emerge seem the result more of wishful thinking than of an accurate reading of current developments.[6] A network of regional and subregional security systems linking military, political, and economic agreements and permitting trade-offs across issue areas may be a less ambitious but more practical alternative. If the arms control process is seen as part of this larger endeavor to structure, manage, and even transform competitive relationships, it may be used to reduce the political incentives, as well as its more traditional concern, the military incentives, to resort to force or to intimidation by the threat of force. The arms control literature, because it remains deeply embedded in Cold War thinking, offers little guidance for navigating the complex, multilateral, and politically charged landscape of today, but a fresh look at the 1920s offers a host of policy-relevant prescriptions.

Novel theoretical insights about arms control may also be gleaned from a careful analysis of the interwar experience. The more familiar, restrictive, Cold War–type, military-based strategies were employed along with more comprehensive political-based strategies that integrate related political concerns with technical issues. We have an opportunity to compare the effectiveness of two approaches to arms control, each grounded in different premises about the sources of instability in interstate relations and the relationship between arms control and the outbreak of war. The interwar process reveals the potential of political-based arms control strategies to bridge and transcend political conflicts,

5. For a discussion of the positive trends, see Stephen Van Evera, "Primed for Peace: Europe After the Cold War," *International Security* 15 (Winter 1990/91): 7–57. For the pessimist's perspective, see John J. Mearsheimer, "Back to the Future: Instability in Europe After the Cold War," *International Security* 15 (Summer 1990): 5–56.

6. For an optimistic appraisal of the chances for collective security, see Charles A. Kupchan and Clifford A. Kupchan, "Concerts, Collective Security, and the Future of Europe," *International Security* 16 (Summer 1991): 114–61. Valid critiques of collective security are offered by Josef Joffe, "Collective Security and the Future of Europe," *Survival* 34 (Spring 1992): 36–50, and by Richard Betts, "Systems for Peace or Causes for War? Collective Security, Arms Control, and the New Europe," *International Security* 17 (Summer 1992): 5–43.

as well as the danger that military-based strategies may exacerbate conflict.

SYSTEM FORMATION

I. *Arms control success varies with the types of interests served, and with the strategies of arms control employed.*

Arms control thinking over the past several decades has been polarized at two extremes. There are those who even though they may have reservations about specific treaties, believe the arms control enterprise is a useful and defensible activity that can contribute to security and peace.[7] And there are those who assume that arms control can be nothing more than the tactics of policy and strategy, that arms control merely reflects the competitive pressures that pervade international politics, and that rather than helping resolve conflict, arms control provides irresistible incentives for cheating, particularly by nondemocracies.[8] In reality, effective arms control is far more complicated.

Athough no arms limitation agreement can emerge if signatories do not agree on what to limit and how limitations should be implemented, the motives underlying decisions to cooperate often differ. Signatories may be driven more by incompatible long-term political and strategic objectives than by a desire to cooperate to enhance mutual security. The degree to which competition is managed varies with the types of interests that motivate cooperation. The strategy of arms control utilized is an equally important factor in the capacity of the system to manage conflict. In 1922, the Washington powers implemented a political-based approach to arms control in the Pacific arena and a military-based approach in the European arena. In 1930, they resorted to a military-based approach in both arenas, as much by choice as by default. Technical force-balance agreements were produced from both sets of negotiations, but the security implications varied across approaches. Political-based strategies integrated technical and nontechnical matters in the arms control process and were more sensitive than military-based

---

7. To include Strobe Talbott, Michael Krepon, and Steven E. Miller.

8. To include Bruce D. Berkowitz, Colin S. Gray, and Robert Gordon Kaufman, who differ in detail on the shortcomings of arms control.

arms control strategies to security concerns that could not be deduced
from the state of technology or the military balance. Military-based
arms control strategies, by electing to treat political dialogues as purely
technical issues, exacerbated insecurities and threat perceptions. As the
events in the Pacific arena show, conflicting political agendas may be
bridged by political-based arms control strategies in the short run. The
events in the European arena demonstrate that despite a mutuality of
security interests, military-based strategies may stunt technical agreement. A political-based approach may at least buy time to resolve political differences, but a military-based approach can erode a foundation
for realizing mutual security that already exists.

In 1922, the Pacific powers acknowledged that the security issues in
question were interrelated so closely that a solution to one issue could
not be worked out in the absence of a simultaneous, coordinated solution to the other issues.[9] According to the Harding administration, the
treaties, resolutions, and declarations of the conference

> should be considered as a whole [for each contributed] in combi-
> nation with the others towards the establishment of conditions
> in which peaceful security will take the place of competitive
> preparation for war. . . . [The Four Power treaty created a] new
> state of mind [and] . . . it would not have been possible except
> as part of a plan including a limitation and reduction of naval
> armaments; but that limitation and reduction would not have
> been possible without the new relations established by the Four
> Power Treaty or something equivalent to it. . . . [The] new
> relations declared in the Four Power treaty could not . . . inspire
> confidence or be reasonably assured of continuance without a
> specific understanding as to the relations of the powers in China.
> . . . [The Nine Power treaty and supplementary resolutions pro-
> vided these understandings and fostered] confidence and good
> will expressed in the Four Power Treaty and upon which the
> reduction of armament in the Naval Treaty may be contem-
> plated with a sense of security.[10]

9. Alexander L. George, "Strategies for Facilitating Cooperation," in George et al., *U.S.-Soviet
Security Cooperation*, pp. 696, 708.

10. "Conference on the Limitation of Armament: Address of President and Report of the American Delegation with Treaties and Resolutions," 67 Cong., 2 sess., 1922, S. Doc. 126, pp. 865–
67.

It would be a mistake to conclude that there was a master plan[11] for the outcomes of bargaining and negotiation frequently diverged from initial expectations. Yet, as Arthur James Balfour stressed to Lloyd George on arrival in Washington, "if satisfactory and durable results are to be achieved in regard to naval disarmament, . . . an agreement must also be reached in regard to certain political problems which have arisen in China and the Pacific [and suggested that] the logical sequence . . . that the business should be conducted is to deal with the political side of the Pacific question before the final decisions have to be taken on the subject of naval diminution of armaments."[12] Balfour later reflected that the agreements were "all necessarily interdependent. The Four Power treaty, carrying with it the termination of the exclusive Anglo-Japanese alliance, the Shantung settlement, the Nine Power treaty, and the Naval Treaty, all these are parts of one connected whole."[13] The successful negotiation of the Washington treaties may be attributed in part to the recognition by the signatories that arms control was not just a technical question of limiting and monitoring force levels, but a way to enhance regional security, provided it was linked to broader political considerations. This meant that the foreign policy objectives of the parties in China had to be linked in some meaningful way to arms control. Integrating political and military understandings in the Pacific in 1922 bridged conflicting agendas and avoided the harsh repercussions that exploded in Japan in 1930 when the first London Naval Treaty confined concessions exclusively to the military level.

Yet as Alexander George points out, "Even systemic linkage of two or more issues cannot work if the respective interests of each negotiating partner in each of the two issues are not adequately accommodated in the proposed over-all agreement."[14] In 1922, important conflicting interests were accommodated, but only superficially. Efforts to bring those differences into alignment and strengthen the delicate political consensus forged in 1922 languished over the years, and a convergence on political fundamentals failed to develop in U.S.-Japanese relations.

11. Nish cautions against viewing the Washington Conference as a system in which "the various aspects of the China and Pacific settlement were cleverly interlocked," arguing that this "reflects a perception . . . influenced by the retrospective writings of American officials." Nish, *Japanese Foreign Policy*, p. 141.

12. Correspondence from Arthur James Balfour to David Lloyd George, November 11, 1921, HLRO, Historical Collection 192, Lloyd George Papers, F/61/1/1.

13. Ibid, February 5, 1922, F/61/3/5.

14. George, "Strategies for Facilitating Cooperation," pp. 696, 708.

With the defeat of Germany, the Japanese began to equate national economic security with autarky and with hegemony over East Asia for secure access to raw materials and markets. Within postwar Japan, the desire for great-power status and the quest for both military and economic security were shared by all civilian and military factions, despite serious disputes over the means to achieve imperial security. U.S. national security, by contrast, "depended upon the reestablishment of global order based on international law. That order would be founded upon the rights of each nation to enjoy political independence and free, equal opportunity to trade with the rest of the world."[15] The Nine Power treaty was a sufficiently ambiguous document to accommodate these conflicting agendas initially, but concerted effort was required to forge a more enduring consensus based on the Washington treaty principles, let alone a new consensus on revised principles.

Cold War arms control theory rejects the notion that agreements on military balances require prior political settlement. Rather, technical arrangements alone may enhance security, despite fundamental conflicts of interest. However, by stressing (and rightly so) that arms control arrangements can be reached without addressing underlying political tensions, these theorists divert attention from the possible long-term effects of agreeing only on technical issues. From the interwar experience, we see the consequences of arms limitation agreements divorced from broader political settlements and built on understandings like the Kellogg-Briand Pact, which merely paper over political differences and slight the sources of general instability and political tension among states. Agreements of this type may undermine international security, despite their positive impact on the military balance, as states, constrained in the military realm, receive inadequate reassurances that the influence they are surrendering in armed force will be compensated for by concessions in other realms.

Cooperation is a multifaceted construct that varies with the interests served and with the nature of the policy process. Negotiating a treaty does not require a political consensus, but the consequences associated with purely technical agreements and with a "technical approach" to arms control may be formidable. A degree of uncertainty accompanies any cooperative agreement between adversaries, but when technical treaties are reached while the sources of general instability are ignored,

15. Barnhart, *Japan Prepares for Total War*, pp. 50–51.

natural mutual suspicions may seriously exacerbate the security dilemma. To manage rivalry, agreements must accurately encode understandings about what constitutes security in its military and political
dimensions. Whether or not the process succeeds in strengthening mutual security over time is contingent on the types of challenges to the
treaty system that emerge from within and without, the strategies of
system maintenance developed and implemented in response to those
challenges, and whether those strategies exacerbate or mitigate the impact of situational factors on the threat perceptions of states.

II.   *Dissimilar doctrines and strategic visions may impede arms control, de-
      spite mutual security interests.*

Military means alone are insufficient for bridging different doctrinal
conceptions of security because it is precisely the technical requisites of
security that are the subject of dispute. The Washington treaties were
handicapped from the outset by disparities in the security requirements
between the maritime and continental members of the system. The
treaties were based on the maritime doctrine of blue-water navies and
failed to address the strategic requirements of continental naval powers.
With no guarantees of security in Europe, the French refused to accept
limits on submarine construction, a weapon uniquely suited to threaten
British lines of communication. Unrestricted submarine construction,
in turn, fueled a renewed arms race in the cruiser category among all
the treaty powers. As long as naval limitation failed to accommodate
the requisites of both continental and maritime doctrine and the political demands of security in Europe, it could only hope to regulate competition in the Pacific.[16]

More generally, developments in the European arena support the
claim that the requirements of security cannot be deduced from any
given state of technology. There is no hard-and-fast relationship between technological change, the military balance, and incentives for
arms control. Rather, doctrine is one important variable that affects
definitions of security and how technological change is perceived to
affect the military balance. These perceptions, in turn, influence the
propensity of states to limit weapon systems. Battleships were limited,
not because they were obsolete, which was far from proven at the time,
but because there existed a consensus among the maritime powers on

16. Chaput, *Disarmament*, p. 194.

the battleship's relationship to the balance of naval power and because of a willingness on the part of the Big Three to accommodate the maritime requisites of security. Submarines were not limited in any meaningful way, not because they were new, but because they were critical to the force requirements of smaller navies, and the traditional maritime nations were not willing to accommodate the continental requisites of security. The submarine and airplane escaped direct limitation in 1922 as much because of their role in French strategic doctrine as because of their being new exploitable systems, not "ripe" for limitation.

REDIRECTION OF MILITARY STRATEGIES AND PROGRAMS

I. *Redirection is a natural product of the arms control process, be it the perverse result of treaty provisions, of technological and bureaucratic forces, or of military professionals attempting to execute strategy within arms control constraints.*

The Washington treaties encouraged technological innovation, force structure change, exploitation of loopholes and ambiguous treaty provisions, cheating, and innovation in strategy and tactics. These developments may not be attributed solely to one cause, and certainly not to the naval treaties alone.[17] However, arms control treaties may alter incentives by creating opportunities that previously did not exist.

In the technological realm, no consideration influenced warship design more during the Washington years than the need to save weight, an incentive created by the arms control agreements. Innovative weight-saving technologies were incorporated into existing and post-treaty ship designs and stimulated capital ship modernization programs in the 1930s. Processes initiated to save weight in accordance with treaty restrictions resulted in weapons of superior strength and accuracy, in efforts to incorporate these developments into existing ship designs,

---

17. Rosen demonstrates how "the transition of the U.S. Navy from a battleship-dominant navy to one in which aircraft carriers had an independent and decisive role" was strongly influenced by "individuals or organizations who consciously redefined the critical military tasks in response to changes in the strategic environment and who had a strategy for gaining control of the officer corps in order to implement the new way of war." Rosen, "New Ways of War," p. 151.

and ultimately in bigger battleships with enhanced combat effectiveness. The Five Power treaty also made modern capital ships available
for weapons tests, and the lessons from these tests—that future battleships should have triple bottoms and that existing deck armor was inadequate—were incorporated into post-treaty building and modernization
programs.

The treaties, by freeing up the hulls of large battle cruisers for conversion to carriers, led directly to the second generation of aircraft carriers, which in all likelihood would never have been built so large.
These hulls, readily adaptable to rapidly evolving aircraft and amenable
to considerable technical growth, permitted experimentation with new
carrier tactics, heralded changes in the role of the U.S. fleet between
the wars, and encouraged experimentation in the U.S. and Japanese
navies with the type of mass carrier attacks that proved very successful
during World War II.[18]

Incentives for compliance may exist that restrain temptations to
cheat or exploit loopholes and ambiguities, such as maintaining one's
reputation, the long shadow of the future, or desires to develop a more
stable and constructive relationship with one's adversary. Yet even with
arms control, militaries are responsible for national defense, and this
may mean exploiting loopholes and ambiguities and pushing treaty provisions to their limits to realize foreign and national security policy
goals. Treaty restrictions on the fortification of the United States's island possessions in the western Pacific, coupled with limits on the offensive capabilities of battleships, accelerated experimentation in fleet
aviation because carrier airpower was one way to solve the paradox of
defending Far Eastern commitments absent modern advanced bases to
project power. The Japanese devised offensive tactics and strategies to
maintain defensive superiority in the western Pacific. To offset the deficiencies of an inferior battleship ratio, the Imperial Navy planned to
wage an attrition campaign against the U.S. fleet as it crossed the Pacific and in the mid-1920s, introduced and refined the attrition stage in
their war plan. The Japanese built high-speed submarines with greater
range and more reliable torpedoes, perfected the tactics and strategy of

---

18. Friedman, U.S. Aircraft Carriers, pp. 7, 44–66; Friedman, Carrier Air Power, pp. 9–10, 39,
54; Melhorn, Two-Block Fox, pp. 108–9.

submarine warfare, and introduced night tactics for destroyers to compensate for limitation of their battleline force.

Exploiting loopholes and ambiguous treaty provisions and devising innovative technologies, tactics, and strategies or changing force structure to adjust to the new arms control environment are not by definition acts of bad faith. Willful cheating is not the same as honest differences in interpretation, normal bending of the rules, or the problems of disorganized bureaucracy. But as military bureaucracies rechannel efforts to enhance the ability to execute strategies given the constraints created by arms control, they may inadvertently develop weapon systems that exacerbate tensions and insecurities, and drive competitive building, particularly when the nonmilitary aspects of security have only been superficially accommodated in the arms control process, or when asymmetries in doctrine, threat environment, or strategic preference persist. Japan developed offensive technologies to execute a defensive strategy. France built submarines, and Great Britain responded with cruisers. The United States laid down large cruisers to patrol the Pacific, and Britain responded in kind, building systems for which it had no independent need.

II. *Expectations about the type of behavior that should follow from agreements, and beliefs about the role of arms control in enhancing security, influence perceptions of rechanneling.*

There will always be differences of opinion over whether abuses and rechanneling mean that treaty provisions are being exploited for purposes outside and contradictory to the spirit if not also the specific terms of an agreement, or whether they simply represent attempts to maximize military effectiveness within the constraints created by arms control. In the 1920s and 1930s, rechanneling—into superior offensive technologies and tactics—exacerbated the security dilemma when different strategic visions fostered conflicting interpretations of the role of arms control in national security strategy.

Whether arms control has a positive or negative impact on the strategic balance and on great-power relations depends to a degree on how it is assimilated into definitions of national security. Different notions of national security may explain why some states abide only by the letter of a treaty or even exploit it, but other states respect its spirit or even overcomply. In principle, neither approach is objectionable. However, when signatories do not share common expectations about the requirements of treaty compliance, the military balance may fail to reflect treaty principles. For example, U.S. expectations after the Washington Conference of 1922 were that the 5:5:3 ratio in capital ship tonnage codified in the Five Power treaty would eventually be extended to all other categories of vessels. With this "extension principle," the 5:5:3 ratio would then represent the overall balance of naval power. This was an assumption, however, the Japanese did not share. So in post-Conference years, the Japanese concentrated construction in ancillary categories, reducing the ratio of U.S. to Japanese naval forces.[19] What creates the predisposition to view arms control itself as evidence that underlying tensions have been eliminated or conversely, that agreements are simply temporary expedients toward security? Although no single explanation will suffice, beliefs about what security entails and the role arms control is perceived to play in enhancing security are important components. These beliefs will vary from state to state and over time.[20]

Though the dynamics involved in post-Washington building programs were complex, disparate definitions of national security influenced treaty interpretation and compliance, particularly between the United States and Japan. The United States was self-sufficient and had attained this state naturally. Not surprisingly, U.S. definitions of national security were very different from those of Japan. For the United States, a global order based on political independence, self-determination, equal opportunity, and free trade would enhance national security. This definition of security was incompatible with Tokyo's belief that their legitimate exclusive rights in Asia were indispensable for economic survival. For the United States, the conclusion of an arms limitation agreement itself was perceived as a significant step toward a global order based on international law and unfettered economic inter-

---

19. Friedman, U.S. Cruisers, p. 218.

20. Kaufman links differing views about arms control to the nature of closed and open societies. He focuses on the role of public opinion in the United States and the institutional arrangements and cultural legacy of Japan that gave the armed services greater influence in politics. Without neglecting the influence of these domestic-level variables, I link differing perspectives on arms control to broader questions of how states define national security and on how arms control facilitates or hinders the realization of national security. These depend on more than domestic political structure. Robert Gordon Kaufman, Arms Control During the Pre-Nuclear Era: The United States and Naval Limitation Between the Two World Wars (New York: Columbia University Press, 1990), pp. 197–99.

action. With strong economic and domestic political pressures, a relax-
ation of defense efforts followed.

The Japanese, by contrast, were committed to achieving great-power
status. As Barnhart puts it, "From the commencement of the Meiji
Restoration to the conclusion of the Pacific War, Japan pursued the
status of a great power through expansion abroad and reform at home.
The requisites of that status, however, changed over the decades."[21]
Japan's acceptance of an inferior naval ratio was temporary. Although
there were pressures that made cooperation with the West an attractive
strategy, arms control was not valued as an end in itself. Rather, the
Japanese were obsessed with economic security, the memory of a Germany competitive at the military level but economically vulnerable to
blockade foremost in mind. Self-sufficiency required territorial expansion and a domestic economy reordered for mobilization. The foundations of these twin policies were laid in the 1920s and continued to
mature, yet demands for international cooperation and arms control
persisted as well. Even in the 1930s, influential civilian and military
factions—including elements of the "total war" clique of the Imperial
Army—wanted continental expansion, but not at the cost of embroil-
ing Japan in a war on the continent that might jeopardize the long-term
goal of autarky. Those committed to economic self-sufficiency recognized that at least minimally cordial relations with the United States
were necessary. Furthermore, the economic constraints of the postwar
world had escalated with the depression. A naval building race would
only squander scarce economic resources and undermine the production
expansion plan designed to augment Japanese war-making potential.
Nevertheless, despite internal debates over tactics and strategy that
continued as late as 1936, the Japanese remained committed to pursuing what they perceived as eminently reasonable objectives: imperial
security and economic self-sufficiency. As S. Tatsuji Takeuchi summarizes it, "In their insistence upon a 'paramount interest' in Manchuria,
the government has always been consistent irrespective of parties and
factions in power. Thus the difference between the so-called 'friendship
policy' of Baron Shidehara and the Minseito Party and the so-called
'positive policy' of the late General Baron Tanaka and the Seiyukai
party existed only in regard to specific methods to be employed to

21. Barnhart, *Japan Prepares for Total War*, p. 17; Barnhart, "Japan's Economic Security," pp.
110–11.

maintain and foster this common aim."[22] Arms control and cooperation with the West were always subservient to the drive for great-power status.

Although arms control coincided with the ends of U.S. national security, for Japan it coincided only with the means for achieving great-power status. The Japanese signed the Nine Power treaty, pledging themselves to enhance the territorial and administrative integrity of China, yet never intending to surrender their special rights in Manchuria. As long as China remained weak and disunited, the treaty powers could coexist peacefully, if uneasily. Once Chinese nationalism became a force to be reckoned with, the veil of the Nine Power treaty could no longer hide the fragile political compromise on which cooperation in China was based. U.S. position statements acknowledged these competing security requisites and cautioned in 1934,

> We should refuse to be drawn into any likely-to-be-proposed "political trading" for, in the process of such trading, the strategy of the Japanese would be to make the most of our reputed devotion to the cause of "peace," to the principle of disarmament and to the process of entering into agreements; they would try to maneuver us into a position such that we would be compelled to make concessions in fact and to their advantage in return for concessions by them in appearance only and not at all of any real value for us.[23]

SYSTEM MAINTENANCE

I. *System maintenance has different, and more demanding, requirements than system formation does.*

System maintenance is a process of changing rules and procedures that are consistent with a set of principles, to accommodate shifting

22. S. Tatsuji Takeuchi, *War and Diplomacy in the Japanese Empire* (Chicago: Doubleday, Doran, 1935), p. 339.

23. "Naval Conference: London Preliminary Conversations; Suggestions for Consideration of the American Government and the American Conferees," October 4, 1934, Norman H. Davis Papers, London Naval Conference, Miscellaneous memos, October–December 1934, Container 36, Library of Congress, Manuscript Division, Washington, D.C.

security problems, evolving foreign policy objectives, and technological developments. System formation may be relatively easy because it does not require reaching a consensus on the spirit and broader intent of an agreement; system maintenance, however, requires just such a consensus. Distilled to its essence, the Washington treaty system endorsed the principles of arms control; security without resort to collusion, alliance, or force, and preservation of the open door and integrity of China. Successful system maintenance between the wars required that the members agree on the principles that defined the purposes they were expected to pursue,[24] and that the principles reflect the values and attitudes of system members. Otherwise, the security system would require "adaptation," or changing the principles to infuse the system with new political content. Adaptation, a profoundly more difficult task, requires a confluence of the perceptions of the parties on the necessity for and direction of change.

Clearly, there are limits to what maintenance may accomplish in an environment rife with political and military challenges. The unification of China, civil war, German rearmament, and economic depression were hardly minor tests for the treaty system. It is doubtful whether the Western powers could have prevented Tokyo's shift toward unilateralism once Japan decided that cooperation with the West was a bankrupt policy. However, most of the interwar strategies of treaty maintenance circumvented rather than tackled the difficult problems created by changes in the external and domestic constraints facing the treaty powers.

The paradox of the interwar years was that as political cooperation diminished, the signatories struggled to extend arms control coverage by resorting to military-based strategies to compensate for their inability or unwillingness to implement political-based strategies. These policies of expediency were wholly inadequate for system maintenance; and as international and domestic politics evolved, the security system proved less and less effective in containing rivalry. The Nationalist unification of China and the growth of the Red Army in the maritime provinces altered the strategic reality facing the Japanese in China and Manchuria.[25] The impact of world economic depression in the Far East and

---

24. Keohane, *After Hegemony*, p. 58.
25. See Akira Iriye, "The Asian Factor," in Gordon Martel, ed., *The Origins of the Second World War Reconsidered* (Boston: Allen & Unwin, 1986), pp. 227–43.

the collapse of the silk market enhanced the economic constraints facing the Japanese and propelled to power domestic factions committed to
imperial self-sufficiency rather than economic cooperation with the
West.[26] The reconstitution of German power altered the strategic reality
facing the French and British. The Washington treaty system began to
unravel when it failed to address these shifting constraints in any meaningful way. In China, the treaty powers began pursuing unilateral courses
of action rather than developing alternative cooperative strategies to
protect respective interests in the face of strong antiforeign sentiment.[27]
In Europe, British attempts to reorient cooperation in the Pacific to
reduce the pressures created by German rearmament met with Japanese
resistance.[28] In 1935 Tokyo rejected London's strategy of using cooperation in China to induce it to accept naval inferiority.[29] In addition,
collapse of the U.S. market and enactment of the Smoot-Hawley tariff
undermined incentives for economic cooperation with the West and
the foundations of Japan's economic diplomacy.[30] When cooperative arrangements ignored the newly emerging domestic and international imperatives affecting national security requirements, the treaty process
collapsed.

II.   *Strategies of system maintenance inconsistent with a political-based ap-
      proach to arms control undermine cooperation in the long run.*

Five strategies were pursued to maintain the Washington security system: (1) delinking technical arms control from political and economic
developments in the Far East; (2) separating the political from the military components of security at London in 1930; (3) incorporating escape and escalator clauses into treaties; (4) attempting to negotiate a
nonaggression pact with Japan in 1934; and (5) negotiating to bring the
reconstituted great power, Germany, into the system. Only the fourth
strategy was consistent with a political-based approach to the arms control process; however, it followed on the heels of a series of military-
based strategies in 1930, and by 1934, the Japanese were convinced
that their security was no longer served by cooperation with the West.

26. Iriye, *After Imperialism*, pp. 242–43, 279; Beasley, *Japanese Imperialism*, p. 173.

27. Louis, *British Strategy*, pp. 158, 164; Borg, *American Policy and the Chinese Revolution*, p. 422;
Iriye, *After Imperialism*, p. 160.

28. Trotter, *Britain and East Asia*, p. 56; Rudoff, "Influence of the German Navy."

29. Trotter, *Britain and East Asia*, p. 96; Pelz, *Race to Pearl Harbor*, pp. 51–52.

30. Iriye, *After Imperialism*, pp. 242–43, 279.

A delinkage strategy is by definition unable to sustain a symmetry between political understandings and military agreements because it attempts to advance arms control and consolidate technical agreements despite a deterioration in political relations in an interrelated issue area. Delinkage may become politically untenable domestically or internationally. In the interwar years, both occurred. Failure to obtain an equilibrium between military and political settlements contributed to a political crisis in Japan and the collapse of the domestic foundations of interstate consensus. At the same time, unification of China made it impossible for the Japanese to reconcile the policies of cooperation with the West with the defense—let alone extension—of continental interests. In 1922, Japanese treaty rights and interests in Manchuria had been linked to cooperation with the Anglo-Saxon powers. By 1933, peace in Asia demanded a Monroe Doctrine for Asia that precluded cooperation, even in arms limitation. In the estimation of the vice-chief of the Naval General Staff, Admiral Suetsugu, the naval and Manchurian questions had become inseparable.[31] In security systems where cooperation rests on the inherent linkage of issues because parties recognize these issues to be interrelated, delinkage is a problematic strategy for system maintenance in the long run. Correspondingly, progress on technical arms control treaties alone is not necessarily an indicator that the security system is healthy.

Separating the political and military components of security was a strategy of treaty maintenance pursued both by intention (vis-à-vis the Pacific) and by default (vis-à-vis Europe) at the London Naval Conference of 1930. In the Pacific, concessions were confined to ships alone without linking arms control agreements to an accommodation of evolving foreign policy pressures in the Far East. The Japanese accepted an inferior ratio in cruiser tonnage, yet received no visible political compensation as they had at Washington. Although this strategy succeeded in consolidating and advancing the arms limitation component of the security system, it failed to address the political sources of arms competition and contributed to the demise of cooperation in the long run.

Equivocating on French demands for enhanced security by separating the political and military requirements of security in Europe also undermined the system. The French continued to demand political guaran-

---

31. Asada, "Japanese Navy and the United States," p. 239.

tees as a prerequisite for disarmament, and the British continued to refuse. Along with the United States, Britain championed the Kellogg-Briand Pact as an adequate basis for arms limitation, yet were reluctant to modify it to secure a reduction in French demands. Not only were French interests not accommodated; even worse from their perspective, they were disregarded. Though the British and French shared mutual security interests, this was not sufficient to ensure cooperation because they could not agree on a policy toward Germany. France preferred Germany to remain weak; Britain preferred Germany to recover. As O'Connor summarizes the standoff, "The political safety pursued by the French was jeopardized by the economic objectives of Britain."[32] Disagreement also reflected asymmetries in strategic doctrine and force structure, as well as different geopolitical and historical legacies such as those that plagued U.S.-Soviet security cooperation during the Cold War.[33] For the French (and Italians), the memory of the First World War reinforced a conception of the national interest that "excluded the pursuit of security through arms limitation, unless this was comprehensive and included guarantees from other powers."[34] This precluded settlement of naval matters alone. Similar obstacles had earlier prevented the negotiation of a more comprehensive arms control agreement in 1922 as the French refused to accept limits on their submarine force without a mutual assistance guarantee from the British. However, the difference in 1930 was that a resurgent Germany was a reality rather than just a hypothetical possibility, and from the French perspective, system maintenance more than ever required adjustment to deal with shifts in the continental military balance.

A third strategy of system maintenance was the inclusion of escape, or escalator, clauses in the first London Naval Treaty. The second London Naval Treaty of 1936 replicated this strategy as well, but by that time, the security system existed in name only. Escape clauses may be quite effective in facilitating agreement because they build into the treaty the reservations of signatories about the behavior of states not party to the agreement, about possible violations of the agreement, or more broadly about changes in circumstance that may affect the security requirements of treaty powers. Article 21 of the 1930 London Treaty

---

32. O'Connor, *Perilous Equilibrium*, p. 91.
33. Alexander L. George, "Factors Influencing Security Cooperation," in George et al., *U.S.-Soviet Security Cooperation*, pp. 661–63.
34. Hall, *Britain, America, and Arms Control*, p. 115.

cited, as a basis for escalation, the new construction of any power not a party to the treaty; Article 25 of the 1936 London Treaty cited the authorization, construction, or acquisition by a nation not a party to the treaty of a warship not in conformity with treaty restrictions; Article 26 of the 1936 London Treaty cited a change of circumstances materially affecting the national security of a high contracting party. Built-in responses designed to protect the building programs of signatories, however, are less effective for system maintenance if, as in 1930, they are triggered by the policies of nonsignatories. As Richard D. Burns and Donald Urquidi conclude, "If the 'escalator clause' granted a theoretical contractual safeguard against unregulated naval competition, it did not in practice prove to be the reassuring safety valve its English originators had hoped. This was especially true with regard to continental building during the early 1930s."[35] An escape clause may affect the reactions of states bound by the treaty, but has little influence over states not bound by the treaty. In addition, there may be domestic political pressures against invoking an escalator clause. Burns and Urquidi note that

> two major drawbacks appeared to mitigate against British invocation of the escalator clause during the early thirties. First, the government feared that the British public would not understand why their officials were breaking a "disarmament agreement" and, consequently, that the resulting disquietude would react adversely in future elections. And secondly, the government found most distasteful, from the standpoint of its effect on general foreign policy, the necessity of publicly justifying that the naval policies of France or Italy (or both) jeopardized British security. The latter situation would compound the former and both would further alienate diplomatic feelings abroad.[36]

In the 1930s, President Roosevelt designed a proportional-response policy to counteract domestic political pressures inhibiting escalatory response to Japanese violations of the Washington and London treaties. The United States employed adversary-triggered specific escalator clauses (in response to particular specified violations) and broader blanket escalator clauses (in response to external changes perceived as

35. Burns and Urquidi, *Disarmament in Perspective*, vol. 3, p. 268.
36. Ibid., p. 269.

threats to national security under treaty limits),[37] to protect strategic force modernization despite fiscal constraints and domestic pressures for preserving the treaty system. Roosevelt also passed the first and second Vinson Acts in 1934 and 1938, "enabling legislation" in Robin Ranger's words, to legitimize U.S. force increases.[38] Escalator clauses, however, are more effective for meeting the long-term challenge of protecting the force modernization of treaty-regulated militaries, particularly when long lead times are required, than of system maintenance.

A fourth strategy of system maintenance was that of bringing Germany into the security system to regulate German rearmament. Actors may agree on treaty provisions for different reasons, and as the U.S.-Japanese compromises reveal, even conflicting interests may nurture cooperation for short-term tension reduction, a not insignificant achievement. Maintenance, a long-term proposition, by contrast requires that the objectives of the signatories be modified or accommodated. Introducing new members into a security system may be achieved relatively easily, but incorporating their concerns is not the same as reaching an accommodation with the rest of the actors affected by the interlocking set of political and military arrangements. There must be a broader political framework of relations that helps coordinate short-term policies, regardless of how loose and general in character.[39] As Bull points out, the "naval treaties [of 1922] were part of a basic political understanding among the original five parties . . . [and the] Washington Naval Treaty itself was part of a wider structure of agreements about political and territorial position in the Pacific."[40]

In contrast, the London Naval Treaty of 1930 put "the control of weapons in the wrong sequence on the road to security."[41] Likewise, the Anglo-German naval agreement of 1935, a technical agreement consistent with a military-based approach to the arms control process, was for the Germans "an instrument for securing undisturbed progress for a number of years until they were ready to repute the limits imposed by it."[42] All of these first four strategies of system maintenance had a com-

37. Robin Ranger, *The Naval Arms Control Record, 1919–1939: Axis Violations and Democratic Compliance Failures*, prepared for OASD/ISP, Contract No. MDA903-87-M-3565 (Fairfax, Va.: National Security Research, April 1987).

38. Ibid., pp. 26–28.

39. George, "Factors Influencing Security Cooperation," pp. 667–69.

40. Bull, "Strategic Arms Limitation," p. 39.

41. O'Connor, *Perilous Equilibrium*, p. 128.

42. Kennedy, *Rise and Fall*, p. 289.

mon deficiency. In an effort to protect and extend the technical arms control dimension of the security system, they slighted the broader political consensus necessary for system maintenance and neglected the more profound political threats to security emerging in the Far East and in Europe.

The only maintenance strategy remotely consistent with a political-based approach to arms control was the attempt by the British to reach a bilateral nonaggression pact with Japan by guaranteeing the Japanese a role in any reconstruction scheme in China in exchange for adherence to the treaty system. Strategies of British imperial defense had depended in one form or another since the turn of the century on political understandings with Japan. From 1902 until 1922, accommodation had taken the form of the Anglo-Japanese alliance. From 1922 on, it had been incorporated within the Washington treaty system. By 1934, however, the Japanese were charting a new course, and British overtures were a desperate and futile attempt that grossly miscalculated how Chinese unification, worldwide depression, and a constitutional crisis had restructured Japanese domestic politics and shifted support away from "international" solutions toward "national" solutions to foreign policy issues. Domestic political developments in Japan were a major catalyst for system breakdown, but these internal dynamics could not be isolated from regional forces operating in the Far East—Chinese nationalism and growing Soviet power—or from the diplomacy of Western powers there, which turned on the adoption of the nonrecognition doctrine regarding Manchukuo and extensive economic and technical support for the Chinese.[43] In October 1933, the Japanese Cabinet adopted three policies: naval supremacy, superiority over the Red Army, and political hegemony in China. The Imperial Navy's "second building program" in 1934–1937 was initiated in response to the Vinson-Tramell bill of March 1934, and by the end of 1935, the Japanese had exceeded the limits set by the Washington and London treaties. On August 7, 1936, Tokyo adopted the "Fundamentals of National Policy," which advanced the navy's aim of "southward advance,"[44] stressed the need to "strengthen naval armaments in order to ensure the command of the western Pacific against the U.S. Navy, and for the first

43. See Dorothy Borg, *The United States and the Far Eastern Crisis, 1933–1938* (Cambridge: Harvard University Press, 1964), pp. 46–99, for details of Western aid to China.

44. The southward advance was premised on the need to secure advance bases for operations or springboards in the South China Sea en route to the South Seas.

time included Great Britain as one of Japan's potential enemies."[45] The Imperial Navy set long-range political objectives, planned shipbuilding schedules to execute these goals, and secured the necessary funds to these ends.[46] The Washington powers had not altered the principles of the treaty system to speak to the major political upheavals in the international system of the 1930s. Clearly, the 1930s demanded entirely new types of cooperative understandings, adapted to new political realities. The inability to bring Japan into the system in any meaningful way prevented a new system from evolving, whereas Japan's rejection of the Washington treaty system signaled, once and for all, its collapse.

LEGACY OF THE PAST

It has become part of the folklore that interwar naval arms control failed because it did not prevent World War II. The issues are far more complex than this charge would indicate, and the tendency to evaluate arms control in black-and-white, either-or terms obscures the important dimensions of success achieved between the wars. It is always easier to argue that a policy failed rather than succeeded, particularly by switching the scope or time frame within which the policy is evaluated.[47] For an enterprise as fragile and delicate as arms control, it is especially easy to expand the time frame and declare that in the long run, arms control failed to prevent war. I find this argument hackneyed and consider the Washington treaty system, in fact, a limited success. It stabilized the balance of power in the 1920s, yet ultimately contributed to a series of unintended and destabilizing consequences in the 1930s. The treaty system regulated the security arena by limiting capital ships: the strategic system of the day, index of great power, and key instrument of world politics. Moreover, it succeeded for a short while in managing competition in the area of greatest postwar instability—China. Since

45. Asada, "Japanese Navy and the United States," p. 244. Marder argues, however, that the Imperial Navy never seriously thought about war with the Royal Navy. Arthur J. Marder, *Old Friends, New Enemies: The Royal Navy and the Imperial Japanese Navy: Strategic Illusions, 1936–1941* (Oxford: Clarendon Press, 1981), p. viii.

46. See Marder, *Old Friends, New Enemies*, pp. 15–19, on the third and fourth naval replenishment programs.

47. I am indebted to Leslie C. Eliason for pointing this out to me.

the political relations of the five powers transcended the Pacific arena, naval limitation had global consequences. The European system of the nineteenth and early twentieth centuries had clearly burst its seams, and two new major powers, the United States and Japan, had to be included in any postwar reconstruction of balance of power. In this sense, the treaty system represented a modest initial step toward the creation of a new international order to fill the vacuum left by the demise of the European system after World War I.

In Anglo-American relations, the treaty system had its most enduring, long-term positive influence. Tensions in Anglo-American relations certainly oscillated throughout the treaty years, but the naval agreements facilitated peaceful evolution away from British naval superiority toward Anglo-American parity. As Hall points out, "In managing the transfer of military superiority from Britain to America, the Washington System eliminated the possibility of conflict between these two 'superpowers' of the interwar period: a conflict that was certainly envisaged from time to time by naval officers and planners on both sides of the Atlantic."[48] The treaty system also realigned political allies in the Far East as Anglo-American interests began to converge with each other and diverge from those of Japan. It displaced the Anglo-Japanese alliance, the cornerstone of both Japan's and Britain's Far Eastern policies since 1902, as Great Britain abandoned its major Far Eastern ally in order to avoid an arms race with the United States.

The system failed to accommodate developments in China where compromise remained tenuous and limited. By the mid-1920s, the treaty powers were sidestepping the task of forging a more robust security order in the Far East, opting instead to retain many elements of the existing status quo. Efforts to cooperate in helping China emerge as an independent nation and as a stabilizing factor in the Far East were made half-heartedly, despite the fact that "China was a key to the successful functioning of the new system."[49] In Iriye's estimation, "China entered the picture only insofar as these powers agreed to limit their expansion and renounce particularistic agreements."[50] In retrospect, however, the system proved weakest in regulating the European naval balance. In the early 1920s, the British could be fairly confident in their ability to se-

---

48. Hall, *Britain, America and Arms Control*, p. 218.
49. Iriye, *Origins of the Second World War*, p. 3.
50. Iriye, *After Imperialism*, p. 22.

cure the home islands and maritime commerce from any European threat. Yet Franco-Italian antagonism escalated steadily throughout the twenties and thirties, curtailed only negligibly by the naval treaties, and German rearmament made it even more difficult for the Royal Navy to divert sufficient resources to meet threats from extra-European powers. Successful regulation of the European balance required meeting the doctrinal requirements of the continental powers and addressing the political dimensions of security in Europe. The system fell short. Conversely, the ability to create political accommodations in the Pacific, however fragile, reduced tension for a while in this major region of postwar instability.

Though the treaty system had unintended side effects on the balance of power in the Pacific, compared to the turbulence of the thirties, the twenties were a decade of relatively successful cooperation. Despite the turmoil in revolutionary China, Britain, the United States, and Japan were able to consolidate and extend the arms control system in 1930. Cooperation based on the Washington principles eventually collapsed in response to shifts in internal and external pressures. Nevertheless, the Washington treaty system should be scrutinized for its successes, however limited and transient, because it teaches that technical agreements rarely provide solutions to political problems, making arms control that lacks a conflict resolution dimension problematic. Arms control and security cooperation must be continually adjusted to the flow of politics as well as technology.

ARMS CONTROL FOR THE FUTURE

The assumptions of the Cold War approach to arms control have been remarkably resilient over the years. Though grounded in a theory of bipolar conflict in the nuclear age, they have permeated thinking about arms control in non-nuclear, nonbipolar, and non–Cold War contexts. In one example, analysts regularly equate "conventional stability" with the first-strike stability of strategic analysis,[51] judging a military balance

51. Michael Moodie, "Conventional Arms Control: An Analytical Survey of Recent Literature," *Washington Quarterly* 12 (Winter 1989): 193–94; Barry Posen, "Crisis Stability and Conventional Arms Control," *Daedalus* 120 (Winter 1991): 217–32.

as force-posture stable "if the defender would be quite likely to prevail if invaded and that fact is correctly perceived by both sides."[52] The primary culprit of instability was held to be the "short-warning offensive capability inherent in Soviet ground forces (tanks and artillery) deployed forward in Eastern Europe" that created the "capability for surprise attack or for the initiation of large scale offensive action."[53] With the end of the Cold War, the overriding contingency that dominated non-nuclear force reduction, namely, the threat of a Soviet conventional superiority in the heart of Europe, has been overtaken by events. The possibility of a surprise attack by the Soviet Union in Europe greatly receded well before the demise of the central Soviet state because of Gorbachev's unilateral cuts. The Conventional Forces in Europe (CFE) process formalized asymmetric cuts that set equal levels of ground and air force weapons in Europe, yet continued enhancing political stability in addition to the more narrow goal of force-posture stability. CFE codified a fundamental change in the balance of power in Europe and succeeded as far as it went because the signatories shared the political goal of dismantling the Soviet empire in Eastern Europe. Manpower reductions to remove the Soviet Army from Eastern Europe have long since been overcome by events, but they illustrate another arms control measure grounded in the political objective of creating a new order by providing breathing room for emerging democracies. The arms control process has codified and contributed to political change in the post–Cold War era. Arms control has not been rendered obsolete. Only the Cold War approach has.

Although it may be easier and more familiar to think of arms control as a means to regulate the military balance rather than as a currency for political change and a constructive tool for restructuring influence, the complex political landscapes shaping the arms control environments in South Asia, the Middle East, and Eurasia reinforce the pitfalls and shortcomings of relying exclusively on military-based strategies for emerging nuclear and non-nuclear issues. In South Asia, ethnic, religious, ideological, and political differences fuel the antagonism between India and Pakistan. In a pattern reminiscent of Italian and French naval competition in the 1920s, Pakistan is intent on achieving parity with India, and India aspires to great-power status on par with China. Not sur-

---

52. Davis et al., *Variables Affecting Central-Region Stability*, pp. 2–3.
53. Moodie, "Conventional Arms Control," p. 193.

prisingly, India's political and military aspirations beyond the subcontinent are perceived as direct threats to Pakistan's regional security. And although diverse "considerations of national independence, security, economic and technological advancement, and diplomatic leverage drive investment" in military arsenals, Janne E. Nolan reminds us that "given an international system in which military prowess has been a leading determinant of national stature, the efforts of third world nations to acquire the most advanced weapons available in the international market should come as no surprise.[54] Only political agreements can address prestige issues, major motivators of India's drive for military superiority.

In the Middle East, the Arab-Israeli conflict pits five military antagonists (Syria, Iraq, Iran, Libya, and Saudi Arabia) against Israel. Defining military balances there is immensely complicated, given that Israel considers the inventories of the Arab states as a collective threat despite the political animosity among the Arab states, which prevents them from acting collectively. This offers one illustration of how the superpower nuclear arms control experience fails to apply to the more complex, multilateral arms control landscapes of the post–Cold War world.[55] The arms control process needs to develop beyond the strategies derived from gaming exercises that assume two actors with irreconcilable political differences. The demand for, and proliferation of, ballistic missiles and conventional weapons in the Middle East will be impossible to curtail with export controls alone as long as the basic political disputes that sustain the rivalries and motivate weapons buildups are treated separately from force limitation discussions.[56] As recent developments in Iraq and North Korea portend, the proliferation of weapons of mass destruction will eventually deliver them into the hands of actors who may view them as usable.[57] Arms controllers must look for

54. Janne E. Nolan, *Trappings of Power: Ballistic Missiles in the Third World* (Washington, D.C.: The Brookings Institution, 1991), p. 16.

55. Ibid., pp. 156–59.

56. The focus of proliferation treaties has generally been on the suppliers. However, focusing on the demand side, which is a political question of reducing the perceived need for arming, may be no more difficult than using arms control to regulate the supply side. See "Potent Office Weaves Web in China Arms," *New York Times*, August 21, 1991, A16, and Aaron Karp, "Controlling Ballistic Missile Proliferation," *Survival* 33 (November/December 1991): 517–30.

57. Some even advocate "managed" nuclear proliferation to enhance international order. See Kenneth N. Waltz, "The Spread of Nuclear Weapons: More May Be Better," *Adelphi Papers* 171 (London: International Institute for Strategic Studies, 1982), and Mearsheimer, "Back to the Future," pp. 37–40.

creative ways to reduce political tensions, like post–World War I leaders did in the Far East and western Pacific.

In Eurasia, a political consensus on the outlines of a European security architecture has yet to develop. The European Community (EC) remains impotent in security affairs, as its response to the Yugoslav crisis confirms.[58] Developing an active role in that arena or fusing the EC with the Western European Union (WEU) is unlikely in the short term as EC members focus on restarting the engine of European union. Emergence of a genuine political identity, with its attendant closer military ties, has far to travel to surmount popular reluctance to transfer loyalty to a European governing body.[59] NATO lacks a clear political and military agenda, and in search of one has turned its attention toward out-of-area operations under the auspices of the Conference on Security and Cooperation in Europe (CSCE) and peace-keeping operations in conjunction with the United Nations. The CSCE, however, is too unwieldy in its present form to function as a pan-European security organization with a clear mandate to use military force. Nevertheless, former Warsaw Pact states have reduced their militaries and adopted strategies of territorial defense, relying on light infantry and quick mobilization of reserves. If "attacked by larger well-equipped forces without sufficient time to mobilize reserves, they would be prepared only to mount a conventional defense of a few days, after which their fate will depend on outside help."[60] Along with force limitation initiatives, mutual defense obligations need to evolve to support scaled-back capabilities so that fledgling democracies may channel resources into building market economies. To date, no security arrangements protect former Warsaw Pact states. Nor is this a trivial concern considering the conflicting national and ethnic priorities that have torn apart Yugoslavia and fostered civil war, border challenges, secession, and pleas for outside intervention.[61] The Commonwealth of Independent States, as well,

58. "Europeans Retreat on a Peace Force for Croatia," New York Times, September 20, 1991.

59. Beverly Crawford, "Creating A New Europe: Opportunities and Challenges," in Beverly Crawford and Peter W. Schulze, eds., The New Europe Asserts Itself: A Changing Role in International Relations (Berkeley and Los Angeles: University of California Press, 1990), pp. 16, 26–28.

60. Daniel N. Nelson, "Europe's Unstable East," Foreign Policy 82 (Spring 1991): 147; Rudolf L. Tokes, "Central European Conflict Resolution: Security Challenges to the New Democracies of East Central Europe" (Paper presented at the 1991 Topical Symposium "From Regionalism to Globalism—New Perspectives on American Foreign and Defense Policies," November 14–15, 1991, National Defense University, Washington, D.C.).

61. Nelson, "Europe's Unstable East," pp. 137–58.

has yet to develop security guarantees for the former Soviet republics or to forge political and military understandings between Ukraine and Russia.[62] Absence of these political understandings seems to be obstructing Ukrainian ratification of the START I treaty as Ukrainian leaders demand guarantees of security as a prerequisite for surrendering their strategic nuclear arsenal.[63] As the French case between the wars reminds us, technical agreements alone are unlikely to enhance long-term security if they are not part of wider understandings about future structures of political order and are not grounded in a convergence of political vision. This is particularly true in Europe today where new national conceptions of interests and priorities are proliferating. That politics and arms control are inextricably integrated in the European context, however, is nothing new.[64] Even during the Cold War, stability depended more on alliance relationships and the credibility of the United States's nuclear guarantee than on force ratios or theoretical deterrence models. As Catherine Kelleher submits, "Survivability of specific weapons systems was probably less important than the political credibility of their possible use."[65]

A range of arms control prescriptions have been offered for post–Cold War Europe. Many methods focus on the design of military strategy, weaponry, deployments, and doctrine and involve changing the composition, structure, and disposition of armed forces on the Continent. Suggestions include limiting the possibility of quick mobilization of reserves through manpower limits and restraints on training and concentration of force; reducing combat-ready troops to the level of reserve units; restricting logistic components such as railways, engineering, and bridging equipment; restricting arms production; dismantling military infrastructure like ammunition and fuel depots; cutting conventional forces more deeply based on size of territory or length of borders; declaring principles for military doctrine that support defensive armed forces. Many of these suggestions are designed to enhance military stability on the Continent and to reduce the threat of surprise attacks and offensive

---

62. "Europe Welcomes Soviet Arms Cuts," *New York Times*, October 7, 1991, A6.

63. "Ukraine Finds Atom Arms Bring Measure of Respect," *New York Times*, January 7, 1993, A1.

64. Catherine M. Kelleher, "Arms Control in a Revolutionary Future: Europe," *Daedalus* 120 (Winter 1991): 114–19.

65. Ibid., p. 119.

actions. They stem from the fear that democratic changes in the former Soviet Union may not be permanent. However, when we reflect on the range of sources of actual and potential conflict in Europe today and in the future—ethnic, nationalist, religious, and linguistic tensions; mass migration; economic crisis—we see that the traditional arms control agenda of regulating military balances seems divorced from the political realities that may drive rearmament. Perhaps this is a bureaucratic artifact of the Cold War. It is probably a conceptual artifact of the Cold War way of thinking as well.

More recent arms control events, particularly in the nuclear arena, validate the relevance of political-based arms control for the more complex post–Cold War structure of conflict. President Bush's initiatives banning tactical nuclear weapons were significant less for their effect on the military balance than for the fact that they symbolized and codified movement toward a convergence of political vision between the United States and Gorbachev's Soviet Union. The same may be said of the Bush-Yeltsin agreements sharply reducing stocks of long-range missile warheads and eliminating all multiple-warhead missiles based on land, which culminated in the signing of the START II treaty. However, whether arms control succeeds over time with the successor states of the Soviet Union is less a function of specific technical provisions than of whether the arms control process can accommodate the legitimate aspirations and security concerns of these newly emerging nation-states. Arms control becomes a technical enterprise only after states agree on underlying political assumptions.

Events surrounding the START II treaty, cutting nuclear arsenals by 75 percent by the year 2003, should make one pause to reconsider the appropriateness of approaching post–Cold War arms control in the Cold War mode. Despite the Lisbon protocols of July 1991, which pledged Ukraine, Kazakhstan, and Belarus to transfer the nuclear missiles stationed on their territory to Russia for dismantling and surrender them in accord with the first START treaty, START II remains a bloc-based agreement, negotiated between two superpowers, one of which no longer exists. Ukrainian resistance to ratifying the first START treaty, a prerequisite for the new START treaty to take effect, suggests how inappropriate this approach to arms control is to the political and military reality of strategic nuclear arsenals in the world. Ukrainian leaders stress they are intent on relinquishing their strategic nuclear weapons, but not without receiving in return compensation for the loss of their status as the world's third largest nuclear power. Nuclear weapons confer power, prestige, and respect. Most Ukrainian deputies support ratification of START I, but only with appropriate guarantees of security and compensation. Specifically, Ukrainian leaders are calling for a security guarantee in the form of a treaty signed by both the United States and Russia, and economic compensation from Russia. Ukraine forfeited its tactical nuclear weapons without compensation. It will not do the same with its strategic nuclear arsenal. As one influential Ukrainian leader put it, "We would never give up the nuclear weapons now, at least without something in return. We don't want to be the fool. The U.S. needs to understand this, to take into account the psychological factor."[66] Technical agreements regulating force balances alone can never address the factors motivating the Ukrainians to cling to their nuclear arsenal. By contrast, tying force reductions to security guarantees and to political and economic compensation is an assumption of the political-based approach to arms control, and this type of strategy can reduce the prestige value of military assets. The START method, while laudable in the reductions it has in theory attained, is inadequate to the post–Cold War political landscape of arms control because it is both bloc-based and military-based.

Major military capabilities, uncertainty, the devolution of political power, and the proliferation of military technology all characterize the post–Cold War strategic landscape of arms control. Political and military leaders need to focus beyond remedying only instabilities in military relationships that provide opportunities for conflict and focus as well on remedying unstable political relationships that could otherwise destabilize military relationships. Technical arms control initiatives should be integrated with broader political efforts such as these five:

1. The promotion of conflict resolution for ethnic and nationalist violence below the level of the United Nations. This has become imperative because, as Yugoslavia demonstrates, ethnic conflict may bleed into territorial conquest, calls for border adjustments, and the formation of competing blocs, which may transform a localized conflict into one with wider regional proportions.[67] It is virtually impossible to anticipate and orchestrate the range of possible future balances.

66. "Ukraine Finds Atom Arms Bring Measure of Respect," p. A6.
67. "All-Out War in Europe," *New York Times*, September 19, 1991.

2. The definition of norms and procedures of intervention to prevent peacekeeping forces from being viewed as invasion forces. This is emerging as a pressing issue with the developing consensus around the sanctioned use of force for peacemaking purposes. Naval force limitation discussions, in particular, seem closely tied to peacekeeping and peacemaking, as the missions of military forces evolve with the political demands for the use of force. Although norms of restraint for intervention are still evolving in the new Europe, history reminds us of the importance of reaching a shared consensus on dealing with instabilities in areas where history, geography, and traditional spheres of influence, like Russia's "near abroad," have created asymmetric degrees of concern.

3. The provision of meaningful security guarantees in the short run for former Warsaw Pact states that have not yet joined NATO or some other security alliance, yet have inadequate forces for sustained self-defense. This is a highly controversial policy, yet one that deserves careful consideration.

4. The exploration of the utility of regional and subregional groups to meet specific security challenges that affect some, but not all states of a region (such as a Baltic-Nordic group). This initiative offers a more realistic short-run objective than a pan-European security structure. It may reduce the incentives to rely on independent military forces to meet goals, interests, and strategic concerns, and at the same time, compensate for the inherent weaknesses of more centralized global institutions. New security architectures will evolve as participants struggle to reach a common conception of how to enhance security, or at least conceptions that substantially overlap. Regional and subregional arrangements supported by outside powers may be more effective for forging new power balances than international institutions. Again, the pattern of the 1920s emerges: shape a stable military-political order in one arena (the Pacific) and extend force levels to other arenas (Europe). Avoid, however, the major flaws of the interwar experiment (in Europe in 1922 and 1930, and in the Pacific in 1930), namely, seeking only a military balance in the absence of related political arrangements. Both are integral to maintaining balances of power and preventing regional hegemonies.

5. The linking of supply restraints on proliferation with political and economic initiatives to reduce regional tensions. This is an initiative taking shape in the Middle East as senior Israeli military and diplomatic

officials begin to relax barriers to Palestinian autonomy and explore
creative deals with Syria.[68]

In sum, a primary objective of arms control should be to make technical treaties part of a web of understandings with the by-product that
weapons become a less critical index of great-power status. This represents one of the greatest hurdles in stemming weapons proliferation
among developing and newly emerging nation-states today. Nonmilitary arrangements should be exploited where possible to reduce the
prestige value of military assets. The arms control dialogue today, as in
the 1920s, can be a way of creating, shaping, and modifying perceptions about status, power, and interests of states, concerns crucial for
newly emerging nation-states like Ukraine. Arms control, as Johan Jørgen Holst puts it, "is not only about crisis stability it is also a currency
for structuring political influence."[69] During periods of political transition, the arms control process can be an important mechanism for relating the military balance to a structurally appropriate political arrangement. The process, however, must be responsive to, or at least cognizant
of, the multidimensional security considerations of newly emerging
powers (like the United States, Japan, China, and the Soviet Union in
the 1920s), as well as of traditional powers that may be experiencing
only limited retrenchment (like Germany between the wars).

"History reveals arms control to be a modest enterprise. . . . None of
the successfully concluded agreements noted [in Kruzel's study] led to
significant disarmament, with the arguable exception of the Washington Conference."[70] The 1920s and 1930s are a case of limited arms
control success that is historical reality rather than an abstract ideal
derived from gaming exercises. Lessons from this period are important
for contemporary policy analysis and theory development, particularly
for refocusing international attention on the complex relationship between the technical aspects of military force and the reshaping of the

68. Leslie H. Gelb, "Israel's Military Superiority," *New York Times*, June 19, 1992, A27; see
also, "Optimism Seen in Mideast Talks As New Ideas Are Being Reported," *New York Times*,
August 27, 1993, A4; and Michael T. Klare, "The Next Great Arms Race," *Foreign Affairs* 72
(Summer 1993): 152.

69. Johan Jørgen Holst, "Arms Control in the Nineties: A European Perspective," *Daedalus* 120
(Winter 1991): 93.

70. Kruzel, "From Rush-Bagot to START," p. 213. The successfully concluded arms control
agreements examined by Kruzel were the Rush-Bagot Agreement (1817), the Washington Naval
Treaty (1922), the Limited Test Ban Treaty (1963), the Outer Space Treaty (1967), the Non-Pro-
liferation Treaty (1970), the SALT I Agreement (1972), and the SALT II Agreement (1979).

political order within and between states. Events in Europe, the former Soviet Union, and the Middle East present challenges for which traditional arms control theory has little to offer. By contrast, the interwar experience illustrates the consequences of reaching arms agreements absent consensus on underlying norms of political behavior. It suggests the importance of harmonizing competing visions of the future and of unmasking how states define national security and assimilate arms control into definitions of national security.

If I have demonstrated how the interwar arms control process is more relevant than Cold War experiences for the challenges that lie ahead, it may encourage scholars and practitioners to move away from an exclusive focus on technical agreements that preclude addressing instabilities in political relationships as part and parcel of the arms control process and enlarge the domain of arms control, a sphere artificially constrained because of how it was practiced at the strategic nuclear level during the Cold War. Enhancing international security is not strictly a military problem. This seems a remarkably simple assertion, but it is one that the Cold War arms control approach by and large ignored in its formalized separation of politics from arms control strategies. History, on the other hand, continues to demonstrate that the soundness of military agreements may only be understood within a broader political context and that the nature of security is multidimensional and subjective. As Arnold Wolfers puts it, "Security, in an objective sense, measures the absence of threats to acquired values, in a subjective sense, the absence of fear that such values will be attacked." He adds, "The chance of attack can never be measured 'objectively'; it must always remain a matter of subjective evaluation and speculation. . . . It is well known that nations, and groups within nations, differ widely in their reaction to one and the same external situation. . . . [T]his difference in the reaction to similar threats suffices to make it probable that nations will differ in their efforts to obtain more security."[71] Arms control is more complex, yet can be more promising, than the orthodox approach ever suggested, if the process, in Wolfers's words, mitigates not only threats but also reduces the fear that values will be attacked. Reducing that fear requires appreciation of how one's adversaries define security and perceive threats to their security. A military-based approach can never

71. Arnold Wolfers, "National Security as an Ambiguous Symbol," in *Discord and Collaboration: Essays on International Politics* (Baltimore: Johns Hopkins University Press, 1962), pp. 150–51.

accommodate the subjective and multidimensional qualities of security because it deduces an objective definition of security from a theory of bipolar conflict in the nuclear age. Debunking the Cold War orthodoxy may reinvigorate the arms control agenda and transform a technical exercise into a powerful tool for restructuring power relationships.

APPENDIXES

APPENDIX 1: TREATIES AND RESOLUTIONS OF THE WASHINGTON CONFERENCE, 1922

Treaties

(1) A treaty between the United States of America, the British Empire, France, Italy, and Japan, limiting naval armament

(2) A treaty between the same Powers, in relation to the use of submarines and noxious gases in warfare

(3) A treaty between the United States of America, the British Empire, France, and Japan, signed December 13, 1921, relating to their insular possessions and insular dominions in the Pacific Ocean

(4) Declaration accompanying the above Four-Power Treaty

(5) A treaty between the same Four Powers, supplementary to the above, signed February 6, 1922

(6) A treaty between all Nine Powers relating to principles and policies to be followed in matters concerning China

(7) A treaty between the Nine Powers relating to Chinese customs tariff

Resolutions

No. 1. Resolution for a Commission of Jurists to consider amendment of Laws of War

No. 2. Resolution limiting jurisdiction of Commission of Jurists provided in Resolution No. 1

No. 3. Resolution regarding a Board of Reference for Far Eastern Questions

No. 4. Resolution regarding Extraterritoriality in China

No. 5. Resolution regarding Foreign Postal Agencies in China

No. 6. Resolution regarding Armed Forces in China

No. 7. Resolution regarding Radio Stations in China and accompanying Declarations

No. 8. Resolution regarding unification of railways in China and accompanying Declaration by China

No. 9. Resolution regarding the reduction of Chinese Military Forces

No. 10. Resolution regarding existing commitments of China or with respect
to China

No. 11. Resolution regarding the Chinese Eastern Railway, approved by all
the Powers, including China

No. 12. Resolution regarding the Chinese Eastern Railway, approved by all
the Powers, other than China

Treaties

(1) A TREATY BETWEEN THE UNITED STATES OF AMERICA, THE BRITISH EMPIRE, FRANCE, ITALY, AND JAPAN, LIMITING NAVAL ARMAMENT.

Chapter I: General Provisions Relating to the Limitation of Naval Armament

ARTICLE I

The Contracting Powers agree to limit their respective naval armament as provided in the present Treaty.

ARTICLE II

The Contracting Powers may retain respectively the capital ships which are specified in Chapter II, Part 1. On the coming into force of the present Treaty, but subject to the following provisions of this Article, all other capital ships, built or building, of the United States, the British Empire and Japan shall be disposed of as prescribed in Chapter II, Part 2.

In addition to the capital ships specified in Chapter II, Part 1, the United States may complete and retain two ships of the *West Virginia* class now under construction. On the completion of these two ships the *North Dakota* and *Delaware* shall be disposed of as prescribed in Chapter II, Part 2.

The British Empire may, in accordance with the replacement table in Chapter II, Part 3, construct two new capital ships not exceeding 35,000 tons (35,560 metric tons) standard displacement each. On the completion of the said two ships the *Thunderer*, *King George V*, *Ajax* and *Centurion* shall be disposed of as prescribed in Chapter II, Part 2.

ARTICLE III

Subject to the provisions of Article II, the Contracting Powers shall abandon their respective capital ship building programs, and no new capital ships shall be constructed or acquired by any of the Contracting Powers except replacement tonnage which may be constructed or acquired as specified in Chapter II, Part 3.

Ships which are replaced in accordance with Chapter II, Part 3, shall be disposed of as prescribed in Part 2 of that Chapter.

ARTICLE IV

The total capital ship replacement tonnage of each of the Contracting Powers shall not exceed in standard displacement, for the United States 525,000 tons (533,400 metric tons); for the British Empire 525,000 tons (533,400 metric tons); for France 175,000 tons (177,800 metric tons); for Italy 175,000 tons (177,800 metric tons); for Japan 315,000 tons (320,040 metric tons).

ARTICLE V

No capital ship exceeding 35,000 tons (35,560 metric tons) standard displacement shall be acquired by, or constructed by, for, or within the jurisdiction of, any of the Contracting Powers.

ARTICLE VI

No capital ship of any of the Contracting Powers shall carry a gun with a calibre in excess of 16 inches (406 millimetres).

ARTICLE VII

The total tonnage for aircraft carriers of each of the Contracting Powers shall not exceed in standard displacement, for the United States 135,000 tons (137,160 metric tons); for the British Empire 135,000 tons (137,160 metric tons); for France 60,000 tons (60,960 metric tons); for Italy 60,000 tons (60,960 metric tons); for Japan 81,000 tons (82,296 metric tons).

ARTICLE VIII

The replacement of aircraft carriers shall be effected only as prescribed in Chapter II, Part 3, provided, however, that all aircraft carrier tonnage in existence or building on November 12, 1921, shall be considered experimental, and may be replaced, within the total tonnage limit prescribed in Article VII, without regard to its age.

Article IX

No aircraft carrier exceeding 27,000 tons (27,432 metric tons) standard displacement shall be acquired by, or constructed by, for or within the jurisdiction of, any of the Contracting Powers.

However, any of the Contracting Powers may, provided that its total tonnage allowance of aircraft carriers is not thereby exceeded, build not more than two aircraft carriers, each of a tonnage of not more than 33,000 tons (33,528 metric tons) standard displacement, and in order to effect economy any of the Contracting Powers may use for this purpose any two of their ships, whether constructed or in course of construction, which would otherwise be scrapped under the provisions of Article II. The armament of any aircraft carriers exceeding 27,000 tons (27,432 metric tons) standard displacement shall be in accordance with the requirements of Article X, except that the total number of guns to be carried in case any of such guns be of a calibre exceeding 6 inches (152 millimetres), except anti-aircraft guns and guns not exceeding 5 inches (127 millimetres), shall not exceed eight.

Article X

No aircraft carrier of any of the Contracting Powers shall carry a gun with a calibre in excess of 8 inches (203 millimetres). Without prejudice to the provisions of Article IX, if the armament carried includes guns exceeding 6 inches (152 millimetres) in calibre the total number of guns carried, except anti-aircraft guns and guns not exceeding 5 inches (127 millimetres), shall not exceed ten. If alternatively the armament contains no guns exceeding 6 inches (152 millimetres) in calibre, the number of guns is not limited. In either case the number of anti-aircraft guns and of guns not exceeding 5 inches (127 millimetres) is not limited.

Article XI

No vessel of war exceeding 10,000 tons (10,160 metric tons) standard displacement, other than a capital ship or aircraft carrier, shall be acquired by, or constructed by, for, or within the jurisdiction of, any of the Contracting Powers. Vessels not specifically built as fighting ships nor taken in time of peace under government control for fighting purposes, which are employed on fleet duties or as troop transports or in some other way for the purpose of assisting in the prosecution of hostilities otherwise than as fighting ships, shall not be within the limitations of this Article.

ARTICLE XII

No vessel of war of any of the Contracting Powers, hereafter laid down, other than a capital ship, shall carry a gun with a calibre in excess of 8 inches (203 millimetres).

ARTICLE XIII

Except as provided in Article IX, no ship designated in the present Treaty to be scrapped may be reconverted into a vessel of war.

ARTICLE XIV

No preparations shall be made in merchant ships in time of peace for the installation of warlike armaments for the purpose of converting such ships into vessels of war, other than the necessary stiffening of decks for the mounting of guns not exceeding 6 inch (152 millimetres) calibre.

ARTICLE XV

No vessel of war constructed within the jurisdiction of any of the Contracting Powers for a non-Contracting Power shall exceed the limitations as to displacement and armament prescribed by the present Treaty for vessels of a similar type which may be constructed by or for any of the Contracting Powers; provided, however, that the displacement for aircraft carriers constructed for a non-Contracting Power shall in no case exceed 27,000 tons (27,432 metric tons) standard displacement.

ARTICLE XVI

If the construction of any vessel of war for a non-Contracting Power is undertaken within the jurisdiction of any of the Contracting Powers, such Power shall promptly inform the other Contracting Powers of the date of the signing of the contract and the date on which the keel of the ship is laid; and shall also communicate to them the particulars relating to the ship prescribed in Chapter II, Part 3, Section I (b), (4) and (5).

ARTICLE XVII

In the event of a Contracting Power being engaged in war, such Power shall not use as a vessel of war any vessel of war which may be under construction within its jurisdiction for any other Power, or which may have been constructed within its jurisdiction for another Power and not delivered.

Article XVIII

Each of the Contracting Powers undertakes not to dispose by gift, sale or any mode of transfer of any vessel of war in such a manner that such vessel may become a vessel of war in the Navy of any foreign Power.

Article XIX

The United States, the British Empire and Japan agree that the status quo at the time of the signing of the present Treaty, with regard to fortifications and naval bases, shall be maintained in their respective territories and possessions specified hereunder:

(1) The insular possessions which the United States now holds or may hereafter acquire in the Pacific Ocean, except (a) those adjacent to the coast of the United States, Alaska and the Panama Canal Zone, not including the Aleutian Islands, and (b) the Hawaiian Islands;

(2) Hongkong and the insular possessions which the British Empire now holds or may hereafter acquire in the Pacific Ocean, east of the meridian of 110° east longitude, except (a) those adjacent to the coast of Canada, (b) the Commonwealth of Australia and its Territories, and (c) New Zealand;

(3) The following insular territories and possessions of Japan in the Pacific Ocean, to wit: the Kurile Islands, the Bonin Islands, Amami-Oshima, the Loochoo Islands, Formosa and the Pescadores, and any insular territories or possessions in the Pacific Ocean which Japan may hereafter acquire.

The maintenance of the status quo under the foregoing provisions implies that no new fortifications or naval bases shall be established in the territories and possessions specified [,] that no measures shall be taken to increase the existing naval facilities for the repair and maintenance of naval forces, and that no increase shall be made in the coast defences of the territories and possessions above specified. This restriction, however, does not preclude such repair and replacement of worn-out weapons and equipment as is customary in naval and military establishments in time of peace.

Article XX

The rules for determining tonnage displacement prescribed in Chapter II, Part 4, shall apply to the ships of each of the Contracting Powers.

Chapter II: Rules Relating to the Execution of the Treaty—Definition of Terms

PART 1: CAPITAL SHIPS WHICH MAY BE RETAINED BY THE CONTRACTING POWERS

In accordance with Article II ships may be retained by each of the Contracting Powers as specified in this Part.

Ships which may be retained by the United States

Name:	Tonnage
Maryland	32,600
California	32,300
Tennessee	32,300
Idaho	32,000
New Mexico	32,000
Mississippi	32,000
Arizona	31,400
Pennsylvania	31,400
Oklahoma	27,500
Nevada	27,500
New York	27,000
Texas	27,000
Arkansas	26,000
Wyoming	26,000
Florida	21,825
Utah	21,825
North Dakota	20,000
Delaware	20,000
Total tonnage	500,650

On the completion of the two ships of the *West Virginia* class and the scrapping of the *North Dakota* and *Delaware*, as provided in Article II, the total tonnage to be retained by the United States will be 525,850 tons.

Ships which may be retained by the British Empire

Name:	Tonnage
Royal Sovereign	25,750
Royal Oak	25,750
Revenge	25,750
Resolution	25,750
Ramillies	25,750

Malaya	27,500
Valiant	27,500
Barham	27,500
Queen Elizabeth	27,500
Warspite	27,500
Benbow	25,000
Emperor of India	25,000
Iron Duke	25,000
Marlborough	25,000
Hood	41,200
Renown	26,500
Repulse	26,500
Tiger	28,500
Thunderer	22,500
King George V	23,000
Ajax	23,000
Centurion	23,000
Total tonnage	580,450

On the completion of the two new ships to be constructed and the scrapping of the *Thunderer, King George V, Ajax* and *Centurion*, as provided in Article II, the total tonnage to be retained by the British Empire will be 558,950 tons.

Ships which may be retained by France

Name:	Tonnage (metric tons)
Bretagne	23,500
Lorraine	23,500
Provence	23,500
Paris	23,500
France	23,500
Jean Bart	23,500
Courbet	23,500
Condorcet	18,890
Diderot	18,890
Voltaire	18,890
Total tonnage	221,170

France may lay down new tonnage in the years 1927, 1929, and 1931, as provided in Part 3, Section II.

Ships which may be retained by Italy

Name:	Tonnage (metric tons)
Andrea Doria	22,700
Caio Duilio	22,700
Conte Di Cavour	22,500
Giulio Cesare	22,500
Leonardo Da Vinci	22,500
Dante Alighieri	19,500
Roma	12,600
Napoli	12,600
Vittorio Emanuele	12,600
Regina Elena	12,600
Total tonnage	182,800

Italy may lay down new tonnage in the years 1927, 1929, and 1931, as provided in Part 3, Section II.

Ships which may be retained by Japan

Name:	Tonnage
Mutsu	33,800
Nagato	33,800
Hiuga	31,260
Ise	31,260
Yamashiro	30,600
Fu-So	30,600
Kirishima	27,500
Haruna	27,500
Hiyei	27,500
Kongo	27,500
Total tonnage	301,320

PART 2: RULES FOR SCRAPPING VESSELS OF WAR

The following rules shall be observed for the scrapping of vessels of war which are to be disposed of in accordance with Articles II and III.

   I. A vessel to be scrapped must be placed in such condition that it cannot be put to combatant use.

II. This result must be finally effected in any one of the following ways:
   (a)   Permanent sinking of the vessel;
   (b)   Breaking the vessel up. This shall always involve the destruction or removal of all machinery, boilers and armour, and all deck, side and bottom plating;
   (c)   Converting the vessel to target use exclusively. In such case all the provisions of paragraph III of this Part, except sub-paragraph (6), in so far as may be necessary to enable the ship to be used as a mobile target, and except sub-paragraph (7), must be previously complied with. Not more than one capital ship may be retained for this purpose at one time by any of the Contracting Powers.
   (d)   Of the capital ships which would otherwise be scrapped under the present Treaty in or after the year 1931, France and Italy may each retain two seagoing vessels for training purposes exclusively, that is, as gunnery or torpedo schools. The two vessels retained by France shall be of the *Jean Bart* class, and of those retained by Italy one shall be the *Dante Alighieri*, the other of the *Giulio Cesare* class. On retaining these ships for the purpose above stated, France and Italy respectively undertake to remove and destroy their conning-towers, and not to use the said ships as vessels of war.

III. (a)   Subject to the special exceptions contained in Article IX, when a vessel is due for scrapping, the first stage of scrapping, which consists in rendering a ship incapable of further warlike service, shall be immediately undertaken.
   (b)   A vessel shall be considered incapable of further warlike service when there shall have been removed and landed, or else destroyed in the ship:
      (1) All guns and essential portions of guns, fire-control tops and revolving parts of all barbettes and turrets;
      (2) All machinery for working hydraulic or electric mountings;
      (3) All fire-control instruments and range-finders;
      (4) All ammunition, explosives and mines;
      (5) All torpedoes, war-heads and torpedo tubes;
      (6) All wireless telegraphy installations;
      (7) The conning tower and all side armour, or alternatively all main propelling machinery; and
      (8) All landing and flying-off platforms and all other aviation accessories.

IV. The periods in which scrapping of vessels is to be effected are as follows:
   (a)   In the case of vessels to be scrapped under the first paragraph of Article II, the work of rendering the vessels incapable of further warlike service, in accordance with paragraph III of the Part, shall be

completed within six months from the coming into force of the present Treaty, and the scrapping shall be finally effected within eighteen months from such coming into force.

(b) In the case of vessels to be scrapped under the second and third paragraphs of Article II, or under Article III, the work of rendering the vessel incapable of further warlike service in accordance with paragraph III of this Part shall be commenced not later than the date of completion of its successor, and shall be finished within six months from the date of such completion. The vessel shall be finally scrapped, in accordance with paragraph II of this Part, within eighteen months from the date of completion of its successor. If, however, the completion of the new vessel be delayed, then the work of rendering the old vessel incapable of further warlike service in accordance with paragraph III of this Part shall be commenced within four years from the laying of the keel of the new vessel, and shall be finished within six months from the date on which such work was commenced, and the old vessel shall be finally scrapped in accordance with paragraph II of this Part within eighteen months from the date when the work of rendering it incapable of further warlike service was commenced.

PART 3: REPLACEMENT

The replacement of capital ships and aircraft carriers shall take place according to the rules in Section I and the tables in Section II of this Part.

SECTION I: RULES FOR REPLACEMENT

(a) Capital ships and aircraft carriers twenty years after the date of their completion may, except as otherwise provided in Article VIII and in the tables in Section II of this Part, be replaced by new construction, but within the limits prescribed in Article IV and Article VII. The keels of such new construction may, except as otherwise provided in Article VIII and in the tables in Section II of this Part, be laid down not earlier than seventeen years from the date of completion of the tonnage to be replaced, provided, however, that no capital ship tonnage, with the exception of the ships referred to in the third paragraph of Article II, and the replacement tonnage specifically mentioned in Section II of this Part, shall be laid down until ten years from November 12, 1921.

(b) Each of the Contracting Powers shall communicate promptly to each of the other Contracting Powers the following information:

(1) The names of the capital ships and aircraft carriers to be replaced by new construction;

(2) The date of governmental authorization of replacement tonnage;

(3) The date of laying the keels of replacement tonnage.

(4) The standard displacement in tons and metric tons of each new ship to be laid down, and the principal dimensions, namely, length at waterline, extreme beam at or below waterline, mean draft at standard displacement;

(5) The date of completion of each new ship and its standard displacement in tons and metric tons, and the principal dimensions, namely, length at waterline, extreme beam at or below waterline, mean draft at standard displacement, at time of completion.

(c) In case of loss or accidental destruction of capital ships or aircraft carriers, they may immediately be replaced by new construction subject to the tonnage limits prescribed in Articles IV and VII and in conformity with the other provisions of the present Treaty, the regular replacement program being deemed to be advanced to that extent.

(d) No retained capital ships or aircraft carriers shall be reconstructed except for the purpose of providing means of defense against air and submarine attack, and subject to the following rules: The Contracting Powers may, for that purpose, equip existing tonnage with bulge or blister or anti-air attack deck protection, providing the increase of displacement thus effected does not exceed 3,000 tons (3,048 metric tons) displacement for each ship. No alterations in side armor, in calibre, number or general type of mounting of main armament shall be permitted except:

(1) in the case of France and Italy, which countries within the limits allowed for bulge may increase their armor protection and the calibre of the guns now carried on their existing capital ships so as not to exceed 16 inches (406 millimeters) and

(2) the British Empire shall be permitted to complete, in the case of the *Renown*, the alterations to armor that have already been commenced but temporarily suspended.

SECTION II: REPLACEMENT AND SCRAPPING OF CAPITAL SHIPS
UNITED STATES

Year	Ships laid down	Ships completed	Ships scrapped (age in parentheses)	Ships retained Summary Pre-Jutland	Post-Jutland
			Maine (20), Missouri (20), Virginia (17), Nebraska (17), Georgia (17), New Jersey (17), Rhode Island (17), Connecticut (17), Louisiana (17), Vermont (16), Kansas (16), Minnesota (16), New Hampshire (15), South Carolina (13), Michigan (13), Washington (0), South Dakota (0), Indiana (0), Montana (0), North Carolina (0), Iowa (0), Massachusetts (0), Lexington (0), Constitution (0), Constellation (0), Saratoga (0), Ranger (0), United States (0). *	17	1
1922		A, B.#	Delaware (12), North Dakota (12)	15	3
1923				15	3
1924				15	3
1925				15	3
1926				15	3
1927				15	3
1928				15	3
1929				15	3
1930				15	3
1931	C, D			15	3
1932	E, F			15	3
1933	G			15	3
1934	H, I	C, D	Florida (23), Utah (23), Wyoming (22)	12	5
1935	J	E, F	Arkansas (23), Texas (21, New York (21)	9	7
1936	K, L	G	Nevada (20), Oklahoma (20)	7	8
1937	M	H, I	Arizona (21), Pennsylvania (21)	5	10
1938	N, O	J	Mississippi (21)	4	11
1939	P, Q	K, L	New Mexico (21), Idaho (20)	2	13
1940		M	Tennessee (20)	1	14
1941		N, O	California (20), Maryland (20)	0	15
1942		P, Q	2 ships West Virginia class	0	15

*The United States may retain the *Oregon* and *Illinois*, for noncombatant purposes, after complying with the provisions of Part 2, III, (b).
#Two West Virginia class.

NOTE:—A, B, C, D, etc., represent individual capital ships of 35,000 tons standard displacement, laid down and completed in the years specified.

REPLACEMENT AND SCRAPPING OF CAPITAL SHIPS
BRITISH EMPIRE

Year	Ships laid down	Ships completed	Ships scrapped (age in parentheses)	Ships retained Summary Pre-Jutland	Post-Jutland
			Commonwealth (16), Agamemnon (13), Dreadnought (15), Bellerophon (12), St. Vincent (11), Inflexible (13), Superb (12), Neptune (10), Hercules (10), Indomitable (13), Temeraire (12), New Zealand (9), Lion (9), Princess Royal (9), Conqueror (9), Monarch (9), Orion (9), Australia (8), Agincourt (7), Erin (7), 4 building or projected.*	21	1
1922		A, B.#		21	1
1923				21	1
1924				21	1
1925		A, B	King George V (13), Ajax (12), Centurion (12), Thunderer (13).	17	3
1926				17	3
1927				17	3
1928				17	3
1929				17	3
1930				17	3
1931	C, D			17	3
1932	E, F			17	3
1933	G			17	3
1934	H, I	C, D	Iron Duke (20), Marlborough (20), Emperor of India (20), Benbow (20).	13	5
1935	J	E, F	Tiger (21), Queen Elizabeth (20), Warspite (20), Barham (20).	9	7
1936	K, L	G	Malaya (20), Royal Sovereign (20)	7	8
1937	M	H, I	Revenge (21), Resolution (21)	5	10
1938	N, O	J	Royal Oak (22)	4	11
1939	P, Q	K, L	Valiant (23), Repulse (23)	2	13
1940		M	Renown (24)	1	14
1941		N, O	Ramillies (24), Hood (21)	0	15
1942		P, Q	A (17), B (17)	0	15

*The British Empire may retain the Colossus and Collingwood for noncombatant purposes, after complying with the provisions of Part 2, III, (b).
#Two 35,000-ton ships, standard displacement.

NOTE:—A, B, C, D, etc., represent individual capital ships of 35,000 tons standard displacement, laid down and completed in the years specified.

REPLACEMENT AND SCRAPPING OF CAPITAL SHIPS
FRANCE

Year	Ships laid down	Ships completed	Ships scrapped (age in parentheses)	Ships retained Summary Pre-Jutland	Post-Jutland
1922				7	0
1923				7	0
1924				7	0
1925				7	0
1926				7	0
1927	35,000 tons			7	0
1928				7	0
1929	35,000 tons			7	0
1930		35,000 tons	Jean Bart (17), Courbet (17)	5	(*)
1931	35,000 tons			5	(*)
1932	35,000 tons	35,000 tons	France (18)	4	(*)
1933	35,000 tons			4	(*)
1934		35,000 tons	Paris (20), Bretagne (20)	2	(*)
1935		35,000 tons	Provence (20)	1	(*)
1936		35,000 tons	Lorraine (20)	0	(*)
1937				0	(*)
1938				0	(*)
1939				0	(*)
1940				0	(*)
1941				0	(*)
1942				0	(*)

*Within tonnage limitations; number not fixed.

NOTE: France expressly reserves the right of employing the capital ship tonnage allotment as she may consider advisable, subject solely to the limitations that the displacement of individual ships should not surpass 35,000 tons, and that the total capital ship tonnage should keep within the limits imposed by the present Treaty.

APPENDIX 1

REPLACEMENT AND SCRAPPING OF CAPITAL SHIPS
ITALY

Year	Ships laid down	Ships completed	Ships scrapped (age in parentheses)	Ships retained Summary Pre-Jutland	Post-Jutland
1922				6	0
1923				6	0
1924				6	0
1925				6	0
1926				6	0
1927	35,000 tons			6	0
1928				6	0
1929	35,000 tons			6	0
1930				6	0
1931	35,000 tons	35,000 tons	Dante Alighieri (19)	5	(*)
1932	45,000 tons			5	(*)
1933	25,000 tons	35,000 tons	Leonardo da Vinci (19)	4	(*)
1934				4	(*)
1935		35,000 tons	Guilio Cesare (21)	3	(*)
1936		45,000 tons	Conte di Cavour (21), Duilio (21)	1	(*)
1937		25,000 tons	Andrea Doria (21)	0	(*)

*Within tonnage limitations; number not fixed.

NOTE: Italy expressly reserves the right of employing the capital ship tonnage allotment as she may consider advisable, subject solely to the limitations that the displacement of individual ships should not surpass 35,000 tons, and that the total capital ship tonnage should keep within the limits imposed by the present Treaty.

REPLACEMENT AND SCRAPPING OF CAPITAL SHIPS
JAPAN

Year	Ships laid down	Ships completed	Ships scrapped (age in parentheses).	Ships retained Summary Pre-Jutland	Post-Jutland
			Hizen (2), Mikasa (2), Kashima (16), Katori (16), Satsuma (12), Aki (11), Settsu (10), Ikoma (14), Ibuki (12), Kurama (11), Amagi (0), Akagi (0), Kaga (0), Tosa (0), Takao (0), Atago (0). Projected program 8 ships not laid down. *	8	
1922				8	2
1923				8	2
1924				8	2
1925				8	2
1926				8	2
1927				8	2
1928				8	2
1929				8	2
1930				8	2
1931	A			8	2
1932	B			8	2
1933	C			8	2
1934	D	A	Kongo (21)	7	3
1935	E	B	Hiyei (21), Haruna (20)	5	4
1936	F	C	Kirishima (21)	4	5
1937	G	D	Fuso (22)	3	6
1938	H	E	Yamashiro (21)	2	7
1939	I	F	Ise (22)	1	8
1940		G	Hiuga (22)	0	9
1941		H	Nagato (21)	0	9
1942		I	Mutsu (21)	0	9

*Japan may retain the Shikishima and Asahi for noncombatant purposes, after complying with the provisions of Part 2, III, (b).

NOTE: A, B, C, D, etc. represent individual capital ships of 35,000 tons standard displacement, laid down and completed in the years specified.

NOTE APPLICABLE TO ALL THE TABLES IN SECTION II

The order above prescribed in which ships are to be scrapped is in accordance with their age. It is understood that when replacement begins according to the above tables the order of scrapping in the case of the ships of each of the Contracting Powers may be varied at its option; provided, however, that such Power shall scrap in each year the number of ships above stated.

PART 4: DEFINITIONS

For the purposes of the present Treaty, the following expressions are to be understood in the sense defined in this Part.

CAPITAL SHIP

A capital ship, in the case of ships hereafter built, is defined as a vessel of war, not an aircraft carrier, whose displacement exceeds 10,000 tons (10,160 metric tons) standard displacement, or which carries a gun with a calibre exceeding 8 inches (203 millimetres).

AIRCRAFT CARRIER

An aircraft carrier is defined as a vessel of war with a displacement in excess of 10,000 tons (10,160 metric tons) standard displacement designed for the specific and exclusive purpose of carrying aircraft. It must be so constructed that aircraft can be launched therefrom and landed thereon, and not designed and constructed for carrying a more powerful armament than that allowed to it under Article IX or Article X as the case may be.

STANDARD DISPLACEMENT

The standard displacement of a ship is the displacement of the ship complete, fully manned, engined, and equipped ready for sea, including all armament and ammunition, equipment, outfit, provisions and fresh water for crew, miscellaneous stores and implements of every description that are intended to be carried in war, but without fuel or reserve feed water on board.

The word "ton" in the present Treaty, except in the expression "metric tons", shall be understood to mean the ton of 2240 pounds (1016 kilos).

Vessels now completed shall retain their present ratings of displacement tonnage in accordance with their national system of measurement. However, a Power expressing displacement in metric tons shall be considered for the application of the present Treaty as owning only the equivalent displacement in tons of 2240 pounds.

A vessel completed hereafter shall be rated at its displacement tonnage when in the standard condition defined herein.

Chapter III: Miscellaneous Provisions

Article XXI

If during the term of the present Treaty the requirements of the national security of any Contracting Power in respect of naval defence are, in the opinion of that Power, materially affected by any change of circumstances, the Contracting Powers will, at the request of such Power, meet in conference with a view to the reconsideration of the provisions of the Treaty and its amendment by mutual agreement.

In view of possible technical and scientific developments, the United States, after consultation with the other Contracting Powers, shall arrange for a conference of all the Contracting Powers which shall convene as soon as possible after the expiration of eight years from the coming into force of the present Treaty to consider what changes, if any, in the Treaty may be necessary to meet such developments.

Article XXII

Whenever any Contracting Power shall become engaged in a war which in its opinion affects the naval defence of its national security, such Power may after notice to the other Contracting Powers suspend for the period of hostilities its obligations under the present Treaty other than those under Articles XIII and XVII, provided that such Power shall notify the other Contracting Powers that the emergency is of such a character as to require such suspension.

The remaining Contracting Powers shall in such case consult together with a view to agreement as to what temporary modifications if any should be made in the Treaty as between themselves. Should such consultation not produce agreement, duly made in accordance with the constitutional methods of the respective Powers, any one of said Contracting Powers may, by giving notice to the other Contracting Powers, suspend for the period of hostilities its obligations under the present Treaty, other than those under Articles XIII and XVII.

On the cessation of hostilities the Contracting Powers will meet in conference to consider what modifications, if any, should be made in the provisions of the present Treaty.

Article XXIII

The present Treaty shall remain in force until December 31st, 1936, and in case none of the Contracting Powers shall have given notice two years before that date of its intention to terminate the Treaty, it shall continue in force until the expiration of two years from the date on which notice of termination shall be given by one of the Contracting Powers, whereupon the Treaty shall terminate as regards all the Contracting Powers. Such notice shall be communicated in writing to the Government of the United States, which shall immediately transmit a certified copy of the notification to the other Powers and inform them of the date on which it was received. The notice shall be deemed to have been given and shall take effect on that date. In the event of notice of termination being given by the Government of the United States, such notice shall be given to the diplomatic representatives at Washington of the other Contracting Powers, and the notice shall be deemed to have been given and shall take effect on the date of the communication made to the said diplomatic representatives.

Within one year of the date on which a notice of termination by any Power has taken effect, all the Contracting Powers shall meet in conference.

Article XXIV

The present Treaty shall be ratified by the Contracting Powers in accordance with their respective constitutional methods and shall take effect on the date of the deposit of all the ratifications, which shall take place at Washington as soon as possible. The Government of the United States will transmit to the other Contracting Powers a certified copy of the procès-verbal of the deposit of ratifications.

The present Treaty, of which the French and English texts are both authentic, shall remain deposited in the archives of the Government of the United States, and duly certified copies thereof shall be transmitted by that Government to the other Contracting Powers.

In faith whereof the above-named Plenipotentiaries have signed the present Treaty.

Done at the City of Washington the sixth day of February, One Thousand Nine Hundred and Twenty-Two.

[For the United States]
CHARLES EVANS HUGHES
HENRY CABOT LODGE
OSCAR W. UNDERWOOD
ELIHU ROOT

[For the United Kingdom]
ARTHUR JAMES BALFOUR
LEE OF FAREHAM
A. C. GEDDES
[For the Dominion of Canada]
R. L. BORDEN
[For the Commonwealth of Australia]
G. F. PEARCE
[For the Dominion of New Zealand]
JOHN W. SALMOND
[For the Union of South Africa]
ARTHUR JAMES BALFOUR
[For India]
V. S. SRINIVASA SASTRI
[For France]
A. SARRAUT
JUSSERAND
[For Italy]
CARLO SCHANZER
V. ROLANDI RICCI
LUIGI ALBERTINI
[For Japan]
T. KATO
K. SHIDEHARA
M. HANIHARA

(2) A TREATY BETWEEN THE SAME POWERS, IN RELATION TO THE USE OF SUBMARINES AND NOXIOUS GASSES IN WARFARE

ARTICLE I

The Signatory Powers declare that among the rules adopted by civilized nations for the protection of the lives of neutrals and noncombatants at sea in time of war, the following are to be deemed an established part of international law;

(1) A merchant vessel must be ordered to submit to visit and search to determine its character before it can be seized.

A merchant vessel must not be attacked unless it refuse to submit to visit and search after warning, or to proceed as directed after seizure.

A merchant vessel must not be destroyed unless the crew and passengers have been first placed in safety.

(2) Belligerent submarines are not under any circumstances exempt from the universal rules above stated; and if a submarine can not capture a merchant vessel in conformity with these rules the existing law of nations requires it to desist from attack and from seizure and to permit the merchant vessel to proceed unmolested.

ARTICLE II

The Signatory Powers invite all other civilized Powers to express their assent to the foregoing statement of established law so that there may be a clear public understanding throughout the world of the standards of conduct by which the public opinion of the world is to pass judgment upon future belligerents.

ARTICLE III

The Signatory Powers, desiring to insure the enforcement of the humane rules of existing law declared by them with respect to attacks upon and the seizure and destruction of merchant ships, further declare that any person in the service of any Power who shall violate any of those rules, whether or not such person is under orders of a governmental superior, shall be deemed to have violated the laws of war and shall be liable to trial and punishment as if for an act of piracy and may be brought to trial before the civil or military authorities of any Power within the jurisdiction of which he may be found.

ARTICLE IV

The Signatory Powers recognize the practical impossibility of using submarines as commerce destroyers without violating, as they were violated in the recent war of 1914–1918, the requirements universally accepted by civilized nations for the protection of the lives of neutrals and noncombatants, and to the end that the prohibition of the use of submarines as commerce destroyers shall be universally accepted as a part of the law of nations they now accept that prohibition as henceforth binding as between themselves and they invite all other nations to adhere thereto.

ARTICLE V

The use in war of asphyxiating, poisonous or other gases, and all analogous liquids, materials or devices, having been justly condemned by the general opinion of the civilized world and a prohibition of such use having been declared in treaties to which a majority of the civilized Powers are parties,

The Signatory Powers, to the end that this prohibition shall be universally accepted as a part of international law binding alike the conscience and practice of nations, declare their assent to such prohibition, agree to be bound thereby as between themselves and invite all other civilized nations to adhere thereto.

ARTICLE VI

The present Treaty shall be ratified as soon as possible in accordance with the constitutional methods of the Signatory Powers and shall take effect on the deposit of all the ratifications, which shall take place at Washington.

The Government of the United States will transmit to all the Signatory Powers a certified copy of the procès-verbal of the deposit of ratifications.

The present Treaty, of which the French and English texts are both authentic, shall remain deposited in the Archives of the Government of the United States, and duly certified copies thereof will be transmitted by that Government to each of the Signatory Powers.

ARTICLE VII

The Government of the United States will further transmit to each of the Non-Signatory Powers a duly certified copy of the present Treaty and invite its adherence thereto.

Any Non-Signatory Power may adhere to the present Treaty by communicating an Instrument of Adherence to the Government of the United States, which will thereupon transmit to each of the Signatory and Adhering Powers a certified copy of each Instrument of Adherence.

In faith whereof, the above named Plenipotentiaries have signed the present Treaty.

Done at the City of Washington, the sixth day of February, one thousand nine hundred and twenty-two.

[L. S.] CHARLES EVANS HUGHES
[L. S.] HENRY CABOT LODGE
[L. S.] OSCAR W UNDERWOOD
[L. S.] ELIHU ROOT
[L. S.] ARTHUR JAMES BALFOUR
[L. S.] LEE OF FAREHAM.
[L. S.] A. C. GEDDES
R. L. BORDEN [L. S.]
G. F. PEARCE [L. S.]
JOHN W SALMOND [L. S.]

Arthur James Balfour [L. S.]
V S Srinivasa Sastri [L. S.]
A Sarraut [L. S.]
Jusserand [L. S.]
Carlo Schanzer [L. S.]
[L. S.] V. Rolandi Ricci
[L. S.] Luigi Albertini
[L. S.] T. Kato
[L. S.] K. Shidehara
[L. S.] M. Hanihara

(3) A TREATY BETWEEN THE UNITED STATES OF AMERICA, THE BRITISH EMPIRE, FRANCE, AND JAPAN, SIGNED DECEMBER 13, 1921, RELATING TO THEIR INSULAR POSSESSIONS AND INSULAR DOMINIONS IN THE PACIFIC OCEAN

I

The High Contracting Parties agree as between themselves to respect their rights in relation to their insular possessions and insular dominions in the region of the Pacific Ocean.

If there should develop between any of the High Contracting Parties a controversy arising out of any Pacific question and involving their said rights which is not satisfactorily settled by diplomacy and is likely to affect the harmonious accord now happily subsisting between them, they shall invite the other High Contracting Parties to a joint conference to which the whole subject will be referred for consideration and adjustment.

II

If the said rights are threatened by the aggressive action of any other Power, the High Contracting Parties shall communicate with one another fully and frankly in order to arrive at an understanding as to the most efficient measures to be taken, jointly or separately, to meet the exigencies of the particular situation.

III

This Treaty shall remain in force for ten years from the time it shall take effect, and after the expiration of said period it shall continue to be in force subject to the right of any of the High Contracting Parties to terminate it upon twelve months' notice.

IV

This Treaty shall be ratified as soon as possible in accordance with the constitutional methods of the High Contracting Parties and shall take effect on the deposit of ratifications, which shall take place at Washington, and thereupon the agreement between Great Britain and Japan, which was concluded at London on July 13, 1911, shall terminate. The Government of the United States will transmit to all the Signatory Powers a certified copy of the *procès-verbal* of the deposit of ratifications.

The present Treaty, in French and in English, shall remain deposited in the Archives of the Government of the United States, and duly certified copies thereof will be transmitted by that Government to each of the Signatory Powers.

In faith whereof the above named Plenipotentiaries have signed the present Treaty.

Done at the City of Washington, the thirteenth day of December, One Thousand Nine Hundred and Twenty-One.

	[For the United States]	
	CHARLES EVANS HUGHES	[L. S.]
	HENRY CABOT LODGE	[L. S.]
	OSCAR W UNDERWOOD	[L. S.]
	ELIHU ROOT	[L. S.]
	[For the United Kingdom]	
	A M JAMES BALFOUR	[L. S.]
	LEE OF FAREHAM	[L. S.]
	A. C. GEDDES	[L. S.]
	[For the Dominion of Canada]	
[L. S.]	R. L. BORDEN	
	[For the Commonwealth of Australia]	
[L. S.]	G. F. PEARCE	
	[For the Dominion of New Zealand]	
[L. S.]	JOHN W SALMOND	
	[For the Union of South Africa]	
[L. S.]	A M JAMES BALFOUR	
	[For India]	
[L. S.]	V S SRINIVASA SASTRI	
	[For France]	
[L. S.]	RENÉ VIVIANI	
[L. S.]	A. SARRAUT	
[L. S.]	JUSSERAND	
	[For Japan]	
[L. S.]	T. KATO	

[L. S.]   K. Shidehara
[L. S.]   Tokugawa Iyesato
[L. S.]   M. Hanihara

(4) DECLARATION ACCOMPANYING THE ABOVE
FOUR-POWER TREATY

In signing the Treaty this day between The United States of America, The British Empire, France and Japan, it is declared to be the understanding and intent of the Signatory Powers:

1. That the Treaty shall apply to the Mandated Islands in the Pacific Ocean; provided, however, that the making of the Treaty shall not be deemed to be an assent on the part of The United States of America to the mandates and shall not preclude agreements between The United States of America and the Mandatory Powers respectively in relation to the mandated islands.

2. That the controversies to which the second paragraph of Article I refers shall not be taken to embrace questions which according to principles of international law lie exclusively within the domestic jurisdiction of the respective Powers.

Washington, D. C., December 13, 1921.

Charles Evans Hughes	A M James Balfour
Henry Cabot Lodge	V S Srinivasa Sastri
Oscar W Underwood	René Viviani
Elihu Root	A Sarraut
A M James Balfour	Jusserand
Lee of Fareham	T. Kato
A. C. Geddes	K. Shidehara
R. L. Borden	Tokugawa Iyesato
G. F. Pearce	M. Hanihara
John W Salmond	

(5) A TREATY BETWEEN THE SAME FOUR POWERS,
SUPPLEMENTARY TO THE ABOVE, SIGNED FEBRUARY 6, 1922

The United States of America, the British Empire, France and Japan have, through their respective Plenipotentiaries, agreed upon the following stipulations supplementary to the Quadruple Treaty signed at Washington on December 13, 1921:

The term "insular possessions and insular dominions" used in the aforesaid Treaty shall, in its application to Japan, include only Karafuto (or the Southern portion of the island of Sakhalin), Formosa and the Pescadores, and the islands under the mandate of Japan.

The present agreement shall have the same force and effect as the said Treaty to which it is supplementary.

The provisions of Article IV of the aforesaid Treaty of December 13, 1921, relating to ratification shall be applicable to the present Agreement, which in French and English shall remain deposited in the Archives of the Government of the United States, and duly certified copies thereof shall be transmitted by that Government to each of the other Contracting Powers.

In faith whereof the respective Plenipotentiaries have signed the present Agreement.

Done at the City of Washington, the sixth day of February, One Thousand Nine Hundred and Twenty-two.

	CHARLES EVANS HUGHES	[L. S.]
	HENRY CABOT LODGE	[L. S.]
	OSCAR W UNDERWOOD	[L. S.]
[L. S.]	ELIHU ROOT	
[L. S.]	ARTHUR JAMES BALFOUR	
[L. S.]	LEE OF FAREHAM	
[L. S.]	A. C. GEDDES	
[L. S.]	R. L. BORDEN	
[L. S.]	G. F. PEARCE	
[L. S.]	JOHN W SALMOND	
[L. S.]	ARTHUR JAMES BALFOUR	
[L. S.]	V S SRINIVASA SASTRI	
	A SARRAUT	[L. S.]
	JUSSERAND	[L. S.]
	T. KATO	[L. S.]
	K. SHIDEHARA	[L. S.]
	M. HANIHARA	[L. S.]

(6) A TREATY BETWEEN ALL NINE POWERS RELATING TO PRINCIPLES AND POLICIES TO BE FOLLOWED IN MATTERS CONCERNING CHINA

ARTICLE I

The Contracting Powers, other than China, agree:

(1) To respect the sovereignty, the independence, and the territorial and administrative integrity of China;

(2) To provide the fullest and most unembarrassed opportunity to China to develop and maintain for herself an effective and stable government;

(3) To use their influence for the purpose of effectually establishing and maintaining the principle of equal opportunity for the commerce and industry of all nations throughout the territory of China;

(4) To refrain from taking advantage of conditions in China in order to seek special rights or privileges which would abridge the rights of subjects or citizens of friendly States, and from countenancing action inimical to the security of such States.

ARTICLE II

The Contracting Powers agree not to enter into any treaty, agreement, arrangement, or understanding, either with one another, or, individually or collectively, with any Power or Powers, which would infringe or impair the principles stated in Article I.

ARTICLE III

With a view to applying more effectually the principles of the Open Door or equality of opportunity in China for the trade and industry of all nations, the Contracting Powers, other than China, agree that they will not seek, nor support their respective nationals in seeking:

(a) any arrangement which might purport to establish in favour of their interests any general superiority of rights with respect to commercial or economic development in any designated region of China;

(b) any such monopoly or preference as would deprive the nationals of any other Power of the right of undertaking any legitimate trade or industry in China, or of participating with the Chinese Government, or with any local authority, in any category of public enterprise, or which by reason of its scope, duration or geographical extent is calculated to frustrate the practical application of the principle of equal opportunity.

It is understood that the foregoing stipulations of this Article are not to be so construed as to prohibit the acquisition of such properties or rights as may be necessary to the conduct of a particular commercial, industrial, or financial undertaking or to the encouragement of invention and research.

China undertakes to be guided by the principles stated in the foregoing stipulations of this Article in dealing with applications for economic rights and privileges from Governments and nationals of all foreign countries, whether parties to the present Treaty or not.

Article IV

The Contracting Powers agree not to support any agreements by their respective nationals with each other designed to create Spheres of Influence or to provide for the enjoyment of mutually exclusive opportunities in designated parts of Chinese territory.

Article V

China agrees that, throughout the whole of the railways in China, she will not exercise or permit unfair discrimination of any kind. In particular there shall be no discrimination whatever, direct or indirect, in respect of charges or of facilities on the ground of the nationality of passengers or the countries from which or to which they are proceeding, or the origin or ownership of goods or the country from which or to which they are consigned, or the nationality or ownership of the ship or other means of conveying such passengers or goods before or after their transport on the Chinese Railways.

The Contracting Powers, other than China, assume a corresponding obligation in respect of any of the aforesaid railways over which they or their nationals are in a position to exercise any control in virtue of any concession, special agreement or otherwise.

Article VI

The Contracting Powers, other than China, agree fully to respect China's rights as a neutral in time of war to which China is not a party; and China declares that when she is a neutral she will observe the obligations of neutrality.

Article VII

The Contracting Powers agree that, whenever a situation arises which in the opinion of any one of them involves the application of the stipulations of the present Treaty, and renders desirable discussion of such application, there shall be full and frank communication between the Contracting Powers concerned.

Article VIII

Powers not signatory to the present Treaty, which have Governments recognized by the Signatory Powers and which have treaty relations with China, shall be invited to adhere to the present Treaty. To this end the Government of the United States will make the necessary communications to nonsignatory Powers and will inform the Contracting Powers of the replies received. Adherence by any Power shall become effective on receipt of notice thereof by the Government of the United States.

ARTICLE IX

The present Treaty shall be ratified by the Contracting Powers in accordance with their respective constitutional methods and shall take effect on the date of the deposit of all the ratifications, which shall take place at Washington as soon as possible. The Government of the United States will transmit to the other Contracting Powers a certified copy of the procès-verbal of the deposit of ratifications.

The present Treaty, of which the French and English texts are both authentic, shall remain deposited in the archives of the Government of the United States, and duly certified copies thereof shall be transmitted by that Government to the other Contracting Powers.

In faith whereof the above-named Plenipotentiaries have signed the present Treaty.

Done at the City of Washington the Sixth day of February One Thousand Nine Hundred and Twenty-Two.

[For the United States]
CHARLES EVANS HUGHES   [L. S.]
HENRY CABOT LODGE   [L. S.]
OSCAR W UNDERWOOD   [L. S.]
ELIHU ROOT   [L. S.]
[For Belgium]
BARON DE CARTIER DE MARCHIENNE   [L. S.]
[For the United Kingdom]
ARTHUR JAMES BALFOUR   [L. S.]
LEE OF FAREHAM   [L. S.]
A. C. GEDDES   [L. S.]
[For the Dominion of Canada]
R. L. BORDEN   [L. S.]
[For the Commonwealth of Australia]
G. F. PEARCE   [L. S.]
[For the Dominion of New Zealand]
JOHN W SALMOND   [L. S.]
[For the Union of South Africa]
ARTHUR JAMES BALFOUR   [L. S.]
[For India]

	V S Srinivasa Sastri	[L. S.]
	[For China]	
[L. S.]	Sao-Ke Alfred Sze	
[L. S.]	V. K. Wellington Koo	
[L. S.]	Chung-Hui Wang	
	[For France]	
[L. S.]	A Sarraut	
[L. S.]	Jusserand	
	[For Italy]	
[L. S.]	Carlo Schanzer	
[L. S.]	V. Rolandi Ricci	
[L. S.]	Luigi Albertini	
	[For Japan]	
	T. Kato	[L. S.]
	K. Shidehara	[L. S.]
	M. Hanihara	[L. S.]
	[For the Netherlands]	
	Beelaerts van Blokland	[L. S.]
	W. de Beaufort	[L. S.]
	[For Portugal]	
	Alte	[L. S.]
	Ernesto de Vasconcellos	[L. S.]

(7) A TREATY BETWEEN THE NINE POWERS RELATING TO CHINESE CUSTOMS TARIFF

Article I

The representatives of the Contracting Powers having adopted, on the fourth day of February, 1922, in the City of Washington, a Resolution, which is appended as an Annex to this Article, with respect to the revision of Chinese Customs duties, for the purpose of making such duties equivalent to an effective 5 per centum *ad valorem*, in accordance with existing treaties concluded by China with other nations, the Contracting Powers hereby confirm the said Resolution and undertake to accept the tariff rates fixed as a result of such revision. The said tariff rates shall become effective as soon as possible but not earlier than two months after publication thereof.

Annex

With a view to providing additional revenue to meet the needs of the Chinese Government, the Powers represented at this Conference, namely the

United States of America, Belgium, the British Empire, China, France, Italy, Japan, The Netherlands, and Portugal agree:

That the customs schedule of duties on imports into China adopted by the Tariff Revision Commission at Shanghai on December 19, 1918, shall forthwith be revised so that the rates of duty shall be equivalent to 5 per cent. effective, as provided for in the several commercial treaties to which China is a party.

A Revision Commission shall meet at Shanghai, at the earliest practicable date, to effect this revision forthwith and on the general lines of the last revision.

This Commission shall be composed of representatives of the Powers above named and of representatives of any additional Powers having Governments at present recognized by the Powers represented at this Conference and who have treaties with China providing for a tariff on imports and exports not to exceed 5 per cent. ad valorem and who desire to participate therein.

The revision shall proceed as rapidly as possible with a view to its completion within four months from the date of the adoption of this Resolution by the Conference on the Limitation of Armament and Pacific and Far Eastern Questions.

The revised tariff shall become effective as soon as possible but not earlier than two months after its publication by the Revision Commission.

The Government of the United States, as convener of the present Conference, is requested forthwith to communicate the terms of this Resolution to the Governments of Powers not represented at this Conference but who participated in the Revision of 1918, aforesaid.

ARTICLE II

Immediate steps shall be taken, through a Special Conference, to prepare the way for the speedy abolition of likin and for the fulfillment of the other conditions laid down in Article VIII of the Treaty of September 5th, 1902, between Great Britain and China, in Articles IV and V of the Treaty of October 8th, 1903, between the United States and China, and in Article I of the Supplementary Treaty of October 8th, 1903, between Japan and China, with a view to levying the surtaxes provided for in those articles.

The Special Conference shall be composed of representatives of the Signatory Powers, and of such other Powers as may desire to participate and may adhere to the present Treaty, in accordance with the provisions of Article VIII, in sufficient time to allow their representatives to take part. It shall meet in China within three months after the coming into force of the present Treaty, on a day and at a place to be designated by the Chinese Government.

ARTICLE III

The Special Conference provided for in Article II shall consider the interim provisions to be applied prior to the abolition of likin and the fulfillment of the other conditions laid down in the articles of the treaties mentioned in Article II; and it shall authorize the levying of a surtax on dutiable imports as from such date, for such purposes, and subject to such conditions as it may determine.

The surtax shall be at a uniform rate of 2½ per centum *ad valorem*, provided, that in case of certain articles of luxury which, in the opinion of the Special Conference, can bear a greater increase without unduly impeding trade, the total surtax may be increased but may not exceed 5 per centum *ad valorem*.

ARTICLE IV

Following the immediate revision of the customs schedule of duties on imports into China, mentioned in Article I, there shall be a further revision thereof to take effect at the expiration of four years following the completion of the aforesaid immediate revision, in order to ensure that the customs duties shall correspond to the *ad valorem* rates fixed by the Special Conference provided for in Article II.

Following this further revision there shall be, for the same purpose, periodical revisions of the customs schedule of duties on imports into China every seven years, in lieu of the decennial revision authorized by existing treaties with China.

In order to prevent delay, any revision made in pursuance of this Article shall be effected in accordance with rules to be prescribed by the Special Conference provided for in Article II.

ARTICLE V

In all matters relating to customs duties there shall be effective equality of treatment and opportunity for all the Contracting Powers.

ARTICLE VI

The principle of uniformity in the rates of customs duties levied at all the land and maritime frontiers of China is hereby recognized. The Special Conference provided for in Article II shall make arrangements to give practical effect to this principle; and it is authorized to make equitable adjustments in those cases in which a customs privilege to be abolished was granted in return for some local economic advantage.

In the meantime, any increase in the rates of customs duties resulting from tariff revision, or any surtax hereafter imposed in pursuance of the present Treaty, shall be levied at a uniform rate *ad valorem* at all land and maritime frontiers of China.

ARTICLE VII

The charge for transit passes shall be at the rate of 2½ per centum *ad valorem* until the arrangements provided for by Article II come into force.

ARTICLE VIII

Powers not signatory to the present Treaty whose Governments are at present recognized by the Signatory Powers, and whose present treaties with China provide for a tariff on imports and exports not to exceed 5 per centum *ad valorem*, shall be invited to adhere to the present Treaty.

The Government of the United States undertakes to make the necessary communications for this purpose and to inform the Governments of the Contracting Powers of the replies received. Adherence by any Power shall become effective on receipt of notice thereof by the Government of the United States.

ARTICLE IX

The provisions of the present Treaty shall override all stipulations of treaties between China and the respective Contracting Powers which are inconsistent therewith, other than stipulations according most favored nation treatment.

ARTICLE X

The present Treaty shall be ratified by the Contracting Powers in accordance with their respective constitutional methods and shall take effect on the date of the deposit of all the ratifications, which shall take place at Washington as soon as possible. The Government of the United States will transmit to the other Contracting Powers a certified copy of the procès-verbal of the deposit of ratifications.

The present Treaty, of which the English and French texts are both authentic, shall remain deposited in the archives of the Government of the United States, and duly certified copies thereof shall be transmitted by that Government to the other Contracting Powers.

In faith whereof the above-named Plenipotentiaries have signed the present Treaty.

Done at the City of Washington the sixth day of February, One Thousand Nine Hundred and Twenty-two.

Charles Evans Hughes	V. K. Wellington Koo
Henry Cabot Lodge	Chung-Hui Wang
Oscar W. Underwood	A. Sarraut
Elihu Root	Jusserand
Baron de Cartier de Marchienne	Carlo Schanzer
Arthur James Balfour	V. Rolandi Ricci
Lee of Fareham	Luigi Albertini
A. C. Geddes	T. Kato
R. L. Borden	K. Shidehara
G. F. Pearce	M. Hanihara
John W. Salmond	Beelaerts van Blokland
Arthur James Balfour	W. de Beaufort
V. S. Srinivasa Sastri	Alte
Sao-Ke Alfred Sze	Ernesto de Vasconcellos

APPENDIX 2: THE LONDON NAVAL TREATY OF 1930

1. Text of the London Naval Treaty,[2] April 22, 1930

The President of the United States of America, the President of the French Republic, His Majesty the King of Great Britain, Ireland, and the British Dominions beyond the Seas, Emperor of India, His Majesty the King of Italy, and His Majesty the Emperor of Japan,

Desiring to prevent the dangers and reduce the burdens inherent in competitive armaments, and

Desiring to carry forward the work begun by the Washington Naval Conference and to facilitate the progressive realization of general limitation and reduction of armaments,

Have resolved to conclude a Treaty for the limitation and reduction of naval armament, and have accordingly appointed as their Plenipotentiaries: . . . who, having communicated to one another their full powers, found in good and due form, have agreed as follows:

2. Cmd. 3758.

Part I

ARTICLE 1

The High Contracting Parties agree not to exercise their rights to lay down the keels of capital ship replacement tonnage during the years 1931–6 inclusive as provided in Chapter II, Part 3 of the Treaty for the Limitation of Naval Armament signed between them at Washington on the 6th February, 1922, and referred to in the present Treaty as the Washington Treaty.

This provision is without prejudice to the disposition relating to the replacement of ships accidentally lost or destroyed contained in Chapter II, Part 3, Section I, paragraph (c) of the said Treaty.

France and Italy may, however, build the replacement tonnage which they were entitled to lay down in 1927 and 1929 in accordance with the provisions of the said Treaty.

ARTICLE 2

1. The United States, the United Kingdom of Great Britain and Northern Ireland, and Japan shall dispose of the following capital ships as provided in this Article:

United States: *Florida, Utah, Arkansas* or *Wyoming.*
United Kingdom: *Benbow, Iron Duke, Marlborough, Emperor of India, Tiger.*
Japan: *Hiyei.*

(a) Subject to the provisions of sub-paragraph (b), the above ships, unless converted to target use exclusively in accordance with Chapter II, Part 2, paragraph II (c) of the Washington Treaty, shall be scrapped in the following manner:

One of the ships to be scrapped by the United States, and two of those to be scrapped by the United Kingdom shall be rendered unfit for warlike service, in accordance with Chapter II, Part 2, paragraph III (b) of the Washington Treaty, within twelve months from the coming into force of the present Treaty. These ships shall be finally scrapped, in accordance with paragraph II (a) or (b) of the said Part 2, within twenty-four months from the said coming into force. In the case of the second of the ships to be scrapped by the United States, and of the third and fourth of the ships to be scrapped by the United Kingdom, the said periods shall be eighteen and thirty months respectively from the coming into force of the present Treaty.

(b) Of the ships to be disposed of under this Article, the following may be retained for training purposes:

by the United States: *Arkansas* or *Wyoming.*
by the United Kingdom: *Iron Duke.*
by Japan: *Hiyei.*

These ships shall be reduced to the condition prescribed in Section V of Annex II to Part II of the present Treaty. The work of reducing these vessels to the required condition shall begin, in the case of the United States and the United Kingdom, within twelve months, and in the case of Japan within eighteen months from the coming into force of the present Treaty; the work shall be completed within six months of the expiration of the above-mentioned periods.

Any of these ships which are not retained for training purposes shall be rendered unfit for warlike service within eighteen months, and finally scrapped within thirty months, of the coming into force of the present Treaty.

2. Subject to any disposal of capital ships which might be necessitated, in accordance with the Washington Treaty, by the building by France or Italy of the replacement tonnage referred to in Article 1 of the present Treaty, all existing capital ships mentioned in Chapter II, Part 3, Section II of the Washington Treaty and not designated above to be disposed of may be retained during the term of the present Treaty.

3. The right of replacement is not lost by delay in laying down replacement tonnage, and the old vessel may be retained until replaced even though due for scrapping under Chapter II, Part 3, Section II of the Washington Treaty.

ARTICLE 3

1. For the purposes of the Washington Treaty, the definition of an aircraft carrier given in Chapter II, Part 4 of the said Treaty is hereby replaced by the following definition:

The expression 'aircraft carrier' includes any surface vessel of war, whatever its displacement, designed for the specific and exclusive purpose of carrying aircraft and so constructed that aircraft can be launched therefrom and landed thereon.

2. The fitting of a landing-on or flying-off platform or deck on a capital ship, cruiser or destroyer, provided such vessel was not designed or adapted exclusively as an aircraft carrier, shall not cause any vessel so fitted to be charged against or classified in the category of aircraft carriers.

3. No capital ship in existence on April 1, 1930, shall be fitted with a landing-on platform or deck.

ARTICLE 4

1. No aircraft carrier of 10,000 tons (10,160 metric tons) or less standard displacement mounting a gun above 6·1-inch (155 mm.) calibre shall be acquired by or constructed by or for any of the High Contracting Parties.

2. As from the coming into force of the present Treaty in respect of all the High Contracting Parties, no aircraft carrier of 10,000 tons (10,160 metric tons) or less standard displacement mounting a gun above 6·1-inch (155 mm.) calibre shall be constructed within the jurisdiction of any of the High Contracting Parties.

Article 5

An aircraft carrier must not be designed and constructed for carrying a more powerful armament than that authorized by Article IX or Article X of the Washington Treaty, or by Article 4 of the present Treaty, as the case may be.

Wherever in the said Articles IX and X the calibre of 6 inches (152 mm.) is mentioned, the calibre of 6·1 inches (155 mm.) is substituted therefor.

Part II

Article 6

1. The rules for determining standard displacement prescribed in Chapter II, Part 4 of the Washington Treaty shall apply to all surface vessels of war of each of the High Contracting Parties.

2. The standard displacement of a submarine is the surface displacement of the vessel complete (exclusive of the water in non-watertight structure), fully manned, engined, and equipped ready for sea, including all armament and ammunition, equipment, outfit, provisions for crew, miscellaneous stores, and implements of every description that are intended to be carried in war, but without fuel, lubricating oil, fresh water or ballast water or any kind on board.

3. Each naval combatant vessel shall be rated at its displacement tonnage when in the standard condition. The word 'ton', except in the expression 'metric tons', shall be understood to be the ton of 2,240 pounds (1,016 kilos.).

Article 7

1. No submarine the standard displacement of which exceeds 2,000 tons (2,032 metric tons) or with a gun above 5·1-inch (130 mm.) calibre shall be acquired by or constructed by or for any of the High Contracting Parties.

2. Each of the High Contracting Parties may, however, retain, build or acquire a maximum number of three submarines of a standard displacement not exceeding 2,800 tons (2,845 metric tons); these submarines may carry guns not above 6·1-inch (155 mm.) calibre. Within this number, France may retain one

unit, already launched, of 2,880 tons (2,926 metric tons), with guns the calibre of which is 8 inches (203 mm.).

3. The High Contracting Parties may retain the submarines which they possessed on April 1, 1930, having a standard displacement not in excess of 2,000 tons (2,032 metric tons) and armed with guns above 5·1-inch (130 mm.) calibre.

4. As from the coming into force of the present Treaty in respect of all the High Contracting Parties, no submarine the standard displacement of which exceeds 2,000 tons (2,032 metric tons) or with a gun above 5.1-inch (130 mm.) calibre shall be constructed within the jurisdiction of any of the High Contracting Parties, except as provided in paragraph 2 of this Article.

ARTICLE 8

Subject to any special agreements which may submit them to limitation, the following vessels are exempt from limitation:

(a) naval surface combatant vessels from 600 tons (610 metric tons) standard displacement and under;

(b) naval surface combatant vessels exceeding 600 tons (610 metric tons), but not exceeding 2,000 tons (2,032 metric tons) standard displacement, provided they have none of the following characteristics:
   (1) mount a gun above 6·1-inch (155 mm.) calibre;
   (2) mount more than four guns above 3-inch (76 mm.) calibre;
   (3) are designed or fitted to launch torpedoes;
   (4) are designed for a speed greater than twenty knots;

(c) naval surface vessels not specifically built as fighting ships which are employed on fleet duties or as troop transports or in some other way than as fighting ships, provided they have none of the following characteristics:
   (1) mount a gun above 6·1-inch (155 mm.) calibre;
   (2) mount more than four guns above 3-inch (76 mm.) calibre;
   (3) are designed or fitted to launch torpedoes;
   (4) are designed for a speed greater than twenty knots;
   (5) are protected by armour plate;
   (6) are designed or fitted to launch mines;
   (7) are fitted to receive aircraft on board from the air;
   (8) mount more than one aircraft-launching apparatus on the centre line; or two, one on each broadside;
   (9) if fitted with any means of launching aircraft into the air, are designed or adapted to operate at sea more than three aircraft.

ARTICLE 9

The rules as to replacement contained in Annex I to this Part II are applicable to vessels of war not exceeding 10,000 tons (10,160 metric tons) standard displacement, with the exception of aircraft carriers, whose replacement is governed by the provisions of the Washington Treaty.

ARTICLE 10

Within one month after the date of laying down and the date of completion respectively of each vessel of war, other than capital ships, aircraft carriers and the vessels exempt from limitation under Article 8, laid down or completed by or for them after the coming into force of the present Treaty, the High Contracting Parties shall communicate to each of the other High Contracting Parties the information detailed below:

(a) the date of laying the keel and the following particulars:
classification of the vessel;
standard displacement in tons and metric tons;
principal dimensions, namely: length at water-line, extreme beam at or below water-line;
mean draft at standard displacement;
calibre of the largest gun.
(b) the date of completion together with the foregoing particulars relating to the vessel at that date.
The information to be given in the case of capital ships and aircraft carriers is governed by the Washington Treaty.

ARTICLE 11

Subject to the provisions of Article 2 of the present Treaty, the rules for disposal contained in Annex II to this Part II shall be applied to all vessels of war to be disposed of under the said Treaty, and to aircraft carriers as defined in Article 3.

ARTICLE 12

1. Subject to any supplementary agreements which may modify, as between the High Contracting Parties concerned, the lists in Annex III to this Part II, the special vessels shown therein may be retained and their tonnage shall not be included in the tonnage subject to limitation.
2. Any other vessel constructed, adapted, or acquired to serve the purposes for which these special vessels are retained shall be charged against the ton-

nage of the appropriate combatant category, according to the characteristics of the vessel, unless such vessel conforms to the characteristics of vessels exempt from limitation under Article 8.

3. Japan may, however, replace the minelayers *Aso* and *Tokiwa* by two new minelayers before December 31, 1936. The standard displacement of each of the new vessels shall not exceed 5,000 tons (5,080 metric tons); their speed shall not exceed twenty knots, and their other characteristics shall conform to the provisions of paragraph (*b*) of Article 8. The new vessels shall be regarded as special vessels and their tonnage shall not be chargeable to the tonnage of any combatant category. The *Aso* and *Tokiwa* shall be disposed of in accordance with Section I or II of Annex II to this Part II, on completion of the replacement vessels.

4. The *Asama*, *Yakumo*, *Izumo*, *Iwate*, and *Kasuga* shall be disposed of in accordance with Section I or II of Annex II to this Part II when the first three vessels of the *Kuma* class have been replaced by new vessels. These three vessels of the *Kuma* class shall be reduced to the condition prescribed in Section V, sub-paragraph (*b*) 2 of Annex II to this Part II, and are to be used for training ships, and their tonnage shall not thereafter be included in the tonnage subject to limitation.

ARTICLE 13

Existing ships of various types, which, prior to April 1, 1930, have been used as stationary training establishments or hulks, may be retained in a non-seagoing condition.

[Here follow: *Annex I*. Rules for replacement. *Annex II*. Rules for disposal of vessels of war. *Annex III*. List of special vessels.]

Part III

The President of the United States of America, His Majesty the King of Great Britain, Ireland, and the British Dominions beyond the Seas, Emperor of India, and His Majesty the Emperor of Japan, have agreed as between themselves to the provisions of this Part III:

ARTICLE 14

The naval combatant vessels of the United States, the British Commonwealth of Nations and Japan, other than capital ships, aircraft carriers and all vessels exempt from limitation under Article 8, shall be limited during the term of the present Treaty as provided in this Part III, and, in the case of special vessels, as provided in Article 12.

Article 15

For the purpose of this Part III the definition of the cruiser and destroyer categories shall be as follows:

Cruisers

Surface vessels of war, other than capital ships or aircraft carriers, the standard displacement of which exceeds 1,850 tons (1,880 metric tons), or with a gun above 5·1-inch (130 mm.) calibre.

The cruiser category is divided into two sub-categories, as follows:

(a) cruisers carrying a gun above 6·1-inch (155 mm.) calibre;
(b) cruisers carrying a gun not above 6·1-inch (155 mm.) calibre.

Destroyers

Surface vessels of war the standard displacement of which does not exceed 1,850 tons (1,880 metric tons), and with a gun not above 5·1-inch (130 mm.) calibre.

Article 16

1. The completed tonnage in the cruiser, destroyer, and submarine categories which is not to be exceeded on December 31, 1936, is given in the following table:

Categories	United States	British Commonwealth of Nations	Japan
Cruisers:			
(a) with guns of more than 6·1- inch (155 mm.) calibre	180,000 tons (182,880 metric tons)	146,800 tons (149,149 metric tons)	108,400 tons (110,134 metric tons)
(b) with guns of 6·1-inch (155 mm) calibre or less	143,500 tons (145,796 metric tons)	192,200 tons (192,275 metric tons)	100,450 tons (102,057 metric tons)
Destroyers	150,000 tons (152,400 metric tons)	150,000 tons (152,400 metric tons)	105,500 tons (107,188 metric tons)
Submarines	52,700 tons (53,543 metric tons)	52,700 tons (53,543 metric tons)	52,700 tons (53,543 metric tons)

2. Vessels which cause the total tonnage in any category to exceed the figures given in the foregoing table shall be disposed of gradually during the period ending on December 31, 1936.

3. The maximum number of cruisers of sub-category (a) shall be as follows: for the United States, eighteen; for the British Commonwealth of Nations, fifteen; for Japan, twelve.

4. In the destroyer category not more than 16 per cent. of the allowed total tonnage shall be employed in vessels of over 1,500 tons (1,524 metric tons) standard displacement. Destroyers completed or under construction on April 1, 1930, in excess of this percentage may be retained, but no other destroyers exceeding 1,500 tons (1,524 metric tons) standard displacement shall be constructed or acquired until a reduction to such 16 per cent. has been effected.

5. Not more than 25 per cent. of the allowed total tonnage in the cruiser category may be fitted with a landing-on platform or deck for aircraft.

6. It is understood that the submarines referred to in paragraphs 2 and 3 of Article 7 will be counted as part of the total submarine tonnage of the High Contracting Party concerned.

7. The tonnage of any vessels retained under Article 13 or disposed of in accordance with Annex II to Part II of the present Treaty shall not be included in the tonnage subject to limitation.

ARTICLE 17

A transfer not exceeding 10 per cent. of the allowed total tonnage of the category or sub-category into which the transfer is to made shall be permitted between cruisers of sub-category (b) and destroyers.

ARTICLE 18

The United States contemplates the completion by 1935 of fifteen cruisers of sub-category (a) of an aggregate tonnage of 150,000 tons (152,400 metric tons). For each of the three remaining cruisers of sub-category (a) which it is entitled to construct, the United States may elect to substitute 15,166 tons (15,409 metric tons) of cruisers of sub-category (b). In case the United States shall construct one or more of such three remaining cruisers of sub-category (a), the sixteenth unit will not be laid down before 1933 and will not be completed before 1936; the seventeenth will not be laid down before 1934 and will not be completed before 1937; the eighteenth will not be laid down before 1935 and will not be completed before 1938.

ARTICLE 19

Except as provided in Article 20, the tonnage laid down in any category subject to limitation in accordance with Article 16 shall not exceed the amount necessary to reach the maximum allowed tonnage of the category, or to replace vessels that become 'over-age' before December 31, 1936. Nevertheless, replacement tonnage may be laid down for cruisers and submarines that become 'over-age' in 1937, 1938, and 1939, and for destroyers that become 'over-age' in 1937 and 1938.

Article 20

Notwithstanding the rules for replacement contained in Annex I to Part II:

(a) The *Frobisher* and *Effingham* (United Kingdom) may be disposed of during the year 1936. Apart from the cruisers under construction on April 1, 1930, the total replacement tonnage of cruisers to be completed, in the case of the British Commonwealth of Nations, prior to December 31, 1936, shall not exceed 91,000 tons (92,456 metric tons).

(b) Japan may replace the *Tama* by new construction to be completed during the year 1936.

(c) In addition to replacing destroyers becoming 'over-age' before December 31, 1936, Japan may lay down, in each of the years 1935 and 1936, not more than 5,200 tons (5,283 metric tons) to replace part of the vessels that become 'over-age' in 1938 and 1939.

(d) Japan may anticipate replacement during the term of the present Treaty by laying down not more than 19,200 tons (19,507 metric tons) of submarine tonnage, of which not more than 12,000 tons (12,192 metric tons) shall be completed by December 31, 1936.

Article 21

If, during the term of the present Treaty, the requirements of the national security of any High Contracting Party in respect of vessels of war limited by Part III of the present Treaty are in the opinion of that Party materially affected by new construction of any Power other than those who have joined in Part III of this Treaty, that High Contracting Party will notify the other Parties to Part III as to the increase required to be made in its own tonnages within one or more of the categories of such vessels of war, specifying particularly the proposed increases and the reasons therefor, and shall be entitled to make such increase. Thereupon the other Parties to Part III of this Treaty shall be entitled to make a proportionate increase in the category or categories specified; and the said other Parties shall promptly advise with each other through diplomatic channels as to the situation thus presented.

Part IV

ARTICLE 22

The following are accepted as established rules of International Law:

(1) In their action with regard to merchant ships, submarines must conform to the rules of International Law to which surface vessels are subject.

(2) In particular, except in the case of persistent refusal to stop on being duly summoned, or of active resistance to visit or search, a warship, whether surface vessel or submarine, may not sink or render incapable of navigation a merchant vessel without having first placed passengers, crew, and ship's papers in a place of safety. For this purpose the ship's boats are not regarded as a place of safety unless the safety of the passengers and crew is assured, in the existing sea and weather conditions, by the proximity of land, or the presence of another vessel which is in a position to take them on board.

The High Contracting Parties invite all other Powers to express their assent to the above rules.

Part V

ARTICLE 23

The present Treaty shall remain in force until December 31, 1936, subject to the following exceptions:

(1) Part IV shall remain in force without limit of time;

(2) the provisions of Articles 3, 4, and 5, and of Article 11 and Annex II to Part II so far as they relate to aircraft carriers, shall remain in force for the same period as the Washington Treaty.

Unless the High Contracting Parties should agree otherwise by reason of a more general agreement limiting naval armaments, to which they all become parties, they shall meet in conference in 1935 to frame a new treaty to replace and to carry out the purposes of the present Treaty, it being understood that none of the provisions of the present Treaty shall prejudice the attitude of any of the High Contracting Parties at the conference agreed to.

ARTICLE 24

1. The present Treaty shall be ratified by the High Contracting Parties in accordance with their respective constitutional methods, and the ratifications shall be deposited at London as soon as possible. Certified copies of all the

procès-verbaux of the deposit of ratifications will be transmitted to the Governments of all the High Contracting Parties.

2. As soon as the ratifications of the United States of America, of His Majesty the King of Great Britain, Ireland, and the British Dominions beyond the Seas, Emperor of India, in respect of each and all of the Members of the British Commonwealth of Nations as enumerated in the preamble of the present Treaty, and of His Majesty the Emperor of Japan, have been deposited, the Treaty shall come into force in respect of the said High Contracting Parties.

3. On the date of the coming into force referred to in the preceding paragraph, Parts I, II, IV, and V of the present Treaty will come into force in respect of the French Republic and the Kingdom of Italy if their ratifications have been deposited at that date; otherwise these Parts will come into force in respect of each of those Powers on the deposit of its ratification.

4. The rights and obligations resulting from Part III of the present Treaty are limited to the High Contracting Parties mentioned in paragraph 2 of this Article. The High Contracting Parties will agree as to the date on which, and the conditions under which, the obligations assumed under the said Part III by the High Contracting Parties mentioned in paragraph 2 of this Article will bind them in relation to France and Italy: such agreement will determine at the same time the corresponding obligations of France and Italy in relation to the other High Contracting Parties.

ARTICLE 25

After the deposit of the ratifications of all the High Contracting Parties, His Majesty's Government in the United Kingdom of Great Britain and Northern Ireland will communicate the provisions inserted in Part IV of the present Treaty to all Powers which are not signatories of the said Treaty, inviting them to accede thereto definitely and without limit of time.

Such accession shall be effected by a declaration addressed to His Majesty's Government in the United Kingdom of Great Britain and Northern Ireland.

ARTICLE 26

The present Treaty, of which the French and English texts are both authentic, shall remain deposited in the archives of His Majesty's Government in the United Kingdom of Great Britain and Northern Ireland. Duly certified copies thereof shall be transmitted to the Governments of all the High Contracting Parties.

In faith whereof the above-named Plenipotentiaries have signed the present Treaty and have affixed thereto their seals.

Done at London, the twenty-second day of April, nineteen hundred and thirty.

[For the United States]
HENRY L. STIMSON
CHARLES G. DAWES
CHARLES F. ADAMS
JOSEPH T. ROBINSON
DAVID A. REED
HUGH GIBSON
DWIGHT W. MORROW
[For France]
ARISTIDE BRIAND
J. L. DUMESNIL
A. DE FLEURIAU
[For the United Kingdom]
J. RAMSAY MACDONALD
ARTHUR HENDERSON
A. V. ALEXANDER
W. WEDGWOOD BENN
[For the Dominion of Canada
PHILIPPE ROY
[For the Commonwealth of Australia]
JAMES E. FENTON
[For the Dominion of New Zealand]
T. M. WILFORD
C. T. TE WATER
[For the Irish Free State]
T. A. SMIDDY
[For India]
ATUL C. CHATTERJEE
[For Italy]
G. SIRIANNI
A. C. BORDONARO
ALFREDO ACTON
[For Japan]
R. WAKATSUKI
TAKESHI TAKARABE
T. MATSUDAIRA
M. NAGAL

APPENDIX 3: NOMINAL NAVAL STRENGTH, 1921, 1929, and 1935

Table A–1   Nominal naval strength, 1921

	Great Britain	United States	Japan	France	Italy
Battleships (BS) & battle cruisers (BC)	29 BS 8 BC	36 BS (+11 BS + 6 BC bldg)	12 BS 7 BC (+3 BS +2 BC bldg)	11 BS	9 BS
Aircraft carriers	4 (+2 bldg)	1 (+1 bldg)	(1 bldg)	1 (+1 bldg)	0
Cruisers*	3	15	4	10	3
Light cruisers**	45 (+9 bldg) &6 (+1 bldg) for Dominions	15 (+10 bldg)	9 (+8 bldg)	5 (+6 bldg)	10
Torpedo boat destroyers & flotilla leaders	188 (+8 bldg) & 13 for Dominions	278 (+40 bldg)	84 (+9 bldg)	71 (+13 bldg +12 projected)	60 (+15 bldg)
Submarines	81 (+8 bldg) & 8 for Dominions	103 (+46 bldg)	23 (+15 bldg)	48 (+17 bldg)	65 (+3 bldg)

SOURCE: "Fleets (Great Britain and Foreign Countries)," H.C. 164, *Parliamentary Papers* 1921, Vol. 21.
*"Cruiser" designates all vessels classified as armored cruisers or protected cruisers first class.
**"Light Cruiser" designates all vessels classified as protected cruisers second class, protected cruisers third class, unprotected cruisers, and scouts.

Table A–2   Nominal naval strength (effective/overage*), 1929

	Great Britain	United States	Japan	France	Italy
Battleships (BS) & battle cruisers (BC)	16 BS 4 BC	18 BS	6 BS 4 BC	9 BS	4 BS
Aircraft carriers	6	3 (+1 authorized)	3	1	1
Heavy cruisers (Guns > 6.1 caliber)	9 (+4 bldg)	(13 bldg +5 appropriated +5 authorized)	8/2 (+4 bldg)	4 & 3/4 armored cruisers	5 (+4 bldg)
Light cruisers (Guns ≤ 6.1 caliber)	39	10/22	21	6/1 (+3 bldg)	7/1 (+6 bldg)
Destroyers & flotilla leaders (Torpedo boats = TB)	142 (+18 bldg +9 projected)	284/25	95 (+24 bldg +15 projected)	10 (+12 bldg) & 50/6 TB (+8 bldg)	45 (+11 bldg) & 36 TB
Submarines	51 (+10 bldg +6 authorized)	108/14 (+2 bldg +3 appropriated)	68/4 (+6 bldg)	45/7 (+42 bldg)	45 (+14 bldg)

SOURCE: League of Nations, *Armaments Year-Book* (1929).
*According to Annex I of the London Naval Treaty of 1930, effective age of cruisers = 20 years, destroyers = 16 years, submarines = 13 years from date of completion. (Cruisers = 16 years if laid *before* 1/1/20 and destroyers = 12 years if laid *before* 1/1/21; I use longer effective age limits for consistency.)

Table A–3   Nominal naval strength (effective/overage*), 1935

	Great Britain	United States	Japan	France	Italy
Battleships (BS) & battle cruisers (BC)	12 BS 3 BC	12/3 BS	8/1 BS	3/6 BS (+2 bldg)	4/1 BS (+2 bldg)
Aircraft carriers	6	3/1 (+2 bldg)	4 (+2 bldg)	1	1
Heavy cruisers (Guns > 6.1 caliber)	17	15 (+10 bldg)	12	7/3	7/4
Light cruisers (Guns ≤ 6.1 caliber)	27 (+9 bldg)	10	20/3 (+3 bldg)	6/2 (+6 bldg)	8/5 (+6 bldg)
Destroyers & flotilla leaders (Torpedo boats = TB)	94/53 (+17 bldg)	193/22 (+44 bldg)	96/5 (+15 bldg) & 7 TB (+5 bldg)	24/1 (+8 bldg) & 27/18 TB (+15 bldg)	37/3 (+2 bldg) & 13/13 TB (+10 bldg) & 16/4 scouts
Submarines	51 (+6 bldg)	45/39 (+10 bldg)	60/1 (+6 bldg)	70/25 (+15 bldg)	48/21** (+8 bldg)

SOURCE: League of Nations, *Armaments Year-Book* (1935 and 1936).
*According to Annex I of the London Naval Treaty of 1930, effective age of cruisers = 20 years, destroyers = 16 years, submarines = 13 years from date of completion. (Cruisers = 16 years if laid *before* 1/1/20 and destroyers = 12 years if laid *before* 1/1/21; I use longer effective age limits for consistency.)
**19/17 of total are coastal submarines.

BIBLIOGRAPHY

DOCUMENTS

Official Papers

Great Britain
  Admiralty Papers. Public Records Office, London.
    ADM 116 series.
  Cabinet Papers. Public Records Office, London.
    CAB 2, *Minutes of Committee of Imperial Defense (CID).*
    CAB 4, *CID Miscellaneous Papers.*
    CAB 23, *Cabinet Conclusions.*
    CAB 27, *Cabinet Committee Records.*
    CAB 29, *Records of International Conferences.*
United States
  Department of the Navy Papers. National Archives, Washington D.C. Record Group 80, General Board Studies.

  Department of State Papers. National Archives, Washington D.C. Record Group 43, International Conferences.

Private Papers

Great Britain
  Arthur James Balfour. British Library, London.
  Admiral Earl Beatty. National Maritime Museum, Greenwich.
  Viscount Cecil of Chelwood. British Library, London.
  David Lloyd George. House of Lords Records Office, London.
  Vice-Admiral Sir W. A. Howard Kelly. National Maritime Museum, Greenwich.
  Rear Admiral Sir Herbert W. Richmond. National Maritime Museum, Greenwich.
United States
  Norman H. Davis. Library of Congress, Washington, D.C.
  Herbert Hoover. Presidential Library, West Branch, Iowa.
  Charles Evan Hughes. Library of Congress, Washington, D.C.
  Rear Admiral Hilary P. Jones. Library of Congress, Washington, D.C.
  William V. Pratt. Library of Congress, Washington, D.C. (Microfilm copies, originals at U.S. Naval War College, Newport, R.I.)

PUBLISHED PRIMARY SOURCES

League of Nations
  Armaments Year-Books: General and Statistical Information. Geneva, 1924–1936.

United Kingdom
  Command Papers
    Cmd. 3758. April 1930. *Treaty of London of April 22, 1930.*
    Cmd. 4930. June 1935. *Exchange of Notes Between His Majesty's Government in the
    United Kingdom and the German Government Regarding the Limitation of Naval Arma-
    ments.*
    Cmd. 5302. November 1936. *Procès-Verbal Relating to the Rules of Submarine War-
    fare Set Forth in Part IV of the Treaty of London of April 22, 1930.*
    Cmd. 5519. July 1937. *Agreement Between His Majesty's Government in the United
    Kingdom and the German Goverment Providing for the Limitation of Naval Armament
    and the Exchange of Information Concerning Naval Construction.*
    Cmd. 5561. March 1936. *Treaty for the Limitation of Naval Armaments of March 25,
    1936.*

Parliamentary Papers, House of Commons, February 1921, Volume 21. "Fleets (Great
Britain and Foreign Countries). Return showing the Fleets of Great Britain, France,
Russia, Germany, Italy, Austria-Hungary, United States of America, and Japan, on
1st February 1921; and showing Date of Launch, Date of Completion, Displacement,
Horse-Power, and Armaments reduced to one common scale (in continuation of No.
113 of 1914)."

United States

Foreign Relations of the United States. Washington, D.C.: Government Printing
Office, 1921–1930.

U.S. Congress. Senate. *Armament Conference Treaties.* 67th Cong., 2d sess., 1922.
S. Doc. 126.
U.S. Congress. *Treaties and Resolutions of the Conference on the Limitation of
Armament as Ratified by the United States Senate.* New York: Federal Trade
Information Service, 1922.

BOOKS AND ARTICLES

Adler, Selig. *The Uncertain Giant, 1921–1941: American Foreign Policy Between the
    Wars.* New York: Macmillan, 1965.
Agawa, Hiroyuki. *The Reluctant Admiral: Yamamoto and the Imperial Navy.* Tokyo: Ko-
    dansha International, 1979.
Albion, Robert Greenhalgh. *Makers of Naval Policy, 1798–1947.* Annapolis: Naval
    Institute Press, 1980.
Allison, Graham T., and Frederic A. Morris. "Armaments and Arms Control: Exploring
    the Determinants of Military Weapons." *Daedalus* 104 (Summer 1975): 99–129.
"All-Out War in Europe." *New York Times*, September 19, 1991.
Almond, Gabriel A., and G. Bingham Powell, Jr. *Comparative Politics: System, Process
    and Policy.* Second edition. Boston: Little, Brown, 1978.
Andrade, Ernest, Jr. "United States Naval Policy in the Disarmament Era, 1921–
    1937." Ph.D. diss., Michigan State University, 1966.
Angell, Norman. "Why the Disarmament Deadlock?" *The Nineteenth Century and After*
    116 (July 1934): 16–28.

Asada, Sadao. "Japanese Admirals and the Politics of Naval Limitation: Kato Tomo-saburo vs Kato Kanji." In Gerald Jordan, ed., *Naval Warfare in the Twentieth Century, 1900–1945: Essays in Honor of Arthur Marder*. New York: Crane Russak, 1977.

———. "The Japanese Navy and the United States." In Dorothy Borg and Shumpei Okamoto, eds., *Pearl Harbor as History: Japanese-American Relations, 1931–1941*. New York: Columbia University Press, 1973.

———. "Japan's Special Interests and the Washington Conference, 1921–1922." *American Historical Review* 67 (October 1961): 62–70.

Axelrod, Robert, and Robert O. Keohane. "Achieving Cooperation Under Anarchy: Strategies and Institutions." *World Politics* 37 (October 1985): 226–54.

Bacon, Admiral Sir Reginald. *The Life of John Rushworth Earl Jellicoe*. London: Cassell, 1936.

Ballard, Vice-Admiral G. A., C.B. *The Influence of the Sea on the Political History of Japan*. London: John Murray, 1921.

Bamba, Nobuya. *Japanese Diplomacy in a Dilemma: New Light on Japan's China Policy, 1924–1929*. Vancouver: University of British Columbia Press, 1972.

Barnhart, Michael A. *Japan Prepares for Total War: The Search for Economic Security, 1919–1941*. Ithaca: Cornell University Press, 1987.

———. "Japan's Economic Security and the Origins of the Pacific War." *Journal of Strategic Studies* 4 (June 1981): 105–24.

Barton, John H. *The Politics of Peace: An Evaluation of Arms Control*. Stanford: Stanford University Press, 1981.

Beard, Charles A. *American Foreign Policy in the Making, 1932–1940: A Study in Responsibilities*. New Haven: Yale University Press, 1946.

Beasley, W. G. *Japanese Imperialism, 1894–1945*. Oxford: Clarendon Press, 1987.

Beaver, Paul. *The British Aircraft Carrier*. Wellingborough, Northamptonshire: Patrick Stephens, 1982.

Bechhoeffer, Bernard B. *Postwar Negotiations for Arms Control*. Washington, D.C.: The Brookings Institution, 1961.

Beloff, Max. *Imperial Sunset: Britain's Liberal Empire, 1897–1921*. Vol. 1. New York: Knopf, 1970.

Belote, James H., and William M. Belote. *Titans of the Sea: The Development and Operations of Japanese and American Carrier Task Forces in World War II*. New York: Harper & Row, 1975.

Berg, Meredith William. "The United States and the Breakdown of Naval Limitation, 1934–1939." Ph.D. diss., Tulane University, 1966.

Berkowitz, Bruce. *Calculated Risks: A Century of Failed Arms Control, Why It Has Failed, and How It Can Be Made to Work*. New York: Simon & Schuster, 1987.

Betts, Richard. "Systems for Peace or Causes for War? Collective Security, Arms Control, and the New Europe." *International Security* 17 (Summer 1992): 5–43.

Birn, Donald S. "Open Diplomacy at the Washington Conference of 1921–1922: The British and French Experience." *Comparative Studies in Society and History* 12 (July 1970): 297–319.

Blacker, Coit D., and Gloria Duffy, eds. *International Arms Control: Issues and Agreements*. Stanford: Stanford University Press, 1984.

Blackwill, Robert D. "Conceptual Problems and Conventional Arms Control." *International Security* 12 (Spring 1988): 28–47.

Blanton, Lieutenant Commander Sankey L. "Learning the Wrong Lessons." *U.S. Naval Institute Proceedings* 113 (October 1987): 178–82.

Blechman, Barry M. *The Control of Naval Armaments: Prospects and Possibilities*. Washington, D.C.: The Brookings Institution, 1975.

Bloch, Charles. "Great Britain, German Rearmament, and the Naval Agreement of 1935." In Hans W. Gatzke, ed., *European Diplomacy Between Two Wars, 1919–1939*. Chicago: Quadrangle Books, 1972.

Boggs, Marion William. "Attempts To Define and Limit 'Aggressive' Armament in Diplomacy and Strategy." *The University of Missouri Studies 16*. Columbia: University of Missouri, 1941.

Borg, Dorothy. *American Policy and the Chinese Revolution, 1925–1928*. New York: Macmillan, 1947.

———. *The United States and the Far Eastern Crisis, 1933–1938*. Cambridge: Harvard University Press, 1964.

Borg, Dorothy, and Shumpei Okamoto, eds. *Pearl Harbor as History: Japanese-American Relations, 1931–1941*. New York: Columbia University Press, 1973.

Boudon, Raymond. *The Unintended Consequences of Social Action*. London: Macmillan, 1982.

Brassey's Naval Annual. London, 1929.

Braisted, William Reynolds. *The United States Navy in the Pacific*. Austin: University of Texas Press, 1971.

Brennan, Donald G., ed. *Arms Control, Disarmament, and National Security*. New York: George Braziller, 1961.

Breslauer, George. "Why Detente Failed." In Alexander L. George, ed., *Managing U.S.-Soviet Rivalry: Problems of Crisis Prevention*. Boulder: Westview Press, 1983.

Breyer, Siegfried. *Battleships of the World, 1905–1970*. New York: Mayflower Books, 1980.

Bright, C. C. "Britain's Search for Security, 1930–1936: The Diplomacy of Naval Disarmament and Imperial Defense." Ph.D. diss., Yale University, 1970.

Brodie, Bernard. *A Guide to Naval Strategy*. Princeton: Princeton University Press, 1944.

———. "On the Objectives of Arms Control." *International Security 1* (Summer 1976): 17–36.

———. *Sea Power in the Machine Age: Major Naval Inventions and Their Consequences on International Politics, 1814–1940*. Princeton: Princeton University Press, 1941.

———. "Technological Change, Strategic Doctrine, and Political Outcomes." In Klaus Knorr, ed., *Historical Dimensions of National Security Problems*. Lawrence: University Press of Kansas, 1976.

Brown, Sidney DeVere. "Shidehara Kijuro: The Diplomacy of the Yen." In Richard Dean Burns and Edward M. Bennett, eds., *Diplomats in Crisis: United States–Chinese-Japanese Relations, 1919–1941*. Santa Barbara: American Bibliographical Center-Clio Press, 1974.

Buckley, Thomas A. *The United States and the Washington Conference, 1921–1922*. Knoxville: University of Tennessee Press, 1970.

Buell, Raymond Leslie. *The Washington Conference*. New York: D. Appleton, 1922.

Bull, Hedley. "The Classical Approach to Arms Control Twenty Three Years After." In Clive Nerlich, ed., *Soviet Power and Western Negotiating Policies 2*. New York: Ballinger, 1983. Reprinted in Robert O'Neill and David N. Schwartz, eds., *Hedley Bull on Arms Control*. New York: St. Martin's Press, 1987.

———. *The Control of the Arms Race*. Second edition. New York: Praeger, 1965.

———. "Strategic Arms Limitation: The Precedent of the Washington and London Naval Treaties." In Morton A. Kaplan, ed., *SALT: Problems and Prospects*. Morristown, N.J.: General Learning Press, 1973.

Burns, Richard Dean, and Edward M. Bennett. *Diplomats in Crisis: United States–Chinese–Japanese Relations, 1919–1941*. Santa Barbara: American Bibliographical Center-Clio Press, 1974.

Burns, Richard Dean, and Donald Urquidi. *Disarmament in Perspective: An Analysis of Selected Arms Control and Disarmament Agreements Between the World Wars, 1919–1939*. Vol. 3, *Limitation of Sea Power*. The U.S. Arms Control and Disarmament Agency, Contract No. ACDA/RS–55 III, July 1968.

Bywater, Hector. *The Great Pacific War: A History of the American-Japanese Campaign of 1931–33*. London: Constable, 1925.

———. *Navies and Nations: A Review of Naval Developments Since the Great War*. London: Constable, 1927.

———. *Sea Power in the Pacific: A Study of the American-Japanese Naval Problem*. Boston: Houghton Mifflin, 1921.

Caporaso, James A. "Global Political Economy." In Ada A. Finifter, ed., *Political Science: State of the Discipline*. Washington, D.C.: American Political Science Association, 1993.

Carnesale, Albert, and Richard N. Haass. "Lessons Learned from Superpower Arms Control." *Washington Quarterly* 10 (Summer 1987): 29–45.

———, eds. *Superpower Arms Control: Setting the Record Straight*. Cambridge: Ballinger, 1987.

Chaput, Rolland A. *Disarmament in British Foreign Policy*. London: G. Allen & Unwin, 1935.

Christopher, James William. *Conflict in the Far East: American Diplomacy in China from 1928–1933*. Leiden: E. J. Brill, 1950.

Clinard, Outen Jones. *Japan's Influence on American Naval Power, 1897–1917*. Berkeley and Los Angeles: University of California Press, 1947.

Cohen, Eliot. "The Future of Force." *National Interest* 21 (Fall 1990): 3–15.

Corbett, Julian S. *The Campaign at Trafalgar*. Vol. 1. London: Longmans, 1919. Reprint, New York: AMS Press, 1976.

———. *Some Principles of Maritime Strategy*. Second edition. London: Longmans, 1918.

Crawford, Beverly. "Creating a New Europe: Opportunities and Challenges." In Beverly Crawford and Peter W. Schulze, eds., *The New Europe Asserts Itself: A Changing Role in International Relations*. Berkeley and Los Angeles: University of California Press, 1990.

Crowley, James B. "A New Deal for Japan: One Road to Pearl Harbor." In James B. Crowley, ed., *Modern East Asia: Essays in Interpretation*. New York: Harcourt, Brace & World, 1970.

———. *Japan's Quest for Autonomy: National Security and Foreign Policy, 1930–1938*. Princeton: Princeton University Press, 1966.

Davis, George T. *A Navy Second to None: The Development of Modern American Naval Policy*. New York: Harcourt, Brace, 1940.

Davis, Paul K., Robert D. Howe, Richard L. Kugler, and William G. Wild, Jr. *Variables Affecting Central-Region Stability: The "Operational Minimum" and Other Issues at Low Force Levels*. (N-2976-USDP). Santa Monica: The Rand Corporation, September 1989.

Davis, Vincent. *The Admirals Lobby*. Chapel Hill: University of North Carolina Press, 1967.

Dayer, Roberta A. *Bankers and Diplomats in China, 1917–25*. London: Frank Cass, 1981.

Dingman, Roger. *Power in the Pacific: The Origin of Naval Arms Limitation, 1914–1922*. Chicago: University of Chicago Press, 1976.

————. *Statesmen, Admirals, and SALT: The United States and the Washington Confer-ence, 1921–1922.* Los Angeles: The California Arms Control and Foreign Policy Seminar, 1972.

Dougherty, James E. *How to Think About Arms Control and Disarmament.* New York: Crane, Russak, 1973.

Dougherty, James E., and Robert L. Pfaltzgraff, Jr. *Contending Theories of International Relations.* Second edition. New York: Harper & Row, 1981.

Douglas, Lawrence H. "The Submarine and the Washington Conference of 1921." In Richard B. Lillich and John Norton Moore, eds., *U.S. Naval War College International Law Studies.* Vol. 62. *The Use of Force. Human Rights and General International Legal Issues.* Newport: Naval War College Press, 1980.

Downs, George W., David M. Rocke, and Randolph M. Siverson. "Arms Races and Cooperation." *World Politics* 38 (October 1985): 118–46.

Duus, Peter. "The Era of Party Rule: Japan, 1905–1932." In James B. Crowley, ed., *Modern East Asia: Essays in Interpretation.* New York: Harcourt, Brace and World, 1970.

Easton, David. *A Framework for Political Analysis.* Englewood Cliffs: Prentice-Hall, 1965.

————. *A Systems Analysis of Political Life.* New York: John Wiley, 1965.

————. *The Political System.* New York: Alfred A. Knopf, 1953.

Eckstein, Harry. "Case Study and Theory in Political Science." In Fred I. Greenstein and Nelson W. Polsby, eds., *Handbook of Political Science 7.* Reading, Mass: Addison-Wesley, 1975.

English, Howard L., Jr. "Great Britain and the Problem of Imperial Defense." Ph.D. diss., Fordham University, 1971.

"Europe Welcomes Soviet Arms Cuts." *New York Times,* October 7, 1991, A6.

"Europeans Retreat on a Peace Force for Croatia." *New York Times,* September 20, 1991.

Evangelista, Matthew. *Innovation and the Arms Race: How the United States and the Soviet Union Develop New Military Technologies.* Ithaca: Cornell University Press, 1988.

Fagan, George Vincent. "Anglo-American Naval Relations, 1927–1937." Ph.D. diss., University of Pennsylvania, 1954.

Fairbanks, Charles H., Jr. "Arms Races: The Metaphor and the Facts." *The National Interest* 1 (Fall 1985): 75–90.

————. "The Washington Naval Treaty, 1922–1936." *The Wall Street Journal* (1979). Reprinted in Robert J. Art and Kenneth N. Waltz, eds., *The Use of Force.* Second edition. Lanham, Md.: University Press of America, 1983.

Fairbanks, Charles H., Jr., and Abram N. Shulsky. "From 'Arms Control' to Arms Reductions: The Historical Experience." *Washington Quarterly* 10 (Summer 1987): 59–73.

Feis, Herbert. *The Road to Pearl Harbor: The Coming of the War Between the United States and Japan.* Princeton: Princeton University Press, 1950.

Ferris, John. "A British 'Unofficial' Aviation Mission and Japanese Naval Developments, 1919–1929." *Journal of Strategic Studies* 5 (September 1982): 416–39.

————. *Men, Money, and Diplomacy: The Evolution of British Strategic Policy, 1919–26.* Ithaca: Cornell University Press, 1989.

Floweree, Charles C. "On Tending Arms Control Agreements." *Washington Quarterly* 13 (Winter 1990): 199–214.

Forbes, Henry W. *The Strategy of Disarmament.* Washington, D.C.: Public Affairs Press, 1962.

Freedman, Lawrence. *The Evolution of Nuclear Strategy*. New York: St. Martin's Press, 1981.

———. "Weapons, Doctrines, and Arms Control." *Washington Quarterly* 7 (Spring 1984): 8–16.

Friedman, Norman. *Battleship Design and Development, 1905–1945*. New York: Mayflower Books, 1978.

———. *Carrier Air Power*. Annapolis: Naval Institute Press, 1981.

———. *Submarine Design and Development*. Annapolis: Naval Institute Press, 1984.

———. *U.S. Aircraft Carriers: An Illustrated Design History*. Annapolis: Naval Institute Press, 1983.

———. *U.S. Battleships: An Illustrated Design History*. Annapolis: Naval Institute Press, 1985.

———. *U.S. Cruisers: An Illustrated Design History*. Annapolis: Naval Institute Press, 1984.

Frisch, David H., ed. *Arms Reduction: Program and Issues*. New York: The Twentieth Century Fund, 1961.

Fry, M. G. "The North Atlantic Triangle and the Abrogation of the Anglo-Japanese Alliance." *Journal of Modern History* 39 (March 1967): 46–64.

Gallagher, John, and Ronald E. Robinson. "The Imperialism of Free Trade." *Economic History Review*, 2d series, 6 (August 1953): 1–15.

Garzke, William H., Jr., and Robert O. Dulin, Jr. *Battleships: Axis and Neutral Battleships in World War II*. Annapolis: Naval Institute Press, 1985.

———. *Battleships: United States Battleships and World War II*. Annapolis: Naval Institute Press, 1976.

Gelb, Leslie H. "Israel's Military Superiority." *New York Times*, June 19, 1992, A27.

Genda, General Minoru. "Evolution of Aircraft Carrier Tactics of the Imperial Japanese Navy." In Paul Stillwell, ed., *Air Raid: Pearl Harbor! Recollections of a Day of Infamy*. Annapolis: Naval Institute Press, 1981.

George, Alexander L. "Case Studies and Theory Development." Paper presented to the Second Annual Symposium on Information Processing in Organizations, Carnegie-Mellon University, October 15–16, 1982.

———. "Detente: The Search for a Constructive Relationship." In Alexander L. George, ed., *Managing U.S.-Soviet Rivalry: Problems of Crisis Prevention*. Boulder: Westview Press, 1983.

———. "Domestic Constraints on Regime Change in U.S. Foreign Policy: The Need for Policy Legitimacy." In Ole R. Holsti, Randolph M. Siverson, and Alexander L. George, eds., *Change in the International System*. Boulder: Westview Press, 1980.

———. "Factors Influencing Security Cooperation." In Alexander L. George, Philip J. Farley, and Alexander Dallin, eds., *U.S.-Soviet Security Cooperation: Achievements, Failures, Lessons*. New York: Oxford University Press, 1988.

———. "Incentives for U.S.-Soviet Security Cooperation and Mutual Adjustment." In Alexander L. George, Philip J. Farley, and Alexander Dallin, eds., *U.S.-Soviet Security Cooperation: Achievements, Failures, Lessons*. New York: Oxford University Press, 1988.

———. "Strategies for Facilitating Cooperation." In Alexander L. George, Philip J. Farley, and Alexander Dallin, eds., *U.S.-Soviet Security Cooperation: Achievements, Failures, Lessons*. New York: Oxford University Press, 1988.

George, Alexander L. and Timothy J. McKeown. "Case Studies and Theories of Organizational Decision Making." *Advances in Information Processing in Organizations* 2 (1985): 21–58.

George, Margaret. *The Warped Vision: British Foreign Policy, 1933–1939.* Pittsburgh: University of Pittsburgh Press, 1965.

George, Roger Zane. "The Economics of Arms Control." *International Security* 3 (Winter 1978–79): 94–125.

Gibbs, N. H. *Grand Strategy: History of the Second World War.* Vol. 1, *Rearmament Policy.* United Kingdom Military History Series. London: Her Majesty's Stationery Office, 1977.

Gittings, John. *The World and China, 1922–1927.* London: Eyre Metheun, 1974.

Gray, Colin S. "Across the Nuclear Divide—Strategic Studies, Past and Present." *International Security* 1 (Summer 1977): 24–46.

———. "The Arms Race Is About Politics." *Foreign Policy* 9 (Winter 1972–73): 117–29.

———. "The Arms Race Phenomenon." *World Politics* 24 (October 1971): 39–79.

———. *The Soviet-American Arms Race.* London: D. C. Heath, 1976.

———. "The Urge to Compete: Rationales for Arms Racing." *World Politics* 26 (January 1974): 207–33.

Griswold, A. Whitney. *Far Eastern Policy of the United States.* New York: Harcourt, Brace, 1938.

Groeling, Dorothy T. "Submarines, Disarmament, and Naval Warfare." Ph.D. diss., Columbia University, 1950.

Hadley, Arthur T. *The Nation's Safety and Arms Control.* New York: Viking, 1961.

Haftendorn, Helga. "The Security Puzzle: Theory-Building and Discipline-Building in International Security." *International Studies Quarterly* 35 (March 1991): 3–17.

Hall, Christopher. *Britain, America, and Arms Control.* New York: St. Martin's Press, 1987.

Hamill, Ian. *The Strategic Illusion: The Singapore Strategy and the Defense of Australia and New Zealand, 1919–1942.* Kent Ridge: Singapore University Press, 1981.

Harada, Baron Kumao. *Fragile Victory: The 1930 London Treaty Issue.* Translated by Thomas Francis Mayer-Oakes. Detroit: Wayne State University Press, 1968.

"Has Arms Control Worked?" *Bulletin of the Atomic Scientists* 45 (May 1989): 26–45.

Hawkins, William R. "Arms Control: Three Centuries of Failure." *National Review* 37 (August 9, 1985): 26–32.

Henkin, Louis, ed. *Arms Control: Issues for the Public.* New York: Prentice-Hall, 1961.

Henry, David. "British Submarine Policy, 1918–1939." In Bryan Ranft, ed., *Technical Change and British Naval Policy, 1860–1939.* New York: Holmes & Meier, 1977.

Herzog, James. *Closing the Open Door: Anglo-Japanese Diplomatic Negotiations, 1936–1941.* Annapolis: Naval Institute Press, 1973.

Hezlet, Vice Admiral Sir Arthur. *Aircraft and Sea Power.* New York: Stein & Day, 1970.

Higham, Robin. *Armed Forces in Peacetime: Britain, 1918–1940, A Case Study.* Hamden, Conn.: Archon Books, 1962.

Hinds, Cpt. A. W. "Changes in the Naval Situation of the Pacific Due to the World War." *Army and Navy Journal* 59 (October 15, 1921): 149, 153.

Hoag, C. Leonard. *Preface to Preparedness: The Washington Disarmament Conference and Public Opinion.* Washington, D.C.: American Council on Public Affairs, 1941.

Hodges, Peter. *The Big Gun: Battleship Main Armament, 1860–1945.* Annapolis: Naval Institute Press, 1981.

Holst, Johan Jørgen. "Arms Control in the Nineties: A European Perspective." *Daedalus* 120 (Winter 1991): 83–110.

Hone, Thomas C. "Spending Patterns of the United States Navy, 1921–1941." *Armed Forces and Society* 8 (Spring 1982): 443–62.

Hoover, Robert A. *Arms Control: The Interwar Naval Limitation Agreements*. Monograph Series in World Affairs. Denver: University of Denver, 1980.

Hosoya, Chihiro. "Britain and the United States in Japan's View of the International System, 1919–37." In Ian H. Nish, ed., *Anglo-Japanese Alienation, 1919–1952*. Cambridge: Cambridge University Press, 1982.

———. "Retrogression in Japan's Foreign Policy Decision-Making Process." In James William Morley, ed., *Dilemmas of Growth in Prewar Japan*. Princeton: Princeton University Press, 1971.

Howard, Michael. *The British Way in Warfare*. London: Trinity Press, 1975.

Howarth, Stephen. *The Fighting Ships of the Rising Sun: The Drama of the Imperial Japanese Navy, 1895–1945*. New York: Atheneum, 1983.

Hunt, B. D. "Smaller Navies and Disarmament: Sir Herbert Richmond's 'Small Ship' Theories and the Development of British Naval Policy in the 1920s." In A.M.J. Hyatt, ed., *Dreadnought to Polaris: Maritime Strategy Since Mahan*. Toronto: Copp Clark, 1973.

Huntington, Samuel P. "Arms Races: Prerequisites and Results." *Public Policy* (1958): 41–83. Reprinted in Robert J. Art and Kenneth N. Waltz, eds., *The Use of Force*. Second edition. Lanham, Md.: University Press of America, 1983.

Hyatt, A.M.J., ed. *Dreadnought to Polaris: Maritime Strategy Since Mahan*. Toronto: Copp Clark, 1973.

Ichihashi, Yamato. *The Washington Conference and After: A Historical Survey*. Stanford: Stanford University Press, 1928.

Ikle, Fred Charles. "After Detection—What?" *Foreign Affairs* 39 (January 1961): 208–20.

Iriye, Akira. *Across the Pacific: An Inner History of American–East Asian Relations*. New York: Harcourt, Brace, & World, 1967.

———. *After Imperialism: The Search for a New Order in the Far East, 1921–1931*. Cambridge: Harvard University Press, 1965.

———. "The Asian Factor." In Gordon Martel, ed., *The Origins of the Second World War Reconsidered*. Boston: Allen & Unwin, 1986.

———. "The Failure of Economic Expansionism: 1918–1931." In Bernard Silberman and Harry Harootunian, eds., *Japan in Crisis*. Princeton: Princeton University Press, 1974.

———. "The Failure of Military Expansionism." In James William Morley, ed., *Dilemmas of Growth in Prewar Japan*. Princeton: Princeton University Press, 1971.

———. "Imperialism in East Asia." In James B. Crowley, ed., *Modern East Asia: Essays in Interpretation*. New York: Harcourt, Brace & World, 1970.

———. *Mutual Images: Essays in American-Japanese Relations*. Cambridge: Harvard University Press, 1975.

———. *The Origins of the Second World War in Asia and the Pacific*. London: Longman, 1987.

———. *Pacific Estrangement: Japanese and American Expansion, 1897–1911*. Cambridge: Harvard University Press, 1972.

Iwasaki, Uichi. *The Working Forces in Japanese Politics*. New York: Columbia University Press, 1921.

Jane, Fred T. *Heresies of Sea Power*. London: Longmans, 1906.

Jentschura, Hansgeorg, Dieter Jung, and Peter Mickel. *Warships of the Imperial Japanese Navy, 1869–1945*. Annapolis: Naval Institute Press, 1977.

Jervis, Robert. "Cooperation Under the Security Dilemma." *World Politics* 30 (January 1978): 167–214.

———. "From Balance to Concert: A Study of International Security Cooperation."
   World Politics 38 (October 1985): 58–79.
———. *Perception and Misperception in International Politics*. Princeton: Princeton University Press, 1976.
———. "Realism, Game Theory, and Cooperation." *World Politics* 40 (April 1988): 317–49.
Joffe, Josef. "Collective Security and the Future of Europe." *Survival* 34 (Spring 1992):36–50.
Johnson, Lt. Paul G. "Arms Control: Upping the Ante." *U.S. Naval Institute Proceedings* 109 (August 1983): 28–34.
Jordan, Gerald, ed. *Naval Warfare in the Twentieth Century, 1900–1945: Essays in Honor of Arthur Marder*. New York: Crane Russak, 1977.
Karp, Aaron. "Controlling Ballistic Missile Proliferation." *Survival* 33 (November/December 1991): 517–30.
Kaufman, Robert Gordon. *Arms Control During the Pre-Nuclear Era: The United States and Naval Limitation Between the Two World Wars*. New York: Columbia University Press, 1990.
Kelleher, Catherine. "Arms Control in a Revolutionary Future: Europe." *Daedalus* 120 (Winter 1991): 111–31.
Kemp, Geoffrey, and John Maurer. "The Logistics of the Pax Britannica: Lessons for America." In Uri Ra'anan, Robert L. Pfaltzgraff, Jr., and Geoffrey Kemp, eds., *Projection of Power: Perspectives, Perceptions, and Problems*. Hamden: Archon, 1982.
Kennedy, Malcolm D. *The Estrangement of Great Britain and Japan, 1917–1935*. Berkeley and Los Angeles: University of California Press, 1969.
———. *The Problem of Japan*. London: Nisbet, 1935.
Kennedy, Paul M. *The Realities Behind Diplomacy: Background Influences on British External Policy, 1865–1980*. Glasgow: William Collins Sons, 1981.
———. *The Rise and Fall of British Naval Mastery*. London: Macmillan, 1983.
Keohane, Robert O. *After Hegemony: Cooperation and Discord in the World Political Economy*. Princeton: Princeton University Press, 1984.
Kiralfly, Alexander. "Japanese Naval Strategy." In Edward Mead Earle, ed., *Makers of Modern Strategy: Military Thought from Machiavelli to Hitler*. Princeton: Princeton University Press, 1941.
Klachko, Mary. "Anglo-American Naval Competition 1918–1922." Ph.D. diss., Columbia University, 1962.
Klare, Michael T. "The Next Great Arms Race." *Foreign Affairs* 72 (Summer 1993: 136–52.
Klein, Ira. "Whitehall, Washington, and the Anglo-Japanese Alliance, 1919–1921." *Pacific Historical Review* 41 (November 1972): 460–83.
Krasner, Stephen D. *Defending the National Interest*. Princeton: Princeton University Press, 1978.
———. "Structural Causes and Regime Consequences." In Stephen D. Krasner, ed., *International Regimes*. Ithaca: Cornell University Press, 1983.
Kruzel, Joseph. "Arms Control, Disarmament, and Stability of the Postwar Era." In Charles W. Kegley, Jr., ed., *The Long Postwar Peace: Contending Explanations and Projections*. New York: HarperCollins, 1991.
———. "From Rush Bagot to START: The Lessons of Arms Control." *Orbis* 30 (Spring 1986): 193–216.
———. "The Preconditions and Consequences of Arms Control Agreements." Ph.D. diss., Harvard University, 1975.

———. "What's Wrong with the Traditional Approach?" *Washington Quarterly* 8 (Spring 1985): 121–32.

Kupchan, Charles A., and Clifford A. Kupchan. "Concerts, Collective Security, and the Future of Europe." *International Security* 16 (Summer 1991): 114–61.

Lacroix, Eric. "The Development of the 'A Class' Cruisers in the Imperial Japanese Navy," Parts 1– 7. *Warship International* 14:4 (1977): 337–57; 16:1 (1979): 41–62; 16:4 (1979): 329–61; 18:1 (1981): 40–76; 18:4 (1981): 323–67; 20:3 (1983): 232–82; 21:3 (1984): 246–305.

Latimer, Hugh. *Naval Disarmament: A Brief Record from the Washington Conference to Date.* London: The Royal Institute of International Affairs, 1930.

Lautenschlager, Karl. "The Submarine in Naval Warfare, 1901–2001." *International Security* 2 (Winter 1986–87): 94–140.

Lengerer, Hans. "Akagi and Kaga," Parts 1–3. *Warship* 22 (April 1982): 127–39; 23 (July 1982): 170–77; 24 (October 1982): 305–10.

———. "The Japanese Super Battleship Strategy," Parts 1–3. *Warship* 25 (January 1983): 30–39; 26 (April 1983): 88–96; 27 (July 1983): 161–69.

Levy, Jack S. "The Offensive/Defensive Balance of Military Technology: A Theoretical and Historical Analysis." *International Studies Quarterly* 28 (June 1984): 219–38.

Livezey, William E. *Mahan on Sea Power.* Norman: University of Oklahoma Press, 1947.

Louis, W. Roger. *British Strategy in the Far East, 1919–1939.* Oxford: Clarendon Press, 1971.

Lowe, Peter. *Britain in the Far East: A Survey from 1819 to the Present.* London: Longman, 1981.

———. *Great Britain and Japan, 1911–1915: A Study of British Far Eastern Policy.* London: St. Martin's Press, 1969.

Luttwak, Edward M. *The Political Uses of Sea Power.* Baltimore: Johns Hopkins University Press, 1974.

———. *Strategy: The Logic of War and Peace.* Cambridge: The Belknap Press of Harvard University Press, 1987.

Lynn-Jones, Sean M. "Lulling and Stimulating Effects of Arms Control." In Albert Carnesale and Richard N. Haass, eds., *Superpower Arms Control: Setting the Record Straight.* Cambridge: Ballinger, 1987.

Lyon, Hugh. "The Relations Between the Admiralty and Private Industry in the Development of Warships." In Bryan Ranft, ed., *Technical Change and British Naval Policy, 1860–1939.* New York: Holmes & Meier, 1977.

McDonald, J. Kenneth. "Lloyd George and the Search for a Postwar Naval Policy, 1919." In A.J.P. Taylor, ed., *Lloyd George: Twelve Essays.* London: Hamish Hamilton, 1971.

McKercher, B.J.C., and D. J. Moss, eds. *Shadow and Substance in British Foreign Policy, 1895–1939.* Edmonton: University of Alberta Press, 1984.

Mahan, Alfred T. *The Influence of Sea Power Upon History, 1660–1783.* Boston: Little, Brown, 1890.

———. *The Interest of America in Sea Power, Present and Future.* Boston: Little, Brown, 1911.

———. *Naval Strategy: Compared and Contrasted with the Principles and Practice of Military Operations on Land.* Boston: Little, Brown, 1911.

———. *Retrospect and Prospect: Studies in International Relations Naval and Political.* Boston: Little, Brown, 1903.

Mandelbaum, Michael. *The Nuclear Revolution: International Politics Before and After Hiroshima.* Cambridge: Cambridge University Press, 1981.

Marder, Arthur J. *From the Dardenelles to Oran: Studies of the Royal Navy in War and Peace, 1915–1940.* London: Oxford University Press, 1974.

————. *From the Dreadnought to Scapa Flow: The Royal Navy in the Fisher Era, 1904–1919.* 5 vols. London: Oxford University Press, 1961–1970.

————. "The Influence of History on Sea Power: The Royal Navy and the Lessons of 1914–1918." *Pacific Historical Review* 41 (November 1972): 413–43.

————. *Old Friends, New Enemies: The Royal Navy and the Imperial Japanese Navy; Strategic Illusions, 1936–1941.* Oxford: Clarendon Press, 1981.

Maxon, Yale Candee. *Control of Japanese Foreign Policy: A Study of Civil-Military Rivalry, 1930–1945.* Berkeley and Los Angeles: University of California Press, 1957.

Mearsheimer, John J. "Back to the Future: Instability in Europe After the Cold War." *International Security* 15 (Summer 1990): 5–56.

Melhorn, Charles M. *Two-Block Fox: The Rise of the Aircraft Carrier, 1911–1929.* Annapolis: Naval Institute Press, 1974.

Mets, David Raymond. "A Case Study in Arms Control: Naval Limitation Before Pearl Harbor and Post-War Arms Control Theory." Ph.D. diss., University of Denver, 1972.

Michelson, Mark Charles. "A Place in the Sun: The Foreign Ministry and Perceptions and Policies in Japan's International Relations, 1931–1941." Ph.D. diss., University of Illinois at Urbana-Champaign, 1979.

Mihalka, Michael. *German Strategic Deception in the 1930s* (N-1557-NA). Santa Monica: The RAND Corporation, 1980.

Miller, Steven E. "Politics over Promise: Domestic Impediments to Arms Control." *International Security* 8 (Spring 1984): 67–90.

Moodie, Michael. "Conventional Arms Control: An Analytical Survey of Recent Literature." *Washington Quarterly* 12 (Winter 1989): 189–201.

Morgenthau, Hans J. "Some Political Aspects of Disarmament." In David Carlton and Carlo Schaerf, eds., *The Dynamics of the Arms Race.* London: Croom Helm, 1975.

Morison, Elting. *Admiral Sims and the Modern American Navy.* Boston: Houghton Mifflin, 1942.

Morison, Samuel Eliot. *History of the United States Naval Operations in World War II.* Vol. 3, *The Rising Sun in the Pacific, 1931–April 1942.* Boston: Little, Brown, 1957.

Morley, James William, ed. *Dilemmas of Growth in Prewar Japan.* Princeton: Princeton University Press, 1971.

————, ed. *The Fateful Choice: Japan's Advance into Southeast Asia, 1939–1941.* Japan's Road to the Pacific War Series. New York: Columbia University Press, 1980.

————, ed. *Japan Erupts: The London Naval Conference and the Manchurian Incident, 1928–1932.* Japan's Road to the Pacific War Series. New York: Columbia University Press, 1984.

Mueller, John. "The Essential Irrelevance of Nuclear Weapons." *International Security* 13 (Fall 1988): 55–79.

Murray, Williamson. "Neither Navy was Ready." *U.S. Naval Institute Proceedings* 107 (April 1981): 38–47.

Mushakoji, Kinhide. "The Structure of Japanese-American Relations in the 1930s." In Dorothy Borg and Shumpei Okamoto, eds., *Pearl Harbor as History: Japanese-American Relations, 1931–1941.* New York: Columbia University Press, 1973.

Nelson, Daniel N. "Europe's Unstable East." *Foreign Policy* 82 (Spring 1991): 137–58.

Neu, Charles. *The Troubled Encounter: The United States and Japan.* New York: John Wiley, 1975.

Neumann, William. *America Encounters Japan: From Perry to MacArthur.* Baltimore: Johns Hopkins University Press, 1963.

Nish, Ian H. *A Short History of Japan.* New York: Praeger, 1968.

———. *Alliance in Decline: A Study in Anglo-Japanese Relations, 1908–1923.* London: Athlone Press, 1972.

———, ed. *Anglo-Japanese Alienation, 1919–1952.* Cambridge: Cambridge University Press, 1982.

———. *The Anglo-Japanese Alliance: The Diplomacy of Two Island Empires, 1894–1907.* London: Athlone Press, 1966.

———. "Japan in Britain's View of the International System, 1919–1937." In Ian H. Nish, ed., *Anglo-Japanese Alienation, 1919–1952.* Cambridge: Cambridge University Press, 1982.

———. *Japanese Foreign Policy, 1869–1942.* London: Routledge & Kegan Paul, 1977.

Noel-Baker, Philip. *The First World Disarmament Conference, 1932–1933, and Why It Failed.* New York: Pergamom Press, 1979.

Nolan, Janne E. *Trappings of Power: Ballistic Missiles in the Third World.* Washington, D.C.: The Brookings Institution, 1991.

Northedge, F. S. *Freedom and Necessity in British Foreign Policy.* London: C. Tinling, 1972.

———. *The Troubled Giant: Britain Among the Great Powers, 1916–1939.* New York: Praeger, 1966.

O'Connor, Raymond G. *Perilous Equilibrium: The United States and the London Naval Conference of 1930.* Lawrence: University of Kansas Press, 1962.

———. "The 'Yardstick' and Naval Disarmament in the 1920s." *The Mississippi Valley Historical Review* 45 (December 1958): 441–63.

Oelrich, Ivan. "The Changing Rules of Arms Control Verification." *International Security* 14 (Spring 1990): 176–84.

Ogata, Sadako. *Defiance in Manchuria: The Making of Japanese Foreign Policy, 1931–1932.* Berkeley and Los Angeles: University of California Press, 1964.

Olson, Mancur, Jr. and Richard Zeckhauser. "An Economic Theory of Alliances." In Bruce M. Russett, ed., *Economic Theories of International Alliances.* Chicago: Markham, 1966.

O'Neill, Robert, and David N. Schwartz, eds. *Hedley Bull on Arms Control.* New York: St. Martin's Press, 1987.

"Optimism Seen in Mideast Talks As New Ideas Are Being Reported," *New York Times,* August 27, 1993, A4.

Osborne, Sidney. *The Problem of Japan.* Amsterdam: C. L. van Langenhuysen, 1918.

Osgood, Robert. *Ideals and Self-Interest in American Foreign Policy: The Great Transformation of the Twentieth Century.* Chicago: University of Chicago Press, 1953.

Padfield, Peter. *The Battleship Era.* London: Rupert Hart-Davis, 1972.

Peattie, Mark R. "Akiyama Saneyuki and the Emergence of Modern Japanese Naval Doctrine." *U.S. Naval Institute Proceedings* 103 (January 1977): 61–69.

———. *Ishiwara Kanji and Japan's Confrontation with the West.* Princeton: Princeton University Press, 1975.

Pelz, Stephen E. *Race to Pearl Harbor: The Failure of the Second London Naval Conference and the Onset of World War II.* Cambridge: Harvard University Press, 1974.

Perrett, William Gregory. "French Naval Policy and Foreign Affairs, 1930–1939." Ph.D. diss., Stanford University, 1977.

Polmar, Norman. *Aircraft Carriers: A Graphic History of Carrier Aviation and Its Influence on World Events*. London: MacDonald, 1969.

Posen, Barry. "Crisis Stability and Conventional Arms Control." *Daedalus* 120 (Winter 1991): 217–32.

―――. *The Sources of Military Doctrine*. Ithaca: Cornell University Press, 1984.

"Potent Office Weaves Web in China Arms." *New York Times*, August 21, 1991, A16.

Potter, E. B., ed. *Sea Power: A Naval History*. Second edition. Annapolis: Naval Institute Press, 1981.

―――. ed. *The United States and World Sea Power*. Englewood Cliffs: Prentice-Hall, 1955.

Potter, E. B. and Chester W. Nimitz, eds. *Sea Power: A Naval History*. Englewood Cliffs: Prentice-Hall, 1961.

Potter, John Deare. *Yamamoto: The Man Who Menaced America*. New York: Viking Press, 1979.

Preston, Anthony. *An Illustrated History of the Navies of World War II*. London: Bison Books, 1976.

―――. *Cruisers*. London: Bison Books, 1980.

Puleston, W. D. *The Armed Forces of the Pacific: A Comparison of the Military and the Naval Power of the United States and Japan*. New Haven: Yale University Press, 1941.

Putnam, Robert D. "Diplomacy and Domestic Politics: The Logic of Two-Level Games." *International Organization* 42 (Summer 1988): 427–60.

Quester, George H. *Deterrence Before Hiroshima: The Airpower Background to Modern Strategy*. New Brunswick: Transaction, 1986.

―――. "Naval Armaments: The Past as Prologue." In George Quester, ed., *Navies and Arms Control*. New York: Praeger, 1980.

―――. *Offense and Defense in the International System*. New York: John Wiley, 1977.

Ranft, Bryan, ed. *Technical Change and British Naval Policy, 1860–1939*. New York: Holmes & Meier, 1977.

Ranger, Robin. *Arms and Politics, 1958–1978: Arms Control in a Changing Political Context*. Toronto: Macmillan, 1979.

―――. *Arms Control in Theory and Practice, 1958–1981*. National Security Series. Kingston, Canada: Queens University, 1981.

―――. "Learning from the Naval Arms Control Experience." *Washington Quarterly* 10 (Summer 1987): 47–58.

―――. *The Naval Arms Control Record, 1919–1939: Axis Violations and Democratic Compliance Failures*. Prepared for OASD/ISP, Contract No. MDA903-87-M-3565. Fairfax, Va.: National Security Research, April 1987.

Ransom, Harry H. "The Battleship Meets the Airplane." *Military Affairs* 23 (Spring 1959): 21–27.

Raven, Alan, and John Roberts. *British Battleships of World War II*. Annapolis: Naval Institute Press, 1976.

―――. *British Cruisers of World War II*. Annapolis: Naval Institute Press, 1980.

Reynolds, Clark G. *Command of the Sea: The History and Strategy of Maritime Empires*. New York: William Morrow, 1974.

―――. "The Continental Strategy of Imperial Japan." *U.S. Naval Institute Proceedings* 109 (August 1983): 65–71.

―――. *The Fast Carriers: The Forging of an Air Navy*. New York: McGraw-Hill, 1968. Reprint, Huntington, N.Y.: Robert E. Krieger, 1978.

―――. "John H. Towers, the Morrow Board, and the Reform of the Navy's Aviation." *Military Affairs* 52 (April 1988): 78–84.

Rice, Condoleezza. "SALT and the Search for a Security Regime." In Alexander L. George, Philip J. Farley, and Alexander Dallin, eds., *U.S.-Soviet Security Cooperation: Achievements, Failures, Lessons*. New York: Oxford University Press, 1988.

Richardson, Dick. *The Evolution of British Disarmament Policy in the 1920s*. New York: St. Martin's Press, 1989.

Ropp, Theodore. "Continental Doctrines of Sea Power." In Edward Meade Earle, ed., *Makers of Modern Strategy: Military Thought from Machiavelli to Hitler*. Princeton: Princeton University Press, 1941.

———. "German Seapower: A Study in Failure." In A.M.J. Hyatt, ed., *Dreadnought to Polaris: Maritime Strategy Since Mahan*. Toronto: Copp Clark, 1973.

Rosecrance, Richard N. *Action and Reaction in World Politics*. Boston: Little, Brown, 1963.

Rosen, Stephen Peter. "New Ways of War: Understanding Military Innovation." *International Security* 13 (Summer 1988): 134–68.

Rosinski, Herbert. "Command of the Sea." In B. Mitchell Simpson III, ed., *The Development of Naval Thought: Essays by Herbert Rosinski*. Newport: Naval War College Press, 1977.

———. "Mahan and World War II." In B. Mitchell Simpson III, ed., *The Development of Naval Thought: Essays by Herbert Rosinski*. Newport: Naval War College Press, 1977.

———. "The Strategy of Japan." In B. Mitchell Simpson III, ed., *The Development of Naval Thought: Essays by Herbert Rosinski*. Newport: Naval War College Press, 1977.

Roskill, Stephen. *Naval Policy Between the Wars*. Vol. 1, *The Period of Anglo-American Antagonism, 1919–1929*. New York: Walker, 1968.

———. *Naval Policy Between the Wars*. Vol. 2, *The Period of Reluctant Rearmament, 1930–1939*. London: Collins Press, 1976.

Royama, Masamichi. *Foreign Policy of Japan, 1914–1939*. Tokyo: Japanese Council, Institute of Pacific Relations, 1941.

Rudoff, Robin. "The Influence of the German Navy on the British Search for Naval Arms Control, 1928–1935." Ph.D. diss., Tulane University, 1964.

Schelling, Thomas C., and Morton H. Halperin. *Strategy and Arms Control*. New York: The Twentieth Century Fund, 1961. Reprint, Washington: Pergamom Press, 1985.

Schilling, Warner R. "Civil-Naval Politics in World War I." *World Politics* 7 (July 1955): 572–91.

Seaman, L.C.B. *Post-Victorian Britain, 1902–1951*. London: Methuen, 1966.

Semmel, Bernard. *Liberalism and Naval Strategy: Ideology, Interest, and Sea Power During the Pax Britannica*. Boston: Allen & Unwin, 1986.

Simpson, B. Mitchell, III, ed. *The Development of Naval Thought: Essays by Herbert Rosinski*. Newport: Naval War College Press, 1977.

———. *War, Strategy, and Maritime Power*. New Brunswick: Rutgers University Press, 1977.

Sims, Rear-Admiral William Sowden. *The Victory at Sea*. New York: Doubleday, Page, 1921.

Skinner, Kiron K. "Linkage." In Albert Carnesale and Richard N. Haass, eds., *Superpower Arms Control: Setting the Record Straight*. Cambridge, Mass.: Ballinger, 1987.

Smith, Malcolm. *British Air Strategy Between the Wars*. Oxford: Clarendon Press, 1984.

Snyder, Glenn H., and Paul Diesing. *Conflict Among Nations*. Princeton: Princeton University Press, 1977.

Sprout, Harold, and Margaret Sprout. *The Rise of American Naval Power, 1776–1918*. Princeton: Princeton University Press, 1939.

———. *Toward a New Order of Sea Power: American Naval Policy and the World Scene, 1918–1922*. Princeton: Princeton University Press, 1940.

Sprout, Margaret Tuttle. "Mahan: Evangelist of Sea Power." In Edward Meade Earle, ed., *Makers of Modern Strategy: Military Thought from Machiavelli to Hitler*. Princeton: Princeton University Press, 1941.

Stein, Arthur A. "Coordination and Collaboration." In Stephen D. Krasner, ed., *International Regimes*. Ithaca: Cornell University Press, 1983.

Steven, R.P.G. "Hybrid Constitutionalism in Prewar Japan." *Journal of Japanese Studies* 3 (Winter 1977): 99–133.

Takeuchi, S. Tatsuji. *War and Diplomacy in the Japanese Empire*. Chicago: Doubleday, Doran, 1935.

Tate, Merze. *The United States and Armaments*. Cambridge: Harvard University Press, 1948.

Tatsuo, Kobayashi. "The London Naval Treaty, 1930." In James William Morley, ed., *Japan Erupts: The London Naval Conference and the Manchurian Incident, 1928–1932*. Japan's Road to the Pacific War Series. New York: Columbia University Press, 1984.

Teichman, Sir Eric. *Affairs of China: A Survey of the Recent History and Present Circumstances of the Republic of China*. London: Methuen, 1938.

Thorne, Christopher. "The Shanghai Crisis of 1932: The Basis of British Policy." *American Historical Review* 75 (October 1970): 1616–39.

Till, Geoffrey. "Airpower and the Battleship in the 1920s." In Bryan Ranft, ed., *Technical Change and British Naval Policy, 1860–1939*. New York: Holmes & Meier, 1977.

———. *Airpower and the Royal Navy, 1914–1945*. London: Jane's, 1979.

———. *Maritime Strategy and the Nuclear Age*. London: Macmillan, 1982.

Titus, David Anson. *Palace and Politics in Prewar Japan*. New York: Columbia University Press, 1974.

Tokes, Rudolf L. "Central European Conflict Resolution: Security Challenges to the New Democracies of East Central Europe." Paper presented at the 1991 Topical Symposium "From Regionalism to Globalism—New Perspectives on American Foreign and Defense Policies," November 14–15, 1991, National Defense University, Washington, D.C.

Toyama, Saburo. "Lessons From the Past." *U.S. Naval Institute Proceedings* 108 (September 1982): 62–69.

Trotter, Ann. *Britain and East Asia, 1933–1937*. London: Cambridge University Press, 1975.

Turnbull, Archibald D., and Clifford L. Lord. *History of United States Naval Aviation*. New Haven: Yale University Press, 1949.

"Ukraine Finds Atom Arms Bring Measure of Respect." *New York Times*, January 7, 1993, A1.

Van Evera, Stephen. "Primed for Peace: Europe After the Cold War." *International Security* 15 (Winter 1990/91): 7–57.

Vinacke, Harold M. *A History of the Far East in Modern Times*. Fifth edition. New York: Appleton-Century-Crofts, 1950.

Vinson, John Chalmers. *The Parchment Peace: The United States Senate and the Washington Conference, 1921–1922*. Athens: University of Georgia Press, 1955.

Waltz, Kenneth. "The Spread of Nuclear Weapons: More May Be Better." *Adelphi Papers* 171. London: International Institute for Strategic Studies, 1982.
———. *Theory of International Politics.* New York: Random House, 1979.
Warner, Edward. "Douhet, Mitchell, Seversky: Theories of Air Warfare." In Edward Meade Earle, ed., *Makers of Modern Strategy: Military Thought from Machiavelli to Hitler.* Princeton: Princeton University Press, 1941.
Watt, D. C. "The Anglo-German Naval Agreement of 1935: An Interim Judgement." *Journal of Modern History* 28 (June 1956): 155–75.
———. "The Possibility of a Multilateral Arms Race: A Note." *International Relations* 2 (October 1962): 372–77, 397.
Watts, Anthony J., and Brian G. Gordon. *The Imperial Japanese Navy.* London: Macdonald, 1971.
Weale, Putnam [Bertram Lenox Simpson]. *An Indiscreet Chronicle from the Pacific.* New York: Dodd, Mead, 1922.
Weinrod, Bruce W. "Strategic Defense and the ABM Treaty." *Washington Quarterly* 9 (Summer 1986): 73–87.
Whaley, Barton. *Covert German Rearmament, 1919–1939: Deception and Misperception.* Frederick, Md.: University Publications of America, 1984.
Wheeler, Gerald E. "Isolated Japan: Anglo-American Diplomatic Cooperation, 1927–1936." *Pacific Historical Review* 30 (May 1961): 165–78.
———. *Prelude to Pearl Harbor: The United States Navy and the Far East, 1921–1931.* Columbia: University of Missouri Press, 1963.
———. "The United States Navy and the Japanese 'Enemy,' 1919–1931." *Military Affairs* 21 (Summer 1957): 61–74.
Wheeler-Bennett, Sir John. *Disarmament and Security Since Locarno, 1925–1931.* London: Allen & Unwin, 1932.
Wieseltier, Leon. *Nuclear War and Nuclear Peace.* New York: Holt, Rinehart & Winston, 1983.
Willmott, H. P. *Empires in the Balance: Japanese and Allied Pacific Strategies to April 1942.* Annapolis: Naval Institute Press, 1982.
Wilmott, Ned. *Strategy and Tactics of Sea Warfare.* Secaucus, New Jersey: Chartwell Books, 1979.
Wilson, Hugh R. *Disarmament and the Cold War in the Thirties.* New York: Vantage Press, 1963.
Wolfers, Arnold. "National Security as an Ambiguous Symbol." In Arnold Wolfers, *Discord and Collaboration: Essays on International Politics.* Baltimore: Johns Hopkins University Press, 1962.
Wragg, David. *A History of Naval Aviation: Wings Over the Sea.* New York: Arco, 1979.
Yoshihaski, Takehiko. *Conspiracy at Mukden: The Rise of the Japanese Military.* New Haven: Yale University Press, 1963.

INDEX

Scheer, R., 88, 90
Schelling, T., 17–18
sea power
 airpower and, 99
 Anglo-Japanese alliance and, 45
 in national defense, 85, 95, 106
 See also specific countries
security systems
 arms control and, 14, 15–17
 China and, 7–8
 delinkage strategy in, 192, 255
 European, 4, 265, 269
 Five Power treaty and, 8
 international, 21, 271
 Japan and, 14, 15
 maintenance of, 189–91
 military components of, 21
 multilateral, 7–8
 Pacific naval powers and, 143
 political vs. military, 255
 post–Cold War and, 241
 requisites in, 246
 state-specific perceptions of, 16
 strategies for, 190–91
 See also specific countries
Seiyukai party, 251
Senate Naval Affairs Committee, U.S.
 and, 58
Shanghai, 196, 199, 210, 216
Shantung settlement, 71, 133–35, 244
Shidehara diplomacy, 62–63, 200, 206–7,
 209
 on China, 232
 London Naval Treaty and, 209, 230
 vs. Tanaka's policy, 200, 251
 undermining of, 203
Ship Improvement Law (1932), 178
ships
 aircraft carriers and. See aircraft carriers
 capital ship tonnage, 8, 114, 118, 126
 carriers vs. battleships, 160
 conversion ships and, 178
 cruisers and. See cruisers
 design of, 90, 248
 dive-bombers and, 160
 dreadnoughts, 138. See also battleships;
  super-dreadnoughts
 Improvement Law (1932), 178
 Mutsu-class, 125
 post-Jutland, 118

Settsu-class, 125
 standard displacement and. See standard
  displacement
 submarines and. See submarines
 super-dreadnoughts, 116n.6, 125. See also
  dreadnoughts
 technology and, 247–48
 tonnage limits and, 10, 12, 114, 179
 U-boats and. See submarines
 warship design and, 157, 162–63, 168
 wartime conversion of, 177
 Washington treaty and, 10, 154, 158–59
 See also specific ship types
Siberia, 54, 63
silk market, collapse of, 203–4, 253–54
Simon, J., 218, 221–23
Singapore, 220
Smoot-Hawley tariff, 204, 254
Smuts Committee, 104–5
South Manchurian Railway, 200
Soviet Union
 arms control treaty and, 18
 China and, 72
 democratic change in, 267
 Europe and, 263
 Japan and, 60, 67, 192
 maritime army and, 209
 October Revolution and, 35
 rearmament and, 231
 Red Army and, 253
Spanish-American War (1898), 48
standard displacement
 aircraft carriers and, 159
 battleships and, 156–57
 definition of, 156n.8
 Five Power treaty and, 156–57
 France and, 180
 Italy and, 180
 Japan and, 179–80
 technological innovations in, 156–58
 Washington treaty and, 164
 See also specific ships
steam, technology of, 81
steel guns, 157
Strategic Arms Limitation Treaty (SALT),
 19, 136, 190
Strategic Arms Reduction Treaty
 (START), 266–68
submarines
 antisubmarine craft, 139